W9-BXE-456

THE EMPEROR RECEIVING THE DIPLOMATIC CORPS

China, Frontispiece

CHINA

BY

DEMETRIUS CHARLES BOULGER

WITH TWO SUPPLEMENTARY CHAPTERS OF RECENT EVENTS

BY MAYO W. HAZELTINE

ILLUSTRATED

NEW YORK
PETER FENELON COLLIER & SON
· M C M I ·

I DEDICATE THIS SHORT

HISTORY OF CHINA

TO

SIR HALLIDAY MACARTNEY, K.C.M.G.

AS A SLIGHT TRIBUTE OF PERSONAL RESPECT AND ADMIRATION FOR ONE WHO
HAS MAINTAINED THE RIGHT OF CHINA TO BE TREATED BY THE
GOVERNMENTS OF EUROPE WITH THE DIGNITY AND
CONSIDERATION THAT BECOME A

GREAT EMPIRE.

IF TO LORD MACARTNEY WE OWE THE FIRST SUCCESSFUL ATTEMPT TO OBTAIN
AUDIENCE OF THE EMPEROR OF CHINA ON THE SAME CONDI-
TIONS AS THOSE ON WHICH FOREIGN EMBASSADORS
ARE RECEIVED AT EUROPEAN COURTS, TO

SIR HALLIDAY MACARTNEY

A SCION OF THE SAME FAMILY

CHINA

OWES MUCH OF THE SUCCESS THAT HAS ATTENDED HER DIPLOMACY
IN FOREIGN COUNTRIES

3

CONTENTS

LIST OF ILLUSTRATIONS

CHINA

PREFACE

As China has now fairly taken her place in the family of nations, it is unnecessary to elaborate an argument in support of even the humblest attempt to elucidate her history. It is a subject to which we can no longer remain indifferent, because circumstances are bringing every day more clearly into view the important part China must play in the changes that have become imminent in Asia, and that will affect the security of our position and empire in that continent. A good understanding with China should be the first article of our Eastern policy, for not only in Central Asia, but also in Indo-China, where French ambition threatens to create a fresh Egypt, hor interests coincide with ours and furnish the sound basis of a fruitful alliance.

This book, which I may be pardoned for saying is not an abridgment of my original work, but entirely rewritten and rearranged with the view of giving prominence to the modern history of the Chinese Empire, may appeal, although they generally treat Asiatic subjects with regrettable indifference, to that wider circle of English readers on whose opinion and efforts the development of our political and commercial relations with the greatest of Oriental States will mainly depend.

D. C. BOULGER.

April 28, 1893.

(9)

A SHORT
HISTORY OF CHINA

CHAPTER I

THE EARLY AGES

THE Chinese are unquestionably the oldest nation in the world, and their history goes back to a period to which no prudent historian will attempt to give a precise date. They speak the language and observe the same social and political customs that they did several thousand years before the Christian era, and they are the only living representatives to-day of a people and government which were contemporary with the Egyptians, the Assyrians, and the Jews. So far as our knowledge enables us to speak, the Chinese of the present age are in all essential points identical with those of the time of Confucius, and there is no reason to doubt that before his time the Chinese national character had been thoroughly formed in its present mold. The limits of the empire have varied from time to time under circumstances of triumph or disunion, but the Middle Kingdom, or China Proper, of the eighteen provinces has always possessed more or less of its existing proportions. Another striking and peculiar feature about China is the small amount of influence that the rest of the world has exercised upon it. In fact, it is only during the present century that that influence can be said to have existed at all. Up to that point China had pursued a course of her own, carrying on her own struggles within a definite limit, and completely indifferent to, and

(11)

ignorant of, the ceaseless competition and contests of mankind outside her orbit, which make up the history of the rest of the Old World. The long struggles for supremacy in Western Asia between Assyrian, Babylonian and Persian, the triumphs of the Greek, followed by the absorption of what remained of the Macedonian conquests in the Empire of Rome, even the appearance of Islam and the Mohammedan conquerors, who changed the face of Southern Asia from the Ganges to the Levant, and long threatened to overrun Europe, had no significance for the people of China, and reacted as little on their destiny as if they had happened in another planet. Whatever advantages the Chinese may have derived from this isolation, it has entailed the penalty that the early history of their country is devoid of interest for the rest of the world, and it is only when the long independent courses of China and Europe are brought into proximity by the Mongol conquests, the efforts of the medieval travelers, the development of commerce, and the wars carried on for the purpose of obtaining a secure position for foreigners in China—four distinct phases covering the last seven centuries—that any confidence can be felt in successfully attracting notice to the affairs of China. Yet, as a curiosity in human existence, the earlier history of that country may justly receive some notice. Even though the details are not recited, the recollection of the antiquity of China's institutions must be ever present with the student, as affording an indispensable clew to the character of the Chinese people and the composition of their government.

The first Chinese are supposed to have been a nomad tribe in the province of Shensi, which lies in the northwest of China, and among them at last appeared a ruler, Fohi, whose name at least has been preserved. His deeds and his person are mythical, but he is credited with having given his country its first regular institutions. One of his successors was Hwangti (which means Heavenly Emperor), who was the first to employ the imperial style of Emperor, the earlier rulers having been content with the inferior title of

Wang, or prince. He adopted the convenient decimal division in his administration as well as his coinage. His dominions were divided into ten provinces, each of these into ten
departments, these again into ten districts, each of which
held ten towns. He regulated the calendar, originating the
Chinese cycle of sixty years, and he encouraged commerce.
He seems to have been a wise prince and to have been the
first of the great emperors. His grandson, who was also
emperor, continued his good work and earned the reputation
of being "the restorer or even founder of true astronomy."

But the most famous of Hwangti's successors was his
great-grandson Yao, who is still one of the most revered of
all Chinese rulers. He was "diligent, enlightened, polished
and prudent," and if his words reflected his actions he must
have been most solicitous of the welfare of his people. He
is specially remarkable for his anxiety to discover the best
man to succeed him in the government, and during the last
twenty-eight years of his reign he associated the minister
Chun with him for that purpose. On his death he left the
crown to him, and Chun, after some hesitation, accepted the
charge; but he in turn hastened to secure the co-operation of
another minister named Yu in the work of administration,
just as he had been associated with Yao. The period covered by the rule of this triumvirate is considered one of the
most brilliant and perfect in Chinese history, and it bears a
resemblance to the age of the Antonines. These rulers seem
to have passed their leisure from practical work in framing
moral axioms, and in carrying out a model scheme of government based on the purest ethics. They considered that
"a prince intrusted with the charge of a State has a heavy
task. The happiness of his subjects absolutely depends
upon him. To provide for everything is his duty; his ministers are only put in office to assist him," and also that "a
prince who wishes to fulfill his obligations, and to long preserve his people in the ways of peace, ought to watch without ceasing that the laws are observed with exactitude."
They were stanch upholders of temperance, and they ban-

ished the unlucky discoverer of the fact that an intoxicating drink could be obtained from rice. They also held fast to the theory that all government must be based on the popular will. In fact, the reigns of Yao, Chun and Yu are the ideal period of Chinese history, when all questions were decided by moral right and justice, and even now Chinese philosophers are said to test their maxims of morality by the degree of agreement they may have with the conduct of those rulers.

With them passed away the practice of letting the most capable and experienced minister rule the State. Such an impartial and reasonable mode of selecting the head of a community can never be perpetuated. The rulers themselves may see its advantages and may endeavor as honestly as these three Chinese princes to carry out the arrangement, but the day must come when the family of the able ruler will assert its rights to the succession, and take advantage of its opportunities from its close connection with the government to carry out its ends. The Emperor Yu, true to the practice of his predecessors, nominated the president of the council as his successor, but his son Tiki seized the throne, and became the founder of the first Chinese dynasty, which was called the Hia, from the name of the province first ruled by his father. This event is supposed to have taken place in the year 2197 B.C., and the Hia dynasty, of which there were seventeen emperors, ruled down to the year 1776 B.C. These Hia princes present no features of interest, and the last of them, named Kia, was deposed by one of his principal nobles, Ching Tang, Prince of Chang.

This prince was the founder of the second dynasty, known as Chang, which held possession of the throne for 654 years, or down to 1122 B.C. With the exception of the founder, who seems to have been an able man, this dynasty of twenty-eight emperors did nothing very noteworthy. The public morality deteriorated very much under this family, and it is said that when one of the emperors wanted an honest man as minister he could only find one in the person of a common laborer. At last, in the twelfth century before our era, the enormities of the Chang rulers reached a climax in the person of Chousin, who was deposed by a popular rising headed by Wou Wang, Prince of Chow.

This successful soldier, whose name signifies the Warrior King, founded the third Chinese dynasty of Chow, which governed the empire for the long space of 867 years down to 255 B.C. During that protracted period there were necessarily good and bad emperors; and the Chow dynasty was rendered specially illustrious by the appearance of the great social and religious reformers, Laoutse, Confucius and Mencius, during the existence of its power. The founder of the dynasty instituted the necessary reforms to prove that he was a national benefactor, and one of his successors, known as the Magnificent King, extended the authority of his family over some of the States of Turkestan. But, on the whole, the rulers of the Chow dynasty were not particularly distinguished, and one of them in the eighth century B.C. was weak enough to resign a portion of his sovereign rights to a powerful vassal, Siangkong, the Prince of Tsin, in consideration of his undertaking the defense of the frontier against the Tartars. At this period the authority of the central government passed under a cloud. The emperor's prerogative became the shadow of a name, and the last three centuries of the rule of this family would not call for notice but for the genius of Laoutse and Confucius, who were both great moral teachers and religious reformers.

Laoutse, the founder of Taouism, was the first in point of time, and in some respects he was the greatest of these reformers. He found his countrymen sunk in a low state of moral indifference and religious infidelity which corresponded with the corruption of the times and the disunion in the kingdom. He at once set himself to work with energy and devotion to repair the evils of his day, and to raise before his countrymen a higher ideal of duty. He has been called the Chinese Pythagoras, the most erudite of sinologues have pronounced his text obscure, and the mysterious Taouism which he founded holds the smallest or the least assignable part in what passes for the religion of the Chinese. As a philosopher and minister Laoutse will always attract attention and excite speculation, but as a practical reformer and politician he was far surpassed by his younger and less theoretical contemporary Confucius.

Confucius was an official in the service of one of the great princes who divided the governing power of China among themselves during the whole of the seventh century before our era, which beheld the appearance of both of these religious teachers and leaders. He was a trained administrator with long experience when he urged upon his prince the necessity of reform, and advocated a policy of union throughout the States. His exhortations were in vain, and so far ill-timed that he was obliged to resign the service of one prince after another. In his day the authority of the Chow emperor had been reduced to the lowest point. Each prince was unto himself the supreme authority. Yet one cardinal point of the policy of Confucius was submission to the emperor, as implicit obedience to the head of the State throughout the country as was paid to the father of every Chinese household. Although he failed to find a prince after his own heart, his example and precepts were not thrown away, for in a later generation his reforms were executed, and down to the present day the best points in Chinese government are based on his recommendations. If "no intelligent monarch arose" in his time, the greatest emperors have since sought to conform with his usages and to rule after the ideal of the great philosopher. His name and his teachings were perpetuated by a band of devoted disciples, and the book which contained the moral and philosophical axioms of Confucius passed into the classic literature of the country and stood in the place of a Bible for the Chinese. The list of the great Chinese reformers is completed by the name of Mencius, who, coming two centuries later, carried on with better opportunities the reforming work of Confucius, and left behind him in his Sheking the most popular book of Chinese poetry and a crowning tribute to the great Master.

From teachers we must again pass to the chronicle of kings, although few of the later Chow emperors deserve their names to be rescued from oblivion. One emperor suffered a severe defeat while attempting to establish his authority over the troublesome tribes beyond the frontier; of another it was written that "his good qualities merited a happier day," and the general character of the age may be inferred from its being designated by the native chroniclers "The warlike period." At last, after what seemed an interminable old age, marked by weakness and vice, the Chow dynasty came to an end in the person of Nan Wang, who, although he reigned for nearly sixty years, was deposed in ignominious fashion by one of his great vassals, and reduced to a humble position. His conqueror became the founder of the fourth Chinese dynasty.

During the period of internal strife which marked the last four centuries of the Chow dynasty, one family had steadily waxed stronger and stronger among the princes of China: the princes of Tsin, by a combination of prudence and daring, gradually made themselves supreme among their follows. It was said of one of them that "like a wolf or a tiger he wished to draw all the other princes into his claws, so that he might devour them." Several of the later Tsin princes, and particularly one named Chow Siang Wang, showed great capacity, and carried out a systematic policy for their own aggrandizement. When Nan Wang was approaching the end of his career, the Tsin princes had obtained everything of the supreme power short of the name and the right to wear the imperial yellow robes. Ching Wang, or, to give him his later name as emperor, Tsin Chi Hwangti, was the reputed great-grandson of Chow Siang Wang, and under him the fame and power of the Tsins reached their culminating point. This prince also proved himself one of the greatest rulers who ever sat on the Dragon throne of China.

only claim to distinction, arises from its having produced the great ruler Hwangti, and its destiny was Napoleonic in its brilliance and evanescence.

Looking back at the long period which connects the mythical age with what may be considered the distinctly historical epoch of the Tsins, we find that by the close of the third century before the Christian era China possessed settled institutions, the most remarkable portion of its still existing literature, and mighty rulers. It is hardly open to doubt that the Chinese annalist finds in these remote ages as much interest and instruction as we should in the record of more recent times, and proof of this may be discovered in the fact that the history of the first four dynasties, which we must dismiss in these few pages, occupies as much space in the national history as the chronicle of events from Tsin Chi Hwangti to the end of the Ming dynasty in 1644, at which date the official history of China stops, because the history of the Manchu dynasty, which has occupied the throne ever since, will only be given to the world after it has ceased to rule. We must not be surprised at this discursiveness, because the teachings of human experience are as clearly marked in those early times as they have been since, and Chinese historians aim as much at establishing moral and philosophical truths as at giving a complete record of events. The consequences of human folly and incompetence are as patent and conspicuous in those days as they are now. The ruling power is lost by one family and transferred to another because the prince neglects his business, gives himself over to the indulgence of pleasure, or fails to see the signs of the times. Cowardice and corruption receive their due and inevitable punishment. The founders of the dynasties are all brave and successful warriors, who are superior to the cant of a hypercivilized state of society, which covers declining vigor and marks the first phase of effeteness, and who see that as long as there are human passions they may be molded by genius to make the many serve the few and to build up an autocracy. Nor are the lessons to be learned from history applicable only to individuals. The faults of an emperor are felt in every household of the community, and injure the State. Indifference and obtuseness at the capital entailed weakness on the frontier and in the provincial capitals. The barbarians grew defiant and aggressive, and defeated the imperial forces. The provincial governors asserted their independence, and founded ruling families. The empire became attenuated by external attack and internal division. But, to use the phrase of the Chinese historians, "after long abiding disunion, union revived." The strong and capable man always appears in one form or another, and the Chinese people, impressed with a belief in both the divine mission of their emperor and also in the value of union, welcome with acclaim the advent of the prince who will restore their favorite and ideal system of one-man government. The time is still hidden in a far-distant and undiscoverable future when it will be otherwise, and when the Chinese will be drawn away from their consistent and ancient practice to pursue the ignis fatuus of European politics that seeks to combine human equality with good practical government and national security. The Chinese have another and more attainable ideal, nor is there any likelihood of their changing it. The fall of dynasties may, needs must, continue in the ordinary course of nature, but in China it will not pave the way to a republic. The imperial authority will rise triumphant after every struggle above the storm.

CHAPTER II

THE FIRST NATIONAL DYNASTY

As the Chinese are still proud to call themselves the sons of Han, it will be understood that the period covered by the Han rulers must be an important epoch in their history, and in more than one respect they were the first national dynasty. When the successors of Tsin Chi Hwangti proved unable to keep the throne, the victorious general who profited by their discomfiture was named Liu Pang. He had been a trusted official of the Emperor Hwangti, but on finding that his descendants could not bear the burden of government, he resolved to take his own measures, and he lost no time in collecting troops and in making a bid for popularity by endeavoring to save all the books that had not been burned. His career bears some resemblance to that of Macbeth, for a soothsayer meeting him on the road predicted, "by the expression of his features, that he was destined to become emperor." He began his struggle for the throne by defeating another general named Pawang, who was also disposed to make a bid for supreme power. After this success Liu Pang was proclaimed emperor as Kao Hwangti, meaning Lofty and August Emperor, which has been shortened into Kaotsou. He named his dynasty the Han, after the small state in which he was born.

Kaotsou began his reign by a public proclamation in favor of peace, and deploring the evils which follow in the train of war. He called upon his subjects to aid his efforts for their welfare by assisting in the execution of many works of public utility, among which roads and bridges occupied the foremost place. He removed his capital from Loyang in Honan to Singanfoo in Shensi, and as Singan was difficult of access in those days, he constructed a great highroad from the center of China to this somewhat remote spot on the western frontier. This road still exists, and has been described by several travelers in our time. It was constructed by the labor of one hundred thousand men through the most difficult country, crossing great mountain chains and broad rivers. The Chinese engineers employed on the making of this road, which has excited the admiration of all who have traversed it, first discovered and carried into execution the suspension bridge, which in Europe is quite a modern invention. One of these "flying bridges," as the Chinese called them, is one hundred and fifty yards across a valley five hundred feet below, and is still in use. At regular intervals along this road Kaotsou constructed rest-houses for travelers, and postal-stations for his couriers. No Chinese ruler has done anything more useful or remarkable than this admirable road from Loyang to Singanfoo. He embellished his new capital with many fine buildings, among which was a large palace, the grandeur of which was intended to correspond with the extent of his power.

The reign of Kaotsou was, however, far from being one of uncheckered prosperity. Among his own subjects his popularity was great because he promoted commerce and improved the administration of justice. He also encouraged literature, and was the first ruler to recognize the claims of Confucius, at whose tomb he performed an elaborate ceremony. He thus acquired a reputation which induced the King of Nanhai—a state composed of the southern provinces of China, with its capital at or near the modern Canton—to tender his allegiance. But he was destined to receive many slights and injuries at the hands of a foreign enemy, who at this time began a course of active aggression that entailed serious consequences for both China and Europe.

Reference has been made to the Hiongnou or Hun tribes, against whom Tsin Hwangti built the Great Wall. In the interval between the death of that ruler and the consolidation of the power of Kaotsou, a remarkable chief named Meha, or Meta, had established his supremacy among the disunited clans of the Mongolian Desert, and had succeeded in combining for purposes of war the whole fighting force of what had been a disjointed and barbarous confederacy. The Chinese rulers had succeeded in keeping back this threatening torrent from overflowing the fertile plains of their country, as much by sowing dissension among these clans and by bribing one chief to fight another, as by superior arms. But Meha's success rendered this system of defense no longer possible, and the desert chieftain, realizing the opportunity of spoil and conquest, determined to make his position secure by invading China. If the enterprise had failed, there would have been an end to the paramounce of Meha, but his rapid success convinced the Huns that their proper and most profitable policy was to carry on implacable war with their weak and wealthy neighbors. Meha's success was so great that in a single campaign he recovered all the districts taken from the Tartars by the general Moungtien. He turned the western angle of the Great Wall, and brought down his frontier to the river Hoangho. His light cavalry raided past the Chinese capital into the province of Szchuen, and returned laden with the spoil of countless cities. These successes were crowned by a signal victory over the emperor in person. Kaotsou was drawn into an ambuscade in which his troops had no chance with their more active adversaries, and, to save himself from capture, Kaotsou had no alternative but to take refuge in the town of Pingching, where he was closely beleaguered. It was impossible to defend the town for any length of time, and the capture of Kaotsou seemed inevitable, when recourse was had to a stratagem. The most beautiful Chinese maiden was sent as a present to propitiate the conqueror, and Meha, either mollified by the compliment, or deeming that nothing was to be gained by driving the Chinese to desperation, acquiesced in a convention which, while it sealed the ignominious defeat of the Chinese, rescued their sovereign from his predicament.

This disaster, and his narrow personal escape, seem to have unnerved Kaotsou, for when the Huns resumed their incursions in the very year following the Pingching convention, he took no steps to oppose them, and contented himself with denouncing in his palace Meha as "a wicked and faithless man, who had risen to power by the murder of his father, and one with whom oaths and treaties carried no weight." Notwithstanding this opinion, Kaotsou proceeded to negotiate with Meha as an equal, and gave this barbarian prince his own daughter in marriage as the price of his abstaining from further attacks on the empire. Never, wrote a historian, "was so great a shame inflicted on the Middle Kingdom, which then lost its dignity and honor." Meha observed this peace during the life of Kaotsou, who found that his reputation was much diminished by his coming to terms with his uncivilized opponent, but although several of his generals rebelled, until it was said that "the very name of revolt inspired Kaotsou with apprehension," he succeeded in overcoming them all without serious difficulty. His troubles probably shortened his life, for he died when he was only fifty-three, leaving the crown to his son, Hoeiti, and injunctions to his widow, Liuchi, as to the conduct of the administration.

The brief reign of Hoeiti is only remarkable for the rigor and terrible acts of his mother, the Empress Liuchi, who is the first woman mentioned in Chinese history as taking a supreme part in public affairs. Another of Kaotsou's widows aspired to the throne for her son, and the chief direction for herself. Liuchi nipped their plotting in the bud by poisoning both of them. She marked out those who differed from her, or who resented her taking the most prominent part in public ceremonies, as her enemies, to be removed from her path by any means. At a banquet she endeavored to poison one of the greatest princes of the empire, but her plot was detected and baffled by her son. It is perhaps not surprising that Hoeiti did not live long after this episode, and then Liuchi ruled in her own name, and without filling up the vacancy on the throne, until the public dissatisfaction warned her that she was going too far. She then adopted a supposititious child as her grandson and governed as regent in his name. The mother of this youth seems to have made inconvenient demands on the empress, who promptly put her out of the way, and when the son showed a disposition to resent this action, she caused him to be poisoned. She again ruled without a puppet emperor, hoping to retain power by placing her relatives in the principal offices; but the dissatisfaction had now reached an acute point, and threatened to destroy her. It may be doubted whether she would have surmounted these difficulties and dangers, when death suddenly cut short her adventurous career. The popular legend is that this Chinese Lucretia Borgia died of fright at seeing the apparitions of her many victims, and there can be no doubt that her crimes did not conduce to make woman government more popular in China.

It says much for the excellence of Kaotsou's work, and for the hold the Han family had obtained on the Chinese people, that when it became necessary to select an emperor after the death of Liuchi the choice should have fallen unanimously on the Prince of Tai, who was the illegitimate son of Kaotsou. On mounting the throne, he took the name of Wenti. He began his reign by remitting taxes and by appointing able and honest governors and judges. He ordered that all old men should be provided with corn, meat and wine, besides silk and cotton for their garments. At the suggestion of his ministers, who were alive to the dangers of a disputed succession, he proclaimed his eldest son heir to the throne. He purified the administration of justice by declaring that prince and peasant must be equally subject to the law; he abolished the too common punishment of mutilation, and had the satisfaction of seeing crime reduced to such low proportions in the empire that the jails contained only four hundred prisoners. Wenti was a strong advocate of peace, which was, indeed, necessary to China, as it had not recovered from the effects of the last Hun invasion. He succeeded by diplomacy in inducing the Prince at Canton, who had shown a disposition to assert his independence, to recognize his authority, and thus averted a civil war. In his relations with the Huns, among whom the authority of Meha had passed to his son, Lao Chang, he strove to preserve the peace, giving that chief one of his daughters in marriage, and showing moderation in face of much provocation. When war was forced upon him by their raids he did everything he could to mitigate its terrors, but the ill success of his troops in their encounters with the Tartars broke his confidence, and he died prematurely after a reign of twenty-three years, which was remarkable as witnessing the consolidation of the Hans. The good work of Wenti was continued during the peaceful reign of sixteen years of his son Kingti.

The next emperor was Vouti, a younger son of Kingti, and one of his earliest conquests was to add the difficult and inaccessible province of Fuhkien to the empire. He also endeavored to propitiate the Huns by giving their chief one of the princesses of his family as a wife, but the opinion was gaining ground that it would be better to engage in a war for the overthrow of the national enemy than to purchase a hollow peace. Wang Kua, a general who had commanded on the frontier, and who knew the Hun mode of warfare, represented that success would be certain, and at last gained the emperor's ear. Vouti decided on war, and raised a large army for the purpose. But the result was not auspicious. Wang Kua failed to bring the Huns to an engagement, and the campaign which was to produce such great results ended ingloriously. The unlucky general who had promised so much anticipated his master's displeasure by committing suicide. Unfortunately for himself, his idea of engaging in a mortal struggle with the Tartars gained ground, and became in time the fixed policy of China. Notwithstanding this check, the authority of Vouti continued to expand. He annexed Szchuen, a province exceeding in site and population most European states, and he received from the ruler of Manchuria a formal tender of submission. In the last years of his reign the irrepressible Hun question again came up for discussion, and the episode of the flight of the Yuchi from Kansuh affords a break in the monotony of the struggle, and is the first instance of that western movement which brought the tribes of the Gobi Desert into Europe. The Yuchi are believed to have been allied with the Jats of India, and there is little or no doubt that the Sacæ, or Scythians, were their descendants. They occupied a strip of territory in Kansuh from Shachow to Lanchefoo, and after suffering much at the hands of the Huns under Meha, they resolved to seek a fresh home in the unknown regions of Western Asia. The Emperor Vouti wished to bring them back, and he sent an envoy named Chang Keen to induce them to return. That officer discovered them in the Oxus region, but all his arguments failed to incline them to leave a quarter in which they had recovered power and prosperity. Powerless against the Huns, they had more than held their own against the Parthians and the Greek kingdom of Bactria. They retained their predominant position in what is now Bokhara and Balkh, until they were gathered up by the Huns in their western march, and hurled, in conjunction with them, on the borders of the Roman Empire.

Meantime, the war with the Huns themselves entered upon a new phase. A general named Wei Tsing obtained a signal victory over them, capturing 15,000 prisoners and the spoil of the Tartar camp. This success restored long-lost confidence to the Chinese troops, and it was followed by several other victories. One Chinese expedition, composed entirely of cavalry, marched through the Hun country to Soponomo on the Tian Shan, carrying everything before it and returning laden with spoil, including some of the golden images of the Hun religion. Encouraged by these successes, Vouti at last took the field in person, and sent a formal summons to the Tartar king to make his submission to China. His reply was to imprison the bearer of the message, and to defy the emperor to do his worst. This boldness had the effect of deterring the emperor from his enterprise. He employed his troops in conquering Yunnan and Leaoutung instead of in waging another war with the Huns. But he had only postponed, not abandoned, his intention of overthrowing, once and for all, this most troublesome and formidable national enemy. He raised an enormous force for the campaign, which might have proved successful but for the mistake of intrusting the command to an incompetent general. In an ill-advised moment, he gave his brother-in-law, Li Kwangli, the supreme direction of the war. His incompetence entailed a succession of disasters, and the only redeeming point amid them was that Li Kwangli was taken prisoner and rendered incapable of further mischief. Liling, the grandson of this general, was intrusted with a fresh army to retrieve the fortunes of the war; but, although successful at first, he was outmaneuvered, and reduced to the unpleasant pass of surrendering to the enemy. Both Li Kwangli and Liling adapted themselves to circumstances, and took service under the Tartar chief. As this conduct obtained the approval of the historian Ssematsien, it is clear that our views of such a proceeding would not be in harmony with the opinion in China of that day. The long war which Vouti waged with the Huns for half a century, and which was certainly carried on in a more honorable and successful manner than any previous portion of that historic struggle, closed with discomfiture and defeat, which dashed to the ground the emperor's hopes of a complete triumph over the most formidable national enemy.

After a reign of fifty-four years, which must be pronounced glorious, Vouti died, amid greater troubles and anxieties than any that had beset him during his long reign. He was unquestionably a great ruler. He added several provinces to his empire, and the success he met with over the Huns was far from being inconsiderable. He was a Nimrod among the Chinese, and his principal enjoyment was to chase the wildest animals without any attendants. Like many other Chinese princes, Vouti was prone to believe in the possibility of prolonging human life, or, as the Chinese put it, in the draught of immortality. In connection with this weakness an anecdote is preserved that will bear telling. A magician offered the emperor a glass containing the pretended elixir of eternal life, and Vouti was about to drink it when a courtier snatched it from his hand and drained the goblet. The enraged monarch ordered him to prepare for instant death, but the ready courtier at once replied, "How can I be executed, since I have drunk the draught of immortality?" To so convincing an argument no reply was possible, and Vouti lived to a considerable age without the aid of magicians or quack medicines. Of him also it may be said that he added to the stability of the Han dynasty, and he left the throne to Chaoti, the youngest of his sons, a child of eight, for whom he appointed his two most experienced ministers to act as governors. As these ministers were true to their duty, the interregnum did not affect the fortunes of the State adversely, and several claimants to the throne paid for their ambition with their lives. The reign of Chaoti was prosperous and successful, but, unfortunately, he died at the early age of thirty-one, and without leaving an heir.

After some hesitation, Chaoti's uncle Liucho was proclaimed emperor, but he proved to be a boor with low tastes, whose sole idea of power was the license to indulge in coarse amusements. The chief minister, Ho Kwang, took upon himself the responsibility of deposing him, and also of placing on the throne Siuenti, who was the great-grandson, or, according to another account, the grandson, of Vouti. The choice was a fortunate one, and "Ho Kwang gave all his care to perfecting the new emperor in the science of government." As a knowledge of his connection with the Imperial family had been carefully kept from him, Siuenti was brought from a very humble sphere to direct the destinies of the Chinese, and his greater energy and more practical disposition were probably due to his not having been bred in the enervating atmosphere of a palace. He, too, was brought at an early stage of his career face to face with the Tartar question, and he had what may be pronounced a unique experience in his wars with them. He sent several armies under commanders of reputation to wage war on them, and the generals duly returned, reporting decisive and easily obtained victories. The truth soon leaked out. The victories were quite imaginary. The generals had never ventured to face the Tartars, and they were given no option by their enraged and disappointed master but to poison themselves. Other generals were appointed, and the Tartars were induced to sue for peace, partly from fear of the Chinese, and partly because they were disunited among themselves. Such was the reputation of Siuenti for justice that several of the Tartar chiefs carried their grievances to the foot of his throne, and his army became known as "the troops of justice." It is said that all the tribes and countries of Central Asia as far west as the Caspian sent him tribute, and to celebrate the event he built a kilin or pavilion, in which he placed statues of all the generals who had contributed toward his triumph. Only one incident marred the tranquillity of Siuenti's reign. The great statesman, Ho Kwang, had sunk quietly into private life as soon as he found the emperor capable of governing for himself; but his wife Hohien was more ambitious and less satisfied with her position, although she had effected a marriage between her daughter and Siuenti. This lady was only one of the queens of the ruler, and not the empress. Hohien, to further her ends, determined to poison the empress, and succeeded only too well. Her guilt would have been divulged by the doctor she employed, but that Ho Kwang, by an exercise of his authority, prevented the application of torture to him when thrown into prison. This narrow escape from detection did not keep Hohien from crime. She had the satisfaction of seeing her daughter proclaimed empress, but her gratification was diminished by the son of the murdered Hiuchi being selected as heir to the throne. Hohien resolved to poison this prince, but her design was discovered, and she and all the members of her family were ordered to take poison. The minister, Ho Kwang, had taken no part in these plots, which, however, injured his reputation, and his statue in the Imperial pavilion was left without a name.

Siuenti did not long survive these events, and Yuenti, the son of Hiuchi, became emperor. His reign of sixteen years presents no features of interest beyond the signal overthrow of the Tartar chief, Chichi, whose head was sent by the victorious general to be hung on the walls of Singan. Yuenti was succeeded by his son Chingti, who reigned twenty-six years, and who gained the reputation of a Chinese Vitellius. His nephew Gaiti, who was the next emperor, showed himself an able and well-intentioned prince, but his reign of six years was too brief to allow of any permanent work being accomplished. One measure of his was not without its influence on the fate of his successors. He had disgraced and dismissed from the service an official named Wang Mang, who had attained great power and influence under Chingti. The ambition of this individual proved fatal to the dynasty. On Gaiti's death he emerged from his retirement, and, in conjunction with that prince's mother, seized the government. They placed a child, grandson of Yuenti, on the throne, and gave him the name of Pingti, or the Peaceful Emperor, but he never governed. Before Pingti was fourteen, Wang Mang resolved to get rid of him, and he gave him the poisoned cup with his own hands. This was not the only, or perhaps the worst, crime that Wang Mang perpetrated to gain the throne. Pressed for money to pay his troops, he committed the sacrilege of stripping the graves of the princes of the Han family of the jewels deposited in them. One more puppet prince was placed on the throne, but he was soon got rid of, and Wang Mang proclaimed himself emperor. He also decreed that the Han dynasty was extinct, and that his family should be known as the Sin.

Wang Mang the usurper was certainly a capable administrator, but in seizing the throne he had attempted a task to which he was unequal. As long as he was minister or regent, respect and regard for the Han family prevented many from revolting against his tyranny, but when he seized the throne he became the mark of popular indignation and official jealousy. The Huns resumed their incursions, and, curiously enough, put forward a proclamation demanding the restoration of the Hans. Internal enemies sprang up on every side, and Wang Mang's attempt to terrify them by severity and wholesale executions only aggravated the situation. It became clear that the struggle was to be one to the death, but this fact did not assist Wang Mang, who saw his resources gradually reduced and his enemies more confident as the contest continued. After twelve years' fighting, Wang Mang was besieged at Singan. The city was soon carried by storm, and Wang Mang retired to the palace to put an end to his existence. But his heart failed him, and

he was cut down by the foe. His last exclamation and the
dirge of his short-lived dynasty, which is denied a place in
Chinese history, was, "If Heaven had given me courage,
what could the family of the Hans have done?"

The eldest of the surviving Han princes, Liu Hiuen, was
placed on the throne, and the capital was removed from
Singan to Loyang, or Honan. Nothing could have been
more popular among the Chinese people than the restoration
of the Hans. It is said that the old men cried for joy when
they saw the banner of the Hans again waving over the
palace and in the field. But Liu Hiuen was not a good
ruler, and there might have been reason to regret the change
if he had not wisely left the conduct of affairs to his able
cousin, Liu Sieou. At last the army declared that Liu Sieou
should be emperor, and when Liu Hiuen attempted to form
a faction of his own he was murdered by Fanchong, the
leader of a confederacy known as the Crimson Eyebrows,
on whose co-operation he counted. The Crimson Eyebrows
were so called from the distinguishing mark which they had
adopted when first organized as a protest against the tyranny
of Wang Mang. At first they were patriots, but they soon
became brigands. After murdering the emperor, Fanchong,
their leader, threw off all disguise, and seizing Singan gave
it over to his followers to plunder. Liu Sieou, on becoming
emperor, took the style of Kwang Vouti, and his first task
was to overthrow the Crimson Eyebrows, who had become a
public enemy. He intrusted the command of the army he
raised for this purpose to Fongy, who justified his reputation
as the most skillful Chinese general of his day by gaining
several victories over a more numerous adversary. Within
two years Kwang Vouti had the satisfaction of breaking up
the formidable faction known as the Crimson Eyebrows, and
of holding its leader Fanchong as a prisoner in his capital.

Kwang Vouti was engaged for many more years in sub-
duing the numerous potentates who had repudiated the
imperial authority. His efforts were invariably crowned
with success, but he acquired so great a distaste for war

that it is said when his son asked him to explain how an army was set in battle array he refused to reply. But the love of peace will not avert war when a State has turbulent or ambitious neighbors who are resolved to appeal to arms, and so Kwang Vouti was engaged in almost constant hostilities to the end of his days. Chingtse, the Queen of Kaochi, which may be identified with the modern Annam, defied the Chinese, and defeated the first army sent to bring her to reason. This reverse necessitated a still greater effort on the part of the Chinese ruler to bring his neighbor to her senses. The occupant of the Dragon throne could not sit down tamely under a defeat inflicted by a woman, and an experienced general named Mayuen was sent to punish the Queen of Kaochi. The Boadicea of Annam made a valiant defense, but she was overthrown, and glad to purchase peace by making the humblest submission. The same general more than held his own on the northern and northwest frontiers. When Kwang Vouti died, in A.D. 57, after a brilliant reign of thirty-three years, he had firmly established the Han dynasty, and he left behind him the reputation of being both a brave and a just prince.

His son and successor, Mingti, was not unworthy of his father. His acts were characterized by wisdom and clemency, and the country enjoyed a large measure of peace through the policy of Mingti and his father. A general named Panchow, who was perhaps the greatest military commander China ever produced, began his long and remarkable career in this reign, and, without the semblance of an effort, kept the Huns in order, and maintained the imperial authority over them. Among other great and important works, Mingti constructed a dike, thirty miles long, for the relief of the Hoangho, and the French missionary and writer, Du Halde, states that so long as this was kept in repair there were no floods. The most remarkable event of Mingti's reign was undoubtedly the official introduction of Buddhism into China. Some knowledge of the great Indian religion and of the teacher Sakya Muni seems to

have reached China through either Tibet, or, more probably, Burma, but it was not until Mingti, in consequence
of a dream, sent envoys to India to study Buddhism, that
its doctrine became known in China. Under the direct
patronage of the emperor it made rapid progress, and although never unreservedly popular, it has held its ground
ever since its introduction in the first century of our era,
and is now inextricably intertwined with the religion of the
Chinese state and people. Mingti died after a successful
reign of eighteen years in 75 A.D. His son, Changti, with
the aid of his mother, Machi, the daughter of the general
Mayuen, enjoyed a peaceful reign of thirteen years, and
died at an early age lamented by his sorrowing people.

After Changti came his son, Hoti, who was only ten at
the time of his accession, and who reigned for seventeen
years. He was a virtuous and well-intentioned prince, who
instituted many internal reforms, and during his reign a
new writing paper was invented, which is supposed to have
been identical with the papyrus of Egypt. But the reign
of Hoti is rendered illustrious by the remarkable military
achievements of Panchow. The success of that general in
his operations with the Huns has already been referred to,
and he at last formed a deliberate plan for driving them
away from the Chinese frontier. Although he enjoyed the
confidence of his successive sovereigns, the imperial sanction
was long withheld from this vast scheme, but during the life
of Changti he began to put in operation measures for the
realization of this project that were only matured under
Hoti. He raised and trained a special army for frontier
war. He enlisted tribes who had never served the emperor
before, and who were specially qualified for desert warfare.
He formed an alliance with the Sienpi tribes of Manchuria,
who were probably the ancestors of the present Manchus,
and thus arranged for a flank attack on the Huns. This
systematic attack was crowned with success. The pressure brought against them compelled the Hiongnou to give
way, and, as they were ousted from their possessions, to

seek fresh homes further west. In this they were, no doubt, stimulated by the example of their old opponents, the Yuchi, but Panchow's energy supplied a still more convincing argument. He pursued them wherever they went, across the Gobi Desert and beyond the Tian Shan range, taking up a strong position at modern Kuldja and Kashgar, sending his expeditions on to the Pamir, and preparing to complete his triumph by the invasion of the countries of the Oxus and Jaxartes. When Hoti was still a youth, he completed this programme by overrunning the region as far as the Caspian, which was probably at that time connected with the Aral, and it may be supposed that Khiva marked the limit of the Chinese general's triumphant progress. It is affirmed with more or less show of truth that he came into contact with the Roman empire or the great Thsin, as the Chinese called it, and that he wished to establish commercial relations with it. But however uncertain this may be, there can be no doubt that he inflicted a most material injury on Rome, for before his legions fled the Huns, who, less than four centuries later, debased the majesty of the imperial city, and whose leader, Attila, may have been a descendant of that Meha at whose hands the Chinese suffered so severely.

After this brilliant and memorable war, Panchow returned to China, where he died at the great age of eighty. With him disappeared the good fortune of the Han dynasty, and misfortunes fell rapidly on the family that had governed China so long and so well. Hoti's infant son lived only a few months, and then his brother, Ganti, became emperor. The real power rested in the hands of the widow of Hoti, who was elevated to the post of regent. Ganti was succeeded in A.D. 124 by his son, Chunti, in whose time several rebellions occurred, threatening the extinction of the dynasty. Several children were then elevated to the throne, and at last an ambitious noble named Leangki, whose sister was one of the empresses, acquired the supreme direction of affairs. He gave a great deal of trouble, but at last, finding that his ambitious schemes did not prosper, he took poison, thus anticipating a decree passed for his execution. Hwanti, the emperor who had the courage to punish this powerful noble, was the last able ruler of the Hans. His reign was, on the whole, a brilliant one, and the Sienpi tribes, who had taken the place of the Hiongnou, were, after one arduous campaign, defeated in a pitched battle. The Chinese were on the verge of defeat when their general, Twan Kang, rushed to the front, exclaiming: "Recall to your minds how often before you have beaten these same opponents, and teach them again to-day that in you they have their masters."

After Hwanti's death the decline of the Hans was rapid. They produced no other ruler worthy of the throne. In the palace the eunuchs, always numerous at the Chinese court, obtained the upper hand, and appointed their own creatures to the great governing posts. Fortunately this dissension at the capital was not attended by weakness on the frontier, and the Sienpi were again defeated. The battle is chiefly memorable because the Sienpi endeavored to frighten the Chinese general by threatening to kill his mother, who was a prisoner in their hands, if he attacked. Not deterred by this menace, Chow Pow attacked the enemy, and gained a decisive victory, but at the cost of his mother's life, which so affected him that he died of grief shortly afterward. After some time dissensions rose in the Han family, and two half-brothers claimed the throne. Pienti became emperor by the skillful support of his uncle, General Hotsin, while his rival, Hienti, enjoyed the support of the eunuchs. A deadly feud ensued between the two parties, which was aggravated by the murder of Hotsin, who rashly entered the palace without an escort. His soldiers avenged his death, carrying the palace by storm and putting ten thousand eunuchs to the sword. After this the last emperors possessed only the name of emperor. The practical authority was disputed among several generals, of whom Tsow Tsow was the most distinguished and successful; and he and his son Tsowpi founded a dynasty, of which more will be heard hereafter. In A.D. 220

Hienti, the last Han ruler, retired into private life, thus bringing to an end the famous Han dynasty, which had governed China for four hundred and fifty years.

Among the families that have reigned in China none has obtained as high a place in popular esteem as the Hans. They rendered excellent work in consolidating the empire and in carrying out what may be called the imperial mission of China. Yunnan and Leaoutung were made provinces for the first time. Cochin China became a vassal state. The writ of the emperor ran as far as the Pamir. The wealth and trade of the country increased with the progress of its armies. Some of the greatest public works, in the shape of roads, bridges, canals, and aqueducts, were constructed during this period, and still remain to testify to the glory of the Hans. As has been seen, the Hans produced several great rulers. Their fame was not the creation of one man alone, and as a consequence the dynasty enjoyed a lengthened existence equaled by few of its predecessors or successors. No ruling family was ever more popular with the Chinese than this, and it managed to retain the throne when less favored rulers would have expiated their mistakes and shortcomings by the loss of the empire. With the strong support of the people, the Hans overcame innumerable difficulties, and even the natural process of decay; and when they made their final exit from history it was in a graceful manner, and without the execration of the masses. That this feeling retains its force is shown in the pride with which the Chinese still proclaim themselves to be the sons of Han.

CHAPTER III

A LONG PERIOD OF DISUNION

THE ignominious failure of the usurper Wang Mang to found a dynasty was too recent to encourage any one to take upon himself the heavy charge of administering the whole

of the Han empire, and so the state was split up into three
principalities, and the period is known from this fact as the
Sankoue.   One prince, a member of the late ruling family,
held possession of Szchuen, which was called the principality of Chow.   The southern provinces were governed by a
general named Sunkiuen, and called Ou.   The central and
northern provinces, containing the greatest population and
resources, formed the principality of Wei, subject to Tsowpi,
the son of Tsow Tsow.   A struggle for supremacy very soon
began between these princes, and the balance of success gradually declared itself in favor of Wei.   It would serve no useful purpose to enumerate the battles which marked this struggle, yet one deed of heroism deserves mention, the defense
of Sinching by Changte, an officer of the Prince of Wei.
The strength of the place was insignificant, and, after a
siege of ninety days, several breaches had been made in the
walls.   In this strait Changte sent a message to the besieging general that he would surrender on the hundredth day
if a cessation of hostilities were granted, "as it was a law
among the princes of Wei that the governor of a place which
held out for a hundred days and then surrendered, with no
prospect of relief visible, should not be considered as guilty."
The respite was short and it was granted.   But the disappointment of the besieger, already counting on success, was
great when a few days later he saw that the breaches had
been repaired, that fresh defenses had been improvised, and
that Sinching was in better condition than ever to withstand
a siege.   On sending to inquire the meaning of these preparations, Changte gave the following reply: "I am preparing my tomb and to bury myself in the ruins of Sinching."
Of such gallantry and resource the internecine strife of the
Sankoue period presents few instances, but the progress of
the struggle steadily pointed in the direction of the triumph
of Wei.

The Chow dynasty of the Later Hans was the first to
succumb to the princes of Wei, and the combined resources
of the two states were then directed against the southern

this campaign, Topatao was murdered by some discontented officers.

Nor was the Song ruler, Wenti, any more fortunate, as he was murdered by his son. The parricide was killed in turn by a brother who became the Emperor Vouti. This ruler was fond of the chase and a great eater, but, on the whole, he did no harm. The next two emperors were cruel and bloodthirsty princes, and during their reigns the executioner was constantly employed. Two more princes, who were, however, not members of the Song family, but only adopted by the last ruler of that house, occupied the throne, but this weakness and unpopularity—for the Chinese, unlike the people of Japan, scout the idea of adoption and believe only in the rights of birth—administered the finishing stroke to the Songs, who now give place to the Tsi dynasty, which was founded by a general named Siaotaoching, who took the imperial name of Kaoti. The change did not bring any improvement in the conditions of China, and it was publicly said that the Tsi family had attained its pride of place "not by merit, but by force." The Tsi dynasty, after a brief and ignominious career, came to an end in the person of a youthful prince named Hoti. After his deposition, in A.D. 502, his successful enemies ironically sent him in prison a present of gold. He exclaimed, "What need have I of gold after my death? A few glasses of wine would be more valuable." They complied with his wish, and while he was drunk they strangled him with his own silken girdle.

After the Tsi came the Leang dynasty, another of those insignificant and unworthy families which occupy the stage of Chinese history during this long period of disunion. The new Emperor Vouti was soon brought into collision with the state of Wei, which during these years had regained all its power, and had felt strong enough to transfer its capital from the northern city of Pingching to Honan, while the Leang capital remained at Nankin. The progress of this contest was marked by the consistent success of Wei, and the prince of that kingdom seems to have been as superior in the capacity of his generals as in the resources of his state. One incident will be sufficient to show the devotion which he was able to inspire in his officers. During the absence of its governor, Vouti attempted to capture the town of Ginching, and he would certainly have succeeded in his object had not Mongchi, the wife of that officer, anticipating by many centuries the conduct of the Countess of Montfort and of the Countess of Derby, thrown herself into the breach, harangued the small garrison, and inspired it with her own indomitable spirit. Vouti was compelled to make an ignominious retreat from before Ginching, and his troops became so disheartened that they refused to engage the enemy, notwithstanding their taunts and their marching round the imperial camp with the head of a dead person decked out in a widow's cap and singing a doggerel ballad to the effect that none of Vouti's generals was to be feared. In the next campaign Vouti was able to restore his declining fortunes by the timely discovery of a skillful general in the person of Weijoui, who, taking advantage of the division of the Wei army into two parts by a river, gained a decisive victory over each of them in turn. If Vouti had listened to his general's advice, and followed up this success, he might have achieved great and permanent results, but instead he preferred to rest content with his laurels, with the result that the Wei prince recovered his military power and confidence. The natural consequence of this was that the two neighbors once more resorted to a trial of strength, and, notwithstanding the valiant and successful defense of a fortress by another lady named Liuchi, the fortune of war declared in the main for Vouti. This may be considered one of the most remarkable periods for the display of female capacity in China, as the great state of Wei was governed by a queen named Houchi; but the general condition of the country does not support an argument in favor of female government.

The tenure of power by Houchi was summarily cut short by the revolt of the Wei commander-in-chief, Erchu Jong, who got rid of his mistress by tying her up in a sack and

CHINA—3

throwing her into the Hoangho. He then collected two thousand of her chief advisers in a plain outside the capital, and there ordered his cavalry to cut them down. Erchu Jong then formed an ambitious project for reuniting the empire, proclaiming to his followers his intention in this speech: "Wait a little while, and we shall assemble all the braves from out our western borders. We will then go and bring to reason the six departments of the north, and the following year we will cross the great Kiang, and place in chains Siaoyen, who calls himself emperor." This scheme was nipped in the bud by the assassination of Erchu Jong. Although the death of its great general signified much loss to the Wei state, the Emperor Vouti experienced bitter disappointment and a rude awakening when he attempted to turn the event to his own advantage. His army was defeated in every battle, his authority was reduced to a shadow, and a mutinous officer completed in his palace the overthrow begun by his hereditary enemy. Vouti was now eighty years of age, and ill able to stand so rude a shock. On being deposed he exclaimed: "It was I who raised my family, and it was I who have destroyed it. I have no reason to complain"; and he died a few days later, from, it is said, a pain in his throat which his jailers refused to alleviate with some honey. On the whole, Vouti was a creditable ruler, although the Chinese annalists blame him for his superstition and denounce his partiality for Buddhism.

Vouti's prediction that his family was destroyed proved correct. He was succeeded in turn by three members of his family, but all of these died a violent death. A general named Chinpasien founded a fresh dynasty known as the Chin, but he died before he had enjoyed power many years. At this period also disappeared the Wei state, which was dissolved by the death of Erchu Jong, and now merged itself into that of Chow. The growth of this new power proved very rapid, and speedily extinguished that of the unfortunate Chins. The Chow ruler took the name of Kaotsou Wenti, and ruled over a great portion of China.

He changed the name of his dynasty to the Soui, which, although it did not hold possession of the throne for long, vindicated its claim to supremacy by successful wars and admirable public works. This prince showed himself a very capable administrator, and his acts were marked by rare generosity and breadth of view. His son and successor, Yangti, although he reached the throne by the murder of a brother, proved himself an intelligent ruler and a benefactor of his people. He transferred his capital from Nankin to Honan, which he resolved to make the most magnificent city in the world. It is declared that he employed two million men in embellishing it, and that he caused fifty thousand merchants to take up their residence there. But of all his works none will compare with the great system of canals which he constructed, and in connection with which his name will live forever in history. Although he reigned no more than thirteen years, he completed nearly five thousand miles of canals. Some of these, such as the Grand Canal, from the Hoangho to the Yangtsekiang, are splendid specimens of human labor, and could be made as useful today as they were when first constructed. The canal named is forty yards wide and is lined with solid stone. The banks are bordered with elms and willows. These works were constructed by a general corvee or levy en masse, each family being required to provide one able-bodied man, and the whole of the army was also employed on this public undertaking. It is in connection with it that Yangti's name will be preserved, as his wars, especially one with Corea, were not successful, and an ignominious end was put to his existence by a fanatic. His son and successor was also murdered, when the Soui dynasty came to an end, and with it the magnificent and costly palace erected at Loyang, which was denounced as only calculated "to soften the heart of a prince and to foment his cupidity."

There now ensues a break in the long period of disunion which had prevailed in China, and for a time the supreme authority of the emperor recovered the general respect and vigor which by right belonged to it. The deposer of the Souis was Liyuen, who some years before had been given the title of Prince of Tang. In the year A.D. 617 he proclaimed himself emperor under the style of Kaotsou, and he began his reign in an auspicious manner by proclaiming an amnesty and by stating his "desire to found his empire only on justice and humanity." While he devoted his attention to the reorganization of the administration at Singan, which he chose for his capital, his second son, Lichimin, was intrusted with the command of the army in the field, to which was assigned the task of subjecting all the provinces. Lichimin proved himself a great commander, and his success was both rapid and unqualified. He was equally victorious over Chinese rebels and foreign enemies. His energy and skill were not more conspicuous than his courage. At the head of his chosen regiment of cuirassiers, carrying black tiger skins, he was to be found in the front of every battle, and victory was due as often to his personal intrepidity as to his tactical skill. Within a few years the task of Lichimin was brought to a glorious completion, and on his return to Singan he was able to assure his father that the empire was pacified in a sense that had not been true for many centuries. His entry into Singan at the head of his victorious troops reminds the reader of a Roman triumph. Surrounded by his chosen bodyguard, and followed by forty thousand cavalry, Lichimin, wearing a breastplate of gold and accompanied by the most important of his captives, rode through the streets to make public offering of thanks for victory achieved, at the temple of his ancestors. His success was enhanced by his moderation, for he granted his prisoners their lives, and his reputation was not dimmed by any acts of cruelty or bloodshed.

The magnitude of Lichimin's success and his consequent popularity aroused the envy and hostility of his elder brother, who aspired to the throne. The intrigues against him were so far successful that he fell into disgrace with the emperor, and for a time withdrew from the court. But his brother

was not content with anything short of taking his life, and
formed a conspiracy with his other brothers and some prominent officials to murder him.   The plot was discovered, and
recoiled upon its authors, who were promptly arrested and
executed.   Then Lichimin was formally proclaimed heir to
the throne; but the event sinks into comparative insignifi-
cance beside the abdication of the throne by Kaotsou in the
same year.   The real cause of this step was probably not
disconnected with the plot against Lichimin, but the official
statement was that Kaotsou felt the weight of years, and
that he wished to enjoy rest and the absence of responsibility during his last days.   Kaotsou must be classed among
the capable rulers of China, but his fame has been over-
shadowed by and merged in the greater splendor of his son.
He survived his abdication nine years, dying in A.D. 635 at
the age of seventy-one.

On ascending the throne, Lichimin took the name of
Taitsong, and he is one of the few Chinese rulers to whom
the epithet of Great may be given without fear of its being
challenged.   The noble task to which he at once set himself
was to prove that the Chinese were one people, that the interests of all the provinces, as of all classes of the community, were the same, and that the pressing need of the hour
was to revive the spirit of national unity and patriotism.
Before he became ruler in his own name he had accomplished something toward this end by the successful campaigns he had conducted to insure the recognition of his
father's authority.   But Taitsong saw that much more remained to be done, and the best way to do it seemed to him
to be the prosecution of what might be called a national war
against those enemies beyond the northern frontier, who
were always troublesome, and who had occasionally founded
governments within the limits of China like the Topa family
of Wei.   In order to achieve any great or lasting success in
this enterprise, Taitsong saw that it was essential that he
should possess a large and well-trained standing army, on
which he could rely for efficient service beyond the frontier

as well as in China itself. Before his time Chinese armies had been little better than a rude militia, and the military knowledge of the officers could only be described as contemptible. The soldiers were, for the most part, peasants, who knew nothing of discipline, and into whose hands weapons were put for the first time on the eve of a war. They were not of a martial temperament, and they went unwillingly to a campaign; and against such active opponents as the Tartars they would only engage when superiority of numbers promised success. They were easily seized with a panic, and the celerity and dash of Chinese troops only became perceptible when their backs were turned to the foe. So evident had these faults become that more than one emperor had endeavored to recruit from among the Tartar tribes, and to oppose the national enemy with troops not less brave or active than themselves. But the employment of mercenaries is always only a half remedy, and not free from the risk of aggravating the evil it is intended to cure. But Taitsong did not attempt any such palliation; he went to the root of the question, and determined to have a trained and efficient army of his own. He raised a standing army of nine hundred thousand men, which he divided into three equal classes of regiments, one containing one thousand two hundred men, another one thousand, and the third eight hundred. The total number of regiments was eight hundred and ninety-five, of which six hundred and thirty-four were recruited for home service and two hundred and sixty-one for foreign. By this plan he obtained the assured services of more than a quarter of a million of trained troops for operations beyond the frontier. Taitsong also improved the weapons and armament of his soldiers. He lengthened the pike and supplied a stronger bow. Many of his troops wore armor; and he relied on the co-operation of his cavalry, a branch of military power which has generally been much neglected in China. He took special pains to train a large body of officers, and he instituted a Tribunal of War, to which the supreme direction of military matters was intrusted. As these measures greatly shocked the civil mandarins, who regarded the emperor's taking part in reviews and the physical exercises of the soldiers as "an impropriety," it will be allowed that Taitsong showed great moral courage and surmounted some peculiar difficulties in carrying out his scheme for forming a regular army. He overcame all obstacles, and gathered under his banner an army formidable by reason of its efficiency and equipment, as well as for its numerical strength.

Having acquired what he deemed the means to settle it, Taitsong resolved to grapple boldly with the ever-recurring danger from the Tartars. Under different names, but ever with the same object, the tribes of the vast region from Corea to Koko Nor had been a trouble to the Chinese agriculturist and government from time immemorial. Their sole ambition and object in life had been to harry the lands of the Chinese, and to bear back to their camps the spoils of cities. The Huns had disappeared, but in their place had sprung up the great power of the Toukinei or Turks, who were probably the ancestors of the Ottomans. With these turbulent neighbors, and with others of different race but of the same disposition on the southern frontier, Taitsong was engaged in a bitter and arduous struggle during the whole of his life; and there can be little or no doubt that he owed his success to the care he bestowed on his army. The Great Wall of Tsin Hwangti had been one barrier in the path of these enemies, but, held by a weak and cowardly garrison, it had proved inadequate for its purpose. Taitsong supplied another and a better defense in a consistent and energetic policy, and in the provision of a formidable and confident army.

The necessity for this military reform was clearly shown by the experience of his first campaign with these implacable enemies, when, in the year of his accession and before his organization had been completed, a horde of these barbarians broke into the empire and carried all before them, almost to the gates of the capital. On this occasion Taitsong resorted to diplomacy and remonstrance. He rode almost unattended to the Tartar camp, and reproached their chiefs with their breach of faith, reminding them that on his sending one of his sisters to be the bride of their chief they had sworn by a solemn oath to keep the peace. He asked: "Are these proceedings worthy, I will not say of princes, but of men possessing the least spark of honor? If they forget the benefits they have received from me, at the least they ought to be mindful of their oaths. I had sworn a peace with them; they are now violating it, and by that they place the justice of the question on my side." The Chinese chroniclers declare that the Tartars were so impressed by Taitsong's majestic air and remonstrances that they agreed to retire, and fresh vows of friendship and peace were sworn over the body of a white horse at a convention concluded on the Pienkiao bridge across the Weichoui River. The only safe deduction from this figurative narrative is that there was a Tartar incursion, and that the Chinese army did not drive back the invaders. Their retreat was probably purchased, but it was the first and last occasion on which Taitsong stooped to such a measure.

The peace of Pienkiao was soon broken. The tribes again drew their forces to a head for the purpose of invading China, but before their plans were complete Taitsong anticipated them by marching into their territory at the head of a large army. Taken by surprise, the Tartars offered but a feeble resistance. Several of their khans surrendered, and at a general assembly Taitsong proclaimed his intention to govern them as Khan of their khans, or by the title of Tien Khan, which means Celestial Ruler. This was the first occasion on which a Chinese ruler formally took over the task of governing the nomad tribes and of treating their chiefs as his lieutenants. Down to the present day the Chinese emperor continues to govern the Mongol and other nomadic tribes under this very title, which the Russians have rendered as Bogdo Khan. The success of this policy was complete, for not only did it give tranquillity to the Chinese borders, but it greatly extended Chinese authority. Kashgaria was then, for the first time, formed into a province under the name of Lonugsi, and Lichitsi, one of the emperor's best generals, was appointed Warden of the Western Marches. Some of the most influential of Taitsong's advisers disapproved of this advanced policy, and attempted to thwart it, but in vain. Carried out with the vigor and consistency of Taitsong there cannot be two opinions about its wisdom and efficacy.

During this reign the relations between China and two of its neighbors, Tibet and Corea, were greatly developed, and the increased intercourse was largely brought about by the instrumentality of war. The first envoys from Tibet, or, as it was then called, Toufan or Toupo, are reported to have reached the Chinese capital in the year 634. At that time the people of Tibet were rude and unlettered, and their chiefs were little better than savages. Buddhism had not taken that firm hold on the popular mind which it at present possesses, and the power of the lamas had not arisen in what is now the most priest-ridden country in the world. A chief, named the Sanpou—which means the brave lord—had, about the time of which we are speaking, made himself supreme throughout the country, and it was said that he had crossed the Himalaya and carried his victorious arms into Central India. Curiosity, or the desire to wed a Chinese princess, and thus to be placed on what may be termed a favored footing, induced the Sanpou to send his embassy to Singan; but although the envoys returned laden with presents, Taitsong declined to trust a princess of his family in a strange country and among an unknown people. The Sanpou chose to interpret this refusal as an insult to his dignity, and he declared war with China. But success did not attend his enterprise, for he was defeated in the only battle of the war, and glad to purchase peace by paying five thousand ounces of gold and acknowledging himself a Chinese vassal. The Sanpou also agreed to accept Chinese education, and as his reward Taitsong gave him one of his daughters as a wife. It is stated that one of his first reforms was to abolish the national practice of painting the face, and he also built a walled city to proclaim his glory as the son-in-law of the Emperor of China. During Taitsong's life there was no further trouble on the side of Tibet.

Taitsong was not so fortunate in his relations with Corea, where a stubborn people and an inaccessible country imposed a bar to his ambition. Attempts had been made at earlier periods to bring Corea under the influence of the Chinese ruler, and to treat it as a tributary state. A certain measure of success had occasionally attended these attempts, but on the whole Corea had preserved its independence. When Taitsong in the plenitude of his power called upon the King of Corea to pay tribute, and to return to his subordinate position, he received a defiant reply, and the Coreans began to encroach on Sinlo, a small state which threw itself on the protection of China. The name of Corea at this time was Kaoli, and the supreme direction of affairs at this period was held by a noble named Chuen Gaisoowun, who had murdered his own sovereign. Taitsong, irritated by his defiance, sent a large army to the frontier, and when Gaisoowun, alarmed by the storm he had raised, made a humble submission and sent the proper tribute, the emperor gave expression to his displeasure and disapproval of the regicide's acts by rejecting his gifts and announcing his resolve to prosecute the war. It is never prudent to drive an opponent to desperation, and Gaisoowun, who might have been a good neighbor if Taitsong had accepted his offer, proved a bitter and determined antagonist. The first campaign was marked by the expected success of the Chinese army. The Coreans were defeated in several battles, several important towns were captured, but Taitsong had to admit that these successes were purchased at the heavy loss of twenty-five thousand of his best troops. The second campaign resolved itself into the siege and defense of Anshu, an important town near the Yaloo River. Gaisoowun raised an enormous force with the view of effecting its relief, and he attempted to overwhelm the Chinese by superior numbers. But the better discipline and tactics of the Chinese turned the day, and the Corean army was driven in rout from the field. But this signal success did not entail the surrender of Anshu, which was gallantly defended. The scarcity of supplies and the approach of winter compelled the Chinese emperor to raise the siege after he had remained before the place for several months, and it is stated that as the Chinese broke up their camp the commandant appeared on the walls and wished them "a pleasant journey." After this rebuff Taitsong did not renew his attempt to annex Corea, although to the end of his life he refused to hold any relations with Gaisoowun.

During the first portion of his reign Taitsong was greatly helped by the labors of his wife, the Empress Changsun-chi, who was a woman of rare goodness and ability, and set a shining example to the whole of her court. She said many wise things, among which the most quotable was that "the practice of virtue conferred honor upon men, especially on princes, and not the splendor of their appointments." She was a patron of letters, and an Imperial Library and College in the capital owed their origin to her. She was probably the best and most trustworthy adviser the emperor had, and after her death the energy and good fortune of Taitsong seemed to decline. She no doubt contributed to the remarkable treatise on the art of government, called the "Golden Mirror," which bears the name of Taitsong as its author. Taitsong was an ardent admirer of Confucius, whom he exalted to the skies as the great sage of the world, declaring emphatically that "Confucius was for the Chinese what the water is for the fishes." The Chinese annalists tell many stories of Taitsong's personal courage. He was a great hunter, and in the pursuit of big game he necessarily had some narrow escapes, special mention being made of his slaying single-handed a savage boar. Another instance was his struggle with a Tartar attendant who attempted to murder him, and whom he killed in the encounter. He had a still narrower escape at the hands of his eldest son, who formed a plot to assassinate him which very nearly succeeded. The excessive anxiety of Prince Lichingkien to reach the crown cost him the succession, for on the discovery of his plot he was deposed from the position of heir-apparent and disappeared from the scene.

After a reign of twenty-three years, during which he accomplished a great deal more than other rulers had done in twice the time, Taitsong died in A.D. 649, leaving the undisturbed possession of the throne to his son, known as the Emperor Kaotsong. There need be no hesitation in calling Taitsong one of the greatest rulers who ever sat on the Dragon Throne, and his death was received with extraordinary demonstrations of grief by the people he had ruled so well. Several of his generals wished to commit suicide on his bier, the representatives of the tributary nations at his capital cut off their hair or sprinkled his grave with their blood, and throughout the length and breadth of the land there was mourning and lamentation for a prince who had realized the ideal character of a Chinese emperor. Nor does his claim to admiration and respect seem less after the lapse of so many centuries. His figure still stands out boldly as one of the ablest and most humane of all Chinese rulers. He not only reunited China, but he proved that union was for his country the only sure basis of prosperity and power.

Under Kaotsong the power of the Tangs showed for thirty years no diminution, and he triumphed in directions where his father had only pointed the way to victory. He began his reign with a somewhat risky act by marrying one of his father's widows, who then became the Empress Wou. She was perhaps the most remarkable woman in the whole range of Chinese history, acquiring such an ascendency over her husband that she practically ruled the state, and retained this power after his death. In order to succeed in so exceptional a task she had to show no excessive delicacy or scrupulousness, and she began by getting rid of the other wives, including the lawful empress of Kaotsong, in a summary fashion. It is stated that she cast them into a vase filled with wine, having previously cut off their hands and feet to prevent their extricating themselves. But on the whole her influence was exerted to promote the great schemes of her husband.

The Tibetan question was revived by the warlike proclivities of the new Sanpou, who, notwithstanding his blood relationship with the Chinese emperor, sought to extend his dominion at his expense toward the north and the east. A desultory war ensued, in which the Chinese got the worst of it, and Kaotsong admitted that Tibet remained "a thorn in his side for years." A satisfactory termination was given to the struggle by the early death of the Sanpou, whose warlike character had been the main cause of the dispute. Strangely enough the arms of Kaotsong were more triumphant in the direction of Corca, where his father had failed. From A.D. 658 to 670 China was engaged in a bitter war on land and sea with the Coreans and their allies, the Japanese, who thus intervened for the first time in the affairs of the continent. Owing to the energy of the Empress Wou victory rested with the Chinese, and the Japanese navy of four hundred junks was completely destroyed. The kingdom of Sinlo was made a Chinese province, and for sixty years the Coreans paid tribute and caused no trouble. In Central Asia also the Chinese power was maintained intact, and the extent of China's authority and reputation may be inferred from the King of Persia begging the emperor's governor in Kashgar to come to his aid against the Arabs, who were then in the act of overrunning Western Asia in the name of the Prophet. Kaotsong could not send aid to such a distance from his borders, but he granted shelter to several Persian princes, and on receiving an embassy from the Arabs, he impressed upon them the wisdom and magnanimity of being lenient to the conquered. Kaotsong died in 683, and the Empress Wou retained power until the year 704, when, at the age of eighty, she was compelled to abdicate. Her independent rule was marked by as much vigor and success as during the life of Kaotsong. She vanquished the Tibetans and a new Tartar race known as the

Khitans, who appeared on the northern borders of Shensi. She placed her son in confinement and wore the robes assigned for an emperor. The extent of her power may be inferred from her venturing to shock Chinese sentiment by offering the annual imperial sacrifice to heaven, and by her erecting temples to her ancestors. Yet it was not until she was broken down by age and illness that any of her foes were bold enough to encounter her. She survived her deposition one year, and her banished son Chongtsong was restored to the throne.

Chongtsong did not reign long, being poisoned by his wife, who did not reap the advantage of her crime. Several emperors succeeded without doing anything to attract notice, and then Mingti brought both his own family and the Chinese empire to the verge of ruin. Like other rulers, he began well, quoting the maxims of the "Golden Mirror" and proclaiming Confucius King of Literature. But defeats at the hands of the Khitans and Tibetans imbittered his life and diminished his authority. A soldier of fortune named Ganlochan revolted and met with a rapid and unexpected success owing to "the people being unaccustomed, from the long peace, to the use of arms." He subdued all the northern provinces, established his capital at Loyang, and compelled Mingti to seek safety in Szchuen, when he abdicated in favor of his son. The misfortunes of Mingti, whose most memorable act was the founding of the celebrated Hanlin College and the institution of the "Pekin Gazette," the oldest periodical in the world, both of which exist at the present day, foretold the disruption of the empire at no remote date. His son and successor Soutsong did something to retrieve the fortunes of his family, and he recovered Singan from Ganlochan. The empire was then divided between the two rivals, and war continued unceasingly between them. The successful defense of Taiyuen, where artillery is said to have been used for the first time, A.D. 757, by a lieutenant of the Emperor Soutsong, consolidated his power, which was further increased by the murder of Ganlochan shortly afterward.

The struggle continued with varying fortune between the northern and southern powers during the rest of the reign of Soutsong, and also during that of his successor, Taitsong the Second. This ruler showed himself unworthy of his name, abandoning his capital with great pusillanimity when a small Tibetan army advanced upon it. The census returns threw an expressive light on the condition of the empire during this period. Under Mingti the population was given at fifty-two million; in the time of the second Taitsong it had sunk to seventeen million. A great general named Kwo Tsey, who had driven back the Tibetan invaders, enabled Tetsong, the son and successor of Taitsong, to make a good start in the government of his dominion, which was sadly reduced in extent and prosperity. This great statesman induced Tetsong to issue an edict reproving the superstitions of the times, and the prevalent fashion of drawing auguries from dreams and accidents. The edict ran thus: "Peace and the general contentment of the people, the abundance of the harvest, skill and wisdom shown in the administration, these are prognostics which I hear of with pleasure; but 'extraordinary clouds,' 'rare animals,' 'plants before unknown,' 'monsters,' and other astonishing productions of nature, what good can any of these do men as auguries of the future? I forbid such things to be brought to my notice." The early death of Kwo Tsey deprived the youthful ruler of his best adviser and the mainstay of his power. He was a man of magnificent capacity and devotion to duty, and when it was suggested to him that he should not be content with any but the supreme place, he proudly replied that he was "a general of the Tangs." It seems from the inscription on the stone found at Singan that he was a patron of the Nestorian Christians, and his character and career have suggested a comparison with Belisarius.

Tetsong lived twenty-four years after the death of his champion, and these years can only be characterized as unfortunate. The great governors claimed and exacted the privilege that their dignities should be made hereditary, and this surrender of the imperial prerogative entailed the usual deterioration of the central power which preceded a change of dynasty. Unpopularity was incurred by the imposition of taxes on the principal articles of production and consumption, such as tea, and, worst symptom of all, the eunuchs again became supreme in the palace. Although the dynasty survived for another century, it was clear that its knell was sounded before Tetsong died. Under his grandson Hientsong the mischief that had been done became more clearly apparent. Although he enjoyed some military successes, his reign on the whole was unfortunate, and he was poisoned by the chief of the eunuchs. His son and successor, Moutsong, from his indifference may be suspected of having been privy to the occurrence. At any rate, he only enjoyed power for a few years before he was got rid of in the same summary fashion. Several other nonentities came to the throne, until at last one ruler named Wentsong, whose intentions at least were stronger than those of his predecessors, attempted to grapple with the eunuchs and formed a plot for their extermination. His courage failed him and the plot miscarried. The eunuchs exacted a terrible revenge on their opponents, of whom they killed nearly three thousand, and Wentsong passed the last year of his life as a miserable puppet in their hands. He was not allowed even to name his successor. The eunuchs ignored his two sons, and placed his brother Voutsong on the throne.

The evils of the day became specially revealed during the reign of Ytsong, who was scarcely seated on the throne before his troops suffered several defeats at the hands of a rebel prince in Yunnan, who completely wrested that province from the empire. He was as pronounced a patron of Buddhism as some of his predecessors had been oppressors, and he sent, at enormous expense, to India a mission to procure a bone of Buddha's body, and on its arrival he received the relic on bended knees before his whole court. His extravagance of living landed the Chinese government in fresh difficulties, and he brought the exchequer to the verge of bankruptcy. Nor was he a humane ruler. On one occasion he executed twenty doctors because they were unable to cure a favorite daughter of his. His son Hitsong came to the throne when he was a mere boy, and at once experienced the depth of misfortune to which his family had sunk. He was driven out of his capital by a rebel named Hwang Chao, and if he had not found an unexpected ally in the Turk chief Likeyong, there would then have been an end to the Tang dynasty. This chief of the Chato immigrants —a race supposed to be the ancestors of the Mohammedan Tungani of more recent times—at the head of forty thousand men of his own race, who, from the color of their uniform, were named "The Black Crows," marched against Hwang Chao, and signally defeated him. The condition of the country at this time is painted in deplorable colors. The emperor did not possess a palace, and all the great towns of Central China were in ruins. Likeyong took in the situation at a glance, when he said, "The ruin of the Tangs is not far distant." Likeyong, who was created Prince of Tsin, did his best to support the emperor, but his power was inadequate for coping with another general named Chuwen, prince of Leang, in whose hands the emperor became a mere puppet. At the safe moment Chuwen murdered his sovereign, and added to this crime a massacre of all the Tang princes upon whom he could lay his hands. Chao Siuenti, the last of the Tangs, abdicated, and a few months later Chuwen, to make assurance doubly sure, assassinated him. Thus disappeared, after two hundred and eighty-nine years and after giving twenty rulers to the state, the great Tang dynasty which had restored the unity and the fame of China. It forms a separate chapter in the long period of disunion from the fall of the Hans to the rise of the Sungs.

After the Tangs came five ephemeral and insignificant dynasties, with the fate of which we need not long detain the reader. In less than sixty years they all vanished from the page of history. The struggle for power between Chuwen, the founder of the so-called Later Leang dynasty, and

Likeyong was successfully continued by the latter's son, Litsunhiu, who proved himself a good soldier. He won a decisive victory at Houlieoupi, and extinguished the Leang dynasty by the capture of its capital and of Chuwen's son, who committed suicide. Litsunhiu ruled for a short time as emperor of the Later Leangs, but he was killed during a mutiny of his turbulent soldiers. This dynasty had a very brief existence; the last ruler of the line, finding the game was up, retired with his family to a tower in his palace, which he set on fire, and perished, with his wives and children, in the flames. Then came the Later Tsins, who only held their authority on the sufferance of the powerful Khitan king, who reigned over Leaoutung and Manchuria. The fourth and fifth of these dynasties, named the Later Hans and Chows, ran their course in less than ten years; and when the last of these petty rulers was deposed by his prime minister a termination was at last reached to the long period of internal division and weakness which prevailed for more than seven hundred and fifty years. The student reaches at this point firmer ground in the history of China as an empire, and his interest in the subject must assume a more definite form on coming to the beginning of that period of united government and settled authority which has been established for nearly one thousand years, during which no more than four separate families have held possession of the throne.

CHAPTER IV

THE SUNGS AND THE KINS

ONE fact will have been noticed during the latter portion of the period that has now closed, and that is the increasing interest and participation in Chinese affairs of the races neighboring to, but still outside, the empire. A large number of the successful generals, and several of the princely families which attained independence, were of Tartar or Turk

origin; but the founder of the new dynasty, which restored
the unity of the empire, was of pure Chinese race, although
a native of the most northern province of the country.   Chow
Kwang Yn was born in Pechihli, at the small town of Yeou-
tou, on the site of which now stands the modern capital of
Pekin.   His family had provided the governor of this place
for several generations, and Chow himself had seen a good
deal of military service during the wars of the period.   He
is described as a man of powerful physique and majestic
appearance, to whose courage and presence of mind the
result of more than one great battle was due, and who had
become in consequence the idol of the soldiery.   The ingenuity of later historians, rather than the credulity of his con-
temporaries, may have discovered the signs and portents
which indicated that he was the chosen of Heaven; but his
army had a simple and convincing method of deciding the
destiny of the empire.   Like the legionaries of Rome, they
exclaimed, "The empire is without a master, and we wish
to give it one.   Who is more worthy of it than our general?"
Thus did Chow Kwang Yn become the Emperor Taitsou and
the founder of the Sung dynasty.

Taitsou began his reign by proclaiming a general amnesty, and he sent the proclamation of his pardon into provinces where he had not a shred of authority.   The step was
a politic one, for it informed the Chinese people that they
again had an emperor.   At the same time he ordered that
the gates and doors of his palace should always be left open
so that the humblest of his subjects might have access to him
at any time.   His own words were that "his house should
resemble his heart, which was open to all his subjects."   He
also devoted his attention to the improvement of his army
and particularly to the training of his officers, who were
called upon to pass an examination in professional subjects
as well as physical exercises.   A French writer said forty
years ago that "The laws of military promotion in the states
of Europe are far from being as rational and equitable as
those introduced by this Chinese ruler."   His solicitude for

the welfare of his soldiers was evinced during a campaign when the winter was exceedingly severe. He took off his own fur coat and sent it to the general in command, with a letter stating that he was sorry that he had not one to send to every soldier in the camp. A soldier himself, he knew how to win a soldier's heart, and the affection and devotion of his army never wavered nor declined. He had many opportunities of testing it. His first war was with the Prince of Han, aided by the King of Leaoutung, whom he speedily vanquished, and whose capacity for aggression was much curtailed by the loss of the frontier fortress of Loochow. His next contest was with an old comrade-in-arms named Li Chougsin, whom he had treated very well, but who was seized with a foolish desire to be greater than his ability or power warranted. The struggle was brief, and Li Chougsin felt he had no alternative save to commit suicide.

The tranquillity gained by these successes enabled Taitsou to institute a great reform in the civil administration of the empire, and one which struck at the root of the evil arising from the excessive power and irresponsibility of the provincial governors. Up to this date the governors had possessed the power of life and death without reference to the capital. It had enabled them to become tyrants, and had simplified their path to complete independence. Taitsou resolved to deprive them of this prerogative and to retain it in his own hands, for, he said, "As life is the dearest thing men possess, should it be placed at the disposal of an official who is often unjust or wicked?" This radical reform greatly strengthened the emperor's position, and weakened that of the provincial viceroys; and Taitsou thus inaugurated a rule which has prevailed in China down to the present day, where the life of no citizen can be taken without the express authority and order of the emperor. Taitsou then devoted his attention to the subjugation of those governors who had either disregarded his administration or given it a grudging obedience. The first to feel the weight of his hand was the viceroy of Honan; but his measures were so well taken, and the military force he employed so overwhelming, that he succeeded in dispossessing him and in appointing his own lieutenant without the loss of a single man. The governor of Szchuen, believing his power to be greater than it was, or trusting to the remoteness of his province, publicly defied Taitsou, and prepared to invade his dominions. The emperor was too quick for him, and before his army was in the field sixty thousand imperial troops had crossed the frontier and had occupied the province. By these triumphs Taitsou acquired possession of some of the richest provinces and forty millions of Chinese subjects.

Having composed these internal troubles with enemies of Chinese race, Taitsou resumed his military operations against his old opponents in Leaoutung. Both sides had been making preparations for a renewal of the struggle, and the fortress of Taiyuen, which had been specially equipped to withstand a long siege, was the object of the emperor's first attack. The place was valiantly defended by a brave governor and a large garrison, and although Taitsou defeated two armies sent to relieve it, he was compelled to give up the hope of capturing Taiyuen on this occasion. Some consolation for this repulse was afforded by the capture of Canton and the districts dependent on that city. He next proceeded against the governor of Kiangnan, the dual province of Anhui and Kiangsu, who had taken the title of Prince of Tang, and striven to propitiate the emperor at the same time that he retained his own independence. The two things were, however, incompatible. Taitsou refused to receive the envoys of the Prince of Tang, and he ordered him to attend in person at the capital. With this the Tang prince would not comply, and an army was at once sent to invade and conquer Kiangnan. The campaign lasted one year, by which time the Tang power was shattered, and his territory resumed its old form as a province of China. With this considerable success Taitsou's career may be said to have terminated, for although he succeeded in detaching the Leaoutung ruler from the side of the Prince of Han, and was hastening at the head of his forces to crush his old enemy at Taiyuen, death cut short his career in a manner closely resembling that of Edward the First of England. Taitsou died in his camp, in the midst of his soldiers; and, acting on the advice of his mother, given on her death-bed a few years before, "that he should leave the throne to a relation of mature age," he appointed his brother his successor, and as his last exhortation to him said, "Bear yourself as becomes a brave prince, and govern well." Many pages might be filled with the recitation of Taitsou's great deeds and wise sayings; but his work in uniting China and in giving the larger part of his country tranquillity speaks for itself. His character as a ruler may be gathered from the following selection, taken from among his many speeches: "Do you think," he said, "that it is so easy for a sovereign to perform his duties? He does nothing that is without consequence. This morning the thought occurs to me that yesterday I decided a case in a wrong manner, and this memory robs me of all my joy."

The new emperor took the style of Tàitsong, and during his reign of twenty-three years the Sung dynasty may be fairly considered to have grown consolidated. One of his first measures was to restore the privileges of the descendants of Confucius, which included a hereditary title and exemption from taxation, and which are enjoyed to the present day. After three years' deliberation Taitsong determined to renew his brother's enterprise against Taiyuen, and as he had not assured the neutrality of the King of Leaoutung, his task was the more difficult. On the advance of the Chinese army, that ruler sent to demand the reason of the attack on his friend the Prince of Han, to which the only reply Taitsong gave was as follows: "The country of the Hans was one of the provinces of the empire, and the prince having refused to obey my orders I am determined to punish him. If your prince stands aside, and does not meddle in this quarrel, I am willing to continue to live at peace with

him; if he does not care to do this we will fight him." On
this the Leaou king declared war, but his troops were repulsed by the covering army sent forward by Taitsong,
while he prosecuted the siege of Taiyuen in person. The
fortress was well defended, but its doom was never in doubt.
Taitsong, moved by a feeling of humanity, offered the Prince
of Han generous terms before delivering an assault which
was, practically speaking, certain to succeed, and he had
the good sense to accept them. The subjugation of Han
completed the pacification of the empire and the triumph of
Taitsong; but when that ruler thought to add to this success
the speedy overthrow of the Khitan power in Leaoutung he
was destined to a rude awakening. His action was certainly precipitate, and marked by overconfidence, for the
army of Leaoutung was composed of soldiers of a warlike
race accustomed to victory. He advanced against it as if it
were an army which would fly at the sight of his standard,
but instead of this he discovered that it was superior to his
own forces on the banks of the Kaoleang River, where he
suffered a serious defeat. Taitsong was fortunate enough
to retain his conquests over the southern Han states and to
find in his new subjects in that quarter faithful and valiant
soldiers. The success of the Leaou army was also largely
due to the tactical skill of its general, Yeliu Hiuco, who
took a prominent part in the history of this period. When
Taitsong endeavored, some years later, to recover what he
had lost by the aid of the Coreans, who, however, neglected
to fulfill their part of the contract, he only invited fresh
misfortunes. Yeliu Hiuco defeated his army in several
pitched battles with immense loss; on one occasion it was
said that the corpses of the slain checked the course of a
river. The capture of Yangyeh, the old Han defender of
Taiyuen, who died of his wounds, completed the triumph
of the Leaou general, for it was said, "If Yangyeh cannot
resist the Tartars they must be invincible." Taitsong's
reign closed under the cloud of these reverses; but, on the
whole, it was successful and creditable, marking an im-

provement in the condition of the country and the people, and the triumph of the Sungs over at least one of their natural enemies.

His son and successor, Chintsong, must be pronounced fortunate in that the first year of his reign witnessed the death of Yeliu Hiuco. The direct consequence of his death was that the Chinese were, for the first time, successful in their campaign against the Leaous. But this satisfactory state of things did not long continue, and the Leaous became so aggressive and successful that there was almost a panic among the Chinese, and the removal of the capital to a place of greater security was suggested. The firm counsel and the courageous demeanor of the minister Kaochun prevented this course being adopted. He figuratively described the evil consequences of retreat by saying, "Your majesty can, without serious consequences, advance a foot further than is absolutely necessary, but you cannot retire, even to the extent of an inch, without doing yourself much harm." Chintsong, fortunately for himself and his state, adopted this course; and the Tartars thought it best to come to terms, especially as the Chinese emperor was willing to pay annually an allowance in silk and money as the reward of their respecting his frontier. The arrangement could not have been a bad one, as it gave the empire eighteen years of peace. The country, no doubt, increased greatly in prosperity during this period; but the reputation of Chintsong steadily declined. He seems to have been naturally superstitious, and he gave himself up to fortune-tellers and soothsayers during the last years of his reign; and when he died, in A.D. 1022, he had impaired the position and power of the imperial office. Yet, so far as can be judged, the people were contented, and the population rose to over one hundred million.

Chintsong was succeeded by his sixth son, Jintsong, a boy of thirteen, for whom the government was carried on by his mother, a woman of capacity and good sense. She took off objectionable taxes on tea and salt—prime necessaries of life in China—and she instituted surer measures against the spiritualists and magicians who had flourished under her husband and acquired many administrative offices under his patronage. After ruling for ten peaceful years she died and Jintsong assumed the personal direction of affairs. During the tranquillity that had now prevailed for more than a generation a new power had arisen on the Chinese frontier in the principality of Tangut or Hia. This state occupied the modern province of Kansuh, with some of the adjacent districts of Koko Nor and the Gobi Desert. Chao Yuen, the prince of this territory, was an ambitious warrior, who had drawn round his standard a force of one hundred and fifty thousand fighting men. With this he waged successful war upon the Tibetans, and began a course of encroachments on Chinese territory which was not to be distinguished from open hostility. Chao Yuen was not content with the appellation of prince, and "because he came of a family several of whose members had in times past borne the imperial dignity," he adopted the title of emperor. Having taken this step, Chao Yuen wrote to Jintsong expressing "the hope that there would be a constant and solid peace between the two empires." The reply of the Chinese ruler to this insult, as he termed it, was to declare war and to offer a reward for the head of Chao Yuen.

It was soon made evident that Chao Yuen possessed the military power to support an imperial dignity. He defeated the emperor's army in two pitched battles at Sanchuen and Yang Moulong, and many years elapsed before the Sung rulers can be held to have recovered from the loss of their best armies. The Khitans of Leaoutung took advantage of these misfortures to encroach, and as Jintsong had no army with which to oppose them, they captured ten cities with little or no resistance. The Chinese government was compelled to purchase them back by increasing the annual allowance it paid of gold and silk. A similar policy was resorted to in the case of Chao Yuen, who consented to a peace on receiving every year one hundred thousand pieces of silk and thirty thousand pounds of tea. Not content with this payment, Chao Yuen subsequently exacted the right to build fortresses along the Chinese frontier. Soon after this Chao Yuen was murdered by one of his sons, whose betrothed he had taken from him. If Jintsong was not fortunate in his wars he did much to promote education and to encourage literature. He restored the colleges founded by the Tangs, he built a school or academy in every town, he directed the public examinations to be held impartially and frequently, and he gave special prizes as a reward for elocution. Some of the greatest historians China has produced lived in his reign, and wrote their works under his patronage; of these Szemakwang was the most famous. His history of the Tangs is a masterpiece, and his "Garden of Szemakwang" an idyll. He was remarkable for his sound judgment as well as the elegance of his style, and during the short time he held the post of prime minister his administration was marked by ability and good sense. The character of Jintsong was, it will be seen, not without its good points, which gained for him the affection of his subjects despite his bad fortune against the national enemies, and his reign of thirty years was, generally speaking, prosperous and satisfactory. After the brief reign of his nephew, Yngtsong, that prince's son, Chintsong the Second, became emperor.

The career of Wanganchi, an eccentric and socialistic statesman, who wished to pose as a great national reformer, and who long possessed the ear and favor of his sovereign, lends an interest to the reign of the second Chintsong. Wanganchi did not possess the confidence or the admiration of his brother officials, and subsequent writers have generally termed him an impostor and a charlatan. But he may only have been a misguided enthusiast when he declared that "the State should take the entire management of commerce, industry, and agriculture into its own hands, with the view of succoring the working classes, and preventing their being ground to the dust by the rich." The advocacy of such a scheme is calculated to earn popularity, as few of those who are to benefit by it stop to examine its feasibility, and Wan-ganchi might have been remembered as an enlightened thinker and enthusiastic advocate of the rights of the masses if he had not been called upon to carry out his theories. But the proof of experience, like the touch of Ithuriel's spear, revealed the practical value of his sugges-tions, and dissolved the attractive vision raised by his per-fervid eloquence and elevated enthusiasm. His honesty of purpose cannot, however, be disputed. On being appointed to the post of chief minister he took in hand the application of his own project. He exempted the poor from all taxa-tion. He allotted lands, and he supplied the cultivators with seeds and implements. He also appointed local boards to superintend the efforts of the agricultural classes, and to give them assistance and advice. But this paternal govern-ment, this system of making the state do what the individ-ual ought to do for himself, did not work as it was expected. Those who counted on the agricultural laborer working with as much intelligence and energy for himself as he had done under the direction of a master were doomed to disappoint-ment. Want of skill, the fitfulness of the small holder, aggravated perhaps by national calamities, drought, flood, and pestilence, being felt more severely by laborers than by capitalists, led to a gradual shrinkage in the area of cul-tivated land, and at last to the suffering of the classes who were to specially benefit from the scheme of Wanganchi. The failure of his scheme, which, to use his own words, aimed at preventing their being any poor or over-rich per-sons in the state, entailed his disgrace and fall from power. But his work and his name have continued to excite interest and speculation among his countrymen down to the present day. His memory has been aspersed by the writers of China, who have generally denounced him as a free-thinker and a nihilist, and although, twenty years after his death, a tablet bearing his name was placed in the Hall of Confucius as the greatest Chinese thinker since Mencius, it was removed after a brief period, and since then both the name and the works of Wanganchi have been consigned to an oblivion from which only the curiosity of European writers has rescued them.

Chintsong's reign was peaceful, but he seems to have only avoided war by yielding to all the demands of the Tartars, who encroached on the frontier and seized several Chinese cities. His son Chetsong was only ten when he became emperor, and the administration was carried on by his mother, the Empress Tefei, another of the capable women of Chinese history. Her early death left Chetsong to rule as he listed, and his first acts of independent authority were not of happy augury for the future. He had not been on the throne many months before he divorced his principal wife without any apparent justification, and when remonstrated with he merely replied that he was imitating several of his predecessors. The censor's retort was, "You would do better to imitate their virtues, and not their faults." Chetsong did not have any long opportunity of doing either, for he died of grief at the loss of his favorite son, and it is recorded that, as "he did not expect to die so soon," he omitted the precaution of selecting an heir. Fortunately the mischief of a disputed succession was avoided by the unanimous selection of his brother Hoeitsong as the new emperor. He proved himself a vain and superstitious ruler, placing his main faith in fortune-tellers, and expecting his subjects to yield implicit obedience to his opinions as "the master of the law and the prince of doctrine." Among other fallacies, Hoeitsong cherished the belief that he was a great soldier, and he aspired to rank as the conqueror of the old successful enemy of China, the Khitans of Leaoutung. He had no army worthy of the name, and the southern Chinese who formed the mass of his subjects were averse to war, yet his personal vanity impelled him to rush into hostilities which promised to be the more serious because a new and formidable power had arisen on the northern frontier.

The Niuche or Chorcha Tartars, who had assumed a distinct name and place in the vicinity of the modern Kalgan, about the year 1000 A.D., had become subservient to the

great Khitan chief Apaoki, and their seven hordes had remained faithful allies of his family and kingdom for many
years after his death. But some of the clan had preferred
independence to the maintenance of friendly relations with
their greatest neighbor, and they had withdrawn northward
into Manchuria. For some unknown reason the Niuche became dissatisfied with their Khitan allies, and about the year
1100 A.D. they had all drawn their forces together as an independent confederacy under the leadership of a great chief
named Akouta. The Niuche could only hope to establish
their independence by offering a successful resistance to the
King of Leaoutung, who naturally resented the defection of
a tribe which had been his humble dependants. They succeeded in this task beyond all expectation, as Akouta inflicted
a succession of defeats on the hitherto invincible army of
Leaoutung. Then the Niuche conqueror resolved to pose
as one of the arbiters of the empire's destiny, and to found
a dynasty of his own. He collected his troops, and he addressed them in a speech reciting their deeds and his pretensions. "The Khitans," he said, "had in the earlier days
of their success taken the name of Pintiei, meaning the iron
of Pinchow, but although that iron may be excellent, it is
liable to rust and can be eaten away. There is nothing save
gold which is unchangeable and which does not destroy itself. Moreover, the family of Wangyen, with which I am
connected through the chief Hanpou, had always a great
fancy for glittering colors such as that of gold, and I am
now resolved to take this name as that of my imperial family. I therefore give it the name of Kin, which signifies
gold." This speech was made in the year 1115, and it
was the historical introduction of the Kin dynasty, which
so long rivaled the Sung, and which, although it attained
only a brief lease of power on the occasion referred to, was
remarkable as being the first appearance of the ancestors
of the present reigning Manchus.

Like other conquerors who had appeared in the same
quarter, the Kins, as we must now call them, owed their

rise to their military qualifications and to their high spirit.
Their tactics, although of a simpler kind, were as superior
to those of the Leaous as the latter's were to the Chinese.
Their army consisted exclusively of cavalry, and victory
was generally obtained by its furious attacks delivered from
several sides simultaneously. The following description,
taken from Mailla's translation of the Chinese official history, gives the best account of their army and mode of
fighting:

"At first the Niuche had only cavalry. For their sole
distinction they made use of a small piece of braid on which
they marked certain signs, and they attached this to both
man and horse. Their companies were usually composed of
only fifty men each, twenty of whom, clothed in strong cui-
rasses, and armed with swords and short pikes, were placed
in the front, and behind those came the remaining thirty in
less weighty armor, and with bows and arrows or javelins
for weapons. When they encountered an enemy, two men
from each company advanced as scouts, and then arranging
their troops so as to attack from four sides, they approached
the foe at a gentle trot until within a hundred yards of his
line. Thereupon charging at full speed, they discharged
their arrows and javelins, again retiring with the same
celerity. This maneuver they repeated several times until
they threw the ranks into confusion, when they fell upon
them with sword and pike so impetuously that they generally gained the victory."

The novelty, as well as the impetuosity, of their attack
supplied the want of numbers and of weapons, and when
the Khitans raised what seemed an overwhelming force to
crush the new power that ventured to play the rival to theirs
in Northern China, Akouta, confident in himself and in his
people, was not dismayed, and accepted the offer of battle.
In two sanguinary battles he vanquished the Khitan armies,
and threatened with early extinction the once famous dynasty
of Leaoutung. When the Sung emperor heard of the defeats
of his old opponents, he at once rushed to the conclusion that

the appearance of this new power on the flank of Leaoutung must redound to his advantage, and, although warned by the King of Corea that "the Kins were worse than wolves and tigers," he sent an embassy to Akouta proposing a joint alliance against the Khitans. The negotiations were not at first successful. Akouta concluded a truce with Leaoutung, but took offense at the style of the emperor's letter. The peace was soon broken by either the Kins or the Khitans, and Hoeitsong consented to address Akouta as the Great Emperor of the Kins. Then Akouta engaged to attack Leaoutung from the north, while the Chinese assailed it on the south, and a war began which promised a speedy termination. But the tardiness and inefficiency of the Chinese army prolonged the struggle, and covered the reputation of Hoeitsong and his troops with ignominy. It was compelled to beat a hasty and disastrous retreat, and the peasants of Leaoutung sang ballads about its cowardice and inefficiency.

But if it fared badly with the Chinese, the armies of Akouta continued to be victorious, and the Khitans fled not less precipitately before him than the Chinese did before them. Their best generals were unable to make the least stand against the Kin forces. Their capital was occupied by the conqueror, and the last descendant of the great Apaoki fled westward to seek an asylum with the Prince of Hia or Tangut. He does not appear to have received the protection he claimed, for after a brief stay at the court of Hia, he made his way to the desert, where, after undergoing incredible hardships, he fell into the hands of his Kin pursuers. With his death soon afterward the Khitan dynasty came to an end, after enjoying its power for two hundred years; but some members of this race escaped across the Gobi Desert, and founded the brief-lived dynasty of the Kara Khitay in Turkestan. Akouta died shortly before the final overthrow of the Leaoutung power, and his brother Oukimai ruled in his place.

The ill-success of Hoeitsong's army in its joint campaign against Leaoutung cost the emperor his share in the spoil.

The Kins retained the whole of the conquered territory, and the Sung prince was the worse off, because he had a more powerful and aggressive neighbor. The ease of their conquest, and the evident weakness of the Chinese, raised the confidence of the Kins to such a high point that they declared that the Sungs must surrender to them the whole of the territory north of the Hoangho, and they prepared to secure what they demanded by force of arms. The Chinese would neither acquiesce in the transfer of this region to the Kins nor take steps to defend it. They were driven out of that portion of the empire like sheep, and they even failed to make any stand at the passage of the Hoangho, where the Kin general declared that "there could not be a man left in China, for if two thousand men had defended the passage of this river we should never have succeeded in crossing it." Hoeitsong quitted his capital Kaifong to seek shelter at Nankin, where he hoped to enjoy greater safety, and shortly afterward he abdicated in favor of his son Kintsong. The siege of Kaifong which followed ended in a convention binding the Chinese to pay the Kins an enormous sum—ten millions of small gold nuggets, twenty millions of small silver nuggets, and ten million pieces of silk; but the Tartar soldiers soon realized that there was no likelihood of their ever receiving this fabulous spoil, and in their indignation they seized both Hoeitsong and Kintsong, as well as any other members of the royal family on whom they could lay their hands, and carried them off to Tartary, where both the unfortunate Sung princes died as prisoners of the Kins.

Although the Kins wished to sweep the Sungs from the throne, and their general Walipou went so far as to proclaim the emperor of a new dynasty, whose name is forgotten, another of the sons of Hoeitsong, Prince Kang Wang, had no difficulty in establishing his own power and in preserving the Sung dynasty. He even succeeded in imparting a new vigor to it, for on the advice of his mother, who pointed out to him that "for nearly two hundred years the nation appears to have forgotten the art of war," he devoted all his attention to the improvement of his army and the organization of his military resources. Prince Kang Wang, on becoming emperor, took the name of Kaotsong, and finally removed the southern capital to Nankin. He was also driven by his financial necessities to largely increase the issue of paper money, which had been introduced under the Tangs. As both the Kins and the Mongols had recourse to the same expedient, it is not surprising that the Sungs should also have adopted the simplest mode of compensating for a depleted treasury. Considering the unexpected difficulties with which he had to cope, and the low ebb to which the fortunes of China had fallen, much might be forgiven to Kaotsong, who found a courageous counselor in the Empress Mongchi, who is reported to have addressed him as follows: "Although the whole of your august family has been led captive into the countries of the north, none the less does China, which knows your wisdom and fine qualities, preserve toward the Sungs the same affection, fidelity, and zeal as in the past. She hopes and expects that you will prove for her what Kwang Vouti was for the Hans." If Kaotsong did not attain the height of this success, he at least showed himself a far more capable prince than any of his immediate predecessors.

The successful employment of cavalry by the Kins naturally led the Chinese to think of employing the same arm against them, although the inhabitants of the eighteen provinces have never been good horsemen. Kaotsong also devoted his attention especially to the formation of a corps of charioteers. The chariots, four-wheeled, carried twenty-four combatants, and these vehicles drawn up in battle array not only presented a very formidable appearance, but afforded a very material shelter for the rest of the army. Kaotsong seems to have been better in imagining reforms than in the task of carrying them out. After he had originated much good work he allowed it to languish for want of definite support, and he quarreled with and disgraced the minister chiefly responsible for these reforms. A short time after this the Kins again advanced southward, but thanks to the improvement effected in the Chinese army, and to the skill and valor of Tsongtse, one of Kaotsong's lieutenants, they did not succeed in gaining any material advantage. Their efforts to capture Kaifong failed, and their general Niyamoho, recognizing the improvement in the Chinese army, was content to withdraw his army with such spoil as it had been able to collect. Tsongtse followed up this good service against the enemy by bringing to their senses several rebellious officials who thought they saw a good opportunity of shaking off the Sung authority. At this stage of the war Tsongtse exhorted Kaotsong, who had quitted Nankin for Yangchow, to return to Kaifong to encourage his troops with his presence, especially as there never was such a favorable opportunity of delivering his august family out of the hands of the Kins. Tsongtse is reported to have sent as many as twenty formal petitions to his sovereign to do this, but Kaotsong was deaf to them all, and it is said that his obtuseness and want of nerve caused Tsongtse so much pain that he died of chagrin.

The death of Tsongtse induced the Kins to make a more strenuous effort to humiliate the Sungs, and a large army under the joint command of Akouta's son, Olito, and the general Niyamoho, advanced on the capital and captured Yangchow. Kaotsong, who saved his life by precipitate flight, then agreed to sign any treaty drawn up by his conqueror. In his letter to Niyamoho he said, "Why fatigue your troops with long and arduous marches when I will grant you of my own will whatever you demand?" But the Kins were inexorable, and refused to grant any terms short of the unconditional surrender of Kaotsong, who fled to Canton, pursued both on land and sea. The Kin conquerors soon found that they had advanced too far, and the Chinese rallying their forces gained some advantage during their retreat. Some return of confidence followed this turn in the fortune of the war, and two Chinese generals, serving in the hard school of adversity, acquired a military knowledge

and skill which made them formidable to even the best of
the Kin commanders. The campaigns carried on between
1131 and 1134 differed from any that had preceded them in
that the Kin forces steadily retired before Oukiai and Changtsiun, and victory, which had so long remained constant in
their favor, finally deserted their arms. The death of the
Kin emperor, Oukimai, who had upheld with no decline of
luster the dignity of his father Akouta, completed the discomfiture of the Kins, and contributed to the revival of Chinese power under the last emperor of the Sung dynasty.
The reign of Oukimai marks the pinnacle of Kin power,
which under his cousin and successor Hola began steadily
to decline.

The possession of Honan formed the principal bone of
contention between the Kins and Sungs, but after considerable negotiation and some fighting, Kaotsong agreed to leave
it in the hands of the Kins, and also to pay them a large
annual subsidy in silk and money. He also agreed to hold
the remainder of his states as a gift at the hands of his northern neighbor. Thus, notwithstanding the very considerable
successes gained by several of the Sung generals, Kaotsong
had to undergo the mortification of signing a humiliating
peace and retaining his authority only on sufferance. Fortunately for the independence of the Sungs, Hola was murdered by Ticounai, a grandson of Akouta, whose ferocious
character and ill-formed projects for the subjugation of the
whole of China furnished the Emperor Kaotsong with the
opportunity of shaking off the control asserted over his actions and recovering his dignity. The extensive preparations
of the Kin government for war warned the Sungs to lose no
time in placing every man they could in the field, and when
Ticounai rushed into the war, which was all of his own making, he found that the Sungs were quite ready to receive him
and offer a strenuous resistance to his attack. A peace of
twenty years' duration had allowed of their organizing their
forces and recovering from an unreasoning terror of the
Kins. Moreover, there was a very general feeling among

the inhabitants of both the north and the south that the war was an unjust one, and that Ticounai had embarked upon a course of lawless aggression which his tyrannical and cruel proceedings toward his own subjects served to inflame.

The war began in 1161 A.D., with an ominous defeat of the Kin navy, and when Kaotsong nerved himself for the crisis in his life and placed himself at the head of his troops, Ticounai must have felt less sanguine of the result than his confident declaration that he would end the war in a single campaign indicated. Before the two armies came into collision Ticounai learned that a rebellion had broken out in his rear, and that his cousin Oulo challenged both his legitimacy and his authority. He believed, and perhaps wisely, that the only way to deal with this new danger was to press on, and by gaining a signal victory over the Sungs annihilate all his enemies at a blow. But the victory had to be gained, and he seems to have underestimated his opponent. He reached the Yangtsekiang, and the Sungs retired behind it. Ticounai had no means of crossing it, as his fleet had been destroyed and the Sung navy stood in his path. Such river junks as he possessed were annihilated in another encounter on the river. He offered sacrifices to heaven in order to obtain a safe passage, but the powers above were deaf to his prayers. Discontent and disorder broke out in his camp. The army that was to have carried all before it was stopped by a mere river, and Ticounai's reputation as a general was ruined before he had crossed swords with the enemy. In this dilemma his cruelty increased, and after he had sentenced many of his officers and soldiers to death he was murdered by those who found that they would have to share the same fate. After this tragic ending of a bad career, the Kin army retreated. They concluded a friendly convention with the Sungs, and Kaotsong, deeming his work done by the repulse of this grave peril, abdicated the throne, which had proved to him no bed of roses, in favor of his adopted heir Hiaotsong. Kaotsong ruled during the long period of thirty-six years, and when we consider the troubled time through which he passed, and the many vicissitudes of fortune he underwent, he probably rejoiced at being able to spend the last twenty-five years of his life without the responsibility of governing the empire and free from the cares of sovereignty.

The new Kin ruler Oulo wished for peace, but a section of his turbulent subjects clamored for a renewal of the expeditions into China, and he was compelled to bend to the storm. The Kin army, however, had no cause to rejoice in its bellicoseness, for the Chinese general, Changtsiun, defeated it in a battle the like of which had not been seen for ten years. After this a peace was concluded which proved fairly durable, and the remainder of the reigns of both Oulo and Hiaotsong were peaceful and prosperous for northern and southern China. Both of these princes showed an aversion to war and an appreciation of peace which was rare in their day. The Kin ruler is stated to have made this noble retort when he was solicited by a traitor from a neighboring state to seize it: "You deceive yourself if you believe me to be capable of approving an act of treason, whatever the presumed advantage it might procure me. I love all peoples of whatever nation they may be, and I wish to see them at peace with one another." It is not surprising to learn that a prince who was so thoroughly imbued with the spirit of civilization should have caused the Chinese classics to be translated into the Kin language. Of all the Kin rulers he was the most intellectual and the most anxious to elevate the standard of his people, who were far ruder than the inhabitants of southern China.

Hiaotsong was succeeded by his son Kwangtsong, and Oulo by his grandson Madacou, both of whom continued the policy of their predecessors. Kwangtsong was saved the trouble of ruling by his wife, the Empress Lichi, and after a very short space he resigned the empty title of emperor, which brought him neither satisfaction nor pleasure. Ningtsong, the son and successor of Kwangtsong, ventured on one war with the Kins in which he was worsted. This was the last of the Kin successes, for Madacou died soon afterward, just on the eve of the advent of the Mongol peril, which threatened to sweep all before it, and which eventually buried both Kin and Sung in a common ruin. The long competition and the bitter contest between the Kins and Sungs had not resulted in the decisive success of either side. The Kins had been strong enough to found an administration in the north but not to conquer China. The Sungs very naturally represent in Chinese history the national dynasty, and their misfortunes, rather than their successes, appeal to the sentiment of the reader. They showed themselves greater in adversity than in prosperity, and when the Mongol tempest broke over China they proved the more doughty opponent, and the possessor of greater powers of resistance than their uniformly successful adversary the Kin or Golden Dynasty.

CHAPTER V

THE MONGOL CONQUEST OF CHINA

WHILE the Kins were absorbed in their contest with the Southern Chinese, they were oblivious of the growth of a new and formidable power on their own borders. The strength of the Mongols had acquired serious dimensions before the Kins realized that they would have to fight, not only for supremacy, but for their very existence. Before describing the long wars that resulted in the subjection of China by this northern race, we must consider the origin and the growth of the power of the Mongols, who were certainly the most remarkable race of conquerors Asia, or perhaps the whole world, ever produced.

The home of the Mongols, whose name signifies "brave men," was in the strip of territory between the Onon and Kerulon rivers, which are both tributaries or upper courses of the Amour. They first appeared as a separate clan or tribe in the ninth century, when they attracted special attention for their physical strength and courage during one of China's many wars with the children of the desert, and it was on that occasion they gained the appellation under which they became famous. The earlier history of the Mongol tribe is obscure, and baffles investigation, but there seems no reason to doubt their affinity to the Hiongnou, with whose royal house Genghis himself claimed blood relationship. If this claim be admitted, Genghis and Attila, who were the two specially typical Scourges of God, must be considered members of the same race, and the probability is certainly strengthened by the close resemblance in their methods of carrying on war. Budantsar is the first chief of the House of Genghis whose person and achievements are more than mythical. He selected as the abode of his race the territory between the Onon and the Kerulon, a region fertile in itself, and well protected by those rivers against attack. It was also so well placed as to be beyond the extreme limit of any triumphant progress of the armies of the Chinese emperor. If Budantsar had accomplished nothing more than this, he would still have done much to justify his memory being preserved among a free and independent people. But he seems to have incited his followers to pursue an active and temperate life, to remain warriors rather than to become rich and lazy citizens. He wrapped up this counsel in the exhortation, "What is the use of embarrassing ourselves with wealth? Is not the fate of men decreed by heaven?" He sowed the seed of future Mongol greatness, and the headship of his clan remained vested in his family.

In due order of succession the chiefship passed to Kabul Khan, who in the year 1135 began to encroach on the dominion of Hola, the Kin emperor. He seems to have been induced to commit this act of hostility by a prophecy, to the effect that his children should be emperors, and also by discourteous treatment received on the occasion of his visit to the court of Oukimai. Whatever the cause of umbrage, Kabul Khan made the Kins pay dearly for their arrogance or short-sighted policy. Hola sent an army under one of his best generals, Hushahu, to bring the Mongol chief to reason, but the inaccessibility of his home stood him in good stead. The Kin army suffered greatly in its futile attempt to cross the desert, and during its retreat it was harassed by the pursuing Mongols. When the Kin army endeavored to make a stand against its pursuers, it suffered a crushing overthrow in a battle at Hailing, and on the Kins sending a larger force against the Mongols in 1139, it had no better fortune. Kabul Khan, after this second success, caused himself to be proclaimed Great Emperor of the Mongols. His success in war, and his ambition, which rested satisfied with no secondary position, indicated the path on which the Mongols proceeded to the acquisition of supreme power and a paramount military influence whithersoever they carried their name and standards. The work begun by Kabul was well continued by his son Kutula, or Kublai. He, too, was a great warrior, whose deeds of prowess aroused as much enthusiasm among the Mongols as those of Cœur de Lion evoked in the days of the Plantagenets. The struggle with the Kins was rendered more bitter by the execution of several Mongols of importance, who happened to fall into the hands of the Kins. When Kutula died the chiefship passed to his nephew, Yissugei, who greatly extended the influence and power of his family among the tribes neighboring to the Mongol home. Many of these, and even some Chinese, joined the military organization of the dominant tribe, so that what was originally a small force of strictly limited numbers became a vast and ever-increasing confederacy of the most warlike and aggressive races of the Chinese northern frontier. Important as Yissugei's work in the development of Mongol power undoubtedly was, his chief historical interest is derived from the fact that he was the father of Genghis Khan.

There are several interesting fables in connection with the birth of Genghis, which event may be safely assigned to the year 1162. One of these reads as follows: "One day Yissugei was hunting in company with his brothers, and was following the tracks of a white hare in the snow.

They struck upon the track of a wagon, and following it up came to a spot where a woman's yart was pitched. Then said Yissugei, 'This woman will bear a valiant son.' He discovered that she was the damsel Ogelen Eke (*i.e.*, the mother of nations), and that she was the wife of Yeke Yilatu, chief of a Tartar tribe. Yissugei carried her off and made her his wife." Immediately after his overthrow of Temujin, chief of one of the principal Tartar tribes, Yissugei learned that the promised "valiant son" was about to be born, and in honor of his victory he gave him the name of Temujin, which was the proper name of the great Genghis. The village or encampment in which the future conqueror first saw the light of day still bears the old Mongol name, Dilun Boldak, on the banks of the Onon. When Yissugei died, Temujin, or Genghis, was only thirteen, and his clan of forty thousand families refused to recognize him as their leader. At a meeting of the tribe Genghis entreated them with tears in his eyes to stand by the son of their former chief, but the majority of them mocked at him, exclaiming, "The deepest wells are sometimes dry, and the hardest stone is sometimes broken, why should we cling to thee?" Genghis owed to the heroic attitude of his mother, who flung abroad the cow tailed banner of his race, the acceptance of his authority by about half the warriors who had obeyed his father. The great advantage of this step was that it gave Genghis time to grow up to be a warrior as famous as any of his predecessors, and it certainly averted what might have easily become the irretrievable disintegration of the Mongol alliance.

The youth of Genghis was passed in one ceaseless struggle to regain the whole of his birthright. His most formidable enemy was Chamuka, chief of the Juriats, and for a long time he had all the worst of the struggle, being taken prisoner on one occasion, and undergoing the indignity of the cangue. On making his escape he rallied his remaining followers round him for a final effort, and on the advice of his mother, Ogelen Eke, who was his principal adviser and stanchest supporter, he divided his forces into thirteen regiments of one thousand men each, and confined his attention to the defense of his own territory. Chamuka, led away by what he deemed the weakness of his adversary, attacked him on the Onon with as he considered the overwhelming force of thirty thousand men; but the result dispelled his hopes of conquest, for Genghis gained a decisive victory. Then was furnished a striking instance of the truth of the saying that "nothing succeeds like success." The despised Temujin, who was thought to be unworthy of the post of ruling the Mongols, was lauded to the skies, and the tribes declared with one voice, "Temujin alone is generous and worthy of ruling a great people." At this time also he began to show the qualities of a statesman and diplomatist. He formed in 1194 a temporary alliance with the Kin emperor, Madacou, and the richness of his reward seems to have excited his cupidity, while his experience of the Kin army went to prove that they were not so formidable as had been imagined. The discomfiture of Chamuka has been referred to, but he had not abandoned the hope of success, and when he succeeded in detaching the Kerait chief, Wang Khan, from the Mongols, to whom he was bound by ties of gratitude, he fancied that he again held victory in his grasp. But the intrigue did not realize his expectations. Wang Khan deserted Genghis while engaged in a joint campaign against the Naimans, but he was the principal sufferer by his treachery, for the enemy pursued his force, and inflicted a heavy defeat upon it. In fact, he was only rescued from destruction by the timely aid of the man he had betrayed.

But far from inspiring gratitude, this incident inflamed the resentment of Wang Khan, who, throwing off the cloak of simulated-friendship, declared publicly that either the Kerait or the Mongol must be supreme on the great steppe, as there was not room for both. Such was the superiority in numbers of the Kerait, that in the first battle of this long and keenly-contested struggle, Wang Khan defeated Temu-

jin near Ourga, where the mounds that cover the slain are
still shown to the curious or skeptical visitor. After this
serious, and in some degree unexpected reverse, the fortunes of Genghis sank to the lowest ebb. He was reduced
to terrible straits, and had to move his camp rapidly from
one spot to another. A small section of his followers, mindful of his past success and prowess, still clung to him, and
by a sudden and daring coup he changed the whole aspect
of the contest. He surprised Wang Khan in his camp at
night, and overwhelmed him and his forces. Wang Khan
escaped to his old foes, the Naimans, who, disregarding the
laws of hospitality, put him to death. The death of Wang
Khan signified nothing less than the wholesale defection of
the Kerait tribe, which joined Genghis to the last man.
Then Genghis turned westward to settle the question of
supremacy with the Naimans, who were both hostile and
defiant. The Naiman chief shared the opinion of Wang
Khan, that there could not be two masters on the Tian
Shan, and with that vigorous illustration which has never
been wanting to these illiterate tribes, he wrote, "There
cannot be two suns in the sky, two swords in one sheath,
two eyes in one eyepit, or two kings in one empire." Both
sides made strenuous efforts for the fray, and brought every
fighting man they could into the field. The decisive battle
of the war was fought in the heart of Jungaria, and the
star of Genghis rose in the ascendant. The Naimans fought
long and well, but they were borne down by the heavier
armed Mongols, and their desperate resistance only added
to their loss. Their chief died of his wounds, and the triumph of Genghis was rendered complete by the capture of
his old enemy, Chamuka. As Genghis had sworn the oath
of friendship with Chamuka, he would not slay him, but he
handed him over to a relative, who promptly exacted the
rough revenge his past hostility and treachery seemed to
call for. On his way back from this campaign the Mongol
chief attacked the Prince of Hia, who reigned over Kansuh
and Tangut, and thus began the third war he waged for the

extension of his power. Before this assumed serious proportions he summoned a Grand Council or Kuriltai, at his camp on the Onon, and then erected outside his tent the royal Mongol banner of the nine white yak-tails. It was on this occasion that Temujin took, and was proclaimed among the Mongol chiefs by, the highly exalted name of Genghis Khan, which means Very Mighty Khan. The Chinese character for the name signifies "Perfect Warrior," and the earlier European writers affirm that it is supposed to represent the sound of "the bird of heaven." At this assemblage, which was the first of a long succession of Mongol councils, summoned at the same place on critical occasions, it was proposed and agreed that the war should be carried on with the richer and less warlike races of the south. Among soldiers it is necessary to preserve the spirit of pre-eminence and warlike zeal by granting rewards and decorations. Genghis realized the importance of this matter and instituted the order of Baturu or Bahadur, meaning warrior. He also made his two leading generals Muhula and Porshu princes, one to sit on his right hand and the other on his left. He addressed them before the council in the following words: "It is to you that I owe my empire. You are and have been to me as the shafts of a carriage or the arms to a man's body." Seals of office were also granted to all the officials, so that their authority might be the more evident and the more honored.

In 1207 Genghis began his war with the state of Hia, which he had determined to crush as the preliminary to an invasion of China. In that year he contented himself with the capture of Wuhlahai, one of the border fortresses of that principality, and in the following year he established his control over the tribes of the desert more fully, thus gaining many Kirghiz and Naiman auxiliaries. In 1209 he resumed the war with Hia in a determined spirit, and placed himself in person at the head of all his forces. Although the Hia ruler prepared as well as he could for the struggle, he was really unnerved by the magnitude of the danger he had to face. His army was overthrown, his best generals were taken prisoners, and he himself had no resource left but to throw himself on the consideration of Genghis. For good reasons the Mongol conqueror was lenient. He married one of the daughters of the king, and he took him into subsidiary alliance with himself. Thus did Genghis absorb the Hia power, which was very considerable, and prepared to enroll it with all his own resources against the Kin empire. If the causes of Mongol success on this occasion and afterward are inquired for, I cannot do better than repeat what I previously wrote on this subject: "The Mongols owed their military success to their admirable discipline and to their close study of the art of war. Their military supremacy arose from their superiority in all essentials as a fighting power to their neighbors. Much of their knowledge was borrowed from China, where the art of disciplining a large army and maneuvering it in the field had been brought to a high state of perfection many centuries before the time of Genghis. But the Mongols carried the teaching of the past to a further point than any of the former or contemporary Chinese commanders, indeed, than any in the whole world, had done; and the revolution which they effected in tactics was not less remarkable in itself, and did not leave a smaller impression upon the age, than the improvements made in military science by Frederick the Great and Napoleon in their day. The Mongol played in a large way in Asia the part which the Normans on a smaller scale played in Europe. Although the landmarks of their triumph have now almost wholly vanished, they were for two centuries the dominant caste in most of the states of Asia."

Having thus prepared the way for the larger enterprise, it only remained to find a plausible pretext for attacking the Kins. With or without a pretext, Genghis would no doubt have made war, but even the ruthless Mongol sometimes showed a regard for appearances. Many years before, the Kins had sent as envoy to the Mongol encampment Chonghei, a member of their ruling house, and his mission had

been not only unsuccessful, but had led to a personal antipathy between the two men. In the course of time Chonghei succeeded Madacou as emperor of the Kins, and when a
Kin messenger brought intelligence of this event to Genghis,
the Mongol ruler turned toward the south, spat upon the
ground, and said, "I thought that your sovereigns were of
the race of the gods, but do you suppose that I am going
to do homage to such an imbecile as that?" The affront
rankled in the mind of Chonghei, and while Genghis was
engaged with Hia, he sent troops to attack the Mongol outposts. Chonghei thus placed himself in the wrong, and gave
Genghis justification for declaring that the Kins and not he
began the war. The reputation of the Golden dynasty, although not as great as it once was, still stood sufficiently
high to make the most adventurous of desert chiefs wary in
attacking it. Genghis had already secured the co-operation
of the ruler of Hia in his enterprise, and he next concluded
an alliance with Yeliu Liuko, chief of the Khitans, who were
again manifesting discontent with the Kins. Genghis finally
circulated a proclamation among all the desert tribes, calling
upon them to join him in his attack on the common enemy.
This appeal was heartily and generally responded to, and it
was at the head of an enormous force that Genghis set out
in March, 1211, to effect the conquest of China. The Mongol army was led by Genghis in person, and under him his
four sons and his most famous general, Chepe Noyan, held
commands.

The plan of campaign of the Mongol ruler was as simple
as it was bold. From his camp at Karakoram, on the Kerulon, he marched in a straight line through Kuku Khoten and
the Ongut country to Taitong, securing an unopposed passage through the Great Wall by the defection of the Ongut
tribe. The Kins were unprepared for this sudden and vigorous assault directed on their weakest spot, and successfully
executed before their army could reach the scene. During
the two years that the forces of Genghis kept the field on
this occasion they devastated the greater portion of the three

northern provinces of Shensi, Shansi, and Pechihli. But the
border fortress of Taitong and the Kin capital, Tungking,
successfully resisted all the assaults of the Mongols, and
when Genghis received a serious wound at the former place,
he reluctantly ordered the retreat of his army, laden with an
immense quantity of spoil, but still little advanced in its main
task of conquering China. The success of the Khitan Yeliu
Liuko had not been less considerable, and he was proclaimed
King of Leaou as a vassal of the Mongols. The planting of
this ally on the very threshold of Chinese power facilitated
the subsequent enterprises of the Mongols against the Kins,
and represented the most important result of this war.

In 1213 Genghis again invaded the Kin dominions, but
his success was not very striking, and in several engagements of no very great importance the Kin arms met with
some success. The most important events of the year were,
however, the deposition and murder of Chonghei, the murder of a Kin general, Hushahu, who had won a battle against
the Mongols, and the proclamation of Utubu as emperor.
The change of sovereign brought no change of fortune to
the unlucky Kins. Utubu was only able to find safety behind the walls of his capital, and he was delighted when
Genghis wrote him the following letter: "Seeing your
wretched condition and my exalted fortune, what may
your opinion be now of the will of heaven with regard
to myself? At this moment I am desirous to return to
Tartary, but could you allow my soldiers to take their
departure without appeasing their anger with presents?"
In reply Utubu sent Genghis a princess of his family as
a wife, and also "five hundred youths, the same number of
girls, three thousand horses, and a vast quantity of precious
articles." Then Genghis retired once more to Karakoram,
but on his march he stained his reputation by massacring
all his prisoners—the first gross act of inhumanity he committed during his Chinese wars.

When Utubu saw the Mongols retreating, he thought to
provide against the most serious consequences of their return

by removing his capital to a greater distance from the frontier, and with this object he transferred his residence to Kaifong. The majority of his advisers were against this change, as a retirement could not but shake public confidence. It had another consequence, which they may not have contemplated, and that was its providing Genghis with an excuse for renewing his attack on China. The Mongol at once complained that the action of the Kin emperor implied an unwarrantable suspicion of his intentions, and he sent his army across the frontier to recommence his humiliation. On this occasion a Kin general deserted to them, and thenceforward large bodies of the Chinese of the north attached themselves to the Mongols, who were steadily acquiring a unique reputation for power as well as military prowess. The great event of this war was the siege of Yenking on the site of which now stands the capital Pekin—the defense of which had been intrusted to the Prince Imperial; but Utubu, more anxious for his son's safety than the interests of the state, ordered him to return to Kaifong. The governor of Yenking offered a stout resistance to the Mongols, and when he found that he could not hold out, he retired to the temple of the city and poisoned himself. His last act was to write a letter to Utubu begging him to listen no more to the pernicious advice of the man who had induced him to murder Hushahu.

The capture of Yenking, where Genghis obtained a large supply of war materials, as well as vast booty, opened the road to Central China. The Mongols advanced as far as the celebrated Tunkwan Pass, which connects Shensi and Honan, but when their general, Samuka, saw how formidable it was, and how strong were the Kin defenses and garrison, he declined to attack it, and, making a detour through very difficult country, he marched on Kaifong, where Utubu little expected him. The Mongols had to make their own road, and they crossed several ravines by improvised "bridges made of spears and the branches of trees bound together by strong chains." But the Mongol force was too small to accomplish any great result, and the impetuosity of Samuka nearly led to his destruction. A prompt retreat, and the fact that the Hoangho was frozen over, enabled him to extricate his army, after much fatigue and reduced in number, from its awkward position. The retreat of the Mongols inspired Utubu with sufficient confidence to induce him to attack Yeliu Liuko in Leaoutung, and the success of this enterprise imparted a gleam of sunshine and credit to the expiring cause of the Kins. Yeliu Liuko was driven from his newly-created kingdom, but Genghis hastened to the assistance of his ally by sending Muhula, the greatest of all his generals, at the head of a large army to recover Leaoutung. His success was rapid and remarkable. The Kins were speedily overthrown, Yeliu Liuko was restored to his authority, and the neighboring King of Corea, impressed by the magnitude of the Mongol success, hastened to acknowledge himself the vassal of Genghis. The most important result of this campaign was that Genghis intrusted to Muhula the control of all military arrangements for the conquest of China. He is reported to have said to his lieutenant: "North of the Taihing Mountains I am supreme, but all the regions to the south I commend to the care of Muhula," and he "also presented him with a chariot and a banner with nine scalops. As he handed him this last emblem of authority, he spoke to his generals, saying, 'Let this banner be an emblem of sovereignty, and let the orders issued from under it be obeyed as my own.'" The principal reason for intrusting the conquest of China to a special force and commander was that Genghis wished to devote the whole of his personal attention to the prosecution of his new war with the King of Khwaresm and the other great rulers of Western Asia.

Muhula more than justified the selection and confidence of his sovereign. In the year 1218–19 he invaded Honan, defeated the best of the Kin commanders, and not merely overran, but retained possession of the places he occupied in the Kin dominions. The difficulties of Utubu were ag-

CHINA—5

gravated by an attack from Ningtsong, the Sung emperor, who refused any longer to pay tribute to the Kins, as they were evidently unable to enforce the claim, and the Kin armies were as equally unfortunate against their southern opponents as their northern. Then Utubu endeavored to negotiate terms with Muhula for the retreat of his army, but the only conditions the Mongol general would accept were the surrender of the Kin ruler and his resignation of the imperial title in exchange for the principality of Honan. Utubu, low as he had sunk, declined to abase himself further and to purchase life at the loss of his dignity. The sudden death of Muhula gained a brief respite for the distressed Chinese potentate, but the advantage was not of any permanent significance; first of all because the Kins were too exhausted by their long struggle, and, secondly, because Genghis hastened to place himself at the head of his army. The news of the death of Muhula reached him when he was encamped on the frontier of India and preparing to add the conquest of that country to his many other triumphs in Central and Western Asia. He at once came to the conclusion that he must return to set his house in order at home, and to prevent all the results of Muhula's remarkable triumphs being lost. What was a disadvantage for China proved a benefit for India, and possibly for Europe, as there is no saying how much further the Mongol encroachment might have extended westward, if the direction of Genghis had not been withdrawn. While Genghis was hastening from the Cabul River to the Kerulon, across the Hindoo Koosh and Tian Shan ranges, Utubu died and Ninkiassu reigned in his stead.

One of the first consequences of the death of Muhula was that the young king of Hia, believing that the fortunes of the Mongols would then wane, and that he might obtain a position of greater power and independence, threw off his allegiance, and adopted hostile measures against them. The prompt return of Genghis nipped this plan in the bud, but it was made quite evident that the conquest

HONG KONG

China

of Hia was essential to the success of any permanent annexation of Chinese territory, and as its prince could dispose of an army which he boasted numbered half a million of men, it is not surprising to find that he took a whole year in perfecting his arrangements for so grave a contest. The war began in 1225 and continued for two years. The success of the Mongol army was decisive and unqualified. The Hias were defeated in several battles; and in one of them, fought upon the frozen waters of the Hoangho, Genghis broke the ice by means of his engines and the Hia army was almost annihilated. The king Leseen was deposed, and Hia became a Mongol province.

It was immediately after this successful war that Genghis was seized with his fatal illness. Signs had been seen in the heavens which the Mongol astrologers said indicated the near approach of his death. The five planets had appeared together in the southwest, and so much impressed was Genghis by this phenomenon that on his death-bed he expressed "the earnest desire that henceforth the lives of our enemies shall not be unnecessarily sacrificed." The expression of this wish undoubtedly tended to mitigate the terrors of war as carried on by the Mongols. The immediate successors of Genghis conducted their campaigns after a more humane fashion, and it was not until Timour revived the early Mongol massacres that their opponents felt there was no chance in appealing to the humanity of the Mongols. Various accounts have been published of the cause of his death; some authorities ascribing it to violence, either by an arrow, lightning, or drowning, and others to natural causes. The event seems to have unquestionably happened in his camp on the borders of Shansi, August 27, 1227, when he was about sixty-five years of age, during more than fifty of which he had enjoyed supreme command of his own tribe.

The area of the undertakings conducted under his eye was more vast and included a greater number of countries than was the case with any other conqueror. Not a country from the Euxine to the China Sea escaped the tramp of the

Mongol horsemen, and if we include the achievements of his immediate successors, the conquest of Russia, Poland, and Hungary, the plundering of Bulgaria, Roumania, and Bosnia, the final subjection of China and its southern tributaries must be added to complete the tale of Mongol triumph. The sphere of Mongol influence extended beyond this large portion of the earth's surface, just as the consequence of an explosion cannot be restricted to the immediate scene of the disaster. If we may include the remarkable achievements of his descendant Baber, and of that prince's grandson Akbar, in India three centuries later, not a country in Asia enjoyed immunity from the effect of their successes. Perhaps the most important result of their great outpouring into Western Asia—which certainly was the arrest of the Mohammedan career in Central Asia, and the diversion of the current of the fanatical propagators of the Prophet's creed against Europe—is not yet as fully recognized as it should be. The doubt has been already expressed whether the Mongols would ever have risen to higher rank than that of a nomad tribe but for the appearance of Genghis. Leaving that supposition in the category of other interesting but problematical conjectures, it may be asserted that Genghis represented in their highest forms all the qualities which entitled his race to exercise governing authority. He was, moreover, a military genius of the very first order, and it may be questioned whether either Cæsar or Napoleon can as commanders be placed on a par with him. Even the Chinese said that he led his armies like a god. The manner in which he moved large bodies of men over vast distances without an apparent effort, the judgment he showed in the conduct of several wars in countries far apart from each other, his strategy in unknown regions, always on the alert, yet never allowing hesitation or overcaution to interfere with his enterprise, the sieges which he brought to a successful termination, his brilliant victories, a succession of "suns of Austerlitz," all combined make up the picture of a career to which Europe can offer nothing that will surpass, if indeed she has anything to bear comparison with it. After the lapse of centuries, and in spite of the indifference with which the great figures of Asiatic history have been treated, the name of Genghis preserves its magic spell. It is still a name to conjure with when recording the great revolutions of a period which beheld the death of the old system in China, and the advent in that country of a newer and more vigorous government which, slowly acquiring shape in the hands of Kublai and a more national form under the Mings, has attained the pinnacle of its utility and strength under the influence of the great emperors of the Manchu dynasty. But great as is the reputation Genghis has acquired it is probably short of his merits. He is remembered as a relentless and irresistible conqueror, a human scourge; but he was much more. He was one of the greatest instruments of destiny, one of the most remarkable molders of the fate of nations to be met with in the history of the world. His name still overshadows Asia with its fame, and the tribute of our admiration cannot be denied.

The death of Genghis did not seriously retard the progress of the war against the Kins. He expressed the wish that war should be carried on in a more humane and less vindictive manner, but he did not advocate there being no war or the abandonment of any of his enterprises. His son and successor Ogotai was indeed specially charged to bring the conquest of China to a speedy and victorious conclusion. The weakness of the Mongol confederacy was the delay connected with the proclamation of a new Khan and the necessity of summoning to a Grand Council all the princes and generals of the race, although it entailed the suspension and often the abandonment of great enterprises. The death of Genghis saved India but not China. Almost his last instructions were to draw up the plan for attacking and turning the great fortress of Tunkwan, which had provided such an efficient defense for Honan on the north; and, in 1230, Ogotai, who had already partitioned the territory taken from the Kins into ten departments, took the field in person, giving a joint command to his brother Tuli, under whom served the experienced generals Yeliu Chutsia, Antchar, and Subutai.   At first the Mongols met with no great success, and the Kins, encouraged by a momentary gleam of victory, ventured to reject the terms offered by Ogotai and to insult his envoy.   The only important fighting during the years 1230–31 occurred round Fongsian, which after a long siege surrendered to Antchar, and when the campaign closed the Kins presented a bold front to the Mongols and still hoped to retain their power and dominions.

In 1232 the Mongols increased their armies in the field, and attacked the Kins from two sides.   Ogotai led the main force against Honan, while Tuli, marching through Shensi into Szchuen, assailed them on their western flank.   The difficulties encountered by Tuli on this march, when he had to make his own roads, were such that he entered the Kin territories with a much reduced and exhausted army.   The Kin forces gained some advantage over it, but by either a feigned or a forced retreat, Tuli succeeded in baffling their pursuit, and in effecting a junction with his brother Ogotai, who had met with better fortune.   Tuli destroyed everything along his line of march, and his massacres and sacks revived the worst traditions of Mongol ferocity.   In these straits the Kins endeavored to flood the country round their capital, to which the Mongols had now advanced, but the Mongols fell upon the workmen while engaged in the task, and slew ten thousand of them.   When the main Kin army accepted battle before the town of Yuchow, it was signally defeated, with the loss of three of its principal generals, and Ninkiassu fled from Kaifong to a place more removed from the scene of war.   The garrison and townspeople of Kaifong —an immense city with walls thirty-six miles in circumference, and a population during the siege, it is said, of one million four hundred thousand families, or nearly seven million people—offered a stubborn resistance to the Mongols, who intrusted the conduct of the attack to Subutai, the most daring of all their commanders.   The Mongols employed their most formidable engines, catapults hurling immense stones, and mortars ejecting explosives and combustibles, but twelve months elapsed before the walls were shattered and the courage and provisions of the defenders exhausted. Then Kaifong surrendered at discretion, and Subutai wished to massacre the whole of the population. But fortunately for the Chinese, Yeliu Chutsai was a more humane and a more influential general, and under his advice Ogotai rejected the cruel proposal.

At this moment, when it seemed impossible for fate to have any worse experience in store for the unfortunate Kins, their old enemies, the Sungs, wishing to give them the *coup de grâce*, declared war upon them, and placed a large army in the field under their best general, Mongkong, of whom more will be heard. The relics of the Kin army, under their sovereign Ninkiassu, took shelter in Tsaichau, where they were closely besieged by the Mongols on one side and the Sungs on the other. Driven thus into a corner, the Kins fought with the courage of despair and long held out against the combined efforts of their enemies. At last Ninkiassu saw that the struggle could not be prolonged, and he prepared himself to end his life and career in a manner worthy of the race from which he sprang. When the enemy broke into the city, and he heard the stormers at the gate of his palace, he retired to an upper chamber and set fire to the building. Many of his generals, and even of his soldiers, followed his example, preferring to end their existence rather than to add to the triumph of their Mongol and Sung opponents. Thus came to an end in 1234 the famous dynasty of the Kins, who under nine emperors had ruled Northern China for one hundred and eighteen years, and whose power and military capacity may best be gauged by the fact that without a single ally they held out against the all-powerful Mongols for more than a quarter of a century. Ninkiassu, the last of their rulers, was not able to sustain the burden of their authority, but he at least showed himself equal to ending it in a worthy and appropriately dramatic manner.

tinued disputes as to the succession, was followed by the withdrawal of the Mongol forces from Sung territory, and during the last six years of his life Ogotai abstained from war, and gave himself up to the indulgence of his gluttony. He built a great palace at Karakoram, where his ancestors had been content to live in a tent, and he intrusted the government of the old Kin dominions to Yeliu Chutsai, who acquired great popularity among the Chinese for his clemency and regard for their customs. Yeliu Chutsai adopted the Chinese mode of taxation, and when Ogotai's widow, Turakina, who acted as regent after her husband's death, ordered him to alter his system and to farm out the revenues, he sent in his resignation, and, it is said, died of grief shortly afterward. Ogotai was one of the most humane and amiable of all the Mongol rulers, and Yeliu Chutsai imitated his master. Of the latter the Chinese contemporary writers said "he was distinguished by a rare disinterestedness. Of a very broad intellect, he was able, without injustice and without wronging a single person, to amass vast treasures (D'Ohsson says only of books, maps, and pictures), and to enrich his family, but all his care and labors had for their sole object the advantage and glory of his masters. Wise and calculating in his plans, he did little of which he had any reason to repent."

During the five years following the death of Ogotai, the Mongols were absorbed in the question who should be their next Great Khan, and it was only after a warm and protracted discussion, which threatened to entail the disruption of Mongol power, and the revelation of many rivalries among the descendants of Genghis, that Kuyuk, the eldest son of Ogotai, was proclaimed emperor. At the kuriltai held for this purpose, all the great Mongol leaders were present, including Batu, the conqueror of Hungary, and after the Mongol chiefs had agreed as to their chief, the captive kings, Yaroslaf of Russia and David of Georgia, paid homage to their conqueror. We owe to the monk Carpino, who was sent by the Pope to convert the Mongol, a graphic account of one of the most brilliant ceremonies to be met with in the whole course of Mongol history. The delay in selecting Kuyuk, whose principal act of sovereignty was to issue a seal having this inscription: "God in Heaven and Kuyuk on earth; by the power of God the ruler of all men," had given the Sungs one respite, and his early death procured them another. Kuyuk died in 1248, and his cousin, Mangu, the son of Tuli, was appointed his successor. By this time the Mongol chiefs of the family of Genghis in Western Asia were practically independent of the nominal Great Khan, and governed their states in complete sovereignty, and waged war without reference to Karakoram. This change left the Mongols in their original home of the Amour absolutely free to devote all their attention to the final overthrow of the Sungs, and Mangu declared that he would know no rest until he had finally subjected the last of the Chinese ruling families. In this resolution Mangu received the hearty support of his younger but more able brother, Kublai, to whom was intrusted the direction in the field of the armies sent to complete the conquest of China.

Kublai received this charge in 1251, so that the Sungs had enjoyed, first through the pacific disposition of Ogotai, and, secondly, from the family disputes following his death, peace for more than fifteen years. The advantage of this tranquillity was almost nullified by the death of Mongkong, a general whose reputation may have been easily gained, but who certainly enjoyed the confidence of his soldiers, and who was thought by his countrymen to be the best commander of his day. When the Chinese emperor, Litsong, saw the storm again approaching his northern frontier, he found that he had lost the main support of his power, and that his military resources were inferior to those of his enemy. He had allowed himself to be lulled into a false sense of security by the long inaction of the Mongols, and although he seems to have been an amiable prince, and a typical Chinese ruler, honoring the descendants of Confucius with the hereditary title of duke, which still remains in that family, and is the only title of its kind in China, and encouraging the literary classes of his country, he was a bad sovereign to be intrusted with the task of defending his realm and people against a bold and determined enemy.

Kublai prepared the way for his campaigns in Southern China by following a very wise and moderate policy in Northern China similar to that begun by Muhula, and carried out with greater effect by Yeliu Chutsai. He had enjoyed the advantage of a Chinese education, imparted by an able tutor named Yaochu, who became the prince's private secretary and mentor in all Chinese matters. At his instigation, or, at least, with his co-operation, Kublai took in hand the restoration of the southern portion of Honan, which had been devastated during the wars, and he succeeded in bringing back its population and prosperity to that great province of Central China. He thus secured a base for his operations close to the Sung frontier, while he attached to his person a large section of the Chinese nation. There never was any concealment that this patronage of Chinese officials, and these measures for the amelioration of many millions of Chinese subjects, were the well calculated preliminaries to the invasion of Southern China and the extinction of the Sung dynasty.

If Kublai had succeeded in obtaining a wise adviser in Yaochu, he was not less fortunate in procuring a great general in the person of Uriangkadai, the son of Subutai, and his remarkable and unvarying successes were largely due to the efforts of those two men in the cabinet and the field. The plan of campaign, drawn up with great care and forethought by the prince and his lieutenant, had the double merit of being both bold and original. Its main purpose was not one that the Sung generals would be likely to divine. It was determined to make a flank march round the Sung dominions, and to occupy what is now the province of Yunnan; and, by placing an army in the rear of their kingdom, to attack them eventually from two sides.

At this time Yunnan formed an independent state, and its ruler, from his position behind the Sung territory, must have fancied himself secure against any attack by the Mongols. He was destined to a rude awakening. Kublai and Uriangkadai, marching across Szchuen and crossing the Kinchakiang, or "river of golden sand," which forms the upper course of the Great River, on rafts, burst into Yunnan, speedily vanquished the frontier garrisons, and laid siege to the capital, Talifoo. That town did not hold out long, and soon Kublai was in a position to return to his own state, leaving Uriangkadai with a considerable garrison in charge of Yunnan. That general, believing that his position would be improved by his resorting to an active offensive, carried the standard of his race against the many turbulent tribes in his neighborhood, and invaded Burma, whose king, after one campaign, was glad to recognize the supremacy of the Mongols. The success and the boldness, which may have been considered temerity, of this campaign, raised up enemies to Kublai at the court of Karakoram, and the mind of his brother Mangu was poisoned against him by many who declared that Kublai aspired to complete independence. These designs so far succeeded, that in 1257 Mangu finally deprived Kublai of all his commands, and ordered him to proceed to Karakoram. At this harsh and unmerited treatment Kublai showed himself inclined to rebel and dispute his brother's authority. If he had done this, although the provocation was great, he would have confirmed the charges of his accusers, and a war would have broken out among the Mongols which would probably have rent their power in twain in Eastern Asia. But fortunately Yaochu was at hand to give prudent advice, and after much hesitation Kublai yielded to the impressive exhortations of his experienced and sagacious minister. He is reported to have addressed Kublai in the following terms: "Prince! You are the brother of the emperor, but you are not the less his subject. You cannot, without committing a crime, question his decisions, and, moreover, if you were to do so, it would only result in placing you in a more dangerous predicament, out of which you could hardly succeed in extricating yourself, as you are so far distant from the capital where your enemies seek to injure you. My advice is that you should send your family to Mangu, and by this step you will justify yourself and remove any suspicions there may be."

Kublai adopted this wise course, and proceeded in person to Karakoram, where he succeeded in proving his innocence and in discomfiting his enemies. It is said that Mangu was so affected at the mere sight of his brother that he at once forgave him without waiting for an explanation and reinstated him in all his offices. To ratify this reconciliation Mangu proclaimed that he would take the field in person, and that Kublai should hold joint command with himself. When he formed this resolution to proceed to China in person, he appointed his next brother, Arikbuka, to act as his lieutenant in Mongolia. It is necessary to recollect this arrangement, as Mangu died during the campaign, and it led to the separation of the Chinese empire and the Mongolian, which were divided after that event between Kublai and Arikbuka.

Mangu did not come to his resolution to prosecute the war with the Sungs any too soon, for Uriangkadai was beginning to find his isolated position not free from danger. Large as the army of that general was, and skillfully as he had endeavored to improve his position by strengthening the fortresses and recruiting from the warlike tribes of Yunnan, Uriangkadai found himself threatened by the collected armies of the Sungs, who occupied Szchuen with a large garrison and menaced the daring Mongol general with the whole of their power. There seems every reason to believe that if the Sungs had acted with only ordinary promptitude they might have destroyed this Mongol army long before any aid could have reached it from the north. Once Mangu had formed his resolution the rapidity of his movements left the Sungs little or no chance of attacking

Uriangkadai. This campaign began in the winter of 1257, when the troops were able to cross the frozen waters of the Hoangho, and the immense Mongol army was divided into three bodies, while Uriangkadai was ordered to march north and effect a junction with his old chief Kublai in Szchuen. The principal fighting of the first year occurred in this part of China, and Mangu hastened there with another of his armies. The Sung garrison was large, and showed great courage and fortitude. The difficulty of the country and the strength of several of their fortresses seconded their efforts, and after two years' fighting the Mongols felt so doubtful of success that they held a council of war to decide whether they should retreat or continue to prosecute the struggle. It has been said that councils of war do not come to bold resolutions, but this must have been an exception, as it decided not to retreat, and to make one more determined effort to overcome the Chinese. The campaign of 1259 began with the siege of Hochau, a strong fortress, held by a valiant garrison and commander, and to whose aid a Chinese army under Luwenti was hastening. The governor, Wangkien, offered a stout resistance, and Luwenti succeeded in harassing the besiegers; but the fall of the fortress appeared assured, when a new and more formidable defender arrived in the form of dysentery. The Mongol camp was ravaged by this foe, Mangu himself died of the disease, and those of the Mongols who escaped beat a hasty and disorderly retreat back to the north. Once more the Sungs obtained a brief respite.

The death of Mangu threatened fresh disputes and strife among the Mongol royal family. Kublai was his brother's lawful heir, but Arikbuka, the youngest of the brothers, was in possession of Karakoram, and supreme throughout Mongolia. He was hostile to Kublai, and disposed to assert all his rights and to make the most of his opportunities. No Great Khan could be proclaimed anywhere save at Karakoram, and Arikbuka would not allow his brother to gain that place, the cradle of their race and dynasty, unless he could do so by force of arms. Kublai attempted to solve the difficulty by holding a grand council near his favorite city of Cambaluc, the modern Pekin, and he sent forth his proclamation to the Mongols as their Khan. But they refused to recognize one who was not elected in the orthodox fashion at Karakoram; and Arikbuka not merely defied Kublai, but summoned his own kuriltai at Karakoram, where he was proclaimed Khakhan in the most formal manner and with all the accustomed ceremonies. Arikbuka was undoubtedly popular among the Mongols, while Kublai, who was regarded as half a Chinese on account of his education, had a far greater reputation south of the wall than north of it. Kublai could not tolerate the open defiance of his authority, and the contempt shown for what was his birthright, by Arikbuka; and in 1261 he advanced upon Karakoram at the head of a large army. A single battle sufficed to dispose of Arikbuka's pretensions, and that prince was glad to find a place of refuge among the Kirghiz. Kublai proved himself a generous enemy. He sent Arikbuka his full pardon, he reinstated him in his rank of prince, and he left him virtually supreme among the Mongol tribes. He retraced his steps to Pekin, fully resolved to become Chinese emperor in reality, but prepared to waive his rights as Mongol Khan. Mangu Khan was the last of the Mongol rulers whose authority was recognized in both the east and the west, and his successor, Kublai, seeing that its old significance had departed, was fain to establish his on a new basis in the fertile, ancient and wide-stretching dominions of China.

Before Kublai composed the difficulty with Arikbuka he had resumed his operations against the Sungs, and even before Mangu's death he had succeeded in establishing some posts south of the Yangtsekiang, in the impassability of which the Chinese fondly believed. During the year 1260 he laid siege to Wochow, the modern Wouchang, but he failed to make any impression on the fortress on this occasion, and he agreed to the truce which Litsong proposed. By the terms of this agreement Litsong acknowl-

edged himself a Mongol vassal, just as his ancestors had
subjected themselves to the Kins, paid a large tribute, and
forbade his generals anywhere to attack the Mongols. The
last stipulation was partly broken by an attack on the rear
of Uriangkadai's corps, but no serious results followed, for
Kublai was well satisfied with the manner in which the
campaign terminated, as there is no doubt that his advance
across the Yangtsekiang had been precipitate, and he may
have thought himself lucky to escape with the appearance
of success and the conclusion of a gratifying treaty. It was
with the reputation gained by this nominal success, and by
having made the Sungs his tributaries, that Kublai hastened
northward to settle his rivalry with Arikbuka. Having accomplished that object with complete success, he decided to
put an end to the Sung dynasty. The Chinese emperor, acting
with strange fatuity, had given fresh cause of umbrage,
and had provoked a war by many petty acts of discourtesy,
culminating in the murder of the envoys of Kublai, sent
to notify him of his proclamation as Great Khan of the
Mongols. Probably the Sung ruler could not have averted
war if he had shown the greatest forbearance and humility,
but this cruel and inexcusable act precipitated the crisis and
the extinction of his attenuated authority. If there was
any delay in the movements of Kublai for the purpose of
exacting reparation for this outrage, it was due to his first
having to arrange a difficulty that had arisen in his relations with the King of Corea. That potentate had long
preserved the peace with his Mongol neighbors, and perhaps he would have remained a friend without any interruption, had not the Mongols done something which was
construed as an infraction of Corean liberty. The Corean
love of independence took fire at the threatened diminution
of their rights, they rose en masse in defense of their country, and even the king, Wangtien, who had been well disposed to the Mongol rulers, declared that he could not continue the alliance, and placed himself at the head of his
people. Seeing himself thus menaced with a costly war in

a difficult country on the eve of a more necessary and hopeful contest, Kublai resorted to diplomacy. He addressed Wangtien in complimentary terms and disclaimed all intention of injuring the Coreans, with whom he wished to maintain friendly relations, but at the same time he pointed out the magnitude of his power and dilated on the extent of the Mongol conquests. Half by flattery and half by menace Kublai brought the Corean court to reason, and Wangtien again entered into bonds of alliance with Cambaluc and renewed his old oaths of friendship.

At this point of the long struggle with the Sungs it will be appropriate to consider what was the exact position of Kublai with regard to his own Chinese subjects, who now formed the backbone of his power. By this time Kublai had become to all practical intents and purposes a Chinese emperor. He had accepted all the traditional functions of the typical Hwangti, and the etiquette and splendor of his court rivaled that of the Sungs. He had not merely adopted the Chinese system of taxation and the form of administration to which the larger portion of his officials, being of Chinese race, had been accustomed, but he declared himself the patron of learning and of Buddhism, which had gained a hold on the minds of the Mongols that it has not lost to the present day. One of the most popular of his early measures had been the order to liberate all the literate class among his Chinese prisoners, and they had formed the nucleus of the civil service Kublai attached to his interests and utilized as his empire expanded. In his relations with Buddhism Kublai showed not less astuteness, and in realizing that to attain durable success he must appeal to the religious side of human character, he showed that he had the true instincts of a statesman.

At this time two facts were clearly apparent. The Chinese were sunk in a low state of religious disbelief, and the Sung rulers were not disposed to play the part of regenerators of their country. The second fact was that the only vigorous religion in China, or, indeed, in Eastern Asia, was

Buddhism, which, since the establishment of Brahmanism in India, had taken up its headquarters in Tibet, where, however, the supreme authority was still secular—that is to say, it was invested in the hands of a prince or king, and not in those of a priest or Grand Lama. It so happened that there was resident at Kublai's court a Tibetan priest, of the family which had always supplied the Sanpou with his minister, who gained the ear of Kublai, and convinced him how politic and advantageous to him personally it would be if he were to secure the co-operation and sympathy of his priestly order. Kublai fell in with his plans, and proclaimed his friend Pakba Lama, and sent him back to Tibet, there to establish the ecclesiastical authority, which still exists in that country, in intimate alliance and sympathy with the Chinese rulers. By this and other similar proceedings Kublai gained over to his side several influential classes among the Chinese people, and many reflecting persons thought they saw in him a true regenerator of the empire, and a worthy successor of their greatest rulers. It was, therefore, with a thoroughly pacified country, and to a great extent a contented people, that Kublai began his last war with the rulers of Southern China.

In 1263 Kublai issued his proclamation of war, calling on his generals "to assemble their troops, to sharpen their swords and their pikes, and to prepare their bows and arrows," for he intended to attack the Sungs by land and sea. The treason of a Chinese general in his service named Litan served to delay the opening of the campaign for a few weeks, but this incident was of no importance, as Litan was soon overthrown and executed. Brief as was the interval, it was marked by one striking and important event—the death of Litsong, who was succeeded by his nephew, Chowki, called the Emperor Toutsong. Litsong was not a wise ruler, but, compared with many of his successors, he might be more accurately styled unfortunate than incompetent. Toutsong, and his weak and arrogant minister, Kiassetao, hastened to show that there were greater heights of folly than any to which he had attained. Acting on the advice of a renegade

Sung general, well acquainted with the defenses of Southern China, Kublai altered his proposed attack, and prepared for crossing the Yangtsekiang by first making himself supreme on its tributary, the Han River. His earlier attack on Wouchang has been described, and his compulsory retirement from that place had taught him the evil of making a premature attack. His object remained the same, but instead of marching direct to it across the Yangtsekiang he took the advice of the Sung general, and attacked the fortress of Sianyang on the Han River, with the object of making himself supreme on that stream, and wresting from the Sungs the last first-class fortress they possessed in the northwest. By the time all these preliminaries were completed and the Mongol army had fairly taken the field it was 1268, and Kublai sent sixty thousand of his best troops, with a large number of auxiliaries, to lay siege to Sianyang, which was held by a large garrison and a resolute governor. The Mongol lines were drawn up round the town, and also its neighbor of Fanching, situated on the opposite bank of the river, with which communication was maintained by several bridges, and the Mongols built a large fleet of fifty war junks, with which they closed the Han River and effectually prevented any aid being sent up it from Hankow or Wouchang. Liuwen Hoan, the commandant of Sianyang, was a brave man, and he commanded a numerous garrison and possessed supplies, as he said, to stand a ten years' siege. He repulsed all the assaults of the enemy, and, undaunted by his isolation, replied to the threats of the Mongols, to give him no quarter if he persisted in holding out, by boasting that he would hang their traitor general in chains before his sovereign. The threats and vaunts of the combatants did not bring the siege any nearer to an end. The utmost that the Mongols could achieve was to prevent any provisions or reenforcements being thrown into the town. But on the fortress itself they made no impression. Things had gone on like this for three years, and the interest in the siege had begun to languish, when Kublai determined to make a supreme effort to carry the place, and at the same moment the Sung minister came to the conclusion to relieve it at all hazards.

The campaign of 1270 began with a heroic episode—the successful dispatch of provisions into the besieged town, under the direction of two Chinese officers named Changkoua and Changchun, whose names deserve to be long remembered for their heroism. The flotilla was divided into two bodies, one composed of the fighting, the other of the store-ships. The Mongols had made every-preparation to blockade the river, but the suddenness and vigor of the Chinese attack surprised them, and, at first, the Chinese had the best of the day. But soon the Mongols recovered, and from their superior position threatened to overwhelm the assailing Chinese squadron. In this perilous moment Changchun, devoting himself to death in the interest of his country, collected all his war-junks, and making a desperate attack on the Mongols, succeeded in obtaining sufficient time to enable the storeships under Changkoua to pass safely up to Sianyang. The life of so great a hero as Changchun was, however, a heavy price to pay for the temporary relief of Sianyang, which was more closely besieged than ever after the arrival of Kublai in person.

After this affair the Mongols pushed the siege with greater vigor, and instead of concentrating their efforts on Sianyang they attacked both that fortress and Fanching from all sides. The Mongol commander, Alihaya, sent to Persia, where the Mongols were also supreme, for engineers trained in the working of mangonels or catapults, engines capable of throwing stones of 160-pounds' weight with precision for a considerable distance. By their aid the bridges across the river were first destroyed, and then the walls of Sianyang were so severely damaged that an assault appeared to be feasible. But Fanching had suffered still more from the Mongol bombardment, and Alihaya therefore attacked it first. The garrison offered a determined resistance, and the fighting was continued in the streets. Not a man of the garrison escaped, and when the slaughter was over the Mongols found that they had only acquired possession of a mass of ruins. But they had obtained the key to Sianyang, the weakest flank of which had been protected by Fanching, and the Chinese garrison was so discouraged that Liuwen Hoan, despairing of relief, agreed to accept the terms offered by Kublai. Those terms were expressed in the following noble letter from the Mongol emperor: "The generous defense you have made during five years covers you with glory. It is the duty of every faithful subject to serve his prince at the expense of his life, but in the straits to which you are reduced, your strength exhausted, deprived of succor and without hope of receiving any, would it be reasonable to sacrifice the lives of so many brave men out of sheer obstinacy? Submit in good faith to us and no harm shall come to you. We promise you still more; and that is to provide each and all of you with honorable employment. You shall have no grounds of discontent, for that we pledge you our imperial word."

It will not excite surprise that Liuwen Hoan, who had been, practically speaking, deserted by his own sovereign, should have accepted the magnanimous terms of his conqueror, and become as loyal a lieutenant of Kublai as he had shown himself to be of the Sung Toutsong. The death of that ruler followed soon afterward, but as the real power had been in the hands of the Minister Kiassetao, no change took place in the policy or fortunes of the Sung kingdom. At this moment Kublai succeeded in obtaining the services of Bayan, a Mongol general who had acquired a great reputation under Khulagu in Persia. Bayan, whose name signifies the noble or the brave, and who was popularly known as Bayan of the Hundred Eyes, because he was supposed to see everything, was one of the greatest military leaders of his age and race. He was intrusted with the command of the main army, and under him served, it is interesting to state, Liuwen Hoan. Several towns were captured after more or less resistance, and Bayan bore down with all his force on the triple cities of Hankow, Wouchang, and Hanyang. Bayan concentrated all his efforts on the capture of Hanyang, while the Mongol navy under Artchu compelled the Chinese fleet to take refuge under the walls of Wouchang. None of these towns offered a very stubborn resistance, and Bayan had the satisfaction of receiving their surrender one after another. Leaving Alihaya with 40,000 men to guard these places, Bayan marched with the rest of his forces on the Sung capital, Lingan or Hangchow, the celebrated Kincsay of medieval travelers. The retreating fleet and army of the Sungs carried with them fear of the Mongols, and the ever-increasing representation of their extraordinary power and irresistible arms. In this juncture public opinion compelled Kiassetao to take the lead, and he called upon all the subjects of the Sung to contribute arms and money for the purpose of national defense. But his own incompetence in directing this national movement deprived it of half its force and of its natural chances of success. Bayan's advance was rapid. Many towns opened their gates in terror or admiration of his name, and Liuwen Hoan was frequently present to assure them that Kublai was the most generous of masters, and that there was no wiser course than to surrender to his generals.

The Mongol forces at last reached the neighborhood of the Sung capital, where Kiassetao had succeeded in collecting an army of 130,000 men; but many of them were ill-trained, and the splendor of the camp provided a poor equivalent for the want of arms and discipline among the men. Kiassetao seems to have been ignorant of the danger of his position, for he sent an arrogant summons to the Mongols to retire, stating also that he would grant a peace based on the Yangtsekiang as a boundary. Bayan's simple reply to this notice was, "If you had really aimed at peace you would have made this proposition before we crossed the Kiang. Now that we are the masters of it, it is a little too late. Still if you sincerely desire it, come and see me in person, and we will discuss the necessary conditions." Very few of the Sung lieutenants offered a protracted re-

sistance, and even the isolated cases of devotion were confined to the official class, who were more loyal than the mass
of the people. Chao Maofa and his wife Yongchi put an
end to their existence sooner than give up their charge at
Chichow, but the garrison accepted the terms of the Mongols without compunction, and without thinking of their
duty. Kiassetao attempted to resist the Mongol advance
at Kien Kang, the modern Nankin, but after an engagement on land and water the Sungs were driven back, and
their fleet only escaped destruction by retiring precipitately
to the sea. After this success Nankin surrendered without
resistance, although its governor was a valiant and apparently a capable man. He committed suicide sooner than
surrender, and among his papers was found a plan of campaign, after perusing which Bayan exclaimed, "Is it possible
that the Sungs possessed a man capable of giving such prudent counsel? If they had paid heed to it, should we ever
have reached this spot?" After this success Bayan pressed
on with increased rather than diminished energy, and the
Sung emperor and his court fled from the capital. Kublai
showed an inclination to temporize and to negotiate, but
Bayan would not brook any delay. "To relax your grip
even for a moment on an enemy whom you have held by
the throat for a hundred years would only be to give him
time to recover his breath, to restore his forces, and in the
end to cause us an infinity of trouble."

The Sung fortunes showed some slight symptoms of im-
proving when Kiassetao was disgraced, and a more competent general was found in the person of Chang Chikia.
But the Mongols never abated the vigor of their attack or
relaxed in their efforts to cut off all possibility of succor from
the Sung capital. When Chang Chikia hoped to improve
the position of his side by resuming the offensive he was
destined to rude disappointment. Making an attack on the
strong position of the Mongols at Nankin he was repulsed
with heavy loss. The Sung fleet was almost annihilated
and 700 war-junks were taken by the victors. After this

the Chinese never dared to face the Mongols again on the water. This victory was due to the courage and capacity of Artchu. Bayan now returned from a campaign in Mongolia to resume the chief conduct of the war, and he signalized his return by the capture of Changchow. At this town he is said to have sanctioned a massacre of the Chinese troops, but the facts are enwrapped in uncertainty; and Marco Polo declares that this was only done after the Chinese had treacherously cut up the Mongol garrison. Alarmed by the fall of Changchow, the Sung ministers again sued for peace, sending an imploring letter to this effect: "Our ruler is young and cannot be held responsible for the differences that have arisen between the peoples. Kiassetao the guilty one has been punished; give us peace and we shall be better friends in the future." Bayan's reply was severe and uncompromising. "The age of your prince has nothing to do with the question between us. The war must go on to its legitimate end. Further argument is useless." The defenses of the Sung capital were by this time removed, and the unfortunate upholders of that dynasty had no option save to come to terms with the Mongols. Marco Polo describes Kincsay as the most opulent city of the world, but it was in no position to stand a siege. The empress-regent, acting for her son, sent in her submission to Bayan, and agreed to proceed to the court of the conqueror. She abdicated for herself and family all the pretensions of their rank, and she accepted the favors of the Mongol with due humility, saying, "The Son of Heaven (thus giving Kublai the correct imperial style) grants you the favor of sparing your life; it is just to thank him for it and to pay him homage." Bayan made a triumphal entry into the city, while the Emperor Kongtsong was sent off to Pekin. The majority of the Sung courtiers and soldiers came to terms with Bayan, but a few of the more desperate or faithful endeavored to uphold the Sung cause in Southern China under the general, Chang Chikia. Two of the Sung princes were supported by this commander, and one was proclaimed by the empty title of emperor.   Capricious fortune rallied to their side for a brief space, and some of the Mongol detachments which had advanced too far or with undue precipitancy were cut up and destroyed.

The Mongols seem to have thought that the war was over, and the success of Chang Chikia's efforts may have been due to their negligence rather than to his vigor.   As soon as they realized that there remained a flickering flame of opposition among the supporters of the Sungs they sent two armies, one into Kwantung and the other into Fuhkien, and their fleet against Chang Chikia.   Desperate as was his position, that officer still exclaimed, "If Heaven has not resolved to overthrow the Sungs, do you think that even now it cannot restore their ruined throne?"   But his hopes were dashed to the ground by the capture of Canton, and the expulsion of all his forces from the mainland.   One puppet emperor died, and then Chang proclaimed another as Tiping.   The last supporters of the cause took refuge on the island of Tai in the Canton estuary, where they hoped to maintain their position.   The position was strong and the garrison was numerous; but the Mongols were not to be frightened by appearances.   Their fleet bore down on the last Sung stronghold with absolute confidence, and, although the Chinese resisted for three days and showed great gallantry, they were overwhelmed by the superior engines as well as the numbers of the Mongols.   Chang Chikia with a few ships succeeded in escaping from the fray, but the emperor's vessel was less fortunate, and finding that escape was impossible, Lousionfoo, one of the last Sung ministers, seized the emperor in his arms and jumped overboard with him.   Thus died Tiping, the last Chinese emperor of the Sungs, and with him expired that ill-fated dynasty.   Chang Chikia renewed the struggle with aid received from Tonquin, but when he was leading a forlorn hope against Canton he was caught in a typhoon and he and his ships were wrecked.   His invocation to Heaven, "I have done everything I could to sustain on the throne the Sung dynasty.   When one prince died, I caused another to be proclaimed emperor. He also has perished, and I still live! Oh, Heaven, shall I be acting against thy desires if I sought to place a new prince of this family on the throne?" sounded the dirge of the race he had served so well.

Thus was the conquest of China by the Mongols completed. After half a century of warfare the kingdom of the Sungs shared the same fate as its old rival the Kin, and Kublai had the personal satisfaction of completing the work begun by his grandfather Genghis seventy years before. Of all the Mongol triumphs it was the longest in being attained. The Chinese of the north and of the south resisted with extraordinary powers of endurance the whole force of the greatest conquering race Asia had ever seen. They were not skilled in war and their generals were generally incompetent, but they held out with desperate courage and obstinacy long after other races would have given in. The student of history will not fail to see in these facts striking testimony of the extraordinary resources of China, and of the capacity of resistance to even a vigorous conqueror possessed by its inert masses. Even the Mongols did not conquer until they had obtained the aid of a large section of the Chinese nation, or before Kublai had shown that he intended to prove himself a worthy Emperor of China and not merely a great Khan of the Mongol Hordes.

CHAPTER VI

KUBLAI AND THE MONGOL DYNASTY

While Bayan was winning victories for his master and driving the Chinese armies from the field, Kublai was engaged at Pekin in the difficult and necessary task of consolidating his authority. In 1271 he gave his dynasty the name of Yuen or Original, and he took for himself the Chinese title of Chitsou, although it will never supersede his Mongol name of Kublai. Summoning to his court the most experienced Chinese ministers, and aided by many foreigners, he succeeded in founding a government which was imposing by reason of its many-sidedness as well as its inherent strength. It satisfied the Chinese and it was gratifying to the Mongols, because they formed the buttress of one of the most imposing administrations in the world. All this was the distinct work of Kublai, who had enjoyed the special favor of Genghis, who had predicted of him that "one day he will sit in my seat and bring you good fortune such as you have had in my time." He resolved to make his court the most splendid in the world. His capital Cambaluc or Khanbalig—"the city of the Khan"—stood on or near the present site of Pekin, and was made for the first time capital of China by the Mongols. There were, according to Marco Polo, twelve gates, at each of which was stationed a guard of 1,000 men, and the streets were so straight and wide that you could see from one end to the other, or from gate to gate. The extent given of the walls varies: according to the highest estimate they were twenty-seven miles round, according to the lowest eighteen. The khan's palace at Chandu or Kaipingfoo, north of Pekin, where he built a magnificent summer palace, kept his stud of horses, and carried out his love of the chase in the immense park and preserves attached, may be considered the Windsor of this Chinese monarch. The position of Pekin had, and still has, much to recommend it as the site of a capital. The Mings, after proclaiming Nankin the capital, made scarcely less use of it, and Chuntche, the first of the Manchus, adopted it as his. It has since remained the sole metropolis of the empire.

When Kublai permanently established himself at Pekin he drew up consistent lines of policy on all the great questions with which it was likely he would have to deal, and he always endeavored to act upon these set principles. In framing this system of government he was greatly assisted by his old friend and tutor Yaochu, as well as by other Chinese ministers. He was thus able to deal wisely and also vigorously with a society with which he was only imperfectly acquainted; and the impartiality and insight into human character, which were his main characteristics, greatly simplified the difficult task before him. His impartiality was shown most clearly in his attitude on the question of religion; but it partook very largely of a hard materialism which concealed itself under a nominal indifference. At first he treated with equal consideration Buddhism, Mohammedanism, Christianity, and even Judaism, and he said that he treated them all with equal consideration because he hoped that the greatest among them would help him in heaven. If some doubt may be felt as to the sincerity of this statement, there can be none as to Kublai's effort to turn all religions to a political use, and to make them serve his turn. Some persons have thought he showed a predilection for Christianity, but his measures in support of Buddhism, and of his friend the Pakba Lama, are a truer indication of his feelings. But none was admitted into his private confidence, and his acts evinced a politic tolerance toward all creeds. But his religious tolerance or indifference did not extend to personal matters. He insisted on the proper prayers being offered to himself and the extreme reverence of the kow-tow. Priests were appointed and specially enjoined to offer up prayers on his behalf before the people, who were required to attend these services and to join in the responses. Images of himself were also sent to all the provincial towns for reverence to be offered. He also followed the Chinese custom of erecting a temple to his ancestors, and the coins that passed current bore his effigy. Thus did Kublai more and more identify himself with his Chinese subjects, and as he found his measures crowned with success he became himself more wedded to Chinese views, less tolerant of adverse opinions, and more disposed to assert his sovereign majesty.

Having embellished his capital, it is not surprising to find that he drew up a strict court ceremonial, and that he prescribed gorgeous dresses for those who were to be allowed to approach him. His banquets were of the most sumptuous description. Strangers from foreign states were admitted to the presence, and dined at a table set apart for travelers, while the great king himself feasted in the full gaze of his people. His courtiers, guard, and ministers attended by a host of servitors, and protected from enemies by 20,000 guards, the flower of the Mongol army; the countless wealth seized in the capitals of numerous kingdoms; the brilliance of intellect among his chief adherents and supporters; the martial character of the race that lent itself almost as well to the pageantry of a court as to the stern reality of battle; and finally the majesty of the great king himself—all combined to make Kublai's court and capital the most splendid, at that time, in the world. Although Kublai's instincts were martial, he gave up all idea of accompanying his armies in the field after his war with Arikbuka. As he was only forty-four when he formed this decision, it must be assumed that he came to it mainly because he had so many other matters to attend to, and also, no doubt, because he felt that he possessed in Bayan a worthy substitute.

The most fortunate and successful monarch rarely escapes without some misfortune, and Kublai was not destined to be an exception to the rule. The successes of the Mongol navy undoubtedly led Kublai to believe that his arms might be carried beyond the sea, and he formed the definite plan of subjecting Japan to his power. The ruling family in that kingdom was of Chinese descent, tracing back its origin to Taipe, a fugitive Chinese prince of the twelfth century before our era. The Chinese in their usual way had asserted the superior position of a suzerain, and the Japanese had as consistently refused to recognize the claim, and had maintained their independence. As a rule the Japanese abstained from all interference in the affairs of the continent, and the only occasion on which they departed from this rule was when they aided Corea against China. In 1266 Kublai sent two embassadors by way of Corea to Japan with a letter from himself complaining that the Japanese court had taken no notice of his accession to power, and treated him with indifference. The mission never had a chance of success, for the Coreans succeeded in frightening the Mongol envoys with the terrors of the sea, and by withholding their assistance prevented them reaching their destination. The envoys returned without having been able to deliver their letter. Kublai decided that the Japanese were hostile to him, and he resolved to humble them. He called upon the King of Corea to raise an auxiliary force, and that prince promised to supply 1,000 ships and 10,000 men. In 1274 he sent a small force of 300 ships and 15,000 men to begin operations in the direction of Japan; but the Japanese navy came out to meet it, and attacking it off the island of Tsiusima, inflicted a crushing defeat. As this expedition was largely composed of the Corean contingent, Kublai easily persuaded himself that this defeat did not indicate what would happen when he employed his own Mongol troops. He also succeeded in sending several envoys to Japan after his first abortive attempt, and they brought back consistent reports as to the hostility and defiance of the Japanese, who at last, to leave no further doubt on the subject, executed his envoy in 1280. For this outrage the haughty monarch swore he would exact a terrible revenge, and in 1280–81, when the last of his campaigns with the Sungs had been brought to a triumphant conclusion, he collected all his forces in the eastern part of the kingdom, and prepared to attack Japan with all his power.

For the purposes of this war he raised an army of over 100,000 men, of whom about one-third were Mongols; and a fleet large enough to carry this host and its supplies was gathered together with great difficulty in the harbors of Chekiang and Fuhkien. It would have been wiser if the expedition had started from Corea, as the sea voyage would have been greatly reduced; but the difficulty of getting his army to that country, and the greater difficulty of feeding it when it got there, induced him to make his own maritime possessions the base of his operations. From the beginning misfortunes fell thick upon it, and the Japanese, not less than the English when assailed by the Spanish Armada and

Boulogne invasions, owed much to the alliance of the sea.
Kublai had felt bound to appoint a Chinese generalissimo as
well as a Mongol to this host, but it did not work well. One
general fell ill and was superseded, another was lost in a
storm, and there was a general want of harmony in the
Mongol camp and fleet. Still the fleet set sail, but the elements declared themselves against Kublai. His shattered
fleet was compelled to take refuge off the islets to the north
of Japan, where it attempted to refit, but the Japanese
granted no respite, and assailed them both by land and sea.
After protracted but unequal fighting the Mongol commander
had no choice left but to surrender. The conquerors spared
the Chinese and Coreans among their prisoners, but they
put every Mongol to the sword. Only a stray junk or two
escaped to tell Kublai the tale of the greatest defeat the
Mongols had ever experienced. Thirty thousand of their
best troops were slaughtered, and their newly-created fleet,
on which they were founding such great expectations, was
annihilated, while 70,000 Chinese and Coreans remained as
prisoners in the hands of the victor. Kublai executed two
of his generals who escaped, but it is clear no one was to
blame. The Mongols were vanquished because they undertook a task beyond their power, and one with which their
military experience did not fit them to cope. The most formidable portion of their army was cavalry, and they had no
knowledge of the sea. Nor could their Chinese auxiliaries
supply this deficiency; for, strange as it may appear, the
Chinese, although many of them are good fishermen and
sailors, have never been a powerful nation at sea. On the
other hand, the Japanese have always been a bold and capable race of mariners. They have frequently proved that
the sea is their natural element, and all the power and resources of Kublai availed not against the skill and courage
of these hardy islanders. Kublai was reluctant to acquiesce
in his defeat, and he endeavored to form another expedition,
but the Chinese sailors mutinied and refused to embark.
They were supported by all the Chinese ministers at Pekin,

and Kublai felt himself compelled to yield and abandon all designs of conquest beyond the sea.

The old success of the Mongols did not desert them on land, and Kublai received some consolation for his rude repulse by the Japanese in the triumph of his arms in Burma. The momentary submission of the King of Burma, or Mien, as it was, and is still, called by the Chinese, had been followed by a fit of truculence and open hostility. This monarch had crossed over into Indian territory, and had assumed the title of King of Bengala in addition to his own. Emboldened by his success, he did not conceal his hostility to the Mongols, sent a defiant reply to all their representations, and even assumed the offensive with his frontier garrisons. He then declared open war. The Mongol general, Nasiuddin, collected all the forces he could, and when the Burmese ruler crossed the frontier at the head of an immense host of horse, foot, and elephants, he found the Mongol army drawn up on the plain of Yungchang. The Mongols numbered only 12,000 select troops, whereas the Burmese exceeded 80,000 men, with a corps of elephants estimated between 800 and 2,000, and an artillery force of sixteen guns. Notwithstanding this numerical disadvantage the Mongols were in no way dismayed by their opponents' manifest superiority; but seldom has the struggle between disciplined and brute force proved closer or more keenly contested. At first the charge of the Burmese cavalry, aided by the elephants and artillery, carried all before it. But Nasiuddin had provided for this contingency. He had dismounted all his cavalry, and had ordered them to fire their arrows exclusively against the elephant corps; and as the Mongols were then not only the best archers in the world, but used the strongest bows, the destruction they wrought was considerable, and soon threw the elephants into hopeless confusion. The crowd of elephants turned tail before this discharge of arrows, as did the elephants of Pyrrhus, and threw the whole Burmese army into confusion. The Mongols then mounting their horses, charged and completed the discomfiture of the Burmese, who were driven from the field with heavy loss and tarnished reputation.   On this occasion the Mongols did not pursue the Burmese very far, and the King of Burma lost little or no part of his dominions, but Nasiuddin reported to Pekin that it would be an easy matter to add the kingdom of Mien to the Mongol empire.   Kublai did not act on this advice until six years later, when he sent his kinsman Singtur with a large force to subdue Burma. The king took shelter in Pegu, leaving his capital Amien at the mercy of the conqueror.   The Mongol conquests were thus brought down to the very border of Assam.   In Tonquin and Annam the arms of Kublai were not so successful. Kublai's son Togan made an abortive campaign in these regions.   Whenever an open force had to be overcome, the Mongol army was successful, but when the Mongols encountered the difficulties of a damp and inclement climate, of the absence of roads, and other disadvantages, they were disheartened, and suffered heavily in men and morale.   With the loss of his two generals, and the main portion of his army, Togan was lucky in himself escaping to China.   Kublai wished to make another effort to subdue these inhospitable regions and their savage inhabitants, but Chinese public opinion proved too strong, and he had to yield to the representations of his ministers.

Kublai was the more compelled to sacrifice his feelings on this point, because there were not wanting indications that if he did not do so he would find a Chinese rebellion on his hands.   Notwithstanding his many successes, and his evident desire to stand well with his Chinese subjects, it was already clear that they bore their new leader little love.   Several of the principal provinces were in a state of veiled rebellion, showing that the first opportunity would be taken to shake off the Mongol yoke, and that Kublai's authority really rested on a quicksand.   The predictions of a fanatic were sufficient to shake the emperor on his throne, and such was Kublai's apprehension that he banished all the remaining Sung prisoners to Mongolia, and executed their last faithful minister, who went to the scaffold with a smile on his face, exclaiming, "I am content; my wishes are about to be realized." It must not be supposed from this that Kublai's authority had vanished or become effete. It was absolutely supreme over all declared enemies, but below the surface was seething an amount of popular hostility and discontent ominous to the longevity of the Mongol dynasty. The restless ambition of Kublai would not be satisfied with anything short of recognition, in some form or other, of his power by his neighbors, and he consequently sent envoys to all the kingdoms of Southern Asia to obtain, by lavish presents or persuasive language, that recognition of his authority on which he had set his heart. In most cases he was gratified, for there was not a power in Eastern Asia to compare with that of the Mongol prince seated on the Dragon Throne of China, and all were flattered to be brought into connection with it on any terms.

These successful and gratifying embassies had only one untoward result: they induced Kublai to revert to his idea of repairing the overthrow of his son Togan in Annam, and of finally subjugating that troublesome country. The intention was not wise, and it was rendered more imprudent by its execution being intrusted to Togan again. Another commander might have fared better, but great as was his initial success, he could not hope to permanently succeed. Togan began as he formerly commenced by carrying all before him. He won seventeen separate engagements, but the further he advanced into the country the more evident did it appear that he only controlled the ground on which he stood. The King of Annam was a fugitive; his capital was in the hands of the Mongols, and apparently nothing more remained to be done. Apachi, the most experienced of the Mongol commanders, then counseled a prompt retreat. Unfortunately the Mongol prince Togan would not take his advice, and the Annamites, gathering fresh forces on all sides, attacked the exhausted Mongols, and compelled them to beat a precipitate retreat from their country. All the fruits of early victory were lost, and Togan's disgrace was a poor consolation for the culminating discomfiture of Kublai's reign. The people of Annam then made good their independence, and they still enjoy it, so far as China is concerned; though Annam is now a dependency of the French republic.

We cannot doubt that the failure of the emperor's endeavor to popularize his rule was as largely due to the tyrannical acts and oppressive measures of some of his principal ministers as to unpopular and unsuccessful expeditions. Notwithstanding the popular dislike of the system, and Kublai's efforts to put it down, the Mongols resorted to the old plan of farming the revenue, and the extortion of those who purchased the right drove the Chinese to the verge of rebellion, and made the whole Mongol regime hateful. Several tax farmers were removed from their posts, and punished with death, but their successors carried on the same system. The declining years of Kublai's reign were therefore marred by the growing discontent of his Chinese subjects, and by his inability or unwillingness to put down official extortion and mismanagement. But he had to cope with a still greater danger in the hostility of some members of his own family. The rivalry between himself and his brother Arikbuka formed one incident of his earlier career, the hostility of his cousin Kaidu proved a more serious peril when Kublai was stricken in years, and approaching the end of his long reign.

Kaidu was one of the sons of Ogotai, and consequently first cousin to Kublai. He held some high post in Mongolia, and he represented a reactionary party among the Mongols, who wished the administration to be less Chinese, and who, perhaps, sighed for more worlds to conquer. But he hated Kublai, and was jealous of his pre-eminence, which was, perhaps, the only cause of his revolt. The hostility of Kaidu might have remained a personal grievance if he had not obtained the alliance of Nayan, a Mongol general of experience and ability, who had long been jealous of the superior reputation of Bayan. He was long engaged in raising an army, with which he might hope to make a bid for empire, but at last his preparations reached the ear of Kublai, who determined to crush him before his power had grown too great. Kublai marched against him at the head of 100,000 men, and all the troops Nayan could bring into the field were 40,000, while Kaidu, although hastily gathering his forces, was too far off to render any timely aid. Kublai commanded in person, and arranged his order of battle from a tower supported on the backs of four elephants chained together. Both armies showed great heroism and ferocity, but numbers carried the day, and Nayan's army was almost destroyed, while he himself fell into the hands of the victor. It was contrary to the practice of the Mongols to shed the blood of their own princes, so Kublai ordered Nayan to be sewn up in a sack, and then beaten to death. The war with Kaidu dragged on for many years, and there is no doubt that Kublai did not desire to push matters to an extremity with his cousin. Having restored the fortunes of the war by assuming the command in person, Kublai returned in a short time to Pekin, leaving his opponent, as he hoped, the proverbial golden bridge by which to retreat. But his lieutenant, Bayan, to whom he intrusted the conduct of the campaign, favored more vigorous action, and was anxious to bring the struggle to a speedy and decisive determination. He had gained one remarkable victory under considerable disadvantage, when Kublai, either listening to his detractors or desirous of restraining his activity, dismissed him from his military posts and, summoning him to Pekin, gave him the uncongenial office of a minister of State. This happened in 1293, and in the following year Kublai, who was nearly eighty, and who had occupied the throne of China for thirty-five years, sickened and died, leaving behind him a great reputation which has survived the criticism of six centuries in both Europe and China.

Kublai's long reign marked the climax of the Mongol

triumph which he had all the personal satisfaction of extending to China. Where Genghis failed, or attained only partial success, he succeeded to the fullest extent, thus verifying the prophecy of his grandfather. But although he conquered their country, he never vanquished the prejudices of the Chinese, and the Mongols, unlike the Manchus, failed completely to propitiate the good will of the historiographers of the Hanlin. Of Kublai they take some recognition, as an enlightened and well-meaning prince, but for all the other emperors of the Yuen line they have nothing good to say. Even Kublai himself could not assure the stability of his throne, and when he died it was at once clear that the Mongols could not long retain the supreme position in China.

But Kublai's authority was sufficiently established for it to be transmitted, without popular disturbance or any insurrection on the part of the Chinese, to his legal heir, who was his grandson. Such risk as presented itself to the succession arose from the dissensions among the Mongol princes themselves, but the prompt measures of Bayan arrested any trouble, and Prince Timour was proclaimed emperor under the Chinese style of Chingtsong. A few months after this signal service to the ruling family, Bayan died, leaving behind him the reputation of being one of the most capable of all the Mongol commanders. Whether because he could find no general worthy to fill Bayan's place or because his temperament was naturally pacific, Timour carried on no military operations, and the thirteen years of his reign were marked by almost unbroken peace. But peace did not bring prosperity in its train, for a considerable part of China suffered from the ravages of famine, and the cravings of hunger drove many to become brigands. Timour's anxiety to alleviate the public suffering gained him some small measure of popularity, and he also endeavored to limit the opportunities of the Mongol governors to be tyrannical by taking away from them the power of life and death. Timour was compelled by the sustained hostility of Kaidu to continue the struggle with that prince, but he confined himself to the defensive, and the death of Kaidu, in 1301, deprived the contest of its extreme bitterness, although it still continued.

Timour was, however, unfortunate in the one foreign enterprise which he undertook. The ease with which Burma had been vanquished and reduced to a tributary state emboldened some of his officers on the southern frontier to attempt the conquest of Papesifu—a state which may be identified with the modern Laos. The enterprise, commenced in a thoughtless and light-hearted manner, revealed unexpected peril and proved disastrous. A large part of the Mongol army perished from the heat, and the survivors were only rescued from their perilous position, surrounded by the numerous enemies they had irritated, by a supreme effort on the part of Koko, the viceroy of Yunnan, who was also Timour's uncle. The insurrectionary movement was not confined to the outlying districts of Annam and Burma, but extended within the Chinese border, and several years elapsed before tranquillity was restored to the frontier provinces.

Timour died in 1306 without leaving a direct legitimate heir, and his two nephews Haichan and Aiyuli Palipata were held to possess an equal claim to the throne. Haichan was absent in Mongolia when his uncle died, and a faction put forward the pretensions of Honanta, prince of Gansi, who seems to have been Timour's natural son, but Aiyuli Palipata, acting with great energy, arrested the pretender and proclaimed Haichan as emperor. Haichan reigned five years, during which the chief reputation he gained was as a glutton. When he died, in 1311, his brother Palipata was proclaimed emperor, although Haichan left two sons. Palipata's reign of nine years was peaceful and uneventful, and his son Chutepala succeeded him. Chutepala was a young and inexperienced prince who owed such authority as he enjoyed to the courage of Baiju, a brave soldier, who was specially distinguished as the lineal descendant of the great

general, Muhula.   The plots and intrigues which compassed
the ruin of the Yuen dynasty began during this reign, and
both Chutepala and Baiju were murdered by conspirators.
The next emperor, Yesun Timour, was fortunate in a peaceful reign, but on his death, in 1328, the troubles of the dynasty accumulated, and its end came clearly into view.   In
little more than a year, three emperors were proclaimed and
died.   Tou Timour, one of the sons of Haichan, who ruled
before Palipata, was so far fortunate in reigning for a longer
period, but the most interesting episode in his barren reign
was the visit of the Grand Lama of Tibet to Pekin, where
he was received with exceptional honor; but when Tou
Timour attempted to compel his courtiers to pay the representative of Buddhism special obeisance he encountered
the opposition of both Chinese and Mongols.

After Tou Timour's death the imperial title passed to
Tohan Timour, who is best known by his Chinese title of
Chunti.   He found a champion in Bayan, a descendant
of the general of that name, who successfully defended the
palace against the attack of a band of conspirators.   In 1337
the first distinct rebellion on the part of the Chinese took
place in the neighborhood of Canton, and an order for the
disarmament of the Chinese population aggravated the situation because it could not be effectually carried out.   Bayan,
after his defense of the palace, became the most powerful
personage in the state, and to his arrogance was largely due
the aggravation of the Mongol difficulties and the imbittering
of Chinese opinion.   He murdered an empress, tyrannized
over the Chinese, and outshone the emperor in his apparel
and equipages, as if he were a Wolsey or a Buckingham.
For the last offense Chunti could not forgive him, and Bayan
was deposed and disgraced.   While these dissensions were
in progress at Pekin the Chinese were growing more daring
and confident in their efforts to liberate themselves from the
foreign yoke.   They had adopted red bonnets as the mark
of their patriotic league, and on the sea the piratical confederacy of Fangkue Chin vanquished and destroyed such navy

as the Mongols ever possessed. But in open and regular fighting on land the supremacy of the Mongols was still incontestable, and a minister, named Toto, restored the sinking fortunes of Chunti until he fell the victim of a court intrigue—being poisoned by a rival named Hamar. With Toto disappeared the last possible champion of the Mongols, and the only thing needed to insure their overthrow was the advent of a capable leader who could give coherence to the national cause, and such a leader was not long in making his appearance.

The deliverer of the Chinese from the Mongols was an individual named Choo Yuen Chang, who, being left an orphan, entered a monastery as the easiest way of gaining a livelihood. In the year 1345, when Chunti had been on the throne twelve years, Choo quitted his retreat and joined one of the bands of Chinese who had thrown off the authority of the Mongols. His physique and fine presence soon gained for him a place of authority, and when the chief of the band died he was chosen unanimously as his successor. He at once showed himself superior to the other popular leaders by his humanity, and by his wise efforts to convince the Chinese people that he had only their interests at heart. Other Chinese so-called patriots thought mainly of plunder, and they were not less terrible to peaceful citizens than the most exacting Mongol commander or governor. But Choo strictly forbade plundering, and any of his band caught robbing or ill-using the people met with prompt and summary punishment. By this conduct he gained the confidence of the Chinese, and his standard among all the national leaders became the most popular and attracted the largest number of recruits. In 1356 he captured the city of Nankin, which thereupon became the base of his operations, as it was subsequently the capital of his dynasty. He then issued a proclamation declaring that his sole object was to expel the foreigners and to restore the national form of government. In this document he said, "It is the birthright of the Chinese to govern foreign peoples and not of these latter to rule in

China. It used to be said that the Yuen or Mongols, who
came from the regions of the north, conquered our empire
not so much by their courage and skill as by the aid of
Heaven. And now it is sufficiently plain that Heaven itself
wishes to deprive them of that empire, as some punishment
for their crimes, and for not having acted according to the
teaching of their forefathers. The time has now come to
drive these foreigners out of China.'' While the Mongols
were assailed in every province of the empire by insurgents,
Choo headed what was the only organized movement for
their expulsion, and his alliance with the pirate Fangkue
Chin added the command of the sea to the control he had
himself acquired over some of the wealthiest and most populous provinces of Central China. The disunion among the
Mongols contributed to their overthrow as much as the valor
of the Chinese. The Emperor Chunti had quite given himself up to pleasure, and his debaucheries were the scandal of
the day. The two principal generals, Chahan Timour and
Polo Timour, hated each other and refused to co-operate.
Another general, Alouhiya, raised the standard of revolt in
Mongolia, and, while he declared that his object was to
regenerate his race, he, undoubtedly, aggravated the embarrassment of Chunti.

In 1366, Choo, having carefully made all the necessary
preparations for war on a large scale, dispatched from Nankin
two large armies to conquer the provinces north of the
Yangtsekiang, which were all that remained in the possession of the Mongols. A third army was intrusted with the
task of subjecting the provinces dependent on Canton, and
this task was accomplished with rapidity and without a
check. Such Mongol garrisons as were stationed in this
quarter were annihilated. The main Chinese army of 250,-
000 men was intrusted to the command of Suta, Choo's
principal lieutenant and best general, and advanced direct
upon Pekin. In 1367 Suta had overcome all resistance south
of the Hoangho, which river he crossed in the autumn of
that year. The Mongols appeared demoralized, and at-

tempted little or no resistance. Chunti fled from Pekin to Mongolia, where he died in 1370, and Suta carried the capital by storm from the small Mongol garrison which remained to defend it. Choo hastened to Pekin to receive the congratulations of his army, and to prove to the whole Chinese nation that the Yuen dynasty had ceased to rule. The resistance offered by the Mongols proved surprisingly slight, and, considering the value of the prize for which they were fighting, quite unworthy of their ancient renown. The real cause of their overthrow was that the Mongols never succeeded in propitiating the good opinion and moral support of the Chinese, who regarded them to the end as barbarians, and it must also be admitted that the main force of the Mongols had drifted to Western Asia, where the great Timour revived some of the traditions of Genghis. At the end of his career that mighty conqueror prepared to invade China, but he died shortly after he had begun a march that boded ill to the peace and welfare of China. Thus, with the flight of Chunti, the Mongol or Yuen dynasty came to an end, and the Mongols only reappear in Chinese history as the humble allies of the Manchus, when they undertook the conquest of China in the seventeenth century.

CHAPTER VII

THE MING DYNASTY

HAVING expelled the Mongols, Choo assumed the style of Hongwou, and he gave his dynasty the name of Ming, which signifies "bright." He then rewarded his generals and officers with titles and pecuniary grants, and in 1369, the first year of his reign after the capture of Pekin, he erected a temple or hall in that city in honor of the generals who had been slain, while vacant places were left for the statues of those generals who still held command. But while he rewarded his army, Hongwou very carefully avoided giving

the southern extremity of the Great Wall, and as isolating Ninghia on the west. Their loss was so serious that the Mongol chief felt compelled to risk a general engagement. The battle was keenly contested, and at one moment it seemed as if success was going to declare itself in favor of the Mongols. But Suta had sent a large part of his force to attack the Mongol rear, and when this movement was completely executed, he assailed the Mongol position at the head of all his troops. The struggle soon became a massacre, and it is said that as many as 80,000 Mongols were slain, while Kuku Timour, thinking Ninghia no longer safe, fled northward to the Amour. The success of Suta was heightened and rendered complete by the capture of a large number of the ex-Mongol ruling family by Ly Wenchong, another of the principal generals of Hongwou. Among the prisoners was the eldest grandson of Chunti, and several of the ministers advised that he should be put to death. But Hongwou instead conferred on him a minor title of nobility, and expressed his policy in a speech equally creditable to his wisdom as a statesman and his heart as a man:

"The last ruler of the Yuens took heed only of his pleasures. The great, profiting by his indolence, thought of nothing save of how to enrich themselves; the public treasures being exhausted by their malpractices, it needed only a few years of dearth to reduce the people to distress, and the excessive tyranny of those who governed them led to the forming of parties which disturbed the empire even to its foundations. Touched by the misfortunes with which I saw them oppressed, I took up arms, not so much against the Yuens as against the rebels who were engaged in war with them. It was over the same foe that I gained my first successes. And if the Yuen prince had not departed from the rules of wise government in order to give himself up to his pleasures, and had the magnates of his court performed their duty, would all honorable men have taken up arms as they did and declared against him? The misconduct of the race brought me a large number of partisans who were convinced of the

rectitude of my intentions, and it was from their hands and
not from those of the Yuens that I received the empire. If
Heaven had not favored me should I have succeeded in destroying with such ease those who withdrew into the desert
of Shamo? We read in the Chiking that after the destruction of the Chang family there remained more than ten thousand of their descendants who submitted themselves to the
Chow, because it was the will of Heaven. Cannot men
respect its decrees? Let them put in the public treasure-
house all the spoil brought back from Tartary, so that it may
serve to alleviate the people's wants. And with regard to
Maitilipala (Chunti's grandson), although former ages supply
examples of similar sacrifice, did Wou Wang, I ask you,
when exterminating the Chang family, resort to this barbarous policy? The Yuen princes were the masters of this empire for nearly one hundred years, and my forefathers were
their subjects, and even although it were the constant practice to treat in this fashion the princes of a dynasty which
has ceased to reign, yet could I not induce myself to
adopt it."

These noble sentiments, to which there is nothing contra-
dictory in the whole life of Hongwou, would alone place his
reign high among the most civilizing and humanly interesting epochs in Chinese history. To his people he appeared
as a real benefactor as well as a just prince. He was ever
studious of their interests, knowing that their happiness depended on what might seem trivial matters, as well as in
showy feats of arms and high policy. He simplified the
transit of salt, that essential article of life, to provinces
where its production was scanty, and when dearth fell on
the land he devoted all the resources of his treasury to its
mitigation. His thoughtfulness for his soldiers was shown
by sending fur coats to all the soldiers in garrison at Ninghia
where the winter was exceptionally severe. A final instance
of his justice and consideration may be cited in his ordering
certain Mongol colonies established in Southern China, to
whom the climate proved uncongenial, to be sent back at his

expense to their northern homes, when his ministers exhorted him to proceed to extremities against them and to root them out by fire and sword.

The pacification of the northern borders was followed by the dispatch of troops into the southern provinces of Szchuen and Yunnan, where officials appointed by the Mongols still exercised authority. One of these had incurred the wrath of Hongwou by assuming a royal style and proclaiming himself King of Hia. He was soon convinced of the folly of taking a title which he had not the power to maintain, and the conquest of Szchuen was so easily effected that it would not call for mention if it were not rendered interesting as providing Hongwou's other great general Fuyuta with the first opportunity of displaying his skill as a commander. The self-created King of Hia presented himself laden with chains at the Chinese camp and begged the favor of his life. The conquest of Szchuen was little more than completed when the attention of Hongwou was again directed to the northwest frontier, where Kuku Timour was making one more effort to recover the footing he had lost on the fringe of the Celestial Empire, and for a time fortune favored his enterprise. Even when Suta arrived upon the scene and took the command of the Chinese forces in person, the Mongols more than held their own. Twice did Suta attack the strong position taken up by the Mongol chief in the desert, and twice was his assault repulsed with heavy loss. A detachment under one of his lieutenants was surprised in the desert and annihilated. Supplies were difficult to obtain, and discouraged by defeat and the scarcity of food the Chinese army was placed in an extremely dangerous position. Out of this dilemma it was rescued by the heroic Fuyuta, who, on the news of the Mongol recrudescence, had marched northward at the head of the army with which he had conquered Szchuen. He advanced boldly into the desert, operated on the flank and in the rear of Kuku Timour, vanquished the Mongols in many engagements, and so monopolized their attention that Suta was able to retire in safety and without

loss. The war terminated with the Chinese maintaining all
their posts on the frontier, and the retreat of the Mongols,
who had suffered too heavy a loss to feel elated at their
repulse of Suta. At the same time no solid peace had been
obtained, and the Mongols continued to harass the borders,
and to exact blackmail from all who traversed the desert.
When Hongwou endeavored to attain a settlement by a
stroke of policy his efforts were not more successful. His
kind reception of the Mongol Prince Maitilipala has been
referred to, and about the year 1374 he sent him back to
Mongolia, in the hope that he would prove a friendly neighbor on his father's death. The gratitude of Maitilipala
seems to have been unaffected; but, although he was the
legitimate heir, the Mongols refused to recognize him as
Khan on the death of his father. Gradually tranquillity
settled down on those borders. The Chinese officials were
content to leave the Mongols alone, and the Mongols abandoned their customary raids into Chinese territory. The
death of Kuku Timour was followed by the abandonment
of all ideas of reviving Mongol authority in China. Not
long after that event died the great general Suta, of whom
the national historians give the following glowing description
which merits preservation: "Suta spoke little and was en-
dowed with great penetration. He was always on good
terms with the generals acting with him, sharing the good
and bad fortune alike of his soldiers, of whom there was not
one who, touched by his kindness, would not have done his
duty to the death. He was not less pronounced in his mod-
esty. He had conquered a capital, three provinces, several
hundred towns, and on the very day of his return to court
from these triumphs he went without show and without
retinue to his own house, received there some learned pro-
fessors and discussed various subjects with them. Throughout his life he was in the presence of the emperor respectful,
and so reserved that one might have doubted his capacity to
speak." Hongwou was in the habit of speaking thus in his
praise: "My orders received, he forthwith departed; his

task accomplished, he returned without pride and without boasting. He loves not women, he does not amass wealth. A man of strict integrity, without the slightest stain, as pure and clear as the sun and moon, there is none like my first general Suta."

Hongwou had the satisfaction of restoring amicable relations with the King of Corea, a state in which the Chinese have always taken naturally enough a great interest from its proximity, as well as from an apprehension that the Japanese might make use of it as a vantage ground for the invasion of the continent. The King of Corea sent a formal embassy to Nankin, and when he died his son asked for and received investiture in his authority with the royal yellow robes at the hands of the Ming ruler. During this period it will be convenient here to note that the ruling power in Corea passed from the old royal family to the minister Li Chungwei, who was the ancestor of the present king. The last military episode of the reign of Hongwou was the conquest of Yunnan, which had been left over after the recovery of Szchuen, in consequence of the fresh outbreak of the Mongols in the north. This task was intrusted to Fuyuta, who at the head of an army of 100,000 men, divided into two corps, invaded Yunnan. The prince of that state offered the utmost resistance he could, but in the one great battle of the war his army, fighting bravely, was overthrown, and he was compelled to abandon his capital. The conquest of Yunnan completed the pacification of the empire, and the authority of Hongwou was unchallenged from the borders of Burma to the Great Wall and the Corean frontier. The population of the empire thus restored did not much exceed sixty millions. The last ten years of the reign of Hongwou were passed in tranquillity, marred by only one unpleasant incident, the mutiny of a portion of his army under an ambitious general. The plot was discovered in good time, but it is said that the emperor did not consider the exigencies of the case to be met until he had executed twenty thousand of the mutineers.

In 1398 Hongwou was attacked with the illness which ended his life. He was then in his seventy-first year, and had reigned more than thirty years since his proclamation of the Ming dynasty at Nankin. The Emperor Keen Lung, in his history of the Mings, states that Hongwou possessed most of the virtues and few of the vices of mankind. He was brave, patient under suffering, far-seeing, studious of his people's welfare, and generous and forbearing toward his enemies. It is not surprising that he succeeded in establishing the Ming dynasty on a firm and popular basis, and that his family have been better beloved in China than any dynasty with the possible exception of the Hans. In his will, which is a remarkable document, he recites the principal events of his reign, how he had "pacified the empire and restored its ancient splendor." With the view of providing for the stability of his empire, he chose as his successor his grandson Chuwen, because he had remarked in him much prudence, a gentle disposition, good intelligence, and a readiness to accept advice. He also selected him because he was the eldest son of his eldest son, and as his other sons might be disposed to dispute their nephew's authority he ordered them to remain at their posts, and not to come to the capital on his death. They were also enjoined to show the new emperor all the respect and docility owed by subjects to their sovereign. Through these timely precautions Chuwen, who was only sixteen years of age, was proclaimed emperor without any opposition, and took the title of Kien Wenti.

Hongwou had rightly divined that his sons might prove a thorn in the side of his successor, and his policy of employing them in posts at a distance from the capital was only half successful in attaining its object. If it kept them at a distance it also strengthened their feeling of independence, and enabled them to collect their forces without attracting much attention. Wenti, as it is most convenient to call the new emperor, felt obliged to send formal invitations to his uncles to attend the obsequies of their father. Most of them had the tact to perceive that the invitation was dictated by a regard for decency, and not by a wish that it should be accepted, and gave the simplest excuse for not attending the funeral. But Ty, Prince of Yen, the most powerful and ambitious of them all, declared that he accepted the emperor's invitation. This decision raised quite a flutter of excitement, almost amounting to consternation, at Nankin, where the Prince of Yen was regarded as a bitter and vindictive enemy. The only way Wenti saw out of this dilemma was to send his uncle a special intimation that his presence at the capital would not be desirable. Before he had been many weeks on the throne Wenti was thus brought into open conflict with the most powerful and ambitious of all his relatives. He resolved, under the advice of his ministers, to treat all his uncles as his enemies, and he sent his officers with armies at their back to depose them, and bring them as prisoners to his court. Five of his uncles were thus summarily dealt with, one committed suicide, and the other four were degraded to the rank of the people. But the Prince of Yen was too formidable to be tackled in this fashion. Taking warning from the fate of his brothers, he collected all the troops he could, prepared to defend his position against the emperor, and issued a proclamation stating that it was lawful for subjects to revolt for the purpose of removing the pernicious advisers of the sovereign. The last was, he announced, the cause of his taking up arms, and he disclaimed any motive of ambitious turbulence for raising his standard. He said, "I am endeavoring to avert the ruin of my family, and to maintain the emperor on a throne which is placed in jeopardy by the acts of traitors. My cause ought, therefore, to be that of all those who keep the blood of the great Hongwou, now falsely aspersed, in affectionate remembrance." A large number of the inhabitants of the northern provinces joined his side, and proclaimed him as "The Prince." Wenti had recourse to arms to bring his uncle back to his allegiance, and a civil war began, which was carried on, with exceptional bitterness, during five years. The resources of the emperor, in men and money, were the superior, but he did not seem able to turn them to good account; and the prince's troops were generally victorious, and his power gradually increased. In the year 1401 both sides concentrated all their strength for deciding the contest by a single trial of arms. The two armies numbered several hundred thousand men, and it is stated that the imperial force alone mustered 600,-000 strong. The battle—which was fought at Techow in Shantung—considering the numbers engaged, it is not surprising to learn, lasted several days, and its fortune alternated from one side to the other. At last victory declared for the prince, and the imperial army was driven in rout from the field with the loss of 100,000 men.

After this great victory the further progress of the prince was arrested by a capable general named Chinyong, who succeeded in gaining one great victory. If Wenti had known how to profit by this success he might have turned the course of the struggle permanently in his own favor. But instead of profiting by his good fortune, Wenti, believing that all danger from the prince was at an end, resumed his old practices, and reinstated two of the most obnoxious of his ministers, whom he had disgraced in a fit of apprehension. Undoubtedly this step raised against him a fresh storm of unpopularity, and at the same time brought many supporters to his uncle, who, even after the serious disaster described, found himself stronger than he had been before. The struggle must have shown little signs of a decisive issue, for in 1402 the prince made a voluntary offer of peace, with a view to putting an end to all strife and of giving the empire peace; but Wenti could not make up his mind to forgive him. The success of his generals in the earlier part of the struggle seemed to warrant the belief that there was no reason in prudence for coming to terms with his rebellious uncle, and that he would succeed in establishing his indisputable supremacy. The prince seemed reduced to such straits that he had to give his army the option of retreat. Addressing his soldiers he said: "I know how to advance, but not to retreat"; but his army decided to return to their homes in the north, when the extraordinary and unexpected retreat of the greater part of the army of Wenti revived their courage and induced them to follow their leader through one more encounter. Like Frederick the Great, the Prince of Yen was never greater than in defeat. He surprised the lately victorious army of Wenti, smashed it in pieces, and captured Tingan, the emperor's best general. The occupation of Nankin and the abdication of Wenti followed this victory in rapid succession. Afraid to trust himself to the mercy of his relative, he fled, disguised as a priest, to Yunnan, where he passed his life ignominiously for forty years, and his identity was only discovered after that lapse of time by his publishing, in his new character of a Buddhist priest, a poem reciting and lamenting the misfortunes of Wenti. Then he was removed to Pekin, where he died in honorable confinement. As a priest he seems to have been more fortunate than as a ruler, and history contains no more striking example of happiness being found in a private station when unattainable on a throne.

After some hesitation the Prince of Yen allowed himself to be proclaimed emperor, and as such he is best known as Yonglo, a name signifying "Eternal Joy." Considering his many declarations that his only ambition was to reform and not to destroy the administration of his nephew, his first act obliterating the reign of Wenti from the records and constituting himself the immediate successor of Hongwou was not calculated to support his alleged indifference to power. He was scarcely seated on the throne before he was involved in serious troubles on both his northern and his southern frontiers. In Mongolia he attempted to assert a formal supremacy over the khans through the person of an adventurer named Kulitchi, but the agent was unable to fulfill his promises, and met with a speedy overthrow. In Tonquin an ambitious minister named Likimao deposed his master and established himself as ruler in his place. The emperor sent an army to bring him to his senses, and it met with such rapid success that the Chinese were encouraged to annex Tonquin and convert it into a province of the empire. When Yonglo's plans failed on the steppe he was drawn into a struggle with the Mongols, which necessitated annual expeditions until he died. During the last of these he advanced as far as the Kerulon, and on his return march he died in his camp at the age of sixty-five. Although he bore arms so long against the head of the state there is no doubt that he greatly consolidated the power of the Mings, which he extended on one side to the Amour and on the other to the Songcoi. It was during his reign that Tamerlane contemplated the reconquest of China, and perhaps it was well for Yonglo that that great commander died when he had traversed only a few stages of his march to the Great Wall. One of his sons succeeded Yonglo as emperor, but he only reigned under the style of Gintsong for a few months.

Then Suentsong, the son of Gintsong, occupied the throne, and during his reign a vital question affecting the constitution of the civil service, and through it the whole administration of the country, was brought forward and fortunately settled without recourse to blows, as was at one time feared would be the case. Before his reign the public examinations had been open to candidates from all parts of the empire, and it had become noticeable that all the honors were being carried off by students from the southern provinces, who were of quicker intelligence than those of the north. It seemed as if in the course of a short time all the posts would be held by them, and that the natives of the provinces north of the Hoangho would be gradually driven out of the service. Naturally this marked tendency led to much agitation in the north, and a very bitter feeling was spreading when Suentsong and his minister took up the matter and proceeded to apply a sound practical remedy. After a commission of inquiry had certified to the reality of the evil, Suentsong decreed that all competitors for literary honors should be restricted to their native districts, and that for the purpose of the competitive examinations China should be divided into three separate divisions, one for the north, another for the center, and the third for the south. The firmness shown by the Emperor Suentsong in this matter was equally conspicuous in his dealings with an uncle, who showed some inclination to revolt. He took the field in person, and before the country was generally aware of the revolt, Suentsong was conducting his relative to a state prison. The rest of Suentsong's reign was peaceful and prosperous, and he left the crown to his son, Yngtsong, a child eight years old.

During his minority the governing authority was exercised by his grandmother, the Empress Changchi, the mother of the Emperor Suentsong. At first it seemed as if there would be a struggle for power between her and the eunuch Wangchin, who had gained the affections of the young emperor; but after she had denounced him before the court and called for his execution, from which fate he was only rescued by the tears and supplications of the young sovereign, the feud was composed by Wangchin gaining such an ascendency over the empress that she made him her associate in the regency. Unfortunately Wangchin did not prove a wise or able administrator. He thought more of the sweets of office than of the duties of his lofty station. He appointed his relations and creatures to the highest civil and military posts without regard to their qualifications or ability. To his arrogance was directly due the commencement of a disastrous war with Yesien, the most powerful of the Mongol chiefs of the day. When that prince sent the usual presents to the Chinese capital, and made the customary request for a Chinese princess as wife, Wangchin appropriated the gifts for himself and sent back a haughty refusal to Yesien's petition, although it was both customary and rarely refused. Such a reception was tantamount to a declaration of war, and Yesien, who had already been tempted by the apparent weakness of the Chinese frontier to resume the raids which were so popular with the nomadic tribes of the desert, gathered his fighting men together and invaded China. Alarmed by the storm he had raised, Wangchin still endeavored to meet it, and summoning all the garrisons in the north to his aid, he placed himself at the head of an army computed to number half a million of men. In the hope of inspiring his force with confidence he took the boy-emperor, Yngtsong, with him, but his own incompetence nullified the value of numbers, and rendered the presence of the emperor the cause of additional ignominy instead of the inspiration of invincible confidence. The vast and unwieldy Chinese army took up a false position at a place named Toumon, and it is affirmed that the position was so bad that Yesien feared that it must cover a ruse. He accordingly sent some of his officers to propose an armistice, but really to inspect the Chinese lines. They returned to say that there was no concealment, and that if an attack were made at once the Chinese army lay at his mercy. Yesien delayed not a moment in delivering his attack, and it was completely successful. The very numbers of the Chinese, in a confined position, added to their discomfiture, and after a few hours' fighting the battle became a massacre and a rout. Wangchin, the cause of all this ruin, was killed by Fanchong, the commander of the imperial guards, and the youthful ruler, Yngtsong, was taken prisoner. There has rarely been a more disastrous day in the long annals of the Chinese empire than the rout at Toumon.

Then Yesien returned to his camp on the Toula, taking his prisoner with him, and announcing that he would only restore him for a ransom of 100 taels of gold, 200 taels of silver, and 200 pieces of the finest silk. For some unknown reason the Empress Changchi did not feel disposed to pay this comparatively low ransom, and instead of reclaiming Yngtsong from his conqueror she placed his brother, Kingti, on the throne. The struggle with the Mongols under Yesien continued, but his attention was distracted from China by his desire to become the great Khan of the Mongols, a title still held by his brother-in-law, Thotho Timour, of the House of Genghis. Yesien, suddenly releasing of his own accord Yngtsong—who returned to Pekin—hastened to the Kerulon country, where he overthrew and assassinated Thotho Timour, and was in turn himself slain by another chieftain.

While the Mongol was thus pursuing his own ambition, and reaching the violent death which forms so common a feature in the history of his family, the unfortunate Yngtsong returned to China, where, on the refusal of his brother Kingti to resign the throne, he sank quietly into private life. Kingti died seven years after his brother's return, and then, failing a better or nearer prince, Yngtsong was brought from his confinement and restored to the throne. He reigned eight years after his restoration, but he never possessed any real power, his authority being wielded by unscrupulous ministers, who stained his reign by the execution of Yukien, the most honest and capable general of the period. If his reign was not remarkable for political or military vigor, some useful reforms appear to have been instituted. Among others may be named the formation of state farms on waste or confiscated lands, the establishment of military schools for teaching archery and horsemanship, and the completion of some useful and elaborate educational works, of which a geography of China, in ninety volumes, is the most famous.

Yngtsong died in the year 1465, and was succeeded by his son, Hientsong, who began his reign with acts of filial devotion that attracted the sympathy of his subjects. He also rendered posthumous honors to the ill-used general, Yukien, and established his fame as a national benefactor. During the twenty-eight years that he occupied the throne he was engaged in a number of petty wars, none of which requires specific mention. The only unpopular measure associated with his name was the creation of a Grand Council of Eunuchs, to which was referred all questions of capital punishment, and this body soon acquired a power which made it resemble the tyrannical and irresponsible British Star Chamber. After five years this institution became so unpopular and was so deeply execrated by the nation that Hientsong, however reluctantly, had to abolish his own creation, and acquiesce in the execution of some of its most active members.

During Hientsong's reign a systematic attempt was

made to work the gold mines reputed to exist in Central
China, but although half a million men were employed
upon them it is stated that the find did not exceed thirty
ounces. More useful work was accomplished in the building of a canal from Pekin to the Peiho, which thus enabled
grain junks to reach the northern capital by the Euho and
Shaho canals from the Yangtsekiang. Another useful public work was the repairing of the Great Wall, effected along
a considerable portion of its extent, by the efforts of 50,000
soldiers, which gave the Chinese a sense of increased security. In connection with this measure of defense, it may
be stated that the Chinese advanced into Central Asia and
occupied the town of Hami, which then and since has
served them as a useful watch-tower in the direction of the
west. The death of Hientsong occurred in 1487, at a moment when the success and prosperity of the country under
the Mings may be described as having reached its height.

During the reign of his son and successor, Hiaotsong,
matters progressed peacefully, for, although there was some
fighting for the possession of Hami, which was coveted by
several of the desert chiefs, but which remained during the
whole of this reign subject to China, the empire was not
involved in any great war. An insurrection of the black
aborigines of the island of Hainan was put down without
any very serious difficulty. These events do not throw any
very clear light on the character and personality of Hiaotsong, who died in 1505 at the early age of thirty-six; but
his care for his people, and his desire to alleviate the misfortunes that might befall his subjects, was shown by his
ordering every district composed of ten villages to send in
annually to a State granary a specified quantity of grain,
until 100,000 bushels had been stored in every such building throughout the country. The idea was an excellent one;
but it is to be feared that a large portion of this grain was
diverted to the use of the peculating officials, whence arose
the phrase, "The emperor is full of pity, but the Court of
Finance is like the never-dying worm which devours the

richest crops." To Hiaotsong succeeded his son, Woutsong, during whose reign many misfortunes fell upon the land. The emperor's uncles had designs on his authority, but these fell through and came to naught, rather through Woutsong's good fortune than the excellence of his arrangements. In Szchuen a peasant war threatened to assume the dimensions of a rebellion, and in Pechihli bands of mounted robbers, or Hiangmas, raided the open country. He succeeded in suppressing these revolts, but his indifference to the disturbed state of his realm was shown by his passing most of his time in hunting expeditions beyond the Great Wall. His successors were to reap the result of this neglect of business for the pursuit of pleasure; and when he died in 1519, without leaving an heir, the outlook was beginning to look serious for the Ming dynasty. One event, and perhaps the most important of Woutsong's reign, calls for special mention, and that is the arrival at Canton of the first native of Europe to reach China by sea. Of course it will be recollected that Marco Polo and others reached the Mongol court by land, although the Venetian sailed from China on his embassy to southern India. In 1511, Raphael Perestralo sailed from Malacca to China, and in 1517 the Portuguese officer, Dom Fernand Perez d'Andrade, arrived in the Canton River with a squadron, and was favorably received by the mandarins. D'Andrade visited Pekin, where he resided for some time as embassador. The commencement of intercourse between Europeans and China was thus effected most auspiciously; and it might have continued so but that a second Portuguese fleet appeared in Chinese waters, and committed there numerous outrages and acts of piracy. Upon this, D'Andrade was arrested by order of Woutsong, and, after undergoing imprisonment, was executed by his successor in 1523. It was a bad beginning for a connection which, after nearly four hundred years, is neither as stable nor as general as the strivers after perfection could desire.

The death of Woutsong without children, or any recognized heir, threatened to involve the realm in serious dangers; but the occasion was so critical that the members of the Ming family braced themselves to it, and under the auspices of the Empress Changchi, the widow of the late ruler, a secret council was held, when the grandson of the Emperor Hientsong, a youth of fourteen, was placed on the throne under the name of Chitsong. It is said that his mother gave him good advice on being raised from a private station to the lofty eminence of emperor, and that she told him that he was about to accept a heavy burden; but experience showed that he was unequal to it. Still, his shortcomings were preferable to a disputed succession. The earlier years of his reign were marked by some successes over the Tartars, and he received tribute from chiefs who had never paid it before. But Chitsong had little taste for the serious work of administration. He showed himself superstitious in matters of religion, and he cultivated poetry, and may even have persuaded himself that he was a poet. But he did not pay any heed to the advice of those among his ministers who urged him to take a serious view of his position, and to act in a manner worthy of his dignity. It is clear that his influence on the lot of his people, and even on the course of his country's history, was small, and such reigns as his inspire the regret expressed at there being no history of the Chinese people; but such a history is impossible.

It might be more instructive to trace the growth of thought among the masses, or to indicate the progress of civil and political freedom; yet, not only do the materials not exist for such a task, but those we possess all tend to show that there has been no growth to describe, no progress to be indicated, during these comparatively recent centuries. It is the peculiar and distinguishing characteristic of Chinese history that the people and their institutions have remained practically unchanged and the same from a very early period. Even the introduction of a foreign element has not tended to disturb the established order of things. The supreme ruler possesses the same attributes and dis-

It was in the year 1618 that Noorhachu invaded Leaou-tung, and so surprised were the Chinese at his audacity that they offered little or no resistance. The town of Fooshun was captured and made the headquarters of the Manchu prince. From this place he sent a list of his requirements to the governor of Leaoutung, and it is said that he offered, on the Chinese complying with his terms, to withdraw and desist from hostilities. But the Chinese did not appreciate the power of this new enemy. They treated his grievances with indifference and contempt, and they sent an army to drive him out of Leaoutung. The Chinese troops soon had a taste of the quality of the Manchu army. They were defeated in several encounters, and the best Chinese troops fled before the impetuous charge of the Manchu cavalry. Noorhachu then laid siege to the prefectural town of Tsingho, which he captured after a siege of some weeks, and where he massacred nearly 20,000 of the garrison and townspeople. He would have continued the campaign but that his followers demanded to be led back, stating that they feared for the safety of their homes at the hands of Yeho, still hostile and aggressive in their rear. The conquest of Leaoutung was therefore discontinued for the purpose of closing accounts with the last of the Niuche principalities; but enough had been accomplished to whet the appetite of the Manchu leader for more, and to show him how easy it was to vanquish the Chinese. On his return to his capital, Hingking, he prepared to invade Yeho, but his plans were undoubtedly delayed by the necessity of resting his troops and of allowing many of them to return to their homes. This delay, no doubt, induced the Chinese to make a supreme effort to avert the overthrow of Yeho, who had proved so useful an ally, and accordingly the governor of Leaoutung advanced with 100,000 men into Manchuria. He sacrificed the advantage of superior numbers by dividing his army into four divisions, with very inadequate means of inter-communication. Noorhachu could only bring 60,000 men into the field; but, apart from their high training, they represented a compact body subject to the direction of Noorhachu alone. The Manchu leader at once perceived the faulty disposition of the Chinese army, and he resolved to attack and overwhelm each corps in detail before it could receive aid from the others. The strongest Chinese corps was that operating most to the west, and marching from Fooshun on Hingking; and Noorhachu perceived that if he could overthrow it the flank of the rest of the Chinese army would be exposed, and its line of retreat imperiled. The Chinese general in command of this corps was impetuous and anxious to distinguish himself. His courage might on another occasion have helped his country, but under the circumstances his very ardor served the purpose of Noorhachu. Tousong, such was his name, marched more rapidly than any of his comrades, and reached the Hwunho—the Tiber of the Manchus—behind which Noorhachu had, at a little distance, drawn up his army. Without pausing to reconnoiter, or to discover with what force he had to deal, Tousong threw himself across the river, and intrenched himself on Sarhoo Hill. His overconfidence was so extreme and fatuous that he weakened his army by sending a detachment to lay siege to the town of Jiefan. The Manchus had, however, well provided for the defense of that place, and while the Chinese detachment sent against it was being destroyed, Noorhachu attacked Tousong in his position on Sarhoo Hill with the whole of his army. The Chinese were overwhelmed, Tousong was slain, and the majority of those who escaped the fray perished in the waters of the Hwunho, beneath the arrows and javelins of the pursuing Manchus.

Then Noorhachu hastened to attack the second of the Chinese divisions under a capable officer named Malin, who selected a strong position with great care, and wished to stand on the defensive. His wings rested on two hills which he fortified, and he strengthened his center in the intervening valley with a triple line of wagons. If he had only remained in this position he might have succeeded in keeping Noorhachu at bay until he could have been joined by the two remaining Chinese corps; but the impetuosity of his troops, or it may have been the artifice of the Manchu leader, drew him from his intrenchments. At first the Chinese seemed to have the best of the battle, but in a short time victory turned to the side of the Manchus, and Malin fled with the relics of his force back to Chinese territory. After these two successes Noorhachu proceeded to attack the third Chinese corps under Liuyen, who had acquired a cheap reputation by his success over the Miaotze. He had no better fortune than any of his colleagues, and his signal defeat completed the Manchu triumph over the Chinese army of invasion. The defeat of Liuyen was effected by a stratagem as much as by superior force. Noorhachu dressed some of his troops in the Chinese uniforms he had captured, and sent them among the Chinese, who received them as comrades until they discovered their mistake in the crisis of the battle. During this campaign it was computed that the total losses of the Chinese amounted to 310 general officers and 45,000 private soldiers. Among other immediate results of this success were the return of 20,000 Yeho troops to their homes and the defection of 5,000 Coreans, who joined Noorhachu. Like all great commanders, Noorhachu gave his enemies no time to recover from their misfortunes. He pursued Malin to Kaiyuen, which he captured, with so many prisoners that it took three days to count them. He invaded Yeho, which recognized his authority without a blow, and gave him an additional 30,000 fighting men. All the Niuche clans thus became united under his banner, and adopted the name of Manchu. He had succeeded in the great object of his life, the union of his race, and he had well avenged the death of his father and grandfather; but his ambition was not satisfied with this success. It had rather grown with the widening horizon opened by the discomfiture of the Chinese, and with the sense of military superiority.

Amid these national disasters the long reign of Wanleh closed in the year 1620. That unhappy monarch lived long enough to see the establishment on his northern borders of the power which was to destroy his dynasty. The very last act of his reign was, whether by accident or good judgment, the most calculated to prevent the Manchus overrunning the State, and that was the selection of a capable general in the person of Hiung Tingbi. With the death of Wanleh the decadence of Ming power became clearly marked, and the only question that remained was whether it could be arrested before it resulted in absolute ruin.

CHAPTER IX

THE MANCHU CONQUEST OF CHINA

Tingbi, with the wrecks of the Chinese armies, succeeded in doing more for the defense of his country than had been accomplished by any of his predecessors with undiminished resources. He built a chain of forts, he raised the garrison of Leaoutung to 180,000 men, and he spared no effort to place Leaouyang, the capital of that province, in a position to stand a protracted siege. If his counsels had been followed to the end, he might have succeeded in permanently arresting the flood of Manchu conquest; but at the very moment when his plans promised to give assured success, he fell into disgrace at the capital, and his career was summarily ended by the executioner. The greatest compliment to his ability was that Noorhachu remained quiescent as long as he was on the frontier, but as soon as he was removed he at once resumed his aggression on Chinese soil.

Meanwhile, Wanleh had been succeeded on the Chinese throne by his son, Chu Changlo, who took the name of Kwangtsong. He was an amiable and well-meaning prince, whose reign was unquestionably cut short by foul means. There is little doubt that he was poisoned by the mother of his half-brother, from a wish to secure the throne for her son; but if so she never gained the object that inspired her crime, for the princes of the family met in secret conclave.

and selected Kwangtsong's son, a youth of sixteen, as his successor. The choice did not prove fortunate, as this prince became known as Tienki the Unhappy; whose reign witnessed the culmination of Ming misfortunes. One of his first acts was the removal of Tingbi from his command, and this error of judgment, aggravated by the ingratitude it implied to a faithful servant, fitly marked the commencement of a reign of incompetence and misfortune.

In 1621 the Manchu war reopened with an attack on Moukden or Fanyang, which Noorhachu had marked out as his next object. The garrison was numerous, and might have made a good defense, for the walls were strong; but the commandant was brave to the degree of temerity, and, leaving his fortress, marched out to meet the Manchus in the open. The result was a decisive overthrow, and the victors entered Moukden at the heels of the vanquished. The Chinese still resisted, and a terrible slaughter ensued, but the Manchus retained their conquest. At this juncture the Chinese were offered the assistance of the Portuguese at Macao, who sent a small body of 200 men, armed with arquebuses and with several cannon, to Pekin; but after some hesitation the Chinese, whether from pride or contempt of so small a force, declined to avail themselves of their service, and thus lost an auxiliary that might have turned the fortune of the war in their favor. The Portuguese were sent back to Macao, and, although the Chinese kept the cannon, and employed the Jesuit priests in casting others for them, nothing came of an incident which might have exercised a lasting influence not merely on the fortune of the war, but also on the relations between the Chinese and Europeans. The Chinese sent several armies to recover Moukden; but, although they took these guns with them, they met with no success, and Noorhachu made it the base of his plan of attack on Leaouyang, the capital of the province. The defense of this important town was intrusted to Yuen Yingtai, the court favorite and incompetent successor of Tingbi. That officer, unwarned by the past, and regardless of the experience of so many of his predecessors, weakened himself and invited defeat by attempting to oppose the Manchus in the open. He was defeated, losing some of his best soldiers, and compelled to shut himself up in the town with a disheartened garrison. The Manchus gained an entrance into the city. Then a terrible encounter took place. The garrison was massacred to a man, Yuen Yingtai, brave, if incapable, committed suicide, and those of the townspeople who wished to save their lives had to shave their heads in token of subjection. This is the first historical reference to a practice that is now universal throughout China, and that has become what may be called a national characteristic. The badge of conquest has changed to a mark of national pride; but it is strange to find that the Chinese themselves and the most patient inquirers among sinologues are unable to say what was the origin of the pig-tail. They cannot tell us whether shaving the head was the national custom of the Manchus, or whether Noorhachu only conceived this happy idea of distinguishing those who surrendered to his power among the countless millions of the long-haired people of China. All that can be said of the origin of the pig-tail is that it was first enforced as a badge of subjugation by the Manchus at the siege of Leaouyang, and that thenceforward, until the whole of China was conquered, it was made the one condition of immunity from massacre.

The capture of Leaouyang signified the surrender of the remaining places in Leaoutung, which became a Manchu possession, and Noorhachu, to celebrate his triumph, and also to facilitate his plans for the further humiliation of the Chinese, transferred his capital from Moukden to Leaouyang. Misfortunes never come singly. In Szchuen a local chief had raised a force of 30,000 men for service on the frontier in the wars with the Manchus, and the viceroy of the province not only declined to utilize their services, but dismissed them without reward or even recognition of their loyalty. These slighted and disbanded braves easily changed themselves into brigands, and as the government would not have them as supporters, they determined to make it feel their enmity. Chetsong Ming, the chief who had raised them, placed himself at their head, and attracted a large number of the inhabitants to his standard. The local garrisons were crushed, the viceroy killed, and general disorder prevailed among the people of what was the most fertile and prosperous province of the empire. Chetsong attempted to set up an administration, but he does not seem to have possessed the capacity or the knowledge to establish a regular government. While he headed the rebellious movement, a woman named Tsinleang, the hereditary chieftainess of a small district, placed herself at the head of the loyalists in the state, and, leading them herself, succeeded in recovering the principal cities and in driving Chetsong out of the province. She has been not inappropriately called by one of the missionary historians the Chinese Penthesilea. The success she met with in pacifying Szchuen after a two years' struggle was not attained in other directions without a greater effort and at a still heavier cost. In Kweichow and Yunnan a rebel named Ganpangyen raised an insurrection on a large scale, and if his power had not been broken by the long siege of a strong fortress, obstinately defended by a valiant governor, there is no telling to what success he might not have attained. But his followers were disheartened by the delay in carrying this place, and they abandoned him as soon as they found that he could not command success. In Shantung another rising occurred; but after two years' disturbance the rebel leader was captured and executed. These internal disorders, produced by the corruption and inertness of the officials as much as by a prevalent sense of the embarrassment of the Mings, distracted the attention of the central government from Manchuria, and weakened its preparations against Noorhachu.

For a time Noorhachu showed no disposition to cross the River Leaou, and confined his attention to consolidating his position in his new conquest. But it was clear that this lull would not long continue, and the Chinese emperor, Tienki, endeavored to meet the coming storm by once more intrusting the defense of the frontier to Tingbi. That general devised a simple and what might have proved an efficacious line of defense, but his colleague, with more powerful influence at court, would have none of it, and insisted on his own plan being adopted. Noorhachu divined that the councils of the Chinese were divided, and that Tingbi was hampered. He promptly took advantage of the divergence of opinion, and, crossing the frontier, drove the Chinese behind the Great Wall. Even that barrier would not have arrested his progress but for the stubborn resistance offered by the fortress of Ningyuen—a town about seventy miles northeast of Shanhaikwan, once of great importance, but now, for many years past, in ruins. When he reached that place he found that Tingbi had fallen into disgrace and been executed, not for devising his own plan of campaign, but for animadverting on that of his colleague in satirical terms. The Chinese had made every preparation for the resolute defense of Ningyuen, and when Noorhachu sat down before it, its resolute defender, Chungwan, defied him to do his worst, although all the Chinese troops had been compelled to retreat, and there was no hope of re-enforcement or rescue. At first Noorhachu did not conduct the siege of Ningyuen in person. It promised to be an affair of no great importance, and he intrusted it to his lieutenants, but he soon perceived that Chungwan was a resolute soldier, and that the possession of Ningyuen was essential to the realization of his future plans. Therefore, he collected all his forces and sat down before Ningyuen with the full determination to capture it at all costs. But the garrison was resolute, its commander capable, and on the walls were arranged the cannon of European construction. Noorhachu led two assaults in person, both of which were repulsed, and it is said that this result was mainly due to the volleys of the European artillery. At last, Noorhachu was compelled to withdraw his troops, and although he obtained some successes in other parts of the country, he was so chagrined at this repulse that he fell ill and died some months later at Moukden, in September, 1626.

Noorhachu was succeeded by his fourth son, the fourth Beira or Prince, known as Taitsong, who continued both his work and policy. Taitsong was as determined to humiliate the Mings as his father had been. He commenced his offensive measures by an attack on Corea, which he speedily reduced to such a pass that it accepted his authority and transferred its allegiance from the Mings to the Manchus. This was an important success, as it secured his eastern flank and deprived the Chinese of a useful ally in the Forbidden Kingdom. It encouraged Taitsong to think that the time was once more ripe for attacking Ningyuen, and he laid siege to that fortress at the head of a large army, including the flower of his troops. Notwithstanding the energy of his attack, Chungwan, the former bold defender of the place, had again the satisfaction of seeing the Manchus repulsed, and compelled to admit that the ramparts of Ningyuen presented a serious if not insuperable obstacle to their progress. Almost at the very moment of this success the Emperor Tienki died, and was succeeded, in 1627, by his younger brother, Tsongching, who was destined to be the last of the Ming rulers.

The repulse of Taitsong before Ningyuen might have been fatal if he had not been a man of great ability and resource. The occasion called for some special effort, and Taitsong proved himself equal to it by a stroke of genius that showed he was the worthy inheritor of the mission of Noorhachu. Without taking anybody into his confidence he ordered his army and his allies, the Kortsin Mongols, to assemble in the country west of Ningyuen, and when he had thus collected over a hundred thousand men, he announced his intention of ignoring Ningyuen and marching direct on Pekin. At this juncture Taitsong divided his army into eight banners, which still remain the national divisions of the Manchu race. The Manchus seem to have been a little alarmed by the boldness of Taitsong's scheme, and they might have hesitated to follow him if he had given them any time for reflection, but his plans were not fully known until his forces were through the Dangan Pass on the march to the capital. The Chinese, relying altogether on Ningyuen as a defense, had made no preparation to hold their ground on this side, and Taitsong encountered no opposition until he reached Kichow. Then Chungwan, realizing that he had been outmaneuvered, and that the defenses of Ningyuen had been turned, hastened back by forced marches to defend Pekin. Owing to his road being the better of the two he gained the capital in time, and succeeded in throwing himself and his troops into it in order to defend it against the assault of the Manchus. After Taitsong sat down before Pekin he engaged in an intrigue for the ruin of Chungwan, whose disgrace would be equivalent to a great victory. The method is not to be approved on general grounds, but Taitsong conceived that he was justified in bribing persons in Pekin to discredit Chungwan and compass his ruin. The emperor was persuaded that Chungwan was too powerful a subject to be absolutely loyal, and it was asserted that he was in communication with the enemy. Chungwan, who had been so long the buttress of the kingdom, was secretly arrested and thrown into a prison from which he never issued. The disappearance of Chungwan was as valuable to Taitsong as a great victory, and he made his final preparations for assaulting Pekin; but either the want of supplies or the occurrence of some disturbance in his rear prevented the execution of his plan. He drew off his forces and retired behind the Great Wall at the very moment when Pekin seemed at his mercy.

During four years of more or less tranquillity Taitsong confined his attention to political designs, and to training a corps of artillery, and then he resumed his main project of the conquest of China. Instead of availing themselves of the lull thus afforded to improve their position, the Chinese ministers seemed to believe that the danger from the Manchus had passed away, and they treated all the communications from Taitsong with imprudent and unnecessary disdain. Their attention was also distracted by many internal troubles, produced by their own folly, as well as by the perils of the time.

Taitsong, in 1634, resumed his operations in China, and on this occasion he invaded the province of Shansi, at the head of an army composed largely of Mongols as well as of Manchus. Although the people of Shansi had not had any practical experience of Manchu prowess, and notwithstanding that their frontier was exceedingly strong by nature, Taitsong met with little or no resistance from either the local garrisons or the people themselves. One Chinese governor, it is said, ventured to publish a boastful report of an imaginary victory over the Manchus, and to send a copy of it to Pekin. Taitsong, however, intercepted the letter, and at once sent the officer a challenge, matching 1,000 of his men against 10,000 of the Chinese. That the offer was not accepted is the best proof of the superiority of the Manchu army.

It was at the close of this successful campaign in Shansi that Taitsong, in the year 1635, assumed, for the first time among any of the Manchu rulers, the style of Emperor of China. Events had long been moving in this direction, but an accident is said to have determined Taitsong to take this final measure. The jade seal of the old Mongol rulers was suddenly discovered, and placed in the hands of Taitsong. When the Mongols heard of this, forty-nine of their chiefs hastened to tender their allegiance to Taitsong, and the only condition made was that the King of Corea should be compelled to do so likewise. Taitsong, nothing loth, at once sent off letters to the Corean court announcing the adhesion of the Mongols, and calling upon the king of that state to recognize his supremacy. But the Corean ruler had got wind of the contents of these letters and declined to open them, thus hoping to get out of his difficulty without offending his old friends the Chinese. But Taitsong was not to be put off in this fashion. He sent an army to inflict chastisement on his neighbor, and its mission was successfully discharged. The king and his family were taken prisoners, although they had fled to the island of Gangwa for safety, and Corea became a Manchu possession. The last years of Taitsong's life were spent in conducting repeated expeditions into the provinces of Shansi and Pechihli, but the strength of the fortresses of Ningyuen and Shanhaikwan on the Great Wall effectually prevented his renewing his attempt on Pekin. These two places with the minor forts of Kingchow and Songshan formed a quadrilateral that effectually secured Pekin on its northern side, and being intrusted to the defense of Wou Sankwei, a general of great capacity, of whom much more will be heard, all Taitsong's ability and resources were taxed to overcome those obstacles to his progress south of the Great Wall. He succeeded after great loss, and at the end of several campaigns, in taking Kingchow and Songshan, but these were his last successes, for in the year 1643 he was seized with a fatal illness at Moukden, which terminated his career at the comparatively early age of fifty-two. Taitsong's premature death, due, in all probability, to the incompetence of his physicians, cut short a career that had not reached its prime, and retarded the conquest of China, for the supreme authority among the Manchus then passed from a skillful and experienced ruler into the hands of a child.

The possession of a well-trained army, the production of two great leaders of admitted superiority, and forty years of almost continuously successful war, had not availed to bring the authority of the Manchus in any permanent form south of the Great Wall. The barrier of Tsin Che Hwangti still kept out the most formidable adversary who had ever borne down upon it, and the independence of China seemed far removed from serious jeopardy. At this juncture events occurred that altered the whole situation, and the internal divisions of the Chinese proved more serious and entailed a more rapid collapse than all the efforts of the Manchus.

The arch rebel Li Tseching, who proved more formidable

to the Ming ruler than his Manchu opponent, was the son of a peasant in the province of Shansi. At an early age he attached himself to the profession of arms, and became well known as a skillful archer and horseman. In 1629, he first appears on the scene as member of a band of robbers, who were, however, destroyed by a rare display of energy on the part of one of the emperor's lieutenants. Li was one of the few who were fortunate enough to escape with their lives and liberty. He soon gathered round him another band, and under his successful and courageous leading it shortly acquired the size of an army. One reason of his success was his forming an alliance with the Mohammedan settlers in Kansuh, who were already known as Tungani or "Colonists." But the principal cause of his success was his skill and promptitude in coming to terms with the imperial authorities whenever they became too strong for him, and he often purchased a truce when, if the officials had pushed home their advantage, he must have been destroyed. His power thus grew to a high point, while that of other robber chiefs only waxed to wane and disappear; and about the year 1640, when it was said that his followers numbered half a million of men, he began to think seriously of displacing the Ming and placing himself on the throne of China. With this object in view he laid siege to the town of Honan, the capital of the province of the same name. At first the resolution of the governor baffled his attempt, but treachery succeeded when force failed. A traitor opened a gate for a sum of money which he was never paid, and Li's army burst into the city. The garrison was put to the sword, and horrible outrages were perpetrated on the townspeople. From Honan, Li marched on Kaifong, which he besieged for seven days; but he did not possess the necessary engines to attack a place of any strength, and Kaifong was reputed to be the strongest fortress in China. He was obliged to beat a hasty retreat, pursued by an army that the imperial authorities had hurriedly collected. There is reason to think his retreat was a skillful movement to the rear in order to draw the emperor's troops after him. Certain it is that they pursued him in four separate corps, and that he turned upon them and beat them one after the other. When he had vanquished these armies in four separate encounters he again laid siege to Kaifong, and it was thought that he would have taken it, when Li was wounded by an arrow, and called off his troops in consequence. Several times afterward he resumed the attempt, but with no better fortune, until an accident accomplished what all his power had failed to do. The governor had among other precautions flooded the moat from the Hoangho, and this extra, barrier of defense had undoubtedly done much toward discomfiting the besiegers. But in the end it proved fatal to the besieged, for the Hoangho, at all times capricious in its movements, and the source of as much trouble as benefit to the provinces it waters, rose suddenly to the dimensions of a flood, and, overflowing its banks, spread over the country. Many of Li's soldiers were drowned, and his camp was flooded, but the most serious loss befell the Imperialists in Kaifong. The waters of the river swept away the walls and flooded the town. Thousands perished at the time, and those who attempted to escape were cut down by the rebels outside. Kaifong itself was destroyed and has never recovered its ancient importance, being now a town of only the third or fourth rank. This great success established the reputation of Li Tseching on a firm basis, and constituted him one of the arbiters of his country's destiny. He found himself master of one-third of the state; proclaimed himself Emperor of China, under the style of Yongchang, and gave his dynasty the name of Tachun. Having taken this step of open defiance to the Ming government, Li invaded Shansi, which he reduced to subjection with little difficulty or bloodshed. An officer, named Likintai, was sent to organize some measures of defense, but, on arrival, he found the province in the hands of the rebel, and he had no choice save to beat a discreet and rapid retreat. The success of Li continued unchecked. Important places like Taiyuen and Taitong surrendered to him after a merely nominal resistance, and when they fell there was no further impediment in the way of his marching on Pekin.

No preparations had been made to defend Pekin. The defenses were weak, the garrison insufficient, as all the best troops were on the frontier, and the citizens disposed to come to terms with the assailant rather than to die in the breach for their sovereign. When Li pitched his tent outside the western gate of the capital, and sent a haughty demand to the emperor to abdicate his throne, he was master of the situation; but Tsongching, ignorant of his own impotence, defied and upbraided his opponent as a rebel. His indignation was turned to despair when he learned that the troops had abandoned his cause, that the people were crying out for Li Tseching, and that that leader's followers were rapidly approaching his palace. Tsongching strangled himself with his girdle, but only one officer was found devoted enough to share his fate. Although Tsongching had some nominal successors, he was, strictly speaking, the last of the Ming emperors, and with him the great dynasty founded by Hong-wou came to an end. The many disasters that preceded its fall rendered the loss of the imperial station less of a blow to the individual, and the last of the Ming rulers seems to have even experienced relief on reaching the term of his anxieties. The episode of the faithful officer, Li Kweiching, concludes the dramatic events accompanying the capture of Pekin and the fall of the dynasty. After the death of his sovereign he attempted to defend the capital; but overpowered by numbers he surrendered to the victor, who offered him an honorable command in his service. Li Kweiching accepted the offer on the stipulation that he should be allowed to give the Emperor Tsongching honorable burial, and that the surviving members of the Ming family should be spared. These conditions, so creditable to Li Kweiching, were granted; but, at the funeral of his late sovereign, grief or a spirit of duty so overcame him that he committed suicide on the grave of Tsongching. Li Tseching, who had counted on

valuable assistance from this officer, became furious at this
occurrence. He plundered and destroyed the ancestral temple of the Mings, and he caused every member of the imperial family on whom he could lay hands to be executed.
Thus terminated the events at Pekin in the absolute and
complete triumph of the rebel Li Tseching, and the panic
produced by his success and severity blinded observers to
the hollowness of his power, and to the want of solidity
in his administration. Yet it seemed for a time as if he
were left the virtual master of China.

While the Ming power was collapsing before the onset of
Li Tseching, there still remained the large and well-trained
Ming army in garrison on the Manchu frontier, under command of the able general, Wou Sankwei. At the eleventh
hour the Emperor Tsongching had sent a message to Wou
Sankwei, begging him to come in all haste to save the capital; and that general, evacuating Ningyuen, and leaving a
small garrison at Shanhaikwan, had begun his march for
Pekin, when he learned that it had fallen and that the Ming
dynasty had ceased to be. Placed in this dilemma, between
the advancing Manchus, who immediately occupied Ningyuen
on his evacuation of it, and the large rebel force in possession
of Pekin, Wou Sankwei had no choice between coming to
terms with one or other of them. Li Tseching offered him
liberal rewards and a high command, but in vain, for Wou
Sankwei decided that it would be better to invite the Manchus
to enter the country, and to assist them to conquer it. There
can be no doubt that this course was both the wiser and the
more patriotic, for Li Tseching was nothing more than a
successful brigand on a large scale; whereas the Manchu
government was a respectable one, was well organized, and
aspired to revive the best traditions of the Chinese. Having
come to a prompt decision, Wou Sankwei lost no time in
promptly carrying it out. He wrote a letter to the Manchus,
asking them to send an army to co-operate with his in driving Li Tseching out of Pekin; and the Manchus, at once
realizing that the moment had arrived for conquering China,

Sankwei and to retain the command of his useful services. He was given the high-sounding title of Ping-si Wang, or Prince Pacifier of the West, and many other honors. Gratified by these rewards and unable to discover any person who could govern China, Wou Sankwei gradually reconciled himself to the situation and performed his duty faithfully as the most powerful lieutenant of the young Manchu ruler, Chuntche, the son of Taitsong, who, after the fall of Li Tseching, removed his capital to Pekin, and assumed the style and ceremony of a Chinese emperor. The active administration was intrusted to Prince Dorgun, brother of Taitsong, who now became known as Ama Wang, the Father Prince, and who acted as regent during the long minority of his nephew. The new dynasty was inaugurated at Pekin with a grand ceremony and court.

After this formal and solemn assumption of the governing power in China by the young Manchu prince, the activity of the Manchus increased, and several armies were sent south to subject the provinces, and to bring the whole Chinese race under his authority. For some time no serious opposition was encountered, as the disruption of Li's forces entailed the surrender of all the territory north of the Hoangho. But at Nankin, and in the provinces south of the Yangtsekiang, an attempt had been made, and not unsuccessfully, to set up a fresh administration under one of the members of the prolific Ming family. Fou Wang, a grandson of Wanleh, was placed on the Dragon Throne of Southern China in this hope, but his character did not justify the faith reposed in him. He thought nothing of the serious responsibility he had accepted, but showed that he regarded his high station merely as an opportunity for gratifying his own pleasures. There is little or no doubt that if he had shown himself worthy of his station he might have rallied to his side the mass of the Chinese nation, and Wou Sankwei, who had shown some signs of chafing at Manchu authority, might have been won back by a capable and sympathetic sovereign. But notwithstanding the ability of Fou

Wang's minister, Shu Kofa, who strove to repair the errors of his master, the new Ming power at Nankin did not prosper. Wou Sankwei, cautious not to commit himself, rejected the patent of a duke and the money gifts sent him by Shu Kofa, while Ama Wang, on his side, sought to gain over Shu Kofa by making him the most lavish promises of reward. But that minister proved as true to his sovereign as Wou Sankwei did to the Manchu. The result of the long correspondence between them was nil, but it showed the leaders of the Manchus in very favorable colors, as wishing to avert the horrors of war, and to simplify the surrender of provinces which could not be held against them. When Ama Wang discovered that there was no hope of gaining over Shu Kofa, and thus paving his way to the disintegration of the Nankin power, he decided to prosecute the war against the surviving Ming administration with the greatest activity.

While these preparations were being made to extend the Manchu conquest over Central China, all was confusion at Nankin. Jealousies between the commanders, none of whom possessed much merit or experience, bickerings among the ministers, apathy on the part of the ruler, and bitter disappointment and disgust in the ranks of the people, all combined to precipitate the overthrow of the ephemeral throne that had been erected in the Southern capital. Ama Wang waited patiently to allow these causes of disintegration time to develop their full force, and to contribute to the ruin of the Mings, but in the winter of 1644-45 he decided that the right moment to strike had come. Shu Kofa made some effort to oppose the Manchu armies, and even assumed the command in person, although he was only a civilian; but his troops had no heart to oppose the Manchus, and the devices to which he resorted to make his military power appear more formidable were both puerile and ineffective. Yet one passage may be quoted to his credit if it gave his opponent an advantage. It is affirmed on good authority that he could have obtained a material advantage if he would only have flooded the country, but he "refused to do so, on the ground that more civilians would perish than Manchus, and he said, 'First the people, next the dynasty.'" The sentiment was a noble one, but it was too severe a crisis to admit of any sentiment, especially when fighting an up-hill battle, and Shu Kofa, soon realizing that he was not qualified to play the part of a great soldier, resolved to end his existence. He took shelter with a small force in the town of Yangchow, and when he heard that the Manchus were entering the gate, he and his officers committed suicide. The Chinese lamented and were crushed by his death. In him they saw the last of their great men, and, no doubt, they credited him with a higher capacity even than he possessed. Only a military genius of the first rank could have saved the Mings, and Shu Kofa was nothing more than a conscientious and capable civil mandarin, ignorant of war. His fortitude could only be measured by his indifference to life, and by his resolve to anticipate the fall of his sovereign as soon as he saw it to be inevitable.

Fou Wang speedily followed the fate of his faithful minister; for, when the Manchus marched on Nankin, he abandoned his capital, and sought safety in flight. But one of his officers, anxious to make favorable terms for himself with the conqueror, undertook his capture, and coming up with him when on the point of entering a junk to put to sea, Fou Wang had no alternative left between an ignominious surrender and suicide. He chose the latter course, and throwing himself into the river was drowned, thus ending his own career and the Ming dynasty in its southern capital of Nankin.

Meantime dissension further weakened the already discouraged Chinese forces. The pirate Ching Chelong, who was the mainstay of the Ming cause, cherished the hope that he might place his own family on the throne, and he endeavored to induce the Ming prince to recognize his son, Koshinga, as his heir. Low as he had fallen, it is to the credit of this prince that he refused to sign away the birthright of his family. Ching was bitterly chagrined at this refusal, and after detaching his forces from the other Chinese he at last came to the resolution to throw in his lot with the Manchus. He was promised honorable terms, but the Tartars seem to have had no intention of complying with them, so far at least as allowing him to retain his liberty. For they sent him off to Pekin, where he was kept in honorable confinement, notwithstanding his protests and promises, and the defiant threats of his son Koshinga. In preserving his life he was more fortunate than the members of the Ming family, who were hunted down in a remorseless manner and executed with all their relations on capture. The only place that offered any resistance to the Manchus was the town of Kanchow, on the Kan River, in Kiangsi. The garrison defended themselves with desperate valor during two months, and a council of war was held amid much anxiety, to consider whether the siege should be abandoned. Bold counsels prevailed. The Manchus returned to the attack, and had the satisfaction of carrying the town by assault, when the garrison were put to the sword.

The relics of the Chinese armies gathered for a final stand in the city of Canton, but unfortunately for them the leaders were still divided by petty jealousies. One Ming prince proclaimed himself Emperor at Canton, and another in the adjoining province of Kwangsi. Although the Manchus were gathering their forces to overwhelm the Chinese in their last retreat, they could not lay aside their divisions and petty ambitions in order to combine against the national enemy, but must needs assail one another to decide which should have the empty title of Ming emperor. The Manchus had the satisfaction of seeing the two rivals break their strength against each other, and then they advanced to crush the victor at Canton. Strong as the place was said to be, it offered no serious resistance, and the great commercial city of the south passed into the hands of the race who had subdued the whole country from Pekin to the Tonquin frontier. At this moment the fortune of the Manchus underwent a

CHINA—9

sudden and inexplicable change. Two repulses before a fortress southwest of Canton, and the disaffection of a large part of their Chinese auxiliaries, who clamored for their pay, seem to have broken the strength of the advanced Manchu army. A wave of national antipathy drove the Tartars out of Canton and the southern provinces; but it soon broke its force, and the Manchus, returning with fresh troops, speedily recovered all they had lost, and by placing stronger garrisons in the places they occupied consolidated their hold on Southern China. Although the struggle between the Manchus and their new subjects was far from concluded, the conquest of China as such may be said to have reached its end at this stage. How a small Tartar tribe succeeded after fifty years of war in imposing its yoke on the skeptical, freedom-loving, and intensely national millions of China will always remain one of the enigmas of history.

CHAPTER X

THE FIRST MANCHU RULER

WHILE the Manchu generals and armies were establishing their power in Southern China, the young Emperor Chuntche, under the direction of his prudent uncle, the regent Ama Wang, was setting up at Pekin the central power of a ruling dynasty. In doing so, little or no opposition was experienced at the hands of the Chinese, who showed that they longed once more for a settled government; and this acquiescence on the part of the Chinese people in their authority no doubt induced the Manchu leaders to adopt a far more conciliatory and lenient policy toward the Chinese than would otherwise have been the case. Ama Wang gave special orders that the lives and property of all who surrendered to his lieutenants should be scrupulously respected. This moderation was only departed from in the case of some rebels in Shensi, who, after accepting, repudiated the Manchu authority, and laid close siege to the chief town of Singan, which held a garrison of only 3,000 Manchus. The commandant wished to make his position secure by massacring the Chinese of the town, but he was deterred from taking this extreme step by the representations of a Chinese officer, who, binding himself for the good faith of his countrymen, induced him to enroll them in the ranks of the garrison. They proved faithful and rendered excellent service in the siege; and when a relieving Manchu army came from Pekin, the rebels were quickly scattered and pursued with unflagging bitterness to their remotest hiding places.

In the province of Szchuen, a Chinese leader proclaimed himself Si Wang, or King of the West. He was execrated by those who were nominally his subjects. Among the most heinous of his crimes was his invitation to literary men to come to his capital for employment, and when they had assembled to the number of 30,000, to order them to be massacred. He dealt in a similar manner with 3,000 of his courtiers, because one of them happened to omit a portion of his full titles. His excesses culminated in the massacre of Chentu, when 600,000 innocent persons are said to have perished. Even allowing for the Eastern exaggeration of numbers, the crimes of this inhuman monster have rarely, if ever, been surpassed. His rage or appetite for destruction was not appeased by human sacrifices. He made equal war on the objects of nature and the works of man. He destroyed cities, leveled forests, and overthrew all the public monuments that embellished his province. In the midst of his excesses he was told that a Manchu army had crossed the frontier, but he resolved to crown his inhuman career by a deed unparalleled in the records of history, and, what is more extraordinary, he succeeded in inducing his followers to execute his commands. His project was to massacre all the women in attendance on his army.

When the assembly took place, Si Wang slew his wives *coram populo*, and his followers, seized with an extreme frenzy, followed his example. It is said that as many as 400,000 women were slain that day, and Si Wang, intoxicated by his success in inducing his followers to execute his inhuman behests, believed that he had nothing to fear at the hands of the Manchus. But he was soon undeceived, for in one of the earliest affairs at the outposts he was killed by an arrow. His power at once crumbled away, and Szchuen passed under the authority of the Manchus. The conquest of Szchuen paved the way for the recovery of the position that had been lost in Southern China, and close siege was laid to the city of Canton. Outside Canton the Manchus carried everything before them, and that city itself at last was captured, after what passed for a stubborn resistance. Canton was given over to pillage.

At this moment of success, Ama Wang, the wise regent, died, and Chuntche assumed the reins of government. He at once devoted his attention to administrative reforms. Corruption had begun to sway the public examinations, and Chuntche issued a special edict, enjoining the examiners to give fair awards and to maintain the purity of the service. But several examiners had to be executed and others banished beyond the Wall before matters were placed on a satisfactory basis. He also adopted the astronomical system in force in Europe, and he appointed the priest Adam Schaal head of the Mathematical Board at Pekin. But his most important work was the institution of the Grand Council, which still exists, and which is the supreme power under the emperor in the country. It is composed of only four members—two Manchus and two Chinese—who alone possess the privilege of personal audience with the emperor whenever they may demand it. As this act gave the Chinese an equal place with the Manchus in the highest body of the empire it was exceedingly welcome, and explains, among other causes, the popularity and stability of the Manchu dynasty. When allotting Chuntche his place among the founders of Manchu greatness, allowance must be made for this wise and far-reaching measure.

An interesting event in the reign of Chuntche was the arrival at Pekin of more than one embassy from European States. The Dutch and the Russians can equally claim the honor of having had an envoy resident in the Chinese capital during the year 1656.

In 1661 the health of Chuntche became so bad that it was evident to his courtiers that his end was drawing near, although he was little more than thirty years of age. On his deathbed he selected as his successor the second of his sons, who afterward became famous as the Emperor Kanghi. Kanghi assumed the personal direction of affairs when only fourteen years of age. Such a bold step undoubtedly betokened no ordinary vigor on the part of a youth, and its complete success reflected still further credit upon him.

The interest of the period passes from the scenes at court to the camp of Wou Sankwei, who, twenty years earlier, had introduced the Manchus into China. During the Manchu campaign in Southern China he had kept peace on the western frontier, gradually extending his authority from Shensi into Szchuen and thence over Yunnan. When a Ming prince, Kwei Wang, who had fled into Burma, returned with the support of the king of that country to make another bid for the throne, he found himself confronted by all the power and resources of Wou Sankwei, who was still as loyal a servant of the Manchu emperor as when he carried his ensigns against Li Tseching. Kwei Wang does not appear to have expected opposition from Wou Sankwei, and in the first encounter he was overthrown and taken prisoner. The conqueror, who was already under suspicion at the Manchu court, and whom every Chinese rebel persisted in regarding as a natural ally, now hesitated as to how he should treat these important prisoners. Kwei Wang and his son—the last of the Mings—were eventually led forth to execution, although it should be stated that a less authentic report affirms they were allowed to strangle themselves. Having made use of Wou Sankwei, and obtained, as they thought, the full value of his services, the Manchus sought

to treat him with indifference and to throw him into the
shade.   But the splendor of his work was such that they
had to confer on him the title of Prince, and to make him
viceroy of Yunnan and the adjacent territories.   He exerted
such an extraordinary influence over the Chinese subjects
that they speedily settled down under his authority; revenue
and trade increased, and the Manchu authority was maintained without a Tartar garrison, for Wou Sankwei's army
was composed exclusively of Chinese, and its nucleus was
formed by his old garrison of Ningyuen and Shanhaikwan.
There is no certain reason for saying that Wou Sankwei
nursed any scheme of personal aggrandizement, but the
measures he took and the reforms he instituted were calculated to make his authority become gradually independent
of Manchu control.   For a time the Manchu government
suppressed its apprehensions on account of this powerful
satrap, by the argument that in a few years his death in
the course of nature must relieve it from this peril; but Wou
Sankwei lived on and showed no signs of paying the common debt of humanity.   Then it seemed to Kanghi that
Wou Sankwei was gradually establishing the solid foundation of a formidable and independent power.   The Manchu
generals and ministers had always been jealous of the greater
fame of Wou Sankwei.   When they saw that Kanghi wanted
an excuse to fall foul of him, they carried every tale of alleged self-assertion on the part of the Chinese viceroy to the
imperial ears, and represented that his power dwarfed the
dignity of the Manchu throne and threatened its stability.

At last Kanghi resolved to take some decisive step to
bring the question to a climax, and he accordingly sent
Wou Sankwei an invitation to visit him at Pekin.   Wou
Sankwei excused himself from going to court on the
ground that he was very old, and that his only wish was
to end his days in peace.   He also deputed his son to tender
his allegiance to the emperor and to perform the Kotao in
his name.   But Kanghi was not to be put off in this way,
and he sent two trusted officials to Wou Sankwei to repre-

sent that he must comply with the exact terms of his command, and to point out the grave consequences of his refusing. Wou Sankwei cast off his allegiance to the Manchus, and entered upon a war which aimed at the subversion of their authority. Such was the reputation of this great commander, to whose ability and military prowess the Manchus unquestionably were indebted for their conquest of the empire, that a large part of Southern China at once admitted his authority, and from Szchuen to the warlike province of Hunan his lieutenants were able to collect all the fighting resources of the state, and to array the levies of those provinces in the field for the approaching contest with Kanghi.

While Wou Sankwei was making these extensive preparations in the south, his son at Pekin had devised an ingenious and daring plot for the massacre of the Manchus and the destruction of the dynasty. He engaged in his scheme the large body of Chinese slaves who had been placed in servitude under their Tartar conquerors, and these, incited by the hope of liberty, proved very ready tools to his designs. They bound themselves together by a solemn oath to be true to one another, and all the preparations were made to massacre the Manchus on the occasion of the New Year's Festival. This is the grand religious and social ceremony of the Chinese. It takes place on the first day of the first moon, which falls in our month of February. All business is stopped, the tribunals are closed for ten days, and a state of high festival resembling the Carnival prevails. The conspirators resolved to take advantage of this public holiday, and of the excitement accompanying it, to carry out their scheme, and the Manchus appear to have been in total ignorance until the eleventh hour of the plot for their destruction. The discovery of the conspiracy bears a close resemblance to that of the Gunpowder Plot. A Chinese slave, wishing to save his master, gave him notice of the danger, and this Manchu officer at once informed Kanghi of the conspiracy. The son of Wou Sankwei and the other conspirators were immediately arrested and executed without delay. The Manchus thus escaped by the merest accident from a danger which threatened them with annihilation, and Kanghi, having succeeded in getting rid of the son, concentrated his power and attention on the more difficult task of grappling with the father.

But the power and reputation of Wou Sankwei were so formidable that Kanghi resolved to proceed with great caution, and the emperor began his measures of offense by issuing an edict ordering the disbandment of all the native armies maintained by the Chinese viceroys, besides Wou Sankwei. The object of this edict was to make all the governors of Chinese race show their hands, and Kanghi learned the full measure of the hostility he had to cope with by every governor from the sea-coast of Fuhkien to Canton defying him, and throwing in their lot with Wou Sankwei. The piratical confederacy of Formosa, where Ching, the son of Koshinga, had succeeded to his authority, also joined in with what may be called the national party, but its alliance proved of little value, as Ching, at an early period, took umbrage at his reception by a Chinese official, and returned to his island home. But the most formidable danger to the young Manchu ruler came from an unexpected quarter. The Mongols, seeing his embarrassment and believing that the hours of the dynasty were numbered, resolved to take advantage of the occasion to push their claims. Satchar, chief of one of the Banners, issued a proclamation, calling his race to his side, and declaring his intention to invade China at the head of 100,000 men. It seemed hardly possible for Kanghi to extricate himself from his many dangers. With great quickness of perception Kanghi saw that the most pressing danger was that from the Mongols, and he sent the whole of his northern garrisons to attack Satchar before the Mongol clans could gather to his assistance. The Manchu cavalry, by a rapid march, surprised Satchar in his camp and carried him and his family off as prisoners to Pekin. The capture of their chief discouraged the Mongols and interrupted their plans for invading China. Kanghi thus obtained a respite from what seemed his greatest peril. Then he turned his attention to dealing with Wou Sankwei, and the first effort of his armies resulted in the recovery of Fuhkien, where the governor and Ching had reduced themselves to a state of exhaustion by a contest inspired by personal jealousy not patriotism. From Fuhkien his successful lieutenants passed into Kwantung, and the Chinese, seeing that the Manchus were not sunk as low as had been thought, abandoned all resistance and again recognized the Tartar authority. The Manchus did not dare to punish the rebels except in rare instances, and, therefore, the recovery of Canton was unaccompanied by any scenes of blood. But a garrison of Manchus was placed in each town of importance, and it was by Kanghi's order that a walled town, or "Tartar city," was built within each city for the accommodation and security of the dominant race.

But notwithstanding these successes, Kanghi made little or no progress against the main force of Wou Sankwei, whose supremacy was undisputed throughout the whole of southwest China. It was not until 1677 that Kanghi ventured to move his armies against Wou Sankwei in person. Although he obtained no signal success in the field, the divisions among the Chinese commanders were such that he had the satisfaction of compelling them to evacuate Hunan, and when Wou Sankwei took his first step backward the sun of his fortunes began to set. Calamity rapidly followed calamity. Wou Sankwei had not known the meaning of defeat in his long career of fifty years, but now, in his old age, he saw his affairs in inextricable confusion. His adherents deserted him, many rebel officers sought to come to terms with the Manchus, and Kanghi's armies gradually converged on Wou Sankwei from the east and the north. Driven out of Szchuen, Wou Sankwei endeavored to make a stand in Yunnan. He certainly succeeded in prolonging the struggle down to the year 1679, when his death put a sudden end to the contest, and relieved Kanghi from much anxiety; for although the success of the Manchus was no longer uncertain, the military skill of the old Chinese warrior might have indefinitely prolonged the war. Wou Sankwei is one of the most conspicuous and attractive figures to be met with in the long course of Chinese history, and his career covered one of the most critical periods in the modern existence of that empire. From the time of his first distinguishing himself in the defense of Ningyuen until he died, half a century later, as Prince of Yunnan, he occupied the very foremost place in the minds of his fellow-countrymen. The part he had taken, first in keeping out the Manchus, and then in introducing them into the state, reflected equal credit on his ability and his patriotism. In requesting the Manchus to crush the robber Li and to take the throne which the fall of the Mings had rendered vacant, he was actuated by the purest motives. There was only a choice of evils, and he selected that which seemed the less. He gave the empire to a foreign ruler of intelligence, but he saved it from an unscrupulous robber. He played the part of king-maker to the family of Noorhachu, and the magnitude of their obligations to him could not be denied. They were not as grateful as he may have expected, and they looked askance at his military power and influence over his countrymen. Probably he felt that he had not been well treated, and chagrin undoubtedly induced him to reject Kanghi's request to proceed to Pekin. If he had only acceded to that arrangement he would have left a name for conspicuous loyalty and political consistency in the service of the great race, which he had been mainly instrumental in placing over China. But even as events turned out he is one of the most remarkable personages the Chinese race ever produced, and his military career shows that they are capable of producing great generals and brave soldiers.

The death of Wou Sankwei signified the overthrow of the Chinese uprising which had threatened to extinguish the still growing power of the Manchu under its youthful emperor Kanghi. Wou Shufan, the grandson of that prince, endeavored to carry on the task of holding Yunnan as an independent territory, but by the year 1681 his possessions were reduced to the town of Yunnanfoo, where he was closely besieged by the Manchu forces. Although the Chinese fought valiantly, they were soon reduced to extremities, and the Manchus carried the place by storm. The garrison were massacred to the last man, and Wou Shufan only avoided a worse fate by committing suicide. The Manchus, not satisfied with his death, sent his head to Pekin to be placed on its principal gate in triumph, and the body of Wou Sankwei himself was exhumed so that his ashes might be scattered in each of the eighteen provinces of China as a warning to traitors. Having crushed their most redoubtable antagonist, the Manchus resorted to more severe measures against those who had surrendered in Fuhkien and Kwantung, and many insurgent chiefs who had surrendered, and enjoyed a brief respite, ended their lives under the knife of the executioner. The Manchu soldiers are said to have been given spoil to the extent of nearly ten million dollars, and the war which witnessed the final assertion of Manchu power over the Chinese was essentially popular with the soldiers who carried it on to a victorious conclusion. A very short time after the final overthrow of Wou Sankwei and his family, the Chinese *régime* in Formosa was brought to an end. Kanghi, having collected a fleet and concluded a convention with the Dutch, determined on the invasion and conquest of Formosa. In the midst of these preparations Ching, the son of Koshinga, died, and no doubt the plans of Kanghi were facilitated by the confusion that followed. The Manchu fleet seized Ponghu, the principal island of the Pescadore group, and thence the Manchus threw a force into Formosa. It is said that they were helped by a high tide, and by the superstition of the islanders, who exclaimed, ''The first Wang (Koshinga) got possession of Taiwan by a high tide. The fleet now comes in the same manner. It is the will of Heaven.'' Formosa accepted the supremacy of the Manchus without further ado. Those of the islanders who had ever recognized the authority of any government, accepted that of the Emperor Kanghi, shaved their heads in token of submission, and became, so far as in them lay, respectable citizens.

The overthrow of Wou Sankwei and the conquest of Formosa completed what may be called the pacification of China by the Manchus. From that period to the Taeping Rebellion, or for nearly 200 years, there was no internal insurrection on a large scale. On the whole the Manchus stained their conclusive triumph by few excesses, and Kanghi's moderation was scarcely inferior to that of his father, Chuntche. The family of Wou Sankwei seems to have been rooted out more for the personal attempt of the son at Pekin than for the bold ambition of the potentate himself. The family of Koshinga was spared, and its principal representative received the patent of an earl. Thus, by a policy judiciously combined of severity and moderation, did Kanghi make himself supreme, and complete the work of his race. Whatever troubles may have beset the government in the last 220 years, it will be justifiable to speak of the Manchus and the Tatsing dynasty as the legitimate authorities in China, and, instead of foreign adventurers, as the national and recognized rulers of the Middle Kingdom.

CHAPTER XI

THE EMPEROR KANGHI

AMONG the Mongol tribes the noblest at this period were the Khalkas. They prided themselves on being the descendants of the House of Genghis, the representatives of the special clan of the great conqueror, and the occupants of the original home in the valleys of the Onon and Kerulon. Although their military power was slight, the name of the Khalka princes stood high among the Mongol tribes, and they exercised an influence far in excess of their numbers or capacity as a fighting force. Kanghi determined to establish amicable relations with this clan, and by the dispatch of friendly letters and costly presents he succeeded in inducing the Khalka chiefs to enter into formal alliance with himself, and to conclude a treaty of amity with China, which, be it noted, they faithfully observed. Kanghi's efforts in this direction, which may have been dictated by apprehension at the movements of his new neighbors, the Russians, were thus crowned with success, and the adhesion of the Khalkas signified that the great majority of the Mongols would thenceforth abstain from acts of unprovoked aggression on the Chinese frontier. But the advance of China and her influence, even in the form of paying homage to the emperor as the Bogdo Khan, or the Celestial Ruler, so far west as the upper course of the Amour, involved the Pekin Government in fresh complications by bringing it into contact with tribes and peoples of whom it had no cognizance. Beyond the Khalkas were the Eleuths, supreme in Ili and Kashgaria, and divided into four hordes, who obeyed as many chiefs. They had had some relations with the Khalkas, but of China they knew nothing more than the greatness of her name. When the surrender of the Khalka princes became known the Eleuth chiefs held a grand assembly or kuriltai, and at this it was finally, and, indeed, ostentatiously, decided not to yield Kanghi his demands. Important as this decision was, it derived increased weight from the character of the man who was mainly instrumental in inducing the Eleuths to take it.

Much has been written of the desert chiefs from Yenta to Yakoob Beg, but none of these showed greater ability or attained more conspicuous success than Galdan, who strained the power of China, and fought for many years on equal terms with the Emperor Kanghi. Galdan determined that the easiest and most advantageous beginning for his enterprise would be to attack his neighbors the Khalkas, who, by accepting Kanghi's offers, had made themselves the advanced guard of China in Central Asia. He began a systematic encroachment into their lands in the year 1679, but at the same time he resorted to every device to screen his move-

ments from the Chinese court, and such was the delay in
receiving intelligence, and the ignorance of the situation
beyond the border, that in the very year of his beginning to
attack the Khalkas, his envoy at Pekin received a flattering
reception at the hands of Kanghi, still hopeful of a peaceful
settlement, and returned with the seal and patent of a Khan.
Events had not reached a state of open hostility three years
later, when Kanghi sent special envoys to the camp of
Galdan, as well as to the Khalkas. They were instructed
to promise and pay much, but to rest content with nothing
short of the formal acceptance by all the chiefs of the
supremacy of China. Galdan, bound by the laws of hospitality, nowhere more sacred than in the East, gave them
an honorable reception, and lavished upon them the poor
resources he commanded. In hyperbolic terms he declared
that the arrival of an embassy from the rich and powerful
Chinese emperor in his poor State would be handed down as
the most glorious event of his reign. But he refused to
make any tender of allegiance, or to subscribe himself as a
Chinese vassal. The dissensions among the Khalka princes
assisted the development of Galdan's ambition, and added
to the anxiety of the Chinese ruler. Kanghi admonished
them to heal their differences and to abstain from an internecine strife, which would only facilitate their conquest by
Galdan, and he succeeded so far that he induced them to
swear a peace among themselves before an image of Buddha.

At this juncture the Chinese came into collision with the
Russians on the Amour. The Russians had built a fort at
Albazin, on the upper course of that river, and the Chinese
army located in the Khalka country, considering its proximity
a menace to their own security, attacked it in overwhelming
force. Albazin was taken, and those of the garrison who
fell into the hands of the Chinese were carried off to Pekin,
where their descendants still reside as a distinct Russian
colony. But when the Chinese evacuated Albazin the Russians returned there with characteristic obstinacy, and
Kanghi, becoming anxious at the increasing activity of

Galdan, accepted the overtures of the Russian authorities in Siberia, who, in 1688, sent the son of the Governor-general of Eastern Siberia to Pekin to negotiate a peace. After twelve months' negotiation, protracted by the outbreak of war with Galdan, the Treaty of Nerchinsk, the first concluded between China and any European power, was signed, and the brief and only war between Russia and China was thus brought to a speedy and satisfactory termination. The Russians agreed to the destruction of Fort Albazin, but they were allowed to build another at Nerchinsk.

There is reason to believe that Galdan thought that he might derive some advantage from the complications with Russia, for his military movements were hastened when he heard that the two powers were embroiled on the Amour, and he proclaimed his intention of invading the Khalka region, because some of their people had murdered his kinsmen. Galdan endeavored to conclude an alliance with the Russians, who sent an officer to his camp; but they soon came to the determination that it would be more advantageous to keep on friendly terms with the Chinese than to embark on a hazardous adventure with the chief of an Asiatic horde. The mere rumor of a possible alliance between Galdan and the Russians roused Kanghi to increased activity, and all the picked troops of the Eight Manchu Banners, the Forty-nine Mongol Banners, and the Chinese auxiliaries, were dispatched across the steppe to bring the Napoleon of Central Asia to reason. In face of this formidable danger Galdan showed undiminished courage and energy. Realizing the peril of inaction, he did not hesitate to assume the offensive, and the war began with a victory he gained over a general named Horni, within the limits of Chinese territory. The moral of this success was that it showed that Kanghi had not decided a moment too soon in resorting to extreme measures against the ambitious potentate who found the Gobi Desert and the surrounding region too circumscribed for his ambition.

Kanghi intrusted the chief command of his armies to his

brother, Yu Tsing Wang, who justified his appointment by bringing the Eleuth forces speedily to an engagement, and by gaining a more or less decisive victory over them at Oulan Poutong. The loss was considerable on both sides, among the imperial officers killed being an uncle of the emperor; but Galdan's forces suffered a great deal more during the retreat than they had done in the action. After this disaster Galdan signed a treaty with the Chinese commander, Yu Tsing Wang. At first he attempted to gain an advantage by excluding his personal enemies, the Khalkas, from it, but the Chinese were not to be entrapped into any such arrangement, and, standing up for their dependants, the provisions of the treaty provided equally for their safety and for the acceptance by Galdan of the supremacy of China. This new arrangement or treaty was concluded in 1690, but Kanghi himself seems to have placed no great faith in the sincerity of Galdan, and to have regarded it merely as a truce. This view was soon found to be correct, for neither side laid aside their arms, and the unusual vigilance of the Chinese gave Galdan additional cause for umbrage. Kanghi showed that he was resolved not to let the terms, to which Galdan had subscribed, become a dead letter. He summoned a great assemblage of the Khalka tribes on the plain of Dolonor—the Seven Springs near Changtu—and he attended it in person, bestowing gifts and titles with a lavish hand. Kanghi was thus able to convince himself that, so far as the Mongol tribes were concerned, he might count on their loyalty and support. He then began to establish an understanding with Tse Wang Rabdan, and thus obtain an ally in the rear of Galdan. This latter circumstance was the direct cause of the second war with Galdan, for Kanghi's embassador was waylaid and murdered in the neighborhood of Hami. The outrage for which, whether he inspired it or not, Galdan was held blameworthy, aroused the strongest resentment and anger of Kanghi.

Kanghi made extraordinary preparations for the campaign. He placed four armies in the field numbering about

150,000 combatants, and it has been computed that, with non-combatants, the total of men employed did not fall short of a million. The first of these armies numbered 35,600 men, and was intrusted to Feyanku, the Ney of the Manchu army. Kanghi took personal command of the second, and its strength is given at 37,700 men; and the third army, 35,400 men, was placed under the orders of Sapsu. The fourth, of unstated but greatest numerical strength, acted as the reserve force for the others, and did not, properly speaking, come into action at all. In order to render the war popular, Kanghi offered special pay to the soldiers, and undertook to provide for the widows and orphans of those slain. At the same time, Kanghi neglected no precaution to insure the success of his arms. He provided cotton armor which was proof to the bullet for his cavalry and part of his infantry, and he organized a corps of artillerists mounted on camels, which also carried the light pieces, and rendered good service as "flying artillery." Before setting out for the campaign, the emperor reviewed his army, and he chose for the occasion the date of the popular Feast of Lanterns, when all China takes a holiday. After the inspection of the numerous and well-equipped army an impressive ceremony took place. Feyanku approached his sovereign, and received at his hands a cup of wine, which the general took while on his knees, and which, on descending from the steps of the throne, he quaffed in full view of the spectators. Each of his assistant generals and the subordinate officers in groups of ten went through the same ceremony, and the ruin of Galdan was anticipated in the libations of his conquerors. While Feyanku marched to encounter Galdan wherever he should find him, the ministers and courtiers at Pekin made a strenuous effort to prevent Kanghi taking the field in person, expatiating on the dangers of a war in the desert, and of the loss to the empire if anything happened to him. But Kanghi, while thanking them for their solicitude, was not to be deterred from his purpose. He led his army by a parallel route to that pur-

sued by Feyanku across the Gobi Desert to Kobdo, where
Galdan had established his headquarters. The details of
the march are fully described by the Roman Catholic priest,
Gerbillon, in his interesting narrative. They reveal the difficulties of the enterprise as well as its success. Some detachments of the Chinese army were compelled to beat a retreat,
but the main body succeeded in making its way to the valley
of the Kerulon, where some supplies could be obtained. Feyanku's corps, when it reached the neighborhood of the modern Ourga, was reduced to an effective strength of 10,000
men, and of Sapsu's army only 2,000 ever reached the scene
of operations, and they formed a junction with the force
under Feyanku. But Galdan did not possess the military
strength to take any advantage of the enfeebled state in
which the Chinese armies reached his neighborhood. He
abandoned camp after camp, and sought to make good his
position by establishing an empty alliance with the Russians
in Siberia, from whom he asked 60,000 troops to consummate the conquest of China. Such visionary projects as this
provided a poor defense against the active operations of a
Chinese army in his own country. In a fit bordering on
desperation Galdan suddenly determined to risk an attack
on the camp of Feyanku at Chowmodo. That general, less
fortunate than his sovereign, had been reduced to the verge
of distress by the exhaustion of his supplies, and was even
meditating a retreat back to China, when the action of Galdan relieved him from his dilemma. The exact course of
the battle at Chowmodo is not described in any authentic
document. During three hours Feyanku stood on the defensive, but when he gave the order for attack, the Eleuths
broke in confusion before the charge of his cavalry. Two
thousand of their best warriors were slain, their organization
was shattered, and Galdan became a fugitive in the region
where he had posed as undisputed master. This victory undoubtedly relieved the Chinese from serious embarrassment,
and Kanghi felt able to return to Pekin, leaving the further
conduct of the war and the pursuit of Galdan in the hands

of Feyanku. Formidable enemy as Galdan had proved himself, the defeat at Chowmodo put an end to his career, and destroyed all his schemes of greatness. The Chinese pursued him with great persistence, and at last he died in 1697, either of his deprivations or by the act of his own hand. With Galdan disappeared one of the most remarkable of the desert chiefs; but, although Kanghi flattered himself that such would be the case, peace did not settle down on Central Asia as the consequence of the death of his active and enterprising antagonist. The Chinese armies were recalled for this occasion, and the only force left on the remote frontier was a small one under the command of the gallant Feyanku.

The overthrow and death of Galdan brought Tse Wang Rabdan into direct contact with the Chinese. He had from his hostile relations with Galdan—the murderer of his father Tsenka—acted as the ally of Kanghi, but when he became the chief of the Eleuths on the death of his uncle, his ideas underwent a change, and he thought more of his dignity and independence. No rupture might have taken place, but that the Chinese, in their implacable resolve to exterminate the family of their enemy Galdan, demanded from Tse Wang Rabdan not only the bones of that chieftain, but also the persons of his son and daughter, who had taken refuge with him. Tse Wang Rabdan resented both the demand itself and the language in which it was expressed. He evaded the requests sent by Feyanku, and he addressed a letter of remonstrance to Kanghi, in the course of which he said, "The war being now concluded, past injuries ought to be buried in oblivion. Pity should be shown to the vanquished, and it would be barbarous to think of nothing but of how to overwhelm them. It is the first law inspired by humanity, and one which custom has consecrated from the earliest period among us who are Eleuths." Kanghi, undeterred by this homily, continued to press his demand, and sent several missions to the Eleuth camp to obtain the surrender of Galdan's remains and relations. His pertinacity was at last

to treat him as an enemy, throwing his son, who happened to be at Ili, into prison. He then dispatched an army into Tibet to crush Latsan Khan, and at the same time he sent a force against Sining in the hope of gaining possession of the person of the young Dalai Lama. The Eleuth army quitted the banks of the Ili in 1709, under the command of Zeren Donduk, and having crossed Eastern Turkestan appeared in due course before Lhasa. It met with little or no resistance. Latsan Khan was slain, and the Eleuth army collected an incalculable quantity of spoil, with which it returned to the banks of the Ili. The expedition against Sining failed, and the rapid advance of a Chinese army compelled the retreat of Zeren Donduk without having attained any permanent success. As the Eleuth army had evacuated Tibet there was no object in sending Chinese troops into that state, and Kanghi's generals were instructed to march westward from Hami to Turfan. But their movements were marked by carelessness or over-confidence, and the Eleuths surprised their camp and inflicted such loss upon Kanghi's commanders that they had even to evacuate Hami. But this was only a temporary reverse. A fresh Manchu army soon retrieved it, and Hami again became the bulwark of the Chinese frontier. At the same time Kanghi sent a garrison to Tibet, and appointed resident ambans at Lhasa, which officials China has retained there ever since. The war with Tse Wang Rabdan was not ended by these successes, for he resorted to the hereditary tactics of his family, retiring when the Chinese appeared in force, and then advancing on their retreat. As Kanghi wrote, they are "like wolves who, at the sight of the huntsmen, scatter to their dens, and at the withdrawal of danger assemble again round the prey they have abandoned with regret. Such was the policy of these desert robbers." The last year of Kanghi's reign was illustrated by a more than usually decisive victory over the forces of Tse Wang Rabdan, which a courtier declared to be "equivalent to the conquest of Tibet"; but on the whole the utmost success that can be claimed for Kanghi's policy was that it repelled the chronic danger from the desert chiefs and their turbulent followers to a greater distance from the immediate frontier of the empire than had been the case for many centuries. He left the task of breaking the Eleuth power to his grandson, Keen Lung.

The close of Kanghi's reign witnessed a decline in the interest he took in the representatives of Europe, and this was not revived by the splendor of the embassy which Peter the Great sent to Pekin in 1719. The embassy consisted of the embassador himself, M. Ismaloff; his secretary, M. de Lange; the English traveler, Mr. Bell, and a considerable suite. Kanghi received in the most gracious manner the letter which Peter addressed to him in the following terms: "To the emperor of the vast countries of Asia, to the Sovereign Monarch of Bogdo, to the Supreme Majesty of Khitay, friendship and greeting. With the design I possess of holding and increasing the friendship and close relations long established between your Majesty and my predecessors and myself, I have thought it right to send to your court, in the capacity of embassador-extraordinary, Leon Ismaloff, captain in my guards. I beg you will receive him in a manner suitable to the character in which he comes, to have regard and to attach as much faith to what he may say on the subject of our mutual affairs as if I were speaking to you myself, and also to permit his residing at your Court of Pekin until I recall him. Allow me to sign myself your Majesty's good friend, Peter." Kanghi gave the Russian envoy a very honorable reception. A house was set apart for his accommodation, and when the difficulties raised by the mandarins on the question of the kotao ceremony at the audience threatened to bring the embassy to an abortive end, Kanghi himself intervened with a suggestion that solved the difficulty. He arranged that his principal minister should perform the kotao to the letter of the Russian emperor, while the Russian envoy rendered him the same obeisance. The audience then took place without further delay, and it was allowed on all hands that no foreign embassy had ever been received with greater honor in China than this. Ismaloff returned to his master with the most roseate account of his reception and of the opening in China for Russian trade. A large and rich caravan was accordingly fitted out by Peter, to proceed to Pekin; but when it arrived it found a very different state of affairs from what Ismaloff had pictured. Kanghi lay on his deathbed, the anti-foreign ministers were supreme, declaring that "trade was a matter of little consequence, and regarded by them with contempt," and the Russians were ignominiously sent back to Siberia with the final declaration that such intercourse as was unavoidable must be restricted to the frontier. Thus summarily was ended Peter's dream of tapping the wealth of China.

Although Kanghi was not altogether free from domestic trouble, through the ambition of his many sons to succeed him, his life must on the whole be said to have passed along tranquilly enough apart from his cares of state. The public acts and magnificent exploits of his reign prove him to have been wise, courageous, and magnanimous, and his private life will bear the most searching examination, and only render his virtue the more conspicuous. He always showed a tender solicitude for the interests of his people, which was proved, among other things, by his giving up his annual tours through his dominions on account of the expense thrown on his subjects by the inevitable size of his retinue. His active habits as a hunter, a rider, and even as a pedestrian, were subjects of admiring comment on the part of the Chinese people, and he was one of their few rulers who made it a habit to walk through the streets of his capital. He was also conspicuous as the patron of learning; notably in his support of the foreign missionaries as geographers and cartographers. He was also the consistent and energetic supporter of the celebrated Hanlin College, and, as he was no ordinary *litterateur* himself, this is not surprising. His own works filled a hundred volumes, prominent among which were his Sixteen Maxims on the Art of Government, and it is believed that he took a large part in bringing out the Imperial Dictionary of the Hanlin College. His writings were marked by a high code of morality as well as by the lofty ideas of a broad-minded statesman. His enemies have imputed to him an excessive vanity and avarice; but the whole tenor of his life disproves the former statement, and, whatever foundation in fact the latter may have had, he never carried it to any greater length than mere prudence and consideration for the wants of his people demanded. We know that he resorted to gentle pressure to attain his ends rather than to tyrannical force. When he wished to levy a heavy contribution from a too rich subject he had recourse to what may be styled a mild joke, sooner than to threats and corporal punishment. The following incident has been quoted in this connection: One day Kanghi made an official, who had grown very wealthy, lead him, riding on an ass, round his gardens. As recompense the emperor gave him a tael. Then he himself led the mandarin in similar fashion. At the end of the tour he asked how much greater he was than his minister? "The comparison is impossible," said the ready courtier. "Then I must make the estimate myself," replied Kanghi. "I am 20,000 times as great, therefore you will pay me 20,000 taels." His reign was singularly free from the executions so common under even the best of Chinese rulers; and, whenever possible, he always tempered justice with mercy.

Notwithstanding his enfeebled health and the many illnesses from which he had suffered in later life, he persisted in following his usual sporting amusements, and he passed the winter of 1722 at his hunting-box at Haidsu. He seems to have caught a chill, and after a brief illness he died on the 20th of December in that year.

The place of Kanghi among Chinese sovereigns is clearly defined. He ranks on almost equal terms with the two greatest of them all—Taitsong and his own grandson, Keen Lung—and it would be ungracious, if not impossible, to say in what respect he falls short of complete equality with either, so numerous and conspicuous were his talents and his

virtues.   His long friendship and high consideration for the
Christian missionaries have no doubt contributed to bring
his name and the events of his reign more prominently before
Europe than was the case with any other Chinese ruler.
But, although this predilection for European practices may
have had the effect of strengthening his claims to precede
every other of his country's rulers, it can add but little to the
impression produced on even the most cursory reader by the
remarkable achievements in peace and war accomplished by
this gifted emperor.   Kanghi's genius dominates one of the
most critical periods in Chinese history, of which the narrative should form neither an uninteresting nor an uninstruc-
tive theme.   Celebrated as the consolidator and completer
of the Manchu conquest, Kanghi's virtue and moderation
have gained him permanent fame as a wise, just, and beneficent national sovereign in the hearts of the Chinese people.

CHAPTER XII

A SHORT REIGN AND THE BEGINNING OF A LONG ONE

IMMEDIATELY after the death of Kanghi, his fourth son,
who had long been designated as his heir, was proclaimed
emperor, under the style of Yung Ching, which name means
"the indissoluble concord or stable peace."   The late emperor had always favored this prince, and in his will he
publicly proclaimed that he bore much resemblance to himself, and that he was a man of rare and precious character.
His first acts indicated considerable vigor and decision of
mind.   In the edict announcing the death of his father and
his own accession he said that on the advice of his ministers
he had entered upon the discharge of his imperial duties
without giving up precious time to the indulgence of his
natural grief, which would be gratifying to his feelings but
injurious to the public interests.   As Yung Ching was of the
mature age of forty-five, and as he had enjoyed the confi-

dence of his predecessor, he was fully qualified to carry on the administration. He declared that his main purpose was to continue his father's work, and that he would tread as closely as he could in Kanghi's footsteps. While Yung Ching took these prompt steps to secure himself on the throne, some of his brothers assumed an attitude of menacing hostility toward him, and all his energy and vigilance were required to counteract their designs. A very little time was needed, however, to show that Kanghi had selected his worthiest son as his successor, and that China would have no reason to fear under Yung Ching the loss of any of the benefits conferred on the nation by Kanghi. His fine presence, and frank, open manner secured for him the sympathy and applause of the public, and in a very short time he also gained their respect and admiration by his wisdom and justice.

The most important and formidable of his brothers was the fourteenth son of Kanghi, by the same mother, however, as that of Yung Ching. He and his son Poki had been regarded with no inconsiderable favor by Kanghi, and at one time it was thought that he would have chosen them as his successors; but those expectations were disappointed. He was sent instead to hold the chief command against the Eleuths on the western borders. Yung Ching determined to remove him from this post, in which he might have opportunities of asserting his independence, and for a moment it seemed as if he might disobey. But more prudent counsels prevailed, and he returned to Pekin, where he was placed in honorable confinement, and retained there during the whole of Yung Ching's reign. He and his son owed their release thirteen years later to the greater clemency or self-confidence of Keen Lung. Another brother, named Sessaka, also fell under suspicion, and he was arrested and his estates confiscated. He was then so far forgiven that a small military command was given him in the provinces. Others of more importance were involved in his affairs. Lessihin, son of Prince Sourniama, an elder brother of Kanghi, was denounced as a sympathizer and supporter of Sessaka. The charge seems to have been based on slender evidence, but it sufficed to cause the banishment of this personage and all his family to Sining. It appears as if they were specially punished for having become Christians, and there is no doubt that their conversion imbittered the emperor's mind against the Christian missionaries and their religion. It enabled him to say, or at least induced him to accept the statement, that the Christians meddled and took a side in the internal politics of the country. Yung Ching saw and seized his opportunity. His measures of repression against the recalcitrant party in his own family culminated in the summary exile of Sourni-ama and all his descendants down to the fourth generation. Sourniama vainly endeavored to establish his innocence, and he sent three of his sons, laden with chains, to the palace, to protest his innocence and devotion. But they were refused audience, and Sourniama and his family sank into oblivion and wretchedness on the outskirts of the empire.

Having thus settled the difficulties within his own family, Yung Ching next turned his attention to humbling the bold band of foreigners who had established themselves in the capital and throughout the country, as much by their own persistency and indifference to slight as by the acquiescence of the Chinese government, and who, after they had reached some of the highest official posts, continued to preach and propagate their gospel of a supreme power and mercy beyond the control of kings, a gospel which was simply destructive of the paternal and sacred claims on which a Chinese emperor based his authority as superior to all earthly interference, and as transmitted to him direct from Heaven. The official classes confirmed the emperor's suspicions, and encouraged him to proceed to extreme lengths. On all sides offenses were freely laid at the doors of the missionaries. It was said of them that "their doctrine sows trouble among the people, and makes them doubt the goodness of our laws." In the province of Fuhkien their eighteen churches were closed, and the priests were summarily ordered to return to

Macao. At Pekin itself the Jesuits lost all their influence. Those who had been well-disposed toward them were either banished or cowed into silence. The emperor turned his back on them and refused to see them, and they could only wait with their usual fortitude until the period of imperial displeasure had passed over. When they endeavored to enlist in their support the sympathy and influence of the emperor's brother—the thirteenth prince—who in Kanghi's time had been considered their friend, they met with a rebuff not unnatural or unreasonable when the mishaps to his relations for their Christian proclivities are borne in mind. This prince said, in words which have often been repeated since by Chinese ministers and political writers, "What would you say if our people were to go to Europe and wished to change there the laws and customs established by your ancient sages? The emperor, my brother, wishes to put an end to all this in an effectual manner. I have seen the accusation of the Tsongtou of Fuhkien. It is undoubtedly strong, and your disputes about our customs have greatly injured you. What would you say if we were to transport ourselves to Europe and to act there as you have done here? Would you stand it for a moment? In the course of time I shall master this business, but I declare to you that China will want for nothing when you cease to live in it, and that your absence will not cause it any loss. Here nobody is retained by force, and nobody also will be suffered to break the laws or to make light of our customs."

The influence of Yung Ching on the development of the important foreign question arrested the ambition and sanguine flight of the imagination of the Roman Catholic missionaries, who, rendered overconfident by their success under Kanghi, believed that they held the future of China in their own hands, and that persistency alone was needed to secure the adhesion of that country to the Christian Church. Yung Ching dispelled these illusions, and so far as they were illusions, which nearly two subsequent centuries have proved them to be, it was well that they should be so dis-

pelled. He asserted himself in very unequivocal terms as
an emperor of China, and as resolute in maintaining his sovereign position outside the control of any religious potentate
or creed. The progress of the Christian religion of the Roman Catholic Church in China was quite incompatible with
the supposed celestial origin of the emperor, who was alleged
to receive his authority direct from Heaven. It is not surprising that Yung Ching, at the earliest possible moment,
decided to blight these hopes, and to assert the natural and
inherited prerogative of a Chinese emperor. There is no
room to doubt that the Catholic priests had drawn a too
hasty and too favorable deduction from the favor of Kanghi.
They confounded their practical utility with the intrinsic
merit and persuasive force of Christianity. An enlightened
ruler had recognized the former, but a skeptical people showed
themselves singularly obdurate to the latter. The persecution of the Christians, of which the letters from the missionaries at Pekin at this time are so full, did not go beyond the
placing of some restraint on the preaching of their religion.
No wholesale executions or sweeping decrees passed against
their persons attended its course or marked its development.
Yung Ching simply showed by his conduct that they must
count no longer on the favor of the emperor in the carrying
out of their designs. The difficulties inherent in the task
they had undertaken stood for the first time fully revealed,
and having been denounced as a source of possible danger
to the stability of the empire, they became an object of
suspicion even to those who had sympathized with them
personally, if not with their creed.

The early years of the reign of Yung Ching were marked
by extraordinary public misfortunes. The flooding of the
Hoangho entailed a famine, which spread such desolation
throughout the northern provinces that it is affirmed, on
credible authority, that 40,000 persons were fed at the state
expense in Pekin alone for a period of four months. The
taxes in some of the most important cities and wealthiest
districts had to be greatly reduced, and the resources of the

exchequer were severely strained. But the loss and suffering caused by the famine were speedily cast into the shade by a terrible and sudden visitation which carried desolation and destruction throughout the whole of the metropolitan province of Pechihli. The northern districts of China have for many centuries been liable to the frequent recurrence of earthquakes on a terribly vast and disastrous scale, but none of them equaled in its terrific proportions that of the year 1730. It came without warning, but the shocks continued for ten days. Over 100,000 persons were overwhelmed in a moment at Pekin, the suburbs were laid in ruins, the imperial palace was destroyed, the summer residence at Yuen Ming Yuen, on which Yung Ching had lavished his taste and his treasure, suffered in scarcely a less degree. The emperor and the inhabitants fled from the city, and took shelter without the walls, where they encamped. The loss was incalculable, and it has been stated that Yung Ching expended seventy-five million dollars in repairing the damage and allaying the public misfortune. Notwithstanding these national calamities the population increased, and in some provinces threatened to outgrow the production of rice. Various devices were resorted to to check the growth of the population; but they were all of a simple and harmless character, such as the issue of rewards to widows who did not marry again and to bachelors who preserved their state.

The military events of Yung Ching's reign were confined to the side of Central Asia, where Tse Wang Rabdan emulated with more than ordinary success the example of his predecessors, and where he transmitted his power and authority to his son, Galdan Chereng, on his death in 1727. He established his sovereignty over the whole of Kashgaria, which he ruled through a prince named Daniel, and he established relations with the Russians, which at one time promised to attain a cordial character, but which were suddenly converted into hostility by the Russian belief that the Upper Urtish lay in a gold region which they resolved to conquer. Instead of an ally they then found in Tse Wang

Rabdan the successful defender of that region. But the wars of Central Asia had no interest for Yung Ching. He was one of the Chinese rulers who thought that he should regard these matters as outside his concern, and the experience of Kanghi's wars had divided Chinese statesmen into two clearly-defined parties: those who held that China should conquer Central Asia up to the Pamir, and those who thought that the Great Wall was the best practical limit for the exercise of Chinese authority. Yung Ching belonged to the latter school, and, instead of dispatching fresh armies into the Gobi region to complete the triumph of his father, he withdrew those that were there, and publicly proclaimed that the aggressive chiefs and turbulent tribes of that region might fight out their own quarrels, and indulge their own petty ambitions as best they felt disposed. The success of this policy would have been incontestable if it had been reflected in the conduct of the Central Asian princelets, who, however, seemed to see in the moderation and inaction of the Chinese ruler only a fresh incentive to aggression and turbulence. Yung Ching himself died too soon to appreciate the shortcomings of his own policy.

In the midst of his labors as a beneficent ruler the life of Yung Ching was cut short. On October 7, 1735, he gave audience to the high officials of his court in accordance with his usual custom; but feeling indisposed he was compelled to break off the interview in a sudden manner. His indisposition at once assumed a grave form, and in a few hours he had ceased to live. The loss of this emperor does not seem to have caused any profound or widespread sentiment of grief among the masses, although the more intelligent recognized in him one of those wise and prudent rulers whose tenure of power makes their people's happiness.

Yung Ching died so suddenly that he had not nominated his heir. He left three sons, and, after brief consideration, the eldest of these—to whom was given the name of Keen Lung—was placed upon the throne. The choice was justified by the result, although the chroniclers declare that it came as a surprise to the recipient of the honor, as he had passed his life in the pursuit of literary studies rather than in practical administrative work. His skill and proficiency in the field of letters had already been proved before his father's death; but of public affairs and the government of a vast empire he knew little or nothing. He was a student of books rather than of men, and he had to undergo a preliminary course of training in the art of government before he felt himself capable of assuming the reins of power. Moreover, Keen Lung, although the eldest son, was not the offspring of the empress, and the custom of succession in the imperial family was too uncertain to allow any one in his position to feel absolute confidence as to his claims securing the recognition they might seem to warrant. His admission of his being unequal to the duties of his lofty position, notwithstanding that he was twenty-five years of age, was thoroughly characteristic of the man, and augured well for the future of his reign. He appointed four regents, whose special task was to show him how to rule; but in the edict delegating his authority to them he expressly limited its application to the period of mourning, covering a space of four years; and as a measure of precaution against any undue ambition he made the office terminable at his discretion.

Keen Lung began his reign with acts of clemency, which seldom fail to add a special luster to a sovereign's assumption of power. His father had punished with rigor some of the first princes of the court simply because they were his relations, and there is some ground for thinking that he had put forward antipathy to the foreign heresy of the Christians as a cloak to conceal his private animosities and personal apprehensions. Keen Lung at once resolved to reverse the acts of his predecessor, and to offer such reparation as he could to those who had suffered for no sufficient offense. The sons of Kanghi and their children who had fallen under the suspicion of Yung Ching were released from their confinement, and restored to their rank and privileges. They showed their gratitude to their benefactor by sustained loyalty and practical service that contributed to the splendor of his long reign. The impression thus produced on the public mind was also most favorable, and already the people were beginning to declare that they had found a worthy successor to the great Kanghi.

There is nothing surprising to learn that in consequence of the pardon and restitution of the men who had nominally suffered for their Christian proclivities the foreign missionaries began to hope and to agitate for an improvement in their lot and condition. They somewhat hastily assumed that the evil days of persecution were over, and that Keen Lung would accord them the same honorable positions as they had enjoyed under his grandfather, Kanghi. These expectations were destined to a rude disappointment, as the party hostile to the Christians remained as strong as ever at court, and the regents were not less prejudiced against them than the ministers of Yung Ching had been. The emperor's own opinion does not appear to have been very strong one way or the other, but it seems probable that he was slightly prejudiced against the foreigners. He certainly assented to an order prohibiting the practice of Christianity by any of his subjects, and ordaining the punishment of those who should obstinately adhere to it. At the same time the foreign missionaries were ordered to confine their labors to the secular functions in which they were useful, and to give up all attempts to propagate their creed. Still some slight abatement in practice was procured of these rigid measures through the mediation of the painter Castiglione, who, while taking a portrait of the emperor, pleaded, and not ineffectually, the cause of his countrymen. There was one distinct persecution on a large scale in the province of Fuhkien, where several Spanish missionaries were tortured, their chief native supporters strangled, and Keen Lung himself sent the order to execute the missionaries in retaliation for the massacre of Chinese subjects by the Spaniards in the Philippines. After he had been on the throne fifteen years, Keen Lung began to unbend toward the foreigners, and to avail himself of their services in the same manner as his grandfather had done. The artists Castiglione and Attiret were constantly employed in the palace, painting his portrait and other pictures. Keen Lung is said to have been so pleased with that drawn by Attiret that he wished to make him a mandarin. The French in particular strove to amuse the great monarch, and to enable him to while away his leisure with ingeniously constructed automatons worked by clockwork machinery. He also learned from them much about the politics and material condition of Europe, and it is not surprising that he became imbued with the idea that France was the greatest and most powerful state in that continent. Almost insensibly Keen Lung entertained a more favorable opinion of the foreigners, and extended to them his protection with other privileges that had long been withheld. But this policy was attributable to practical considerations and not to religious belief.

Very little detailed information is obtainable about the inner working of the government and the annual course of events, owing to the practice of not giving the official history of the dynasty publicity until after it has ceased to reign; so all that can be said with any confidence of the first fifteen years of Keen Lung's reign, is that they were marked by great internal prosperity arising from the tranquillity of the realm and the content of the people. Any misfortunes that befell the realm were of personal importance to the sovereign rather than of national significance, although some of the foreign priests affected to see in them the retribution of Providence for the apathy and tyranny of the Chinese rulers. In 1751 Keen Lung lost both his principal wife, the empress, and his eldest son. His disagreements with his ministers also proved many and serious, and the letters from Pekin note, with more than a gleam of satisfaction, that those who were most prominent as Anti-Christians suffered most heavily. Keen Lung suffered from physical weakness, and a susceptibility to bodily ailments, that detracted during the first few years of his reign from his capacity to discharge all the duties of his position, and more than their usual share of power consequently fell into the hands of the great tribunals of the state. When Keen Lung resolutely devoted himself to the task of supervising the acts of the official world the evils became less perceptible, and gradually the provincial governors found it to be their best and wisest course to obey and faithfully execute the behests of their sovereign. For a brief space Keen Lung seemed likely to prove more indifferent to the duties of his rank than either of his predecessors; but after a few years' practice he hastened to devote himself to his work with an energy which neither Kanghi nor Yung Ching had surpassed.

Keen Lung seems to have passed his time between his palace at Pekin and his hunting-box at Jehol, a small town beyond the Wall. The latter, perhaps, was his favorite residence, because he enjoyed the quiet of the country, and the purer and more invigorating air of the northern region agreed with his constitution. Here he varied the monotony of rural pursuits—for he never became as keen a hunter as Kanghi—with grand ceremonies which he employed the foreigners in painting. It was at Jehol that he planned most of his military campaigns, and those conquests which carried his banners to the Pamir and the Himalaya. If the earlier period of Keen Lung's reign was tranquil and undisturbed by war, the last forty years made up for it by their sustained military excitement and achievement. As soon as Keen Lung grasped the situation and found that the administration of the country was working in perfect order, he resolved to attain a complete settlement of the questions pending in Central Asia, which his father had shirked. Up to this time Keen Lung had been generally set down as a literary student, as a man more of thought than of action. But his reading had taught him one thing, and that was that the danger to China from the side of Central Asia was one that went back to remote ages, that it had never been allayed, save for brief intervals, and then only by establishing Chinese authority on either side of the Tian Shan. His studies showed Keen Lung what ought to be done, and the aggressions of his neighbors soon gave him the opportunity of carrying out the policy that he felt to be the best.

CHAPTER XIII

KEEN LUNG'S WARS AND CONQUESTS

It was the arrival of a chief named Amursana at his court that first led Keen Lung to seriously entertain the idea of advancing into Central Asia, and having determined on the Central Asian campaign, Keen Lung's military preparations were commensurate with the importance and magnitude of the undertaking. He collected an army of 150,000 men, including the picked Manchu Banners and the celebrated Solon contingent, each of whom was said to be worth ten other soldiers. The command of this army was given to Panti, the best of the Manchu generals, and Amursana, who accompanied it, received a seal and the honorary title of Great General. But Keen Lung superintended all the operations of the war, and took credit to himself for its successful issue.

The triumph of Amursana, by the aid of the Chinese, did not bring tranquillity to Central Asia. He was not contented with the position to which the friendship of Keen Lung had raised him, and, placing too high an estimate on his own ability and resources, he was inclined to dispute the accepted opinion that all his success was due to the Chinese army. On the termination of the campaign the major portion of that army returned to China, but Panti was left with a select contingent, partly to support Amursana, and partly to secure the restoration of China's authority. Amursana, however, considered that the presence of this force detracted from the dignity of his position. Having risen to the greatness he coveted, Amursana meditated casting aside the prop by which he had risen; but before he took an irre-traceable step he resolved to make use of the Chinese forces for extending his authority south of the Tian Shan range into Kashgaria. With some hesitation Panti lent him 500 Chinese soldiers, and with their aid the Eleuth prince cap-tured the cities of Kashgar and Yarkand, and set up a chief named Barhanuddin Khoja as his nominee. This success confirmed Amursana in his good opinion of himself and his resources, and when Keen Lung, who had grown mistrustful of his good faith, summoned him to Pekin, he resolved to throw off the mask and his allegiance to China. At this supreme moment of his fate not the least thought of grati-tude to the Chinese emperor, who had made him what he was, seems to have entered his mind. He determined not merely to disregard the summons to Pekin and to proclaim his independence, but also to show the extent of his hostility by adding to his defiance an act of treachery. Before he fully revealed his plans he surprised the Chinese garrison and massacred it to the last man; the valiant Panti, who had gained his victories for him, being executed by the public executioner.

The impression produced by this event was profound, and when Amursana followed up the blow by spreading abroad rumors of the magnitude of his designs they obtained some credence even among the Mongols. Encouraged by this success he sought to rally those tribes to his side by imputing sinister intentions to Keen Lung. His emissaries declared that Keen Lung wished to deprive them all of their rank and authority, and that he had summoned Amursana to Pekin only for the purpose of deposing him. To com-plete the quarrel, Amursana declared himself King of the Eleuths, and absolutely independent of China. But the energy and indignation of Keen Lung soon exposed the hol-lowness of these designs, and the inadequacy of Amursana's power and capacity to make good his pretensions. Keen Lung collected another army larger than that which had placed him on his throne, to hurl Amursana from the supremacy which had not satisfied him and which he had grossly abused.

The armies of Keen Lung traversed the Gobi Desert and arrived in Central Asia, but the incapacity of his generals prevented the campaigns having those decisive results which he expected. The autocratic Chinese ruler treated his generals who failed like the fickle French Republic. The penalty of failure was a public execution. Keen Lung would accept nothing short of the capture of Amursana as evidence of his victory, and Amursana escaped to the Kirghiz. His celerity or ingenuity cost the lives of four respectable Chinese generals, two of whom were executed at Pekin and two were slain by brigands on their way there to share the same fate. Emboldened by the inability of the Chinese to capture him, Amursana again assembled an army and pursued the retiring Chinese across the desert, where he succeeded in inflicting no inconsiderable loss upon them.

When the Chinese army retired before Amursana one corps maintained its position and successfully defied him, thanks to the capacity of its commander, Tchaohoei. Tchaohoei not merely held his ground, but drew up a scheme for regaining all that had been lost in Central Asia, and Keen Lung was so impressed by it that he at once resolved to intrust the execution of his policy to the only officer who had shown any military capacity. Two fresh armies were sent to the Ili, and placed, on their arrival there, under the command of Tchaohoei, who was exhorted, above all things, to capture Amursana, dead or alive. Tchaohoei at once assumed the offensive, and as Amursana was abandoned by his followers as soon as they saw that China was putting forth the whole of her strength, he had no alternative but once more to flee for shelter to the Kirghiz. But the conditions imposed by Keen Lung were so rigorous that Tchaohoei realized that the capture of Amursana was essential to his gaining the confidence and gratitude of his master. He, therefore, sent his best lieutenant, Fouta, to pursue the Eleuth prince. Fouta pursued Amursana with the energy of one who has to gain his spurs, and he almost succeeded in effecting his capture, but Amursana just made his escape in time across the frontier into Russian territory. But Keen Lung was not satisfied with this result, and he sent both to Fouta and Tchaohoei to rest satisfied with nothing short of the capture of Amursana. The close of that unfortunate prince's career was near at hand, although it was not ended by the act of the Chinese officers. He died in Russian territory of a fever, and when the Chinese demanded of their neighbors that his body should be surrendered they refused, on the ground that enmity should cease with death; but Fouta was able to report to his sovereign that he had seen with his own eyes the mortal remains of the Eleuth chief who had first been the humble friend and then the bitter foe of the Manchu ruler.

Keen Lung decided to administer the country which he had conquered. But another step was seen to be necessary to give stability to the Chinese administration, and that was the annexation of Kashgaria. The great region of Little Bokhara or Eastern Turkestan, known to us now under the more convenient form of Kashgaria, was still ruled by the Khoja Barhanuddin, who had been placed in power by Amursana, and it afforded a shelter for all the disaffected, and a base of hostility against the Chinese. Even if Tchaohoei had not reported that the possession of Kashgaria was essential to the military security of Jungaria, there is no doubt that sooner or later Keen Lung would have proceeded to extreme lengths with regard to Barhanuddin. The Chinese were fully warranted, however, in treating him as an enemy when he seized an envoy sent to his capital by Tchaohoei and executed him and his escort. This outrage precluded all possibility of an amicable arrangement, and the Chinese prepared their fighting men for the invasion and conquest of Kashgaria. They crossed the frontier in two bodies, one under the command of Tchaohoei, the other under that of Fouta. Any resistance that Barhanuddin and his brother attempted was speedily overcome; the principal cities, Kashgar and Yarkand, were occupied, and the ill-advised princes were compelled to seek their personal safety by a precipitate flight. The conquest and annexation of Kashgaria completed the task with which Tchaohoei was charged, and it also realized Keen Lung's main idea by setting up his authority in the midst of the turbulent tribes who had long disturbed the empire, and who first learned peaceful pursuits as his subjects. The Chinese commanders followed up this decided success by the dispatch of several expeditions into the adjoining states.

The ruler of Khokand was either so much impressed by his neighbor's prowess, or, as there is much reason to believe, experienced himself the weight of their power by the occupation of his principal cities, Tashkent and Khokand, that he hastened to recognize the authority of the emperor and to enroll himself among the tributaries of the Son of Heaven. The tribute he bound himself to pay was sent without a break for a period of half a century. The Kirghiz chiefs of low and high degree imitated his example, and a firm peace was thus established from one end of Central Asia to the other. The administration was divided between Chinese and native officials, and if there was tyranny, the people suffered rather from that of the Mohammedan Hakim Beg than that of the Confucian Amban.

Keen Lung was engaged in many more wars than those in Central Asia. On the side of Burma he found his borders disturbed by nomad and predatory tribes not less than in the region of Gobi. These clans had long been a source of annoyance and anxiety to the viceroy of Yunnan, but the weakness of the courts of Ava and Pegu, who stood behind these frontagers, had prevented the local grievance becoming a national danger. But the triumph of the remarkable Alompra, who united Pegu and Burma into a single state, and who controlled an army with which he effected many triumphs, showed that this state of things might not always continue, and that the day would come when China might be exposed to a grave peril from this side. The successors

of Alompra inherited his pretensions if not his ability, and
when the Chinese called upon them to keep the borders in
better order or to punish some evil-doers, they sent back a
haughty and unsatisfactory reply. Sembuen, the grandson
of Alompra, was king when Keen Lung ordered, in the year
1768, his generals to invade Burma, and the conduct of the
war was intrusted to an officer in high favor at court, named
Count Alikouen, instead of to Fouta, the hero of the Central
Asian war, who had fallen under the emperor's grave displeasure for what, after all, appears to have been a trifling
offense. The course of the campaign is difficult to follow,
for both the Chinese and the Burmese claim the same battles
as victories, but this will not surprise those who remember
that the Burmese court chroniclers described all the encounters with the English forces in the wars of 1829 and 1853 as
having been victorious. The advance of the Chinese army,
estimated to exceed 200,000 men, from Bhamo to Ava shows
clearly enough the true course of the war, and that the Chinese were able to carry all before them up to the gates of the
capital. Count Alikouen did not display any striking military capacity, but by retaining possession of the country
above Ava for three years he at last compelled the Burmese
to sue for peace on humiliating terms.

In previous chapters the growth of China's relations with
Tibet has been traced, and especially under the Manchu
dynasty. The control established by Kanghi after the retirement of the Jungarian army was maintained by both his
successors, and for fifty years Tibet had that perfect tranquillity which is conveyed by the expression that it had
no history. The young Dalai Lama, who fled to Sining
to escape from Latsan Khan, was restored, and under the
name of Lobsang Kalsang pursued a subservient policy to
China for half a century. In the year 1749 an unpleasant
incident took place through a collision between the Chinese
ambans and the Civil Regent or Gyalpo, who administered
the secular affairs of the Dalai Lama. The former acted in
a high-handed and arbitrary manner, and put the Gyalpo

to death. But in this they went too far, for both the lamas and the people strongly resented it, and revolted against the Chinese, whom they massacred to the last man. For a time it looked as if the matter might have a very serious ending, but Keen Lung contented himself with sending fresh ambans and an escort to Tibet, and enjoining them to abstain from undue interference with the Tibetans. But at the same time that they showed this moderation the Chinese took a very astute measure to render their position stronger than ever. They asserted their right to have the supreme voice in nominating the Gyalpo, and they soon reduced that high official, the Prime Minister of Tibet, to the position of a creature of their own. The policy was both astute and successful. The Tibetans had welcomed the Chinese originally because they saved them from the Eleuth army, and provided a guarantee against a fresh invasion. But the long peace and the destruction of the Eleuth power had led the Tibetans to think less of the advantage of Chinese protection, and to pine for complete independence. The lamas also bitterly resented the assumption by the ambans of all practical authority. How long these feelings could have continued without an open outbreak must remain a matter of opinion; but an unexpected event brought into evidence the unwarlike character of the Tibetans, and showed that their country was exposed to many dangers from which only China's protection could preserve them. In Kanghi's time the danger had come from Ili; in the reign of Keen Lung it came from the side of Nepaul.

As a general rule the mighty chain of the Himalaya has effectually separated the peoples living north and south of it, and the instances in history are rare of any collision between them. Of all such collisions the most important was that which has now to be described as the main cause of the tightening of the hold of China upon Tibet. The mountain kingdom of Nepaul was equally independent of the British and the Mogul Empire of Delhi. It was ruled by three separate kings, until in the year 1769 the Goorkha chief Prithi

them in their hour of need, for the latter when hard pressed also appealed to us for assistance, China has had no difficulty in effectually closing Tibet to Indian trade. China closed all the passes on the Nepaul frontier, and only allowed the quinquennial mission to enter by the Kirong Pass. Among all the military feats of China none is more remarkable or creditable than the overthrow of the Goorkhas, who are among the bravest of Indian races, and who, only twenty years after their crushing defeat by Sund Fo, gave the Anglo-Indian army and one of its best commanders, Sir David Ochterloney, an infinity of trouble in two doubtful and keenly contested campaigns.

Keen Lung's war in Formosa calls for only brief notice; but, in concluding our notice of his many military conquests and campaigns, some description must be given of the great rising in an island which Chinese writers have styled "the natural home of sedition and disaffection." In the year 1786 the islanders rose, slaughtered the Tartar garrisons, and completely subverted the emperor's authority. The revolt was one not on the part of the savage islanders themselves, but of the Chinese colonists, who were goaded into insurrection by the tyranny of the Manchu officials. At first it did not assume serious dimensions, and it seemed as if it would pass over without any general rising, when the orders of the Viceroy of Fuhkien, to which Formosa was dependent until made a separate province a few years ago, fanned the fuel of disaffection to a flame. The popular leader Ling organized the best government he could, and, when Keen Lung offered to negotiate, laid down three conditions as the basis of negotiation. They were that "the mandarin who had ordered the cruel measures of repression should be executed," that "Ling personally should never be required to go to Pekin," and, thirdly, that "the mandarins should abandon their old tyrannical ways." Keen Lung's terms were an unconditional surrender and trust in his clemency, which Ling, with perhaps the Miaotze incident fresh in his mind, refused. At first Keen Lung sent numerous but detached expeditions to reassert his power; but these were attacked in detail, and overwhelmed by Ling. Keen Lung said that "his heart was in suspense both by night and by day as to the issue of the war in Formosa"; but, undismayed by his reverses, the emperor sent 100,000 men under the command of a member of his family to crush the insurrection. Complete success was attained by weight of numbers, and Formosa was restored to its proper position in the empire.

A rising in Szchuen, which may be considered from some of its features the precursor of the Taeping Rebellion, and the first outbreak of the Tungan Mohammedans in the northwest, whom Keen Lung wished to massacre, marked the close of this long reign, which was rendered remarkable by so many military triumphs. The reputation of the Chinese empire was raised to the highest point, and maintained there by the capacity and energy of this ruler. Within its borders the commands of the central government were ungrudgingly obeyed, and beyond them foreign peoples and states respected the rights of a country that had shown itself so well able to exact obedience from its dependents and to preserve the very letter of its rights. The military fame of the Chinese, which had always been great among Asiatics, attained its highest point in consequence of these numerous and rapidly-succeeding campaigns. The evidences of military proficiency, of irresistible determination, and of personal valor not easily surpassed, were too many and too apparent to justify any in ignoring the solid claims of China to rank as the first military country in Asia—a position which, despite the appearance of England and Russia in that continent, she still retains, and which must eventually enable her to exercise a superior voice in the arrangement of its affairs to that of either of her great and at present more powerful and better prepared neighbors.

CHAPTER XIV

THE COMMENCEMENT OF EUROPEAN INTERCOURSE

KEEN LUNG was the first Manchu prince to receive formal embassies from the sovereigns of Europe. Among these the Portuguese were the first in point of time, although they never attained the advantage derivable from that priority; and indeed the important period of their connection with China may be said to have terminated before the Manchus had established their authority. Still, as the tenants of Macao, the oldest European settlement in China, for more than three centuries and a half, their connection with the Chinese government must always possess some features of interest and originality. The Portuguese paid their rent to and carried on all their business with the mandarins at Canton, who lost no opportunity of squeezing large sums out of the foreigners, as they were absolutely in their power. The Portuguese could only pay with good or bad grace the bribes and extra duty demanded as the price of their being allowed to trade at all. The power of China seemed so overwhelming that they never attempted to make any stand against its arbitrary decrees, and the only mode they could think of for getting an alleviation of the hardships inflicted by the Canton authorities was to send costly embassies to the Chinese capital. These, however, failed to produce any tangible result. Their gifts were accepted, and their representatives were accorded a more or less gratifying reception; but there was no mitigation of the severity shown by the local mandarins, and, for all practical purposes, the money expended on these missions was as good as thrown away. The Portuguese succeeded in obtaining an improvement in their lot only by combining their naval forces with those of the Chinese in punishing and checking the raids of the pirates, who infested the estuary of the Canton River known as the Bogue. But they never succeeded in emancipating themselves from that position of inferiority in which the Chinese have always striven to keep all foreigners; and if the battle of European enterprise against Chinese exclusiveness had been carried on and fought by the Portuguese it would have resulted in the discomfiture of Western progress and enlightenment.

The Dutch sent an embassy to Pekin in 1795, but it was treated with such contumely that it does not reflect much credit on those who sent it. The Spaniards never held any relations with the central government, all their business being conducted with the Viceroy of Fuhkien; and the successive massacres of Manila completely excluded them from any good understanding with the Pekin government. With Russia, China's relations have always been different from those with the other powers, and this is explained partly by the fact of neighborship, and partly by Russia seeking only her own ends, and not advantages for the benefit of every other foreign nation.

With France, the relations of China, owing to a great extent to the efforts and influence of the missionaries, had always been marked with considerable sympathy and even cordiality. The French monarchs had from time to time turned their attention to promoting trade with China and the Far East. Henry the Fourth sanctioned a scheme with this object, but it came to nothing; and Colbert only succeeded in obtaining the right for his countrymen to land their goods at Whampoa, the river port of Canton. But French commerce never flourished in China, and a bold but somewhat Quixotic attempt to establish a trade between that country and the French settlements on the Mississippi failed to achieve anything practical. But what the French were unable to attain in the domain of commerce they succeeded in accomplishing in the region of literature. They were the first to devote themselves to the study of the Chinese literature and language, and what we know of the history of

CHINA—11

China down to the last century is exclusively due to their laborious research and painstaking translations of Chinese histories and annals. They made China known to the polite as well as the political world of Europe. Keen Lung himself appreciated and was flattered by these efforts. His poetry, notably his odes on "Tea," and the "Eulogy of Moukden" as the cradle of his race, was translated by Père Amiot, and attracted the attention of Voltaire, who addressed to the emperor an epistolary poem on the requirements and difficulties of Chinese versification. The French thus rendered a material service in making China better known to Europe and Europe better known in China, which, although it may be hard to gauge precisely, entitles them still to rank among those who have opened up China to Europeans. The history of China, down to the eighteenth century at least, could not have been written but for the labors of the French, of Mailla, Du Halde, Amiot, and many others.

There remains only to summarize the relations with the English, who, early in the seventeenth century, and before the Manchus had established their supremacy, possessed factories at Amoy and on the island of Chusan. But their trade, hampered by official exactions, and also by the jealousy of the Portuguese and Dutch, proved a slow growth; and at Canton, which they soon discovered to be the best and most convenient outlet for the state, they were more hampered than anywhere else, chiefly through the hostile representations of the Portuguese, who bribed the mandarins to exclude all other foreigners. The English merchants, like the Portuguese, believed that the only way to obtain a remedy for their grievances was by approaching the imperial court and obtaining an audience with the emperor; but they were wise in not attempting to send delegates of their own. They saw that if an impression was to be created at Pekin the embassador must come fully accredited by the British government, and not merely as the representative of a body of merchants who were suppliants for commercial privileges.

The war with the Goorkhas had made the Chinese authorities acquainted with the fact that the English, who were only humble suitors for trade on the coast, were a great power in India. The knowledge of this fact undoubtedly created a certain amount of curiosity in the mind of Keen Lung, and when he heard that the King of England contemplated sending an embassy to his court he gave every encouragement to the suggestion, and promised it a welcome and honorable reception. Permission was given it to proceed to Pekin, and thus was a commencement made in the long story of diplomatic relations between England and China, which have at length acquired a cordial character. As great importance was attached to this embassy, every care was bestowed on fitting it out in a worthy manner. Colonel Cathcart was selected as the envoy, but died on the eve of his departure, and a successor was found in the person of Lord Macartney, a nobleman of considerable attainments, who had been Governor of Madras two years before. Sir George Staunton, one of the few English sinologues, was appointed secretary, and several interpreters were sought for and obtained, not without difficulty. The presents were many and valuable, chosen with the double object of gratifying the emperor and impressing him with the wealth and magnificence of the English sovereign. In September, 1792—the same month that witnessed the overthrow of the Goorkhas at Nayakot—the embassy sailed from Portsmouth, but it did not reach the Peiho, on which Pekin is inaccurately said to stand, until the following August.

An honorable and exceedingly gratifying reception awaited it. The embassador and his suite, on landing from the man-of-war, were conducted with all ceremony and courtesy up the Peiho to Tientsin, where they received what was called the unusual honor of a military salute. Visits were exchanged with the Viceroy of Pechihli and some of the other high officials, and news came down from Pekin that "the emperor had shown some marks of great satisfaction at the news of the arrival of the English embassador.'' Keen Lung happened to be residing at his summer palace at Jehol beyond the Wall, but he sent peremptory instructions that there was to be no delay in sending the English up to Pekin. Up to this point all had gone well, but the anti-foreign party began to raise obstructions, and, headed by Sund Fo, the conqueror of the Goorkhas, to advise the emperor not to receive the embassador, and to reject all his propositions. Whether to strengthen his case, or because he believed it to be the fact, Sund Fo declared that the English had helped ''the Goorkha robbers,'' and that he had found among them ''men with hats,'' *i.e.*, Europeans, as well as ''men with turbans.'' As Sund Fo was the hero of the day, and also the viceroy of the Canton province, his views carried great weight, and they were also of unfavorable omen for the future of foreign relations. But for this occasion the inquisitiveness of the aged emperor prevailed over the views of the majority in his council and also over popular prejudice. When the embassy had been detained some time at Pekin, and after it looked as if a period of vexatious delay was to herald the discomfiture of the mission, such positive orders were sent by Keen Lung for the embassy to proceed to Jehol that no one dared to disobey him. Lord Macartney proceeded to Jehol with his suite and a Chinese guard of honor, and he accomplished the journey, about one hundred miles, in an English carriage. The details of the journey and reception are given in Sir George Staunton's excellent narrative; but here it may be said that the emperor twice received the British embassador in personal audience in a tent specially erected for the ceremony in the gardens of the palace. The embassy then returned to Pekin, and, as the Gulf of Pechihli was frozen, it was escorted by the land route to Canton. On this journey Lord Macartney and his party suffered considerable inconvenience and annoyance from the spite and animosity of the Chinese inferior officials; but nothing serious occurred to mar what was on the whole a successful mission. Keen Lung is said to have wished to go further, but his official utterance was limited to the reciprocation of "the friendly sentiments of His Britannic Majesty." His advanced age and his abdication already contemplated left him neither the inclination nor the power to go very closely into the question of the policy of cultivating closer relations with the foreign people who asserted their supremacy on the sea and who had already subjugated one great Asiatic empire. But it may at least be said that he did nothing to make the ultimate solution of the question more difficult, and his flattering reception of Lord Macartney's embassy was an important and encouraging precedent for English diplomacy with China.

The events of internal interest in the history of the country during the last twenty years of this reign call for some brief notice, although they relate to comparatively few matters that can be disentangled from the court chronicles and official gazettes of the period. The great floods of the Hoangho and the destruction caused thereby had been a national calamity from the earliest period. Keen Lung, filled with the desire to crown his reign by overcoming it, intrusted the task of dealing with this difficulty to Count Akoui, whose laurels over the Miaotze had raised him to the highest position in public popularity and his sovereign's confidence. Keen Lung issued his personal instructions on the subject in unequivocal language. He said in his edict, "My intention is that this work should be unceasingly carried on, in order to secure for the people a solid advantage both for the present and in the time to come. Share my views, and, in order to accomplish them, forget nothing in the carrying out of your project, which I regard as my own, since I entirely approve of it, and the idea which originated it was mine. For the rest, it is at my own charge, and not at the cost of the province, that I wish all this to be done. Let expenses not be stinted. I take upon myself the consequences, whatever they may be." Akoui threw himself into his great task with energy, and it is said that he succeeded in no small degree in controlling the waters and restricting their ravages. We are ignorant of the details of his work, but it may certainly be said that the Hoangho has done less damage since Akoui carried out his scheme than it had effected before. The question is still unsolved, and probably there is no undertaking in which China would benefit more from the engineering science of Europe than this, if the Chinese government were to seriously devote its attention to a matter that affects many millions of people and some of the most important provinces of the empire.

A great famine about the same period is chiefly remarkable for the persecution it entailed on the Christian missionaries and those among the Chinese themselves professing the foreign religion. The cause of this scarcity was mainly due to the extraordinary growth of the population, which had certainly doubled in fifty years, and which, according to the official censuses, had risen from sixty millions in 1735 to three hundred millions in 1792. Of course the larger part of this increase was due to the expansion of the empire and the consolidation of the Manchu authority. So great was the national suffering that the gratuitous distribution of grain and other supplies at the cost of the state provided but a very partial remedy for the evil, which was aggravated by the peculation of the mandarins, and the evidence of the few European witnesses shows that the horrors of this famine have seldom been surpassed. The famine was laid to the charge of the Christians, and a commission of mandarins drew up a formal indictment of Christianity, which has stood its ground ever since as the text of the argument of the anti-foreign school. It read as follows: "We have examined into the European religion (or the doctrine) of the Lord of Heaven, and although it ought not to be compared with other different sects, which are absolutely wicked, yet, and that is what we lay to its blame, it has had the audacity to introduce itself, to promulgate itself, and to establish itself in secret. No permission has ever been given to the people of this country to embrace it. Nay, the laws have absolutely long forbidden its adoption. And now all these criminals have had the boldness to come, all of a sudden, into our kingdom, to establish their bishops and priests in order to seduce the people! This is why it is necessary to extinguish this religion by degrees and to prevent its multiplying its votaries." The fury of the Chinese, fortunately, soon exhausted itself; and although many Europeans were injured none lost their lives, but several thousand native converts were branded on the face and sent to colonize the Ili valley.

While Lord Macartney was at Pekin it was known that the emperor contemplated abdicating when he had completed the sixtieth year of his reign—the cycle of Chinese chronology —because he did not desire his reign to be of greater length than that of his illustrious grandfather, Kanghi. This date was reached in 1796, when on New Year's day (6th of February) of the Chinese calendar, he publicly abdicated, and assigned the imperial functions to his son, Kiaking. He survived this event three years, and during that period he exercised, like Charles the Fifth of Germany, a controlling influence over his son's administration; and he endeavored to inculcate in him the right principles of sound government. But in China, where those principles have been expressed in the noblest language, their practical application is difficult, because the official classes are underpaid and because the law of self-preservation, as well as custom, compels them to pay themselves at the equal expense of the subjects and the government. Even Keen Lung had been unable to grapple with this difficulty of the Chinese civil service, which is as formidable at the present time as ever. One of the ablest and most honest of Keen Lung's ministers, when questioned on the subject, said that there was no remedy. "It is impossible, the emperor himself cannot do it, the evil is too widespread. He will, no doubt, send to the scene of these disorders mandarins, clothed with all his authority, but they will only commit still greater exactions, and the inferior mandarins, in order to be left undisturbed, will offer them presents. The emperor will be told that all is well, while everything is really wrong, and while the poor people are being oppressed.'' And so the vicious circle has gone on to the present day, with serious injury to the state and the people. When Keen Lung had the chance of bringing matters under his own personal control he did not hesitate to exercise his right and power, and all capital punishments were carried out at the capital only after he had examined into each case. It is declared that he always tempered justice with mercy, and that none but the worst offenders suffered death. Transportation to Ili, which he wished to develop, was his favorite form of punishment.

To the end of his life Keen Lung retained the active habits which had characterized his youth. Much of his official work was carried on at an early hour of the morning, and it surprised many Europeans to find the aged ruler so keen and eager for business at these early conferences. His vigor was attributed by competent observers to the active life and physical exercises common among the Tartars. It will be proper to give a description of the personal appearance of this great prince. A missionary thus described him: ''He is tall and well built. He has a very gracious countenance, but capable at the same time of inspiring respect. If in regard to his subjects he employs a great severity, I believe it is less from the promptings of his character than from the necessity which would otherwise not render him capable of keeping within the bounds of dependence and duty two empires so vast as China and Tartary. Therefore the greatest tremble in his presence. On all the occasions when he has done me the honor to address me it has been with a gracious air that inspired me with the courage to appeal to him in behalf of our religion. . . . He is a truly great prince, doing and seeing everything for himself.'' Keen Lung survived his abdication about three years, dying on the 8th of February, 1799—which also happened to be the Chinese New Year's day.

With the death of Keen Lung the vigor of China reached a term, and just as the progress had been consistent and rapid during the space of 150 years, so now will its downward course be not less marked or swift, until, in the very hour of apparent dissolution, the empire will find safety in the valor and probity of an English officer, Charles George Gordon, and in the ability and resolution of the empress-regents and their two great soldier-statesmen, Li Hung Chang and Tso Tsung Tang.

CHAPTER XV

THE DECLINE OF THE MANCHUS

THE favorable opinion which his father had held of Kia-king does not seem to have been shared by all his ministers. The most prominent of them all, Hokwan, who held to Keen Lung the relation that Wolsey held to Henry the Eighth, soon fell under the displeasure of the new emperor, and was called upon to account for his charge of the finances. The favor and the age of Keen Lung left Hokwan absolutely without control, and the minister turned his opportunities to such account that he amassed a private fortune of eighty million taels, or more than one hundred and twenty-five million dollars. He was indicted for peculation shortly after the death of Keen Lung, and, without friends, he succumbed to the attack of his many enemies incited to attack him by the greed of Kiaking. But the amount of his peculations amply justified his punishment, and Kiaking in signing his death warrant could not be accused of harshness or injustice. The execution of Hokwan restored some of his ill-gotten wealth to the state, and served as a warning to other officials; but as none could hope to enjoy his opportunities, it did not act as a serious deterrent upon the mass of the Chinese civil service. If arraigned, they might have justified their conduct by the example of their sovereign, who, instead of devoting the millions of Hokwan to the necessities of the state, employed them on his own pleasure, and in a lavish palace expenditure.

The Portuguese were the tenants, as has previously been stated, of Macao, for which they paid an annual rent to the Chinese; but the nature of their tenure was not understood in Europe, where Macao was considered a Portuguese possession. During the progress of the great European struggle, the French, as part of one of their latest schemes for regaining their position in the East, conceived the idea of taking possession of Macao; but while they were contemplating the enterprise, an English squadron had accomplished it, and during the year 1802 Macao was garrisoned by an English force. The Treaty of Amiens provided for its restoration to Portugal, and the incident closed, chiefly because the period of occupation was brief, without the Chinese being drawn into the matter, or without the true nature of the Portuguese hold on Macao being explained. The exigencies of war unfortunately compelled the re-occupation of Macao six years later, when the indignation of the Chinese authorities at the violation of their territory fully revealed itself. Peremptory orders were sent to the Canton authorities from Pekin to expel the foreigners at all costs. The government of India was responsible for what was a distinct blunder in our political relations with China. In 1808, when alarm at Napoleon's schemes was at its height, it sent Admiral Drury and a considerable naval force to occupy Macao. The Chinese at once protested, withheld supplies, refused to hold any intercourse with that commander, and threatened the English merchants at Lintin with the complete suspension of the trade. In his letter of rebuke the chief mandarin at Canton declared that, "as long as there remained a single soldier at Macao," he would not allow any trade to be carried on, and threatened to "block up the entrance to Macao, cut off your provisions, and send an army to surround you, when repentance would be too late." The English merchants were in favor of compliance with.

the Chinese demands, but Admiral Drury held a very exalted opinion of his own power and a corresponding contempt for the Chinese. He declared that, as "there was nothing in his instructions to prevent his going to war with the Emperor of China," he would bring the Canton officials to reason by force. He accordingly assembled all his available forces, and proceeded up the river at the head of a strong squadron of boats with the avowed intention of forcing his way up to the provincial capital. On their side the Chinese made every preparation to defend the passage, and they blocked the navigation of the river with a double line of junks, while the Bogue forts were manned by all the troops of the province. When Admiral Drury came in sight of these defenses, which must have appeared formidable to him, he hesitated, and instead of delivering his attack he sent a letter requesting an interview with the mandarin, again threatening to force his way up to Canton. But the Chinese had by this time taken the measure of the English commander, and they did not even condescend to send him a reply; when Admiral Drury, submitting to their insult, hastily beat a retreat. On several subsequent occasions he renewed his threats, and even sailed up the Bogue, but always retreated without firing a shot. It is not surprising that the Chinese were inflated with pride and confidence by the pusillanimous conduct of the English officer, or that they should erect a pagoda at Canton in honor of the defeat of the English fleet. After these inglorious incidents Admiral Drury evacuated Macao and sailed for India, leaving the English merchants to extricate themselves as well as they could from the embarrassing situation in which his hasty and blundering action had placed them. If the officials at Canton had not been as anxious for their own selfish ends that the trade should go on as the foreign merchants themselves, there is no doubt that the views of the ultra school at Pekin, who wished all intercourse with foreigners interdicted, would have prevailed. But the Hoppo and his associates were the real friends of the foreigner, and opened the back door to foreign commerce at the very moment that they were signing edicts denouncing it as a national evil and misfortune.

The Macartney mission had attracted what may be called the official attention of the British government to the Chinese question, and the East India Company, anxious to acquire fresh privileges to render that trade more valuable, exercised all its influence to sustain that attention. On its representations a costly present was sent to Sung Tajin, one of the ablest and most enlightened of all the Chinese officials who had shown cordiality to Lord Macartney, but the step was ill-advised and had unfortunate consequences. The present, on reaching Pekin, was returned to Canton with a haughty message that a minister of the emperor dare not even see a present from a foreign ruler. The publicity of the act rather than the offer of a present must be deemed the true cause of this unqualified rejection, but the return of the present was not, unfortunately, the worst part of the matter. The Emperor Kiaking sent a letter couched in lofty language to George the Third, declaring that he had taken such British subjects as were in China under his protection, and that there was "no occasion for the exertions of your Majesty's Government." The advice of the Minister Sung, who was suspected of sympathy with the foreigners, was much discredited, and from a position of power and influence he gradually sank into one of obscurity and impotence. This was especially unfortunate at a moment when several foreign powers were endeavoring to obtain a footing at Pekin. The Russian emperor, wishing no doubt to emulate the English, sent, in 1805, an imposing embassy under Count Goloyken to the Chinese capital. The presents were rich and numerous, for the express purpose of impressing the Chinese ruler with the superior wealth and power of Russia over other European states, and great hopes were entertained that Count Goloyken would establish a secure diplomatic base at Pekin. The embassy reached Kalgan on the Great Wall in safety, but there it was detained until reference had been made to the capital. The instructions came back that the Russian envoy would only be received in audience provided he would perform the kotow, or prostration ceremony, and that if he would not promise to do this he was not to be allowed through the Wall. Count Goloyken firmly refused to give this promise, and among other arguments he cited the exemption accorded to Lord Macartney. The Chinese remained firm in their purpose, Count Goloyken was informed that his visit had been prolonged too far, and the most brilliant of all Russian embassies to China had to retrace its steps without accomplishing any of its objects. This was not the only rebuff Russia experienced at this time. The naval officer Krusenstern conceived the idea that it would be possible to attain all the objects of his sovereign, and to open up a new channel for a profitable trade, by establishing communications by sea with Canton, where the Russian flag had never been seen. The Russian government fitted out two ships for him, and he safely arrived at Canton, where he disposed of their cargoes. When it became known at Pekin that a new race of foreigners had presented themselves at Canton, a special edict was issued ordering that "all vessels belonging to any other nation than those which have been in the habit of visiting this port shall on no account whatever be permitted to trade, but merely suffered to remain in port until every circumstance is reported to us and our pleasure made known." Thus in its first attempt to add to its possession of a land trade, via Kiachta and the Mongol steppe, a share in the sea trade with Canton, Russia experienced a rude and discouraging rebuff.

The unsatisfactory state of our relations with the Chinese government, which was brought home to the British authorities by the difficulty our ships of war experienced in obtaining water and other necessary supplies on the China coast, which had generally to be obtained by force, led to the decision that another embassy should be sent to Pekin, for the purpose of effecting a better understanding.

Lord Amherst, who was specially selected for the mission on account of his diplomatic experience, reached the mouth of the Peiho in August, 1816. When the embassy reached Pekin, the Emperor Kiaking's curiosity to see the foreigners overcame his political resolutions, and with the natural resolve of an irresponsible despot to gratify his wish without regard to the convenience of others, he determined to see them at once, and ordered that Lord Amherst and his companions should be brought forthwith into his presence. This sudden decision was most disconcerting to his own ministers, who had practically decided that no audience should be granted unless Lord Amherst performed the kotow, and especially to his brother-in-law Ho Koong Yay, who, at the emperor's repeated wish to see the English representatives, was compelled to abandon his own schemes and to remove all restrictions to the audience. The firmness of Lord Amherst was unexpected and misunderstood. Ho Koong Yay repeated his invitation several times, and even resorted to entreaty; but when the Chinese found that nothing was to be gained they changed their tone, and the infuriated Kiaking ordered that the embassador and his suite should not be allowed to remain at Pekin, and that they should be sent back to the coast at once. Thus ignominiously ended the Amherst mission, which was summarily dismissed, and hurried back to the coast in a highly inconvenient and inglorious manner. In a letter to the Prince Regent, Kiaking suggested that it would not be necessary for the British government to send another embassy to China. He took some personal satisfaction out of his disappointment by depriving Ho Koong Yay of all his offices, and mulcting him in five years of his pay as an imperial duke. The cause of his disgrace was expressly stated to be the mismanagement of the relations with the English embassador and the suppression of material facts from the emperor's knowledge. Sung Tajin, who had been specially recalled from his governorship in Ili to take part in the reception of the Europeans, and whose sympathy for them

was well known, was also disgraced, and did not recover
his position until after the death of Kiaking. The failure
of the Amherst mission put an end to all schemes for diplomatic intercourse with Pekin until another generation had
passed away; but the facts of the case show that its failure
was not altogether due to the hostility of the Chinese emperor. No practical results, in all probability, would have
followed; but if Lord Amherst had gone somewhat out of
his way to humor the Chinese autocrat, there is no doubt
that he would have been received in audience without any
humiliating conditions.

Long before the Amherst mission reached China evidence
had been afforded that there were many elements of disorder
in that country, and that a dangerous feeling of dissatisfaction was seething below the surface. The Manchus, even
in their moments of greatest confidence, had always distrusted the loyalty of their Chinese subjects, and there is no
dispute that one of their chief reasons for pursuing an excluding policy toward Europeans was the fear that they might
tamper with the mass of their countrymen. What had been
merely a sentiment under the great rulers of the eighteenth
century became an absolute conviction when Kiaking found
himself the mark of conspirators and assassins. The first
of the plots to which he nearly fell a victim occurred at such
an early period of his reign that it could not be attributed to
popular discontent at his misgovernment. In 1803, only
four years after the death of Keen Lung, Kiaking, while
passing through the streets of his capital in his chair, carried
by coolie bearers, was attacked by a party of conspirators,
members of one of the secret societies, and narrowly escaped
with his life. His eunuch attendants showed considerable
devotion and courage, and in the struggle several were killed;
but they succeeded in driving off the would-be assassins.
The incident caused great excitement, and much consternation in the imperial palace, where it was noted that out of
the crowds in the streets only six persons came forward to
help the sovereign in the moment of danger. After this the

emperor gave up his practice of visiting the outer city of Pekin,' and confined himself to the imperial city, and still more to the Forbidden Palace which is situated within it. But even here he could not enjoy the sense of perfect security, for the discovery was made that this attempted assassination was part of an extensive plot with ramifications into the imperial family itself. Inquisitorial inquiries were made, which resulted in the disgrace and punishment of many of the emperor's relatives, and thus engendered an amount of suspicion and a sense of insecurity that retained unabated force as long as Kiaking filled the throne. That there was ample justification for this apprehension the second attempt on the person of the emperor clearly revealed. Whatever dangers the emperor might be exposed to in the streets of Pekin, where the members of the hated and dreaded secret societies had as free access as himself, it was thought that he could feel safe in the interior of the Forbidden City— a palace-fortress within the Tartar quarter garrisoned by a large force, and to which admission was only permitted to a privileged few. Strict as the regulations were at all times, the attempt on Kiaking and the rumors of sedition led undoubtedly to their being enforced with greater rigor, and it seemed incredible for any attempt to be made on the person of the emperor except by the mutiny of his guards or an open rebellion. Yet it was precisely at this moment that an attack was made on the emperor in his own private apartments which nearly proved successful, and which he himself described as an attack under the elbow. In the year 1813 a band of conspirators, some two hundred in number, made their way into the palace, either by forcing one of the gates, or, more probably, by climbing the walls at an unguarded spot, and, overpowering the few guards they met, some of them forced their way into the presence of the emperor. There is not the least doubt that Kiaking would then have fallen but for the unexpected valor of his son Prince Meenning, afterward the Emperor Taoukwang, who, snatching up a gun, shot two of the intruders. This prince had been set down as a harmless, inoffensive student, but his prompt action on this occasion excited general admiration, and Kiaking, grateful for his life, at once proclaimed him his heir.

Toward the close of his reign, and very soon after the departure of Lord Amherst, Kiaking was brought face to face with a very serious conspiracy, or what he thought to be such, among the princes of the Manchu imperial family. By an ordinance passed by Chuntche all the descendants of that prince's father were declared entitled to wear a yellow girdle and to receive a pension from the state; while, with a view to prevent their becoming a danger to the dynasty, they were excluded from civil or military employment, and assigned to a life of idleness. This imperial colony was, and is still, one of the most peculiar and least understood of the departments of the Tartar government; and although it has served its purpose in preventing dynastic squabbles, there must always remain the doubt as to how far the dynasty has been injured by the loss of the services of so many of its members who might have possessed useful capacity. They purchased the right to an easy and unlaborious existence, with free quarters and a small income guaranteed, at the heavy price of exclusion from the public service. No matter how great their ambition or natural capability, they had no prospect of emancipating themselves from the dull sphere of inaction to which custom relegated them. Toward the close of Kiaking's reign the number of these useless Yellow Girdles had risen to several thousand, and the emperor, alarmed by the previous attacks, or having some reason to fear a fresh plot, adopted strenuous measures against them. Whether the emperor's apprehensions overcame his reason, or whether there were among his kinsmen some men of more than average ability, it is certain that the princes of the Manchu family were goaded or incited into what amounted to rebellion. The exact particulars remain unknown until the dynastic history sees the light of day; but it is known that many of them were executed, and that many hundreds of them were banished to Manchuria, where they were given employment in taking care of the ancestral tombs of the ruling family.

Special significance was given to these intrigues and palace plots by the remarkable increase in the number and the confidence of the secret societies which, in some form or other, have been a feature of Chinese public life from an early period. Had they not furnished evidence by their increased numbers and daring of the dissatisfaction prevalent among the Chinese masses, whether on account of the hardships of their lot, or from hatred of their Tartar lords, they would scarcely have created so much apprehension in the bosom of the Emperor Kiaking, whose authority met with no open opposition, and whose reign was nominally one of both internal and external peace. These secret societies have always been, in the form of fraternal confederacies and associations, a feature in Chinese life; but during the present century they have acquired an importance they could never previously claim, both in China and among Chinese colonies abroad. The first secret society to become famous was that of the Water-Lily, or Pe-leen-keaou, which association chose as its emblem and title the most popular of all plants in China. Although the most famous of the societies, and the one which is regarded as the parent of all that have come after it, the Water-Lily had, as a distinct organization, a very brief existence. Its organizers seem to have dropped the name, or to have allowed it to sink into disuse in consequence of the strenuous official measures taken against the society by the government for the attempt, in 1803, on Kiaking's life in the streets of Pekin. They merged themselves into the widely extended confederacy of the Society of Celestial Reason—the Theen-te-Hwuy—which became better known by the title given to it by Europeans of the Triads, from their advocacy of the union between Heaven, earth, and man. The Water-Lily Society, before it was dissolved, caused serious disturbances in both Shantung and Szchuen, and especially in the latter province,

where the disbanded army that had rescued Tibet and punished the Goorkhas furnished the material for sedition. With
more or less difficulty, and at a certain expense of life, these
risings were suppressed, and Kiaking's authority was rendered secure against these assailants, while for his successors
was left the penalty of feeling the full force of the national
indignation of which their acts were the expression.

With regard to the organization of these secret societies,
which probably remain unchanged to the present day, China
had nothing to learn from Europe either as to the objects to
be obtained in this way or as to how men are to be bound
together by solemn vows for the attainment of illegal ends.
By signs known only to themselves, and by pass-words, these
sworn conspirators could recognize their members in the
crowded streets, and could communicate with each other
without exciting suspicion as to their being traitors at heart.
In its endeavors to cope with this formidable and widespread
organization under different names, Kiaking's government
found itself placed at a serious disadvantage. Without an
exact knowledge of the intentions or resources of its secret
enemies, it failed to grapple with them, and, as its sole remedy, it could only decree that proof of membership carried
with it the penalty of death.

During the last years of the reign of Kiaking the secret
societies rather threatened future trouble than constituted a
positive danger to the state. They were compelled to keep
quiet and to confine their attention to increasing their numbers rather than to realizing their programme. The emperor
was consequently able to pass the last four years of his life
with some degree of personal tranquillity, and in full indulgence of his palace pleasures, which seem at this period to
have mainly consisted of a theatrical troupe which accompanied him even when he went to offer sacrifice in the temples. His excessive devotion to pleasure did not add to his
reputation with his people, and it is recorded that one of the
chief causes of the minister Sung's disgrace and banishment
to Ili was his making a protest against the emperor's pro-

ceedings. Some time before his death, Kiaking drew up his will, and on account of his great virtues he specially selected as his successor his second son, Prince Meenning, who had saved his life from assassins in the attack on the palace. Kiaking died on September 2, 1820, in the sixty-first year of his age, leaving to his successor a diminished authority, an enfeebled power, and a discontented people. Some mitigating circumstance may generally be pleaded against the adverse verdict of history in its estimation of a public character. The difficulties with which the individual had to contend may have been exceptional and unexpected, the measures which he adopted may have had untoward and unnatural results, and the crisis of the hour may have called for genius of a transcendent order. But in the case of Kiaking not one of these extenuating facts can be pleaded. His path had been smoothed for him by his predecessor, his difficulties were raised by his own indifference, and the consequences of his spasmodic and ill-directed energy were scarcely less unfortunate than those of his habitual apathy. So much easier is the work of destruction than the labor of construction, that Kiaking in twenty-five years had done almost as much harm to the constitution of his country and to the fortunes of his dynasty as Keen Lung had conferred solid advantages on the state in his brilliant reign of sixty years.

On the whole it seems as if the material prosperity of the people was never greater than during the reign of Kiaking. The population by the census of 1812 is said to have exceeded 360 millions, and the revenue never showed a more flourishing return on paper. To the external view all was still fair and prosperous when Kiaking died; under his successor, who was in every sense a worthier prince, the canker and decay were to be clearly revealed.

CHAPTER XVI

THE EMPEROR TAOUKWANG

THE early years of the new reign were marked by a number of events unconnected with each other but all contributing to the important incidents of the latter period which must be described, although they cannot be separated. The name of Taoukwang, which Prince Meenning took on ascending the throne, means Reason's Light, and there were many who thought it was especially appropriate for a prince who was more qualified for a college than a palace. Most of the chroniclers of the period give an unfavorable picture of the new ruler, who is described as "thin and toothless," and as "lank in figure, low of stature, with a haggard face, a reserved look, and a quiet exterior." He was superior to his external aspect, for it may be truly said that although he had to deal with new conditions he evinced under critical circumstances a dignity of demeanor and a certain royal patience which entitled him to the respect of his opponents.

Taoukwang began his reign in every way in a creditable manner. While professing in his proclamations the greatest admiration for his father, his first acts reversed his policy and aimed at undoing the mischief he had accomplished. He released all the political prisoners who had been consigned to jail by the suspicious fear of Kiaking, and many of the banished Manchu princes were allowed to return to Pekin. He made many public declarations of his intention to govern his people after a model and conscientious fashion, and his subsequent acts showed that he was at least sincere in his intentions, if an accumulation of troubles prevented his attaining all the objects he set before himself when he first took the government in hand. Nothing showed his integrity more clearly than his restoration of the minister Sung to the favor and offices of which he had been dispossessed. The vicissitudes of fortune passed through by this official have been previously referred to, and his restoration to power was a practical proof of the new ruler's good resolutions, and meant more than all the virtuous platitudes expressed in vermilion edicts. Sung had gained a popularity that far exceeded that of the emperor, through the lavish way in which he distributed his wealth, consistently refusing to accumulate money for the benefit of himself or his family. But his independent spirit rendered him an unpleasant monitor for princes who were either negligent of their duty or sensitive of criticism, and even Taoukwang appears to have dreaded, in anticipation, the impartial and fearless criticism of the minister whom he restored to favor. Sung was employed in two of the highest possible posts, Viceroy of Pechihli and President of the Board of Censors, and until his death he succeeded in maintaining his position in face of his enemies, and notwithstanding his excessive candor. One of the first reforms instituted by the Emperor Taoukwang was to cut down the enormous palace expenses, which his father had allowed to increase to a high point, and to banish from the imperial city all persons who could not give some valid justification for their being allowed to remain. The troupes of actors and buffoons were expelled, and the harem was reduced to modest dimensions. Taoukwang declared himself to be a monogamist, and proclaimed his one wife empress. He also put a stop to the annual visits to Jehol and to the costly hunting establishment there, which entailed a great waste of public funds. The money thus saved was much wanted for various national requirements, and the sufferings caused by flood and famine were alleviated out of these palace savings. How great the national suffering had become was shown by the marked increase of crime, especially all forms of theft and the coining of false money, for which new and severe penalties were ordained without greatly mitigating the evil. During all these troubles and trials Taoukwang endeavored to play the part of a beneficent and merciful sovereign, tempering the severity of the laws by acts of clemency, and personally superintending every department of the administration. He seems thus to have gained a reputation among his subjects which he never lost, and the blame for any unpopular measures was always assigned to his ministers. But although he endeavored to play the part of an autocrat, there is every ground for saying that he failed to realize the character, and that he was swayed more than most rulers by the advice of his ministers. The four principal officials after Sung, whose death occurred at an early date after Taoukwang's accession, were Hengan, Elepoo, Keying and Keshen.

The first ten years of Taoukwang's reign have been termed prosperous, because they have left so little to record, but this application of the theory that "the country is happy which has no history," does not seem borne out by such facts as have come to our knowledge. There is no doubt that there was a great amount of public suffering, and that the prosperity of the nation declined from the high point it had reached under Kiaking. Scarcity of food and want of work increased the growing discontent, which did not require even secret societies to give it point and expression, and as far as could be judged it was worse than when the Water-Lily Society inspired Kiaking with most apprehension. Kiaking, as has been observed, escaped the most serious consequences of his own acts. There was much popular discontent, but there was no open rebellion. Taoukwang had not been on the throne many years before he was brought face to face with rebels who openly disputed his authority, and, strangely enough, his troubles began in Central Asia, where peace had been undisturbed for half a century.

The conquest of Central Asia had been among the most brilliant and remarkable of the feats of the great Keen Lung. Peace had been preserved there as much by the extraordinary prestige or reputation of China as by the skill of the administration or the soundness of the policy of the govern-

ing power, which left a large share of the work to the subject races. Outside each of the principal towns the Chinese
built a fort or gulbagh, in which their garrison resided, and
military officers or ambans were appointed to every district.
The Mohammedan officials were held responsible for the
good conduct of the people and the due collection of the
taxes, and as long as the Chinese garrison was maintained
in strength and efficiency they discharged their duties with
the requisite good faith.   The lapse of time and the embarrassment of the government at home led to the neglect of
the force in Central Asia, which had once been an efficient
army. The Chinese garrison, ill-paid and unrecruited, gradually lost the semblance of a military force, and was not to
be distinguished from the rest of the civil population. The
difference of religion was the only unequivocal mark of distinction between the rulers and the ruled, and it furnished
an ever-present cause of enmity and dislike, although apart
from this the Mohammedans accepted the Chinese rule as
not bad in itself, and even praised it. The Chinese might
have continued to govern Ili and Kashgar indefinitely, notwithstanding the weakness and decay of their garrison, but
for the ambition of a neighbor. The Chinese are to blame,
however, not merely for having ignored the obvious aggres-
siveness of that neighbor, but for having provided it with
facilities for carrying out its plans. The Khanate of Khokand, the next-door state in Central Asia, had been inti-
mately connected with Kashgar from ancient times, both in
politics and trade. The Chinese armies in the eighteenth
century had advanced into Khokand, humbled its khan,
and reduced him to a state of vassalage. For more than
fifty years the khan sent tribute to China, and was the
humble neighbor of the Chinese. He gave, however, a
place of refuge and a pension to Sarimsak, the last representative of the old Khoja family of Kashgar, and thus retained a hold on the legitimate ruler of that state. Sarimsak
had as a child escaped from the pursuit of Fouta and the
massacre of his relations by the chief of Badakshan, but he

was content to remain a pensioner at Khokand to the end of his days, and he left the assertion of what he considered his rights to his children. His three sons were named, in the order of their age, Yusuf, Barhanuddin, and Jehangir, and each of them attempted at different times to dispossess the Chinese in Kashgar. In the year 1812, when Kiaking's weakness was beginning to be apparent, the Khan of Khokand, a chief of more than usual ability, named Mahomed Ali, refused to send tribute any more to China, and the Viceroy of Ili, having no force at his disposal, acquiesced in the change with good grace, and no hostilities ensued. The first concession was soon followed by others. The khan obtained the right to levy a tax on all Mohammedan merchandise sold in the bazaars of Kashgar and Yarkand, and deputed consuls or aksakals for the purpose of collecting the duties. These aksakals naturally became the center of all the intrigue and disaffection prevailing in the state against the Chinese, and they considered it to be as much their duty to provoke political discontent as to supervise the customs placed under their charge. Before the aksakals appeared on the scene the Chinese ruled a peaceful territory, but after the advent of these foreign officials trouble soon ensued.

Ten years after his refusal to pay tribute the Khan of Khokand decided to support the Khoja pretenders who enjoyed his hospitality, and in 1822 Jehangir was provided with money and arms to make an attempt on the Chinese position in Kashgaria. Although the youngest, Jehangir seems to have been the most energetic of the Khoja princes; and having obtained the alliance of the Kirghiz, he attempted, by a rapid movement, to surprise the Chinese in the town of Kashgar. In this attempt he was disappointed, for the Chinese kept better guard than he expected, and he was compelled to make an ignominious retreat. The Khan of Khokand, disappointed at the result and apprehensive of counter action on the part of the Chinese, repudiated all participation in the matter, and forbade Jehangir to return to his country. That adventurer then fled to Lake Issik Kul, whither the Chinese pursued him; but when his fortunes seemed to have reached their lowest ebb a revulsion suddenly took place, and by the surprise and annihilation of a Chinese force he was again able to pose as an arbiter of affairs in Central Asia. The fortitude of Jehangir confirmed the attachment of his friends, and the Khokandian ruler, encouraged by the defeat of the Chinese, again took up his cause and sent him troops and a general for a fresh descent on Kashgaria. The khan had his own ends in view quite as much as to support the Khoja pretender; but his support encouraged Jehangir to leave his mountain retreat and to cross the Tian Shan into Kashgaria. This happened in the year 1826, and the Chinese garrison of Kashgar very unwisely quitted the shelter of its citadel and went out to meet the invaders. The combat is said to have been fiercely contested, but nothing is known about it except that the Chinese were signally defeated. This overthrow was the signal for a general insurrection throughout the country, and the Chinese garrisons, after more or less resistance, were annihilated. An attempt was then made to restore the old Mohammedan administration, and Jehangir was proclaimed by the style of the Seyyid Jehangir Sultan. One of his first acts was to dismiss the Khokandian contingent, and to inform his ally or patron, Mahomed Ali, that he no longer required his assistance. His confidence received a rude check when he learned a short time afterward that the Chinese were making extraordinary preparations to recover their lost province, and that they had collected an immense army in Ili for the purpose. Then he wished his Khokandian allies back again; but he still resolved to make as good a fight as he could for the throne he had acquired; and when the Chinese general Chang marched on Kashgar, Jehangir took up his position at Yangabad and accepted battle. He was totally defeated; the capture of Kashgar followed, and Jehangir himself fell into the hands of the victors. The Khoja was sent to

Pekin, where, after many indignities, he was executed and quartered as a traitor. The Chinese punished all open rebels with death, and as a precaution against the recurrence of rebellion they removed 12,000 Mohammedan families from Kashgar to Ili, where they became known as the Tarantchis, or toilers. They also took the very wise step of prohibiting all intercourse with Khokand, and if they had adhered to this resolution they would have saved themselves much serious trouble. But Mahomed Ali was determined to make an effort to retain so valuable a perquisite as his trade relations with Kashgar, and as soon as the Chinese had withdrawn the main portion of their force he hastened to assail Kashgar at the head of his army, and put forward Yusuf as a successor to Jehangir. Only desultory fighting ensued, but his operations were so far successful that the Chinese agreed to resort to the previous arrangement, and Mahomed Ali promised to restrain the Khojas. Fourteen years of peace and prosperity followed this new convention.

Serious disorders also broke out in the islands of Formosa and Hainan. In the former the rebellion was only put down by a judicious manipulation of the divisions of the insurgent tribes; but the settlement attained must be pronounced so far satisfactory that the peace of the island was assured. In Hainan, an island of extraordinary fertility and natural wealth, which must some day be developed, the aboriginal tribes revolted against Chinese authority, and massacred many of the Chinese settlers, who had begun to encroach on the possessions of the natives. Troops had to be sent from Canton before the disorders were suppressed, and then Hainan reverted to its tranquil state, from which only the threat of a French occupation during the Tonquin war roused it. These disorders in different parts of the empire were matched by troubles of a more domestic character within the palace. In 1831 Taoukwang's only son, a young man of twenty, whose character was not of the best, gave him some cause of offense, and he struck him. The young prince died of the blow, and the emperor was left for the moment without a child. His grief was soon assuaged by the news that two of his favorite concubines had borne him sons, one of whom became long afterward the Emperor Hienfung. At this critical moment Taoukwang was seized with a severe illness, and his elder brother, Hwuy Wang, whose pretensions had threatened the succession, thinking his chance had at last come, took steps to seize the throne. But Taoukwang recovered, and those who had made premature arrangements in filling the throne were severely punished. These minor troubles culminated in the Miaotze Rebellion, the most formidable internal war which the Chinese government had to deal with between that of Wou Sankwei and the Taepings. From an early period the Miaotze had been a source of trouble to the executive, and the relations between them and the officials had been anything but harmonious. The Manchu rulers had only succeeded in keeping them in order by stopping their supply of salt on the smallest provocation; and in the belief that they possessed an absolutely certain mode of coercing them, the Chinese mandarins assumed an arrogant and dictatorial tone toward their rude and unreclaimed neighbors. In 1832 the Miaotze, irritated past endurance, broke out in rebellion, and their principal chief caused himself to be proclaimed emperor. Their main force was assembled at Lienchow, in the northwest corner of the Canton province, and their leader assumed the suggestive title of the Golden Dragon, and called upon the Chinese people to redress their wrongs by joining his standard. But the Chinese, who regarded the Miaotze as an inferior and barbarian race, refused to combine with them against the most extortionate of officials or the most unpopular of governments. Although they could not enlist the support of any section of the Chinese people, the Miaotze, by their valor and the military skill of their leader, made so good a stand against the forces sent against them by the Canton viceroy that the whole episode is redeemed from oblivion, and may be considered a romantic incident in modern

Chinese history. The Miaotze gained the first successes of the war, and for a time it seemed as if the Chinese authorities would be able to effect nothing against them. The Canton viceroy fared so badly that Hengan was sent from Pekin to take the command, and the chosen braves of Hoonan were sent to attack the Miaotze in the rear. The latter gained a decisive victory at Pingtseuen, where the Golden Dragon and several thousand of his followers were slain. But, although vanquished in one quarter, the Miaotze continued to show great activity and confidence in another, and when the Canton viceroy made a fresh attack on them they repulsed him with heavy loss. The disgrace of this officer followed, and his fall was hastened by the suppression of the full extent of his losses, which excited the indignation of his own troops, who said, "There is no use in our sacrificing our lives in secret; if our toils are concealed from the emperor neither we nor our posterity will be rewarded." This unlucky commander was banished to Central Asia, and after his supersession Hengan had the satisfaction of bringing the war to a satisfactory end within ten days. Some of the leaders were executed, the others swore to keep the peace, and a glowing account of the pacification of the Miaotze region was sent to Pekin. Some severe critics suggested that the whole arrangement was a farce, and that Hengan's triumph was only on paper; but the lapse of time has shown this skepticism to be unjustified, as the Miaotze have remained tranquil ever since, and the formidable Yaoujin, or Wolfmen, as they are called, have observed the promises given to Hengan, which would not have been the case unless they had been enforced by military success. Should they ever break out again, the government would possess the means, from their command of money and modern arms, of repressing their lawlessness with unprecedented thoroughness, and of absolutely subjecting their hitherto inaccessible districts.

If the first ten or twelve years of the reign of the Emperor Taoukwang were marked by these troubles on a minor scale, an undue importance should not be attached to them, for they did not seriously affect the stability of the government or the authority of the emperor. It is true that they caused a decline in the revenue and an increase in the expenditure, which resulted in the year 1834 in an admitted deficit of fifty million dollars, and no state could be considered as flourishing with the public exchequer in such a condition. But this large deficit must be regarded rather as a floating debt than an annual occurrence.

The Chinese authorities continued to hinder and protest against the foreign trade and intercourse between their subjects and the merchants of Europe as much as ever; but their opposition was mainly confined to edicts and proclamations. When Commissioner Lin resorted to force and violence some years later the auspicious moment for expelling all foreigners had passed away, and the weakness of the government contributed in no small degree to this result. Taoukwang, although his claims as occupant of the Dragon Throne were unabated, could not pretend to the power of a great ruler like Keen Lung, who would have known how to enforce his will. Nor was it possible after 1834 to continue the policy of uncompromising hostility to all foreign nations whose governments had become directly interested in, and to a certain extent responsible to, their respective peoples, for the opening of the Chinese empire to civilized intercourse and commerce. Up to this point Taoukwang's only experience of the pretensions of the foreign powers had been the Amherst mission, in the time of his father, which had ended so ignominiously, and the Russian mission which arrived at Pekin every ten years to recruit the Russian college there, and to pay the descendants of the garrison of Albazin the sum allotted by the Czar for their support. But from these trifling matters Taoukwang's attention was suddenly and completely distracted to the important situation at Canton and on the coast, the settlement of the questions arising out of which filled the remainder of his reign.

CHAPTER XVII

THE FIRST FOREIGN WAR

AT the very time that the Emperor Taoukwang, by the dismissal of the Portuguese astronomers at Pekin and by his general indifference to the foreign question, was showing that no concessions were to be expected from him, an unknown legislature at a remote distance from his capital was decreeing, in complete indifference to the susceptibilities of the occupant of the Dragon Throne, that trade with China might be pursued by any English subject. Up to the year 1834 trade with China had, by the royal charter, remained the monopoly of the East India Company; but when the charter was renewed in that year for a further period of twenty years, it was shorn of the last of its commercial privileges, and an immediate change became perceptible in the situation at Canton, which was the principal seat of the foreign trade. The withdrawal of the monopoly was dictated solely by English, and not Chinese, considerations. Far from facilitating trade with the Chinese, it tended to hinder and prevent its developing; for the Chinese officials had no objection to foreigners coming to Canton, and buying or selling articles of commerce, so long as they derived personal profit from the trade, and so long as the laws of the empire were not disputed or violated. The servants of the East India Company were content to adapt themselves to this view, and they might have carried on relations with the Hong merchants for an indefinite period, and without any more serious collision than occasional interruptions. Had the monopoly been renewed things would have been left in precisely the same position as when intercourse was first established, and trade might have continued within its old restricted limits. But the abolition of the monopoly and the opening of the trade created quite a new situation, and, by intensifying the opposition of the Chinese government, paved the way to the only practicable solution of the question of foreign intercourse with China, which was that, however reluctantly, she should consent to take her place in the family of nations.

The Chinese were not left long in doubt as to the significance of this change. In December, 1833, a royal commission was issued appointing Lord Napier chief superintendent of trade with China, and two assistants under him, of whom one was Sir John Davis. The Chinese had to some extent contributed to this appointment, the Hoppo at Canton having written that "in case of the dissolution of the Company it was incumbent on the British government to appoint a chief to come to Canton for the general management of commercial dealings, and to prevent affairs from going to confusion." But in this message the Hoppo seems to have expressed his own view rather than that of the Pekin government or the Canton viceroy; and certainly none of the Chinese were prepared to find substituted for "a chief of commercial dealings" an important commissioner clothed with all the authority of the British ruler. How very different was the idea formed of this functionary by the Chinese and English may be gathered from their official views of his work. What the Chinese thought has been told in the words of the Hoppo. Lord Palmerston was more precise from his point of view. His instruction to Lord Napier read, "Your lordship will announce your arrival at Canton by letter to the viceroy. In addition to the duty of protecting and fostering the trade at Canton, it will be one of your principal objects to ascertain whether it may not be practicable to extend that trade to other parts of the Chinese dominions. It is obvious that, with a view to the attainment of this object, the establishment of direct communication with the imperial court at Pekin would be most desirable." The two points of radical disagreement between these views were that the Chinese wished to deal with an official who thought exclusively of trade, whereas Lord Napier's task was not less diplomatic than commercial; and, secondly, that they expected him to carry on his business with the Hoppo, as the Company's agents had done, while Lord Napier was specially instructed to communicate with the viceroy, whom those agents had never dared to approach.

If it was thought that the Chinese would not realize all the significance of the change, those who held so slight an opinion of their clear-headedness were quickly undeceived. Lord Napier reached the Canton River in July, 1834, and he at once addressed a letter of courtesy to the viceroy announcing his arrival. The Chinese officers, after perusing it, refused to forward it to the viceroy, and returned it to Lord Napier. Such was the inauspicious commencement of the assumption of responsibility by the crown in China. The Chinese refused to have anything to do with Lord Napier, whom they described as "a barbarian eye," and they threatened the merchants with the immediate suspension of the trade. The viceroy issued an order forbidding the new superintendent to proceed to Canton, and commanding him to stay at Macao until he had applied in the prescribed form for permission to proceed up the river. But Lord Napier did not listen to these representations, nor did he condescend to delay his progress a moment at Macao. He proceeded up the river to Canton, but, although he succeeded in making his way to the English factory, it was only to find himself isolated, and that, in accordance with the viceroy's order, the Hoppo had interdicted all intercourse with the English. The Chinese declared that the national dignity was at stake, and so thoroughly did both officials and merchants harmonize that the English factory was at once deserted by all Chinese subjects, and even the servants left their employment. On his arrival at Canton, Lord Napier found himself confronted with the position that the Chinese authorities refused to have anything to do with him, and that his presence effectually debarred his countrymen from carrying on the trade, which it was his first duty to promote. At this conjuncture it happened that the Chinese had discovered what they thought to be a new grievance against the foreign traders in the steady efflux of silver as the natural consequence of the balance of trade being against China. In a report to the throne in 1833 it was stated that as much as 60,000,000 taels of silver, or $100,000,000, had been exported from China in the previous eleven years, and, as the Chinese of course made no allowance for the equivalent value imported into their country, this total seemed in their eyes an incredibly large sum to be lost from the national treasure. It will be easily understood that at this particular moment the foreign trade appeared to possess few advantages, and found few patrons among the Chinese people.

In meeting this opposition Lord Napier endeavored to combine courtesy and firmness. He wrote courteous and argumentative letters to the mandarins, combating their views, and insisting on his rights as a diplomatist to be received by the officials of the empire; and at the same time he issued a notice to the Chinese merchants which was full of threats and defiance. "The merchants of Great Britain," he said, "wish to trade with all China on principles of mutual benefit; they will never relax in their exertions till they gain a point of equal importance to both countries, and the viceroy will find it as easy to stop the current of the Canton River as to carry into effect the insane determinations of the Hong." This notice was naturally enough interpreted as a defiance by the viceroy, who placed the most severe restrictions he could on the trade, sent his troops into the foreign settlements to remove all Chinese servants, and ordered the Bogue forts to fire on any English ship that attempted to pass. The English merchants, alarmed at the situation, petitioned Lord Napier to allay the storm he had raised by retiring from Canton to Macao, and, harassed in mind and enfeebled in body, Lord Napier acquiesced in an arrangement that stultified all his former proceedings. The Chinese were naturally intoxicated by their triumph, which vindicated their principle that no English merchant or emissary should be allowed to come to Canton except by the viceroy's permit, granted only to the petition and on the guarantee of the Hong merchants. The viceroy had also carried his point of holding no intercourse with the English envoy, to whom he had written that "the great ministers of the Celestial Empire, unless with regard to affairs of going to court and carrying tribute, or in consequence of imperial commands, are not permitted to have interviews with outside barbarians." While the Chinese officials had been both consistent and successful, the new English superintendent of trade had been both inconsistent and discomfited. He had attempted to carry matters with a high hand and to coerce the mandarins, and he was compelled to show in the most public manner that he had failed by his retirement to Macao. He had even imperiled the continuance of the trade which he had come specially to promote, and all he could do to show his indignation was to make a futile protest against "this act of unprecedented tyranny and injustice." Very soon after Lord Napier's return to Macao he died, leaving to other hands the settlement of the difficult affair which neither his acts nor his language had simplified.

On Lord Napier's departure from Canton the restrictions placed on trade were removed, and the intercourse between the English and Chinese merchants of the Hong was resumed. But even then the mandarins refused to recognize the trade superintendents, and after a short time they issued certain regulations which had been specially submitted to and approved by the Emperor Taoukwang as the basis on which trade was to be conducted. These Regulations, eight in number, forbade foreign men-of-war to enter the inner seas, and enforced the old practice that all requests on the part of Europeans should be addressed through the Hong in the form of a petition. It therefore looked as if the Chinese had completely triumphed in carrying out their views, that the transfer of authority from the East India Company to the British crown, with the so-called opening of the trade, had effected no change in the situation, and that such commerce as was carried on should be as the Chinese dictated, and in accordance with their main idea, which was to "prevent the English establishing themselves permanently at Canton." The death of the Viceroy Loo and the familiarity resulting from increased intercourse resulted in some relaxation of these severe regulations, and at last, in March, 1837, nearly three years after Lord Napier's arrival in the Bogue, the new superintendent of trade, Captain Elliot, received, at his own request, permission through the Hong to proceed to Canton. The emperor passed a special edict authorizing Captain Elliot to reside in the factory at Canton, where he was to "control the merchants and seamen"; but it was also stipulated that he was to strictly abide by the old regulations, and not to rank above a supercargo. As Captain Elliot was the representative of a government not less proud or exacting than that of China, it was clear that these conditions could not be permanently enforced; and although he endeavored for a period to conciliate the Chinese and to obtain more favorable terms by concessions, there came a time when it was impossible to assent to the arrogant demands of the mandarins, and when resort became necessary to the *ultima ratio regum.* But for the first two critical years Captain Elliot pursued the same policy as Lord Napier, alternating concessions with threats, and, while vaunting the majesty of his sovereign, yielding to demands which were unreasonable and not to be endured.

The balance of trade against China was the principal cause of the export of silver, and the balance of trade was only against China through the increasing import of opium. Without acquiescing in the least with the strong allegations of the anti opium party, there is no reason to doubt that the excessive use of opium, especially in a crowded city like Canton, was attended with sufficient mischief to justify its official denunciation. The Pekin government may be so far credited with the honest intention to reduce the mischief and to prevent a bad habit from becoming more and more of a national vice, when they determined for far other reasons to place it in the front of their tirade against foreign trade generally. They soon found that it would be more convenient and more plausible to substitute the moral opposition to the opium traffic for the political disinclination to foreign intercourse in any form. They scarcely expected that in this project they would receive the assistance and co-operation of many of the Europeans themselves, who shared with them the opinion that opium was detestable, and its use or sale a mark of depravity.

In January, 1839, Taoukwang ordered Lin Tsihseu, viceroy of the double province of Houkwang and an official of high reputation, to proceed to Canton as Special Commissioner to report on the situation, and to propound the best remedy for the opium evil. At this moment the anti-opium party was supreme in the imperial council, and three Manchu princes were disgraced and banished from Pekin for indulging in the practice. The peremptory instructions given to Commissioner Lin, as he is historically known, were "to cut off the fountain of evil, and, if necessary for the attainment of his object, to sink his ships and break his caldrons, for the indignation of the great emperor has been fairly aroused at these wicked practices—of buying and selling and using opium—and that the hourly thought of his heart is to do away with them forever."

Before Lin reached Canton there had been frequent friction between Captain Elliot and the local mandarins, and more than one interruption of the trade. Less than six months after his installation at Canton his official relations were broken off, and he wrote home to his government a dispatch complaining of the difficulty of conducting any sort of amicable relations with the local mandarins, and indorsing the growing demand for the right of dealing direct with the Pekin government. Captain Elliot, acting under instructions from home, issued a public notice warning all English subjects to discontinue the illicit opium trade, and stating that "her Majesty's Government would not in any way interfere if the Chinese Government should think fit to seize and confiscate the same.''

At this juncture Commissioner Lin, whose fervor and energy carried him away, appeared upon the scene, and, whereas a less capable or honest man would have come to an arrangement with Captain Elliot, his very ability and enthusiasm tended to complicate the situation and render a pacific solution unattainable. Commissioner Lin, on taking up his post, lost no time in showing that he was terribly in earnest; but both his language and his acts proved that he had a very much larger programme than was included in his propaganda against the opium traffic. He wished to achieve the complete humiliation of the foreigners, and nothing less would satisfy him. Within a week of his arrival at Canton he issued an edict denouncing the opium trade; throwing all the blame for it on the English, and asserting what was absolutely untrue; viz., that "the laws of England prohibited the smoking of opium, and adjudged the user to death." The language of the edict was unfriendly and offensive. The Europeans were stigmatized as a barbarous people, who thought only of trade and of making their way by stealth into the Flowery Land. At the same time that he issued this edict he gave peremptory orders that no foreigner was to leave Canton or Macao until the opium question had been settled to his satisfaction. Even then English merchants and officials, who felt no great sympathy with the opium traffic, saw that these proceedings indicated an intention to put down the trade in other articles, and to render the position of foreigners untenable. Lin's demands culminated in the request for all stores of opium to be surrendered to him within three days. By the efforts of some of the merchants about a thousand chests were collected and handed over to the Chinese for destruction; but this did not satisfy Lin, who collected a large rabble force, encamped it outside the settlement, and threatened to carry the place by storm. In this crisis Captain Elliot, who had declared that his confidence in the justice and good faith of the provincial government was destroyed, and who had even drawn up a scheme for concentrating all his forces at Hongkong, called upon all the English merchants to surrender to him, for paramount considerations of the lives and property of every one concerned, all the stores of opium in their possession. More than 20,000 chests, of an estimated value of $10,000,000, were placed at his disposal, and in due course handed over by him to Commissioner Lin for destruction. This task was performed at Chuenpee, when the opium was placed in trenches, then mixed with salt and lime, and finally poured off into the sea. After this very considerable triumph, Lin wrote a letter to Queen Victoria—whose reign witnessed the most critical periods of the China question and its satisfactory settlement—calling upon her Majesty to interdict the trade in opium forever. The letter was as offensive in its tone as it was weak in argument, and no answer was vouchsafed to it. Before any reply could be given, the situation, moreover, had developed into one of open hostilities.

But great as were the concessions made by Captain Elliot, in consequence of the threatening attitude of Commissioner Lin, the Chinese were not satisfied, and made fresh and more exacting demands of those who had been weak enough to make any concession at all. They reasserted their old pretension that Europeans in China must be subject to her laws, and as the sale of opium was a penal offense they claimed the right to punish those Englishmen who had been connected with the traffic. They accordingly drew up a list of sixteen of the principal merchants, some of whom had never had anything to do with opium, and they announced their intention to arrest them and to punish them with death. Not only did Commissioner Lin and the Canton authorities claim the right to condemn and punish British subjects, but they showed in the most insolent manner that they would take away their liberty and lives on the flimsiest and falsest pretext. Captain Elliot, weak and yielding as he was on many points, declared that "this law is incompatible with safe or honorable continuance at Canton." Apparently the

Chinese authorities acted on the assumption that so long as there remained even one offending European the mass of his countrymen ought to be hindered in their avocations, and consequently petty restrictions and provocations continued to be enforced. Then Captain Elliot, seeing that the situation was hopeless and that there was no sign of improvement, took the bold, or at least the pronounced, step of ordering all British subjects to leave Canton or to stay at their own peril. It was on this occasion that he explained away, or put a new interpretation on, his action with regard to the opium surrendered for destruction, which most of the merchants thought represented an irrecoverable loss. It will be best to give the precise words used in his notice of the 22d of May, 1839. "Acting on behalf of her Majesty's Government in a momentous emergency, he has, in the first place, to signify that the demand he recently made to her Majesty's subjects for the surrender of British-owned opium under their control had no special reference to the circumstances of that property; but (beyond the actual pressure of necessity) that demand was founded on the principle that these violent compulsory measures being utterly unjust *per se* and of general application for the enforced surrender of any other property, or of human life, or for the constraint of any unsuitable terms or concessions, it became highly necessary to vest and leave the right of exacting effectual security and full indemnity for every loss directly in the queen." Unfortunately, Captain Elliot's language at the time of the surrender of the opium had undoubtedly led to the conclusion that he sympathized with Commissioner Lin, and that he took the same view as the Chinese officials of the moral iniquity of selling or using opium. The whole mercantile community adopted Captain Elliot's counsel, and the English factory at Canton, which had existed for nearly two hundred years, was abandoned. At the same time a memorial was sent home begging the government to protect the English merchants in China against "a capricious and corrupt government," and demanding compensation for the

$10,000,000 worth of opium destroyed by Commissioner Lin. Pending the reply of the home government to that appeal, nothing could be more complete than the triumph of Commissioner Lin. The Emperor Taoukwang rewarded him with the important viceroyship of the Two Kiang, the seat of which administration is at Nankin.

But the limit of endurance had been reached, and the British Government was on the point of taking decisive action at the very moment when the Chinese triumph seemed most complete and unthreatened. Even before the action of the home authorities was known in the Bogue the situation had become critical, and the sailors in particular had thrown off all restraint. Frequent collisions occurred between them and the foreigners, and in one of them a Chinaman was killed. Commissioner Lin characterized this act as "going to the extreme of disobedience to the laws," and demanded the surrender of the sailor who committed the act, so that a life might be given for a life. This demand was flatly refused, and in consequence of the measures taken by the Chinese at Lin's direction to prevent all supplies reaching the English, Captain Elliot felt bound to remove his residence from Macao to Hongkong. The Chinese called out all their armed forces, and incited their people along the Canton River to attack the foreigners wherever found. An official notice said, "Produce arms and weapons; join together the stoutest of your villagers, and thus be prepared to defend yourselves. If any of the said foreigners be found going on shore to cause trouble, all and every of the people are permitted to fire upon them, to withstand and drive them back, or to make prisoners of them." This appeal to a force which the Chinese did not possess was an act of indiscretion that betrayed an overweening confidence or a singular depth of ignorance. When the mandarins refused to supply the ships with water and other necessaries they carried their animosity to a length which the English naval officers at once defined as a declaration of open hostilities. They retaliated by ordering their men to seize by force whatever was necessary, and thus began a state of things which may be termed one of absolute warfare. The two men-of-war on the station had several encounters with the forts in the Bogue, and on November 3, 1839, they fought a regular engagement with a Chinese fleet of twenty-nine junks off Chuenpee. The Chinese showed more courage than skill, and four of their junks were sunk. It is worth noting that the English sailors pronounced both their guns and their powder to be excellent. While this action deterred the Chinese fleet from coming to close quarters, it also imbittered the contest, and there was no longer room to doubt that if the Chinese were to be brought to take a more reasonable view of foreign trade it would have to be by the disagreeable lesson of force. And at the end of 1839 the Chinese were fully convinced that they had the power to carry out their will and to keep the European nations out of their country by the strong hand.

A short time after the action at Chuenpee an Englishman named Mr. Gribble was seized by the Canton officials and thrown into prison. The English men-of-war went up the river as far as the Bogue forts, which they threatened to bombard unless he was released; and, after considerable discussion, Mr. Gribble was set free, mainly because the Chinese heard of the large force that was on its way from England. Before that armament arrived, the Emperor Taoukwang had committed himself still further to a policy of hostility. A report of the fight at Chuenpee was duly submitted to him, but the affair was represented as a very creditable one for his commander, and as a Chinese victory. The misled monarch at once conferred a high honor on his admiral, and commanded his officers at Canton "to at once put a stop to the trade of the English nation." This had, practically speaking, been already accomplished, and the English merchants had taken refuge at Macao or in their ships anchored at Hongkong.

Before describing the military operations now about to take place, a survey may conveniently be taken of events since the abolition of the monopoly, and it may be pardonable to employ the language formerly used. From an impartial review of the facts, and divesting our minds, so far as is humanly possible, of the prejudice of accepted political opinions, and of conviction as to the hurtful or innocent character of opium in the mixture as smoked by the Chinese, it cannot be contended that the course pursued by Lord Napier and Captain Elliot, and particularly by the latter, was either prudent in itself or calculated to promote the advantage and reputation of England. Captain Elliot's proceedings were marked by the inconsistency that springs from ignorance. The more influential English merchants, touched by the appeal to their moral sentiment, or impressed by the depravity of large classes of the Canton population, of which the practice of opium-smoking was rather the mark than the cause, set their faces against the traffic in this article, and repudiated all sympathy and participation in it. The various foreign publications, whether they received their inspirations from Mr. Gutzlaff or not matters little, differed on most points, but were agreed on this, that the trade in opium was morally indefensible, and that we were bound, not only by our own interests, but in virtue of the common obligations of humanity, to cease to hold all connection with it. Those who had surrendered their stores of opium at the request of Captain Elliot held that their claim for compensation was valid, in the first place, against the English Government alone. They had given them up for the service of the country at the request of the queen's representative, and, considering the line which Captain Elliot had taken, many believed that it would be quite impossible for the English Government to put forward any demand upon the government of China. The ten million dollars, according to these large-hearted and unreflecting moralists, would have to be sacrificed by the people of England in the cause of humanity, to which they had given so much by emancipating the slaves, and the revenue of India should, for the future, be poorer by the amount that used to pay the dividend of the great Company! The Chinese authorities could not help being encouraged in their opinions and course of proceeding by the attitude of the English. Their most sweeping denunciations of the iniquity of the opium traffic elicited a murmur of approval from the most influential among the foreigners. No Europeans stood up to say that their allegations as to the evil of using opium were baseless and absurd. What is more, no one thought it. Had the Chinese made sufficient use of this identity of views, and shown a desire to facilitate trade in the so-called innocent and legitimate articles, there is little doubt that the opium traffic would have been reduced to very small dimensions, because there would have been no rupture. But the action of Commissioner Lin revealed the truth that the Chinese were not to be satisfied with a single triumph. The more easily they obtained their objects in the opium matter the more anxious did they become to impress the foreigners with a sense of their inferiority, and to force them to accept the most onerous and unjust conditions for the sake of a continuance of the trade. None the less, Captain Elliot went out of his way to tie his own hands, and to bind his own government, so far as he could, to co-operate with the emperor's officials in the suppression of the opium traffic. That this is no random assertion may be judged from the following official notice, issued several months after the surrender of the stores of opium. In this Captain Elliot announced that "Her Majesty's flag does not fly in the protection of a traffic declared illegal by the emperor, and, therefore, whenever a vessel is suspected of having opium on board Captain Elliot will take care that the officers of his establishment shall accompany the Chinese officers in their search, and that if, after strict investigation, opium shall be found, he will offer no objection to the seizure and confiscation of the cargo."

The British expedition arrived at the mouth of the Canton River in the month of June, 1840. It consisted of 4,000 troops on board twenty-five transports, with a convoy of fifteen men-of-war. If it was thought that this considerable force would attain its objects without fighting and merely by making a demonstration, the expectation was rudely disappointed. The reply of Commissioner Lin was to place a reward on the person of all Englishmen, and to offer $20,000 for the destruction of an English man-of-war. The English fleet replied to this hostile step by instituting a close blockade at the mouth of the river, which was not an ineffectual retort. Sir Gordon Bremer, the commander of the first part of the expedition, came promptly to the decision that it would be well to extend the sphere of his operations, and he accordingly sailed northward with a portion of his force to occupy the island of Chusan, which had witnessed some of the earliest operations of the East India Company two centuries before. The capture of Chusan presented no difficulties to a well-equipped force, yet the fidelity of its garrison and inhabitants calls for notice as a striking instance of patriotism. The officials at Tinghai, the capital of Chusan, refused to surrender, as their duty to their emperor would not admit of their giving up one of his possessions. It was their duty to fight, and although they admitted resistance to be useless, they refused to yield, save to force. The English commander reluctantly ordered a bombardment, and after a few hours the Chinese defenses were demolished, and Tinghai was occupied. Chusan remained in our possession as a base of operations during the greater part of the war, but its insalubrity rather dissipated the reputation it had acquired as an advantageous and well-placed station for operations on the coast of China. Almost at the same time as the attack on Chusan, hostilities were recommenced against the Chinese on the Canton River, in consequence of the carrying off of a British subject, Mr. Vincent Stanton, from Macao. The barrier forts were attacked by two English men-of-war and two smaller vessels. After a heavy bombardment, a force of marines and blue-jackets was landed, and the Chinese positions carried. The forts and barracks were destroyed, and Mr. Stanton released. Then it was said that "China must either bend or break," for the hour of English forbearance had passed away, and unless China could vindicate her policy by force of arms there was no longer any doubt that she would have to give way.

While these preliminary military events were occurring, the diplomatic side of the question was also in evidence. Lord Palmerston had written a letter stating in categorical language what he expected at the hands of the Chinese government, and he had directed that it should be delivered into nobody else's hands but the responsible ministers of the Emperor Taoukwang. The primary task of the English expedition was to give this dispatch to some high Chinese official who seemed competent to convey it to Pekin. This task proved one of unexpected difficulty, for the mandarins, basing their refusal on the strict letter of their duty, which forbade them to hold any intercourse with foreigners, returned the document, and declared that they could not receive it. This happened at Amoy and again at Ningpo, and the occupation of Chusan did not bring our authorities any nearer to realizing their mission. Baffled in these attempts, the fleet sailed north for the mouth of the Peiho, when at last Lord Palmerston's letter was accepted by Keshen, the viceroy of the province, and duly forwarded by him to Pekin. The arrival of the English fleet awoke the Chinese court for the time being from its indifference, and Taoukwang not merely ordered that the fleet should be provided with all the supplies it needed, but appointed Keshen High Commissioner for the conclusion of an amicable arrangement. The difficulty thus seemed in a fair way toward settlement, but as a matter of fact it was only at its commencement, for the wiles of Chinese diplomacy are infinite and were then only partially understood. Keshen was remarkable for his astuteness and for the yielding exterior which covered a purpose of iron, and in the English political officer, the Captain Elliot of Canton, he did not find an opponent worthy of his steel. Although experience had shown how great were the delays of negotiation at Canton, and how inaccessible were the local officials, Captain Elliot allowed himself to be persuaded that the best place to carry on negotiations was at that city, and after a brief delay the fleet was withdrawn from the Peiho and all the advantages of the alarm created by its presence at Pekin were surrendered. Relieved by the departure of the foreign ships, Taoukwang sent orders for the dispatch of forces from the inland provinces, so that he might be able to resume the struggle with the English under more favorable conditions, and at the same time he hastened to relieve his overcharged feelings by punishing the man whom he regarded as responsible for his misfortunes and humiliation. The full weight of the imperial wrath fell on Commissioner Lin, who from the position of the foremost official in China fell at a stroke of the vermilion pencil to a public criminal arraigned before the Board of Punishments to receive his deserts. He was stripped of all his offices, and ordered to proceed to Pekin, where, however, his life was spared.

Keshen arrived at Canton on November 29, 1840, but his dispatch .to the emperor explaining the position he found there shows that his view of the situation did not differ materially from that of Lin. "Night and day I have considered and examined the state of our relations with the English. At first, moved by the benevolence of his Majesty and the severity of the laws, they surrendered the opium. Commissioner Lin commanded them to give bonds that they would never more deal in opium—a most excellent plan for securing future good conduct. This the English refused to give, and then they trifled with the laws, and so obstinate were their dispositions that they could not be made to submit. Hence it becomes necessary to soothe and admonish them with sound instruction, so as to cause them to change their mien and purify their hearts, after which it will not be too late to renew their commerce. It behooves me to instruct and persuade them so that their good consciences may be restored, and they reduced to submission." The language of this document showed that the highest Chinese officers still believed that the English would accept trade facilities as a favor, that they would be treated *de haut en bas*, and that China possessed the power to make good her lofty pretensions. China had learned nothing from her military mishaps at Canton, Amoy, and Chusan, and from the appearance of an English fleet in the Gulf of Pechihli. Keshen had gained a breathing space by procrastination in the north, and he resorted to the same tactics at Canton. Days expanded into weeks, and at last orders were issued for an advance up the Canton River, as it had become evident that the Chinese were not only bent on an obstructive policy, but were making energetic efforts to assemble a large army. On January 7, 1841, orders were consequently issued for an immediate attack on the Bogue forts, which had been placed in a state of defense, and which were manned by large numbers of Chinese. Fortunately for us, the Chinese possessed a very rudimentary knowledge of the art of war, and showed no capacity to take advantage of the strength of their position and forts, or even of their excellent guns. The troops were landed on the coast in the early morning to operate on the flank and rear of the forts at Chuenpee. The advance squadron, under Captain, afterward Sir Thomas, Herbert, was to engage the same forts in front, while the remainder of the fleet proceeded to attack the stockades on the adjoining island of Taikok. The land force of 1,500 men and three guns had not proceeded far along the coast before it came across a strongly intrenched camp in addition to the Chuenpee forts, with several thousand troops and many guns in position. After a sharp cannonade the forts were carried at a rush, and a formidable army was driven ignominiously out of its intrenchments with hardly any loss to the assailants. The forts at Taikok were destroyed by the fire of the ships, and their guns spiked and garrisons routed by storming parties. In all, the Chinese lost 500 killed, besides an incalculable number of wounded, and many junks. The Chinese showed some courage as well as incompetence, and the English officers described their defense as "obstinate and honorable."

The capture of the Bogue forts produced immediate and important consequences. Keshen at once begged a cessation of hostilities, and offered terms which conceded everything we had demanded. These were the payment of a large indemnity, the cession of Hongkong, and the right to hold official communication with the central government. In accordance with these preliminary articles, Hongkong was proclaimed, on January 29, 1841, a British possession, and the troops evacuated Chusan to garrison the new station. It was not considered at the time that the acquisition was of much importance, and no one would have predicted for it the brilliant and prosperous position it has since attained. But the promises given by Keshen were merely to gain time and to extricate him from a very embarrassing situation. The morrow of what seemed a signal reverse was marked by the issue of an imperial notice, breathing a more defiant tone than ever. Taoukwang declared, in this edict, that he was resolved "to destroy and wash the foreigners away without remorse," and he denounced the English by name as "staying themselves upon their pride of power and fierce strength." He, therefore, called upon his officers to proceed with courage and energy, so that "the rebellious foreigners might give up their ringleaders, to be sent encaged to Pekin, to receive the utmost retribution of the laws." So long as the sovereign held such opinions as these it was evident that no arrangement could endure. The Chinese did not admit the principle of equality in their dealings with the English, and this was the main point in contention, far more than the alleged evils of the opium traffic. So long as Taoukwang and his ministers held the opinions which they did not hesitate to express, a friendly intercourse was impossible. There was no practical alternative between withdrawing from the country altogether and leaving the Chinese in undisturbed seclusion, or forcing their government to recognize a common humanity and an equality in national privileges.

It is not surprising that under these circumstances the suspension of hostilities proved of brief duration. The conflict was hastened by the removal of Keshen from his post, in consequence of his having reported that he considered the Chinese forces unequal to the task of opposing the English. His candor in recognizing facts did him credit, while it cost him his position; and his successor, Eleang, was compelled to take an opposite view, and to attempt something to justify it. Eleang refused to ratify the convention signed by Keshen, and, on February 25, the English commander ordered an attack on the inner line of forts which guarded the approaches to Canton. After a brief engagement, the really formidable lines of Anunghoy, with 200 guns in position, were carried at a nominal loss. The many other positions of the Chinese, up to Whampoa, were occupied in succession; and on March 1 the English squadron drew up off Howqua's Folly, in Whampoa Reach, at the very gateway of Canton. On the following day the dashing Sir Hugh Gough arrived to take the supreme direction of the English forces. After these further reverses, the Chinese again begged a suspension of hostilities, and an armistice for a few days was granted. The local authorities were on the horns of a dilemma. They saw the futility of a struggle with the English, and the Cantonese had to bear all the suffering for the obstinacy of the Pekin government; but, on the other hand, no one dared to propose concession to Taoukwang, who, confident of his power, and ignorant of the extent of his misfortunes, breathed nothing but defiance. After a few days' delay, it became clear that the Cantonese had neither the will nor the power to conclude a definite arrangement, and consequently their city was attacked with as much forbearance as possible. The fort called Dutch Folly was captured, and the outer line of defenses was taken possession of, but no attempt was made to occupy the city itself. Sir Hugh Gough stated, in a public notice, that the city was spared because the queen had desired that all peaceful people should be tenderly considered. The first English successes had entailed the disgrace of Lin, the second were not less fatal to Keshen. Keshen was arraigned before the Board

CANTON—THE FLOWER PAGODA

China

at Pekin, his valuable property was escheated to the crown, and he himself sentenced to decapitation, which was commuted to banishment to Tibet, where he succeeded in amassing a fresh fortune. The success of the English was proclaimed by the merchants re-occupying their factories on March 18, 1841, exactly two years after Lin's first fiery edict against opium. It was a strange feature in this struggle that the instant they did so the Chinese merchants resumed trade with undiminished ardor and cordiality. The officials even showed an inclination to follow their example, when they learned that Taoukwang refused to listen to any conclusive peace, and that his policy was still one of expelling the foreigners. To carry out his views, the emperor sent a new commission of three members to Canton, and it was their studious avoidance of all communication with the English authorities that again aroused suspicion as to the Chinese not being sincere in their assent to the convention which had saved Canton from an English occupation. Taoukwang was ignorant of the success of his enemy, and his commissioners, sent to achieve what Lin and Keshen had failed to do, were fully resolved not to recognize the position which the English had obtained by force of arms, or to admit that it was likely to prove enduring. This confidence was increased by the continuous arrival of fresh troops, until at last there were 50,000 men in the neighborhood of Canton, and all seemed ready to tempt the fortune of war again, and to make another effort to expel the hated foreigner. The measure of Taoukwang's animosity may be taken by his threatening to punish with death any one who suggested making peace with the barbarians.

While the merchants were actively engaged in their commercial operations, and the English officers in conducting negotiations with a functionary who had no authority, and who was only put forward to amuse them, the Chinese were busily employed in completing their warlike preparations, which at the same time they kept as secret as possible, in the hope of taking the English by surprise. But it was impossible for such extensive preparations to be made without their creating some stir, and the standing aloof of the commissioners was in itself ground of suspicion. Suspicion became certainty when, on Captain Elliot paying a visit to the perfect in the city, he was received in a disrespectful manner by the mandarins and insulted in the streets by the crowd. He at once acquainted Sir Hugh Gough, who was at Hongkong, with the occurrence, and issued a notice, on May 21, 1841, advising all foreigners to leave Canton that day. This notice was not a day too soon, for, during the night, the Chinese made a desperate attempt to carry out their scheme. The batteries which they had secretly erected at various points in the city and along the river banks began to bombard the factories and the ships at the same time that fire-rafts were sent against the latter in the hope of causing a conflagration. Fortunately the Chinese were completely baffled, with heavy loss to themselves and none to the English; and during the following day the English assumed the offensive, and with such effect that all the Chinese batteries were destroyed, together with forty war-junks. The only exploit on which the Chinese could compliment themselves was that they had sacked and gutted the English factory. This incident made it clearer than ever that the Chinese Government would only be amenable to force, and that it was absolutely necessary to inflict some weighty punishment on the Chinese leaders at Canton, who had made so bad a return for the moderation shown them and their city, and who had evidently no intention of complying with the arrangement to which they had been a party.

Sir Hugh Gough arrived at Canton with all his forces on May 24, and on the following morning the attack commenced with the advance of the fleet up the Macao passage, and with the landing of bodies of troops at different points which appeared well suited for turning the Chinese position and attacking the gates of Canton. The Chinese did not molest the troops in landing, which was fortunate, as the operation proved exceedingly difficult and occupied more than a whole day. The Chinese had taken up a strong position on the hills lying north of the city, and they showed considerable judgment in their selection and no small skill in strengthening their ground by a line of forts. The Chinese were said to be full of confidence in their ability to reverse the previous fortune of the war, and they fought with considerable confidence, while the turbulent Cantonese populace waited impatiently on the walls to take advantage of the first symptoms of defeat among the English troops. The English army, divided into two columns of nearly 2,000 men each, with a strong artillery force of seven guns, four howitzers, five mortars, and fifty-two rockets, advanced on the Chinese intrenchments across paddy fields, rendered more difficult of passage by numerous burial-grounds. The obstacles were considerable and the progress was slow, but the Chinese did not attempt any opposition. Then the battle began with the bombardment of the Chinese lines, and after an hour it seemed as if the Chinese had had enough of this and were preparing for flight, when a general advance was ordered. But the Chinese thought better of their intention or their movement was misunderstood, for when the English streamed up the hill to attack them they stood to their guns and presented a brave front. Three of their forts were carried with little or no loss, but at the fourth they offered a stubborn if ill-directed resistance. Even then the engagement was not over, for the Chinese rallied in an intrenched camp one mile in the rear of the forts, and, rendered confident by their numbers, they resolved to make a fresh stand, and hurled defiance at the foreigners. The English troops never halted in their advance, and, led by the 18th or Royal Irish, they carried the intrenchment at a rush and put the whole Chinese army to flight. The English lost seventy killed and wounded; the Chinese losses were never accurately known. It was arranged that Canton was to be stormed on the following day, but a terrific hurricane and deluge of rain prevented all military movements on May 26, and, as it proved, saved the city from attack. Once more Chinese diplomacy came to the relief of Chinese arms. To save Canton the mandarins were quite prepared to make every concession, if they only attached a temporary significance to their language, and they employed the whole of that lucky wet day in getting round Captain Elliot, who once more allowed himself to place faith in the promises of the Chinese. The result of this was seen on the 27th, when, just as Sir Hugh Gough was giving orders for the assault, he received a message from Captain Elliot stating that the Chinese had come to terms and that all hostilities were to be suspended. The terms the Chinese had agreed to in a few hours were that the commissioners and all the troops should retire to a distance of sixty miles from Canton, and that $6,000,000 should be paid "for the use of the English crown."

Five of the $6,000,000 had been handed over to Captain Elliot, and amicable relations had been established with the city authorities, when the imperial commissioners, either alarmed at the penalties their failure entailed, or encouraged to believe in the renewed chances of success from the impotence into which the English troops might have sunk, made a sudden attempt to surprise Sir Hugh Gough's camp and to retrieve a succession of disasters at a single stroke. The project was not without a chance of success, but it required prompt action and no hesitation in coming to close quarters —the two qualifications in which the Chinese were most deficient. So it was on this occasion. Ten or fifteen thousand Chinese braves suddenly appeared on the hills about two miles north of the English camp; but instead of seizing the opportunity created by the surprise at their sudden appearance and at the breach of armistice, and delivering home their attack, they merely waved their banners and uttered threats of defiance. They stood their ground for some time in face of the rifle and artillery fire opened upon them, and then they kept up a sort of running fight for three miles as they were pursued by the English. They did not suffer any serious loss, and when the English troops retired in consequence of a heavy storm they became in turn the pursuers and inflicted a few casualties. The advantages they obtained were due to the terrific weather more than to their courage, but one party of Madras sepoys lost its way, and was surrounded by so overwhelming a number of Chinese that they would have been annihilated but that their absence was fortunately discovered and a rescuing party of marines, armed with the new percussion gun, which was to a great degree secure against the weather, went out to their assistance. They found the sepoys, under their two English officers, drawn up in a square firing as best they could and presenting a bold front to the foe—"many of the sepoys, after extracting the wet cartridge very deliberately, tore their pocket handkerchiefs or lining from their turbans and, baling water with their hands into the barrel of their pieces, washed and dried them, thus enabling them to fire an occasional volley." Out of sixty sepoys one was killed and fourteen wounded. After this Sir Hugh Gough threatened to bombard Canton if there were any more attacks on his camp, and they at once ceased, and when the whole of the indemnity was paid the English troops were withdrawn, leaving Canton as it was, for a second time "a record of British magnanimity and forbearance."

After this trade reverted to its former footing, and by the Canton convention, signed by the imperial commissioners in July, 1841, the English obtained all the privileges they could hope for from the local authorities. But it was essentially a truce, not a treaty, and the great point of direct intercourse with the central government was no nearer settlement than ever. At this moment Sir Henry Pottinger arrived as Plenipotentiary from England, and he at once set himself to obtaining a formal recognition from the Pekin executive of his position and the admission of his right to address them on diplomatic business. With the view of pressing this matter on the attention of Taoukwang, who personally had not deviated from his original attitude of emphatic hostility, Sir Henry Pottinger sailed northward with the fleet and a large portion of the land forces about the end of August. The important seaport of Amoy was attacked and taken after what was called "a short but animated resistance." This town is situated on an island, the largest of a group lying at the entrance to the estuary of Lungkiang, and it has long been famous as a convenient port and flourishing place of trade. The Chinese had raised a rampart of 1,100 yards in length, and this they had armed with ninety guns, while a battery of forty-two guns protected its flank. Kulangsu was also fortified, and the Chinese had placed in all 500 guns in position. They believed in the impregnability of Amoy, and it was allowed that no inconsiderable skill as well as great expense had been devoted to the strengthening of the place. When the English fleet arrived off the port the Chinese sent a flag of truce to demand what it wanted, and they were informed the surrender of the town. The necessity for this measure would be hard to justify, especially as we were nominally at peace with China, for the people of Amoy had inflicted no injury on our trade, and their chastisement would not bring us any nearer to Pekin. Nor was the occupation of Amoy necessary on military grounds. It was strong only for itself, and its capture had no important consequences. As the Chinese determined to resist the English, the fleet engaged the batteries, and the Chinese, standing to their guns "right manfully," only abandoned their position when they found their rear threatened by a landing party. Then, after a faint resistance, the Chinese sought safety in flight, but some of their officers, preferring death to dishonor, committed suicide, one of them being seen to walk calmly into the sea and drown himself in face of both armies. The capture of Amoy followed.

As the authorities at Amoy refused to hold any intercourse with the English, the achievement remained barren of any useful consequence, and after leaving a small garrison on Kulangsu, and three warships in the roadstead, the English expedition continued its northern course. After being scattered by a storm in the perilous Formosa channel, the fleet reunited off Ningpo, whence it proceeded to attack Chusan for a second time. The Chinese defended Tinghai, the capital, with great resolution. At this place General Keo, the chief naval and military commander, was killed, and all his officers, sticking to him to the last, also fell with him. Their conduct in fact was noble; nothing could have surpassed it. On the reoccupation of Chusan, which it was decided to retain until a formal treaty had been concluded with the emperor, Sir Henry Pottinger issued a proclamation to the effect that years might elapse before that place would be restored to the emperor's authority, and many persons wished that it should be permanently annexed as the best base for commercial operations in China. A garrison of 400 men was left at Tinghai, and then the expedition proceeded to attack Chinhai on the mainland, where the Chinese had made every preparation to offer a strenuous resistance. The Chinese suffered the most signal defeat and the greatest loss they had yet incurred during the war. The victory at Chinhai was followed by the unopposed occupation of the important city of Ningpo, where the inhabitants shut themselves up in their houses, and wrote on their doors "Submissive People." Ningpo was put to ransom and the authorities informed that unless they paid the sum within a certain time their city would be handed over to pillage and destruction. As the Pekin Government had made no sign of giving in, it was felt that no occasion ought to be lost of overawing the Chinese, and compelling them to admit that any further prolongation of the struggle would be hopeless. The arrival of further troops and warships from Europe enabled the English commanders to adopt a more determined and uncompromising attitude, and the capture of Ningpo would have been followed up at once but for the disastrous events in Afghanistan, which distracted attention from the Chinese question, and delayed its settlement. It was hoped, however, that the continued occupation of Amoy, Chusan and Ningpo would cause sufficient pressure on the Pekin Government to induce it to yield all that was demanded.

These anticipations were not fulfilled, for neither the swift-recurring visitation of disaster nor the waning resources of the imperial government in both men and treasure, could shake the fixed hostility of Taoukwang or induce him to abate his proud pretensions. Minister after minister passed into disgrace and exile. Misfortune shared the same fate as incompetence, and the more the embarrassments of the state increased the heavier fell the hand of the ruler and the verdict of the Board of Punishments upon beaten generals and unsuccessful statesmen. The period of inaction which followed the occupation of Ningpo no doubt encouraged the emperor to think that the foreigners were exhausted, or that they had reached the end of their successes, and he ordered increased efforts to be made to bring up troops, and to strengthen the approaches to Pekin. The first proof of his returning spirit was shown in March, 1842, when the Chinese attempted to seize Ningpo by a coup de main. Suddenly, and without warning, a force of between ten and twelve thousand men appeared at daybreak outside the south and west gates of Ningpo, and many of them succeeded in making their way over the walls and gaining the center of the town; but, instead of proving the path to victory, this advance resulted in the complete overthrow of the Chinese. Attacked by artillery and foot in the market-place they were almost annihilated, and the great Chinese attack on Ningpo resulted in a fiasco. Similar but less vigorous attacks were made about the same time on Chinhai and Chusan, but they were both repulsed with heavy loss to the Chinese. In consequence of these attacks and the improved position in Afghanistan it was decided to again assume the offensive, and to break up the hostile army at Hangchow, of which the body that attacked Ningpo was the advanced guard. Sir Hugh Gough commanded the operations in person, and he had the co-operation of a naval force under Sir William Parker. The first action took place outside Tszeki, a small place ten miles from Ningpo, where the Chinese fancied they occupied an exceedingly strong position. But careful inspection showed it to be radically faulty. Their lines covered part of the Segaou hills, but their left was commanded by some higher hills on the right of the English position, and the Chinese left again commanded their own right. It was evident, therefore, that the capture of the left wing of the Chinese encampment would entail the surrender or evacuation of the rest. The difficulties of the ground caused a greater delay in the advance than had been expected, and the assault had to be delivered along the whole line, as it was becoming obvious that the Chinese were growing more confident, and, consequently, more to be feared from the delay in attacking them. The assault was made with the impetuosity good troops always show in attacking inferior ones, no matter how great the disparity of numbers; and here the Chinese were driven out of their position—although they stood their ground in a creditable manner—and chased over the hills down to the rice fields below. The Chinese loss was over a thousand killed, including many of the Imperial Guard, of whom 500 were present, and whom Sir Hugh Gough described as "remarkably fine men," while the English had six killed and thirty-seven wounded. For the moment it was intended to follow up this victory by an attack on the city of Hangchow, the famous Kincsay of medieval travelers; but the arrival of fresh instructions gave a complete turn to the whole war.

Little permanent good had been effected by these successful operations on the coast, and Taoukwang was still as resolute as ever in his hostility; nor is there any reason to suppose that the capture of Hangchow, or any other of the coast towns, would have caused a material change in the situation. The credit of initiating the policy which brought the Chinese Government to its knees belongs exclusively to Lord Ellenborough, then governor-general of India. He detected the futility of operations along the coast, and he suggested that the great waterway of the Yangtsekiang, perfectly navigable for warships up to the immediate neighborhood of Nankin, provided the means of coercing the Chinese and effecting the objects which the English Government had in view. The English expedition, strongly re-enforced from India, then abandoned Ningpo and Chinhai, and, proceeding north, began the final operations of the war with an attack on Chapoo, where the Chinese had made extensive measures of defense. Chapoo was the port appointed for trade with Japan, and the Chinese had collected there a very considerable force from the levies of Chekiang, which ex-Commissioner Lin had been largely instrumental in raising. Sir Hugh Gough attacked Chapoo with 2,000 men, and the main body of the Chinese was routed without much difficulty, but 300 desperate men shut themselves up in a walled inclosure, and made an obstinate resistance. They held out until three-fourths of them were slain, when the survivors, seventy-five wounded men, accepted the quarter offered them from the first. The English lost ten killed and fifty-five wounded, and the Chinese more than a thousand. After this the expedition proceeded northward for the Great River, and it was found necessary to attack Woosung, the port of Shanghai, en route. This place was also strongly fortified with as many as 175 guns in position, but the chief difficulty in attacking it lay in that of approach, as the channel had first to be sounded, and then the sailing ships towed into position by the steamers. Twelve vessels were in this manner placed broadside to the batteries on land, a position which obviously they could not have maintained against a force of anything like equal strength; but they succeeded in silencing the Chinese batteries with comparatively little loss, and then the English army was landed without opposition. Shanghai is situated sixteen miles up the Woosung River, and while part of the force proceeded up the river another marched overland. Both columns arrived together, and the disheartened Chinese evacuated Shanghai after firing one or two random shots. No attempt was made to retain Shanghai, and the expedition re-embarked, and proceeded to attack Chankiang or Chinkiangfoo, a town on the southern bank of the Yangtsekiang, and at the northern entrance of the southern branch of the Great Canal. This town has always been a place of great celebrity, both strategically and commercially, for not merely does it hold a very strong position with regard to the Canal, but it forms, with the Golden and Silver Islands, the principal barrier in the path of those attempting to reach Nankin. At this point Sir Hugh Gough was re-enforced by the 98th Regiment, under Colonel Colin Campbell. The difficulties of navigation and the size of the fleet, which now reached seventy vessels, caused a delay in the operations, and it was not until the latter end of July, or more than a month after the occupation of Shanghai, that the English reached Chinkiangfoo, where, strangely enough, there seemed to be no military preparations whatever. A careful reconnaissance revealed the presence of three strong encampments at some distance from the town, and the first operation was to carry them, and to prevent their garrisons joining such forces as might still remain in the city. This attack was intrusted to Lord Saltoun's brigade, which was composed of two Scotch regiments and portions of two native regiments, with only three guns. The opposition was almost insignificant, and the three camps were carried with comparatively little loss and their garrisons scattered in all directions. At the same time the remainder of the force assaulted the city, which was surrounded by a high wall and a deep moat. Some delay was caused by these obstacles, but at last the western gate was blown in by Captain Pears, of the Engineers, and at the same moment the walls were escaladed at two different points, and the English troops, streaming in on three sides, fairly surrounded a considerable portion of the garrison, who retired into a detached work, where they perished to the last man either by our fire or in the flames of the houses which were ignited partly by themselves and partly by the fire of our soldiers. The resistance did not stop here, for the Tartar or inner city was resolutely defended by the Manchus, and owing to the intense heat the Europeans would have been glad of a rest; but, as the Manchus kept up a galling fire, Sir Hugh Gough felt bound to order an immediate assault before the enemy grew too daring. The fight was renewed, and the Tartars were driven back at all points; but the English troops were so exhausted that they could not press home this advantage. The interval thus gained was employed by the Manchus, not in making good their escape, but in securing their military honor by first massacring their women and children, and then committing suicide. It must be remembered that these were not Chinese, but Manchu Tartars of the dominant race.

The losses of the English army at this battle—40 killed, and 130 wounded—were heavy, and they were increased by several deaths caused by the heat and exhaustion of the day. The Chinese, or rather the Tartars, never fought better, and it appears from a document discovered afterward that if Hailing's recommendations had been followed, and if he had been properly supported, the capture of Chinkiangfoo would have been even more difficult and costly than it proved.

Some delay at Chinkiangfoo was rendered necessary by the exhaustion of the troops and by the number of sick and wounded; but a week after the capture of that place in the manner described the arrangements for the further advance on Nankin were completed. A small garrison was left in an encampment on a height commanding the entrance to the Canal; but there was little reason to apprehend any fresh attack, as the lesson of Chinkiangfoo had been a terrible one. That city lay beneath the English camp like a vast charnel house, its half-burned buildings filled with the self-immolated Tartars who had preferred honor to life; and so thickly strewn were these and so intense the heat that the days passed away without the ability to give them burial, until at last it became absolutely impossible to render the last kind office to a gallant foe. Despite the greatest precautions of the English authorities, Chinkiangfoo became the source of pestilence, and an outbreak of cholera caused more serious loss in the English camp than befell the main force intrusted with the capture of Nankin. Contrary winds delayed the progress of the English fleet, and it was not until the fifth of August, more than a fortnight after the battle at Chinkiangfoo, that it appeared off Nankin, the second city in reputation and historical importance of the empire, with one million inhabitants and a garrison of 15,000 men, of whom two-thirds were Manchus. The walls were twenty miles in length, and hindered, more than they promoted, an efficient defense; and the difficulties of the surrounding country, covered with the debris of the buildings which constituted the larger cities of Nankin at an earlier period of history, helped the assailing party more than they did the defenders. Sir Hugh Gough drew up an admirable plan for capturing this vast and not defenseless city with his force of 5,000 men, and there is no reason to doubt that he would have been completely successful; but by this the backbone of the Chinese Government had been broken, and even the proud and obstinate Taoukwang was compelled to admit that it was imperative to come to terms with the English, and to make some concessions in order to get rid of them.

The minister Elepoo, who once enjoyed the closest intimacy with Taoukwang, and who was the leader of the Peace party, which desired the cessation of an unequal struggle, had begun informal negotiations several months before they proved successful at Nankin. He omitted no opportunity of learning the views of the English officers, and what was the minimum of concession on which a stable peace could be based. He had endeavored also to give something of a generous character to the struggle, and he had more than once proved himself a courteous as well as a gallant foe. After the capture of Chapoo and Woosung he sent back several officers and men who had at different times been taken prisoners by the Chinese, and he expressed at the same time the desire that the war should end. Sir Henry Pottinger's reply to this letter was to inquire if he was empowered by the emperor to negotiate. If he had received this authority the English plenipotentiary would be very happy to discuss any matter with him, but if not the operations of war must proceed. At that moment Elepoo had not the requisite authority to negotiate, and the war went on until the victorious English troops were beneath the walls of Nankin. At the same time as these pourparlers were held with Elepoo at Woosung, Sir Henry Pottinger issued a proclamation to the Chinese stating what the British Government required to be done. In this document the equality of all nations as members of the same human family was pointed out, and the right to hold friendly intercourse insisted on as a matter of duty and common obligation. Sir Henry said that "England, coming from the utmost west, has held intercourse with China in this utmost east for more than two centuries past, and during this time the English have suffered ill-treatment from the Chinese officials, who, regarding themselves as powerful and us as weak, have thus dared to commit injustice." Then followed a list of the many high-handed acts of Commissioner Lin and his successors. The Chinese, plainly speaking, had sought to maintain their exclusiveness and to live outside the comity of nations, and they had not the power to attain their wish. Therefore they were compelled to listen to and to accept the terms of the English plenipotentiary, which were as follows:—The emperor was first of all to appoint a high officer with full powers to negotiate and conclude arrangements on his own responsibility, when hostilities would be suspended. The three principal points on which these negotiations were to be based were compensation for losses and expenses, a friendly and becoming intercourse on terms of equality between officers of the two countries, and the cession of insular territory for commerce and for the residence of merchants, and as a security and guarantee against the future renewal of offensive acts. The first step toward the acceptance of these terms was taken when an imperial commission was formed of three members, Keying, Elepoo, and Niu Kien, viceroy of the Two Kiang; and to the last named, as governor of the provinces most affected, fell the task of writing the first diplomatic communication of a satisfactory character from the Chinese Government to the English plenipotentiary. This letter was important for more reasons than its being of a conciliatory nature. It held out to a certain extent a hand of friendship, and it also sought to assign an origin to the conflict, and Niu Kien could find nothing more handy or convenient than opium, which thus came to give its name to the whole war. With regard to the Chinese reverses, Niu Kien, while admitting them, explained that "as the central nation had enjoyed peace for a long time the Chinese were not prepared for attacking and fighting, which had led to this accumulation of insult and disgrace." In a later communication Niu Kien admitted that "the English at Canton had been exposed to insults and extortions for a series of years, and that steps should be taken to insure in future that the people of your honorable nation might carry on their commerce to advantage, and not receive injury thereby." These documents showed that the Chinese were at last willing to abandon the old and impossible principle of superiority over other nations, for which they had so long contended; and with the withdrawal of this pretension negotiations for the conclusion of a stable peace became at once possible and of hopeful augury

The first step of the Chinese commissioners was to draw up a memorial for presentation to the emperor, asking his sanction of the arrangement they suggested. In this document they covered the whole ground of the dispute, and stated in clear and unmistakable language what the English demanded, and they did not shrink from recommending compliance with their terms. Keying and his colleagues put the only two alternatives with great cogency. Which will be the heavier calamity, they said, to pay the English the sum of money they demand (21,000,000 dollars, made up as follows: Six million for the destroyed opium, 3,000,000 for the debts of the Hong merchants, and 12,000,000 for the expenses of the war), or that they should continue those military operations which seemed irresistible, and from which China had suffered so grievously? Even if the latter alternative were faced and the war continued, the evil day would only be put off. The army expenses would be very great, the indemnity would be increased in amount, and after all there would be only "the name of fighting without the hope of victory." Similar arguments were used with regard to the cession of Hongkong, and the right of trading at five of the principal ports. The English no doubt demanded more than they ought, but what was the use of arguing with them, as they were masters of the situation? Moreover, some solace might be gathered in the midst of affliction from the fact that the English were willing to pay certain duties on their commerce which would in the end repay the war indemnity, and contribute to "the expenditure of the imperial family." With regard to the question of ceremonial intercourse on a footing of equality, they declared that it might be "unreservedly granted." The reply of Taoukwang to this memorial was given in an edict of considerable length, and he therein assented to all the views and suggestions of the commissioners, while he imposed on Keying alone the responsibility of making all the arrangements for paying the large indemnity. All the preliminaries for signing a treaty of peace had therefore been arranged before the English forces reached Nankin, and as the Chinese commissioners were sincere in their desire for peace, and as the emperor had sanctioned all the necessary arrangements, there was no reason to apprehend any delay, and much less a breakdown of the negotiations.

It was arranged that the treaty should be signed on board a British man-of-war, and the Chinese commissioners were invited to pay a visit for the purpose to the "Cornwallis," the flagship of the admiral. The event came off on the 20th of August, 1842, and the scene was sufficiently interesting, if not imposing. The long line of English warships and transports, drawn up opposite to and within short range of the lofty walls of Nankin; the land forces so disposed on the raised causeways on shore as to give them every facility of approach to the city gates, while leaving it doubtful to the last which gate would be the real object of attack; and then the six small Chinese boats, gayly decorated with flags, bearing the imperial commissioners and their attendants, to sign for the first time in history a treaty of defeat with a foreign power. The commissioners were dressed in their plainest clothes, as they explained, because imperial commissioners are supposed to proceed in haste about their business, and have no time to waste on their persons, but there is reason to believe that they thought such clothing best consorted with the inauspicious character for China of the occasion. The ceremony passed off without a hitch, and four days later Sir Henry Pottinger paid the Chinese officers a return visit, when he was received by them in a temple outside the city walls. A third and more formal reception was held on the 26th of August in the College Hall, in the center of Nankin, when Sir Henry Pottinger, twenty officers, and an escort of native cavalry rode through the streets of one of the most famous cities of China. It was noted at the time that on this date an event of great importance had happened in each of the three previous years. On the 26th of August, 1839, Lin had expelled the English from Macao, in 1840 the British fleet anchored off the Peiho, and in 1841 Amoy was captured. Three days after this reception the treaty itself was signed on board the "Cornwallis," when Keying and his colleagues again attended for the purpose. The act of signing was celebrated by a royal salute of twenty-one guns, and the hoisting of the standards of England and China at the masthead of the man-of-war. The Emperor Taoukwang ratified the treaty with commendable dispatch, and the only incident to mar the cordiality of the last scene in this part of the story of Anglo-Chinese relations was the barbarous and inexcusable injury inflicted by a party of English officers and soldiers on the famous Porcelain Tower, which was one of the finest specimens of Chinese art, having been built 400 years before at great expense and the labor of twenty years.

therefore, of the injustice of this war as another instance of the triumph of might over right, they should recollect that China in the first place was wrong in claiming an impossible position in the family of nations. We cannot doubt that if the acts of Commissioner Lin had been condoned the lives of all Europeans would have been at the mercy of a system which recognizes no gradation in crime, which affords many facilities for the manufacture of false evidence, and which inflicts punishment altogether in excess of the fault. It is gratifying to find that many unprejudiced persons declared at the time that the war which resulted in the Nankin treaty was a just one, and so eminent an authority on international law as John Quincy Adams drew up an elaborate treatise to show that "Britain had the righteous cause against China." We may leave the scene of contest and turn from the record of an unequal war with the reflection that the results of the struggle were to be good. However inadequately the work of far-seeing statesmanship may have been performed in 1842, enough was done to make present friendship possible and a better understanding between two great governing peoples a matter of hope and not desponding expectancy.

CHAPTER XVIII

TAOUKWANG AND HIS SUCCESSOR

THE progress and temporary settlement of the foreign question so completely overshadows every other event during Taoukwang's reign that it is difficult to extract anything of interest from the records of the government of the country, although the difficult and multifarious task of ruling three hundred millions of people had to be performed. More than one fact went to show that the bonds of constituted authority were loosened in China, and that men paid only a qualified respect to the imperial edict. Bands of robbers prowled about the country, and even the capital was not free from their presence. While one band made its headquarters within the imperial city, another established itself in a fortified position in the central provinces of China, whence it dominated a vast region. The police were helpless, and such military forces as existed were unable to make any serious attempt to crush an opponent who was stronger than themselves. The foreign war had led to the recruiting of a large number of braves, and the peace to their sudden disbandment, so that the country was covered with a large number of desperate and penniless men, who were not particular as to what they did for a livelihood. It is not surprising that the secret societies began to look up again with so promising a field to work in, and a new association, known as the Green Water-Lily, became extremely formidable among the truculent braves of Hoonan. But none of these troubles assumed the extreme form of danger in open rebellion, and there was still wanting the man to weld all these hostile and dangerous elements into a national party of insurgents against Manchu authority, and so it remained until Taoukwang had given up his throne to his successor.

In Yunnan there occurred, about the year 1846, the first simmerings of disaffection among the Mohammedans, which many years later developed into the Panthay Rebellion, but on that occasion the vigor of the viceroy nipped the danger in the bud. In Central Asia there was a revival of activity on the part of the Khoja exiles, who fancied that the discomfiture of the Chinese by the English and the internal disorders, of which rumor had no doubt carried an exaggerated account into Turkestan, would entail a very much diminished authority in Kashgar. As it happened, the Chinese authority in that region had been consolidated and extended by the energy and ability of a Mohammedan official named Zuhuruddin. He had risen to power by the thoroughness with which he had carried out the severe repressive measures sanctioned after the abortive invasion of Jehangir, and during fifteen years he increased the revenue and trade of the great province intrusted to his care. His loyalty to the Chinese Government seems to have been unimpeachable, and the only point he seems to have erred in was an overconfident belief in the strength of his position. He based this opinion chiefly on the fact of his having constructed strong new forts, or yangyshahr, outside the principal towns. But a new element of danger had in the meantime been introduced into the situation in Kashgar by the appointment of Khokandian consuls, who were empowered to raise custom dues on all Mohammedan goods. These officials became the center of intrigue against the Chinese authorities, and whenever the Khan of Khokand determined to take up the cause of the Khojas he found the ground prepared for him by these emissaries.

In 1842 Mahomed Ali, Khan of Khokand, a chief of considerable ability and character, died, and his authority passed, after some confusion, to his kinsman, Khudayar, who was a man of little capacity and indisposed to meddle with the affairs of his neighbors. But the Khokandian chiefs were loth to forego the turbulent adventures to which they were addicted for the personal feelings of their nominal head, and they thought that a descent upon Kashgar offered the best chance of glory and booty. Therefore they went to the seven sons of Jehangir and, inciting them by the memory of their father's death as well as the hope of a profitable adventure, to make another attempt to drive the Chinese out of Central Asia, succeeded in inducing them to unfurl once more the standard of the Khojas. The seven Khojas—Haft Khojagan—issued their proclamation in the winter of 1845-46, rallied all their adherents to their side, and made allies of the Kirghiz tribes.

When the Mohammedan forces left the hills they advanced with extreme rapidity on Kashgar, to which they laid siege. After a siege of a fortnight they obtained possession of the town through the treachery of some of the inhabitants; but the citadel or yangyshahr continued to hold out, and their excesses in the town so alienated the sympathy of the Kashgarians, that no popular rising took place, and the Chinese were able to collect all their garrisons to expel the invaders. The Khojas were defeated in a battle at Kok Robat, near Yarkand, and driven out of the country. The affair of the seven Khojas, which at one time threatened the Chinese with the gravest danger, thus ended in a collapse, and it is remarkable as being the only invasion in which the Mohammedan subjects of China did not fraternize with her enemies. Notwithstanding the magnitude of his services as an administrator, Zuhuruddin was disgraced and dismissed from his post for what seemed his culpable apathy at the beginning of the campaign.

Another indication of the weakness of the Chinese executive was furnished in the piratic confederacy which established itself at the entrance of the Canton River, and defied all the efforts of the mandarins until they enlisted in their behalf the powerful co-operation of the English navy. The Bogue had never been completely free from those lawless persons who are willing to commit any outrage if it holds out a certain prospect of gain with a minimum amount of danger, and the peace had thrown many desperate men out of employment who thought they could find in piracy a mode of showing their patriotism as well as of profiting themselves. These turbulent and dangerous individuals gathered round a leader named Shapuntsai, and in the year of which we are speaking, 1849, they controlled a large fleet and a well-equipped force, which levied blackmail from Fochow to the Gulf of Tonquin, and attacked every trading ship, European or Chinese, which did not appear capable of defending itself. If they had confined their attacks to their own countrymen it is impossible to say how long they might have gone on in impunity, for the empire possessed no naval power; but, unfortunately for them, and fortunately for China, they seized some English vessels and murdered some English subjects. One man-of-war under Captain Hay was employed in operations against them, and in the course of six months fifty-seven piratical vessels were destroyed, and a thousand of their crews either slain or taken prisoners.

Captain Hay, on being joined by another man-of-war, had the satisfaction of destroying the remaining junks and the depots in the Canton River, whereupon he sailed to attack the headquarters of Shapuntsai in the Gulf of Tonquin. After some search the piratical fleet was discovered off an island which still bears the name of the Pirates' Hold, and after a protracted engagement it was annihilated. Sixty junks were destroyed, and Shapuntsai was compelled to escape to Cochin China, where it is believed that he was executed by order of the king. The dispersion of this powerful confederacy was a timely service to the Chinese, who were informed that the English Government would be at all times happy to afford similar aid at their request. Even at this comparatively early stage of the intercourse it was apparent that the long-despised foreigners would be able to render valuable service of a practical kind to the Pekin executive, and that if the Manchus wished to assert their power more effectually over their Chinese subjects they would be compelled to have recourse to European weapons and military and scientific knowledge. The suppression of the piratical confederacy of the Bogue was the first occasion of that employment of European force, which was carried to a much more advanced stage during the Taeping rebellion, and of which we have certainly not seen the last development.

One of the last acts of Taoukwang's reign showed to what a depth of mental hesitation and misery he had sunk. It seems that the Chinese New Year's Day—February 12, 1850—was to be marked by an eclipse of the sun, which was considered very inauspicious, and as the emperor was especially susceptible to superstitious influences, he sought to get out of the difficulty, and to avert any evil consequences, by decreeing that the new year should begin on the previous day. But all-powerful as a Chinese emperor is, there are some things he cannot do, and the good sense of the Chinese revolted against this attempt to alter the course of nature. The imperial decree was completely disregarded, and received with expressions of derision, and in several towns the placards were torn down and defaced. Notwithstanding the eclipse, the Chinese year began at its appointed time. Some excuse might be made for Taoukwang on the ground of ill-health, for he was then suffering from the illness which carried him off a few weeks later. His health had long been precarious, the troubles of his reign had prematurely aged him, and he had experienced a rude shock from the death, at the end of 1849, of his adopted mother, toward whom he seems to have preserved the most affectionate feelings. From the first day of his illness its gravity seems to have been appreciated, and an unfavorable issue expected. On February 25, a grand council was held in the emperor's bed-chamber, and the emperor wrote in his bed an edict proclaiming his fourth son his heir and chosen successor. Taoukwang survived this important act only a very short time, but the exact date of his death is uncertain. There is some reason for thinking that his end was hastened by the outbreak of a fire within the Imperial City, which threatened it with destruction. The event was duly notified to the Chinese people in a proclamation by his successor, in which he dilated on the virtues of his predecessor, and expressed the stereotyped wish that he could have lived a hundred years.

Taoukwang was in his sixty-ninth year, having been born on September 12, 1781, and the thirty years over which his reign had nearly extended were among the most eventful, and in some respects the most unfortunate, in the annals of his country. When he was a young man, the power of his grandfather, Keen Lung, was at its pinnacle, but the misfortunes of his father's reign had prepared him for the greater misfortunes of his own, and the school of adversity in which he had passed the greater portion of his life had imbued him only with the disposition to bear calamity, and not the vigor to grapple with it. Yet Taoukwang was not without many good points, and he seems to have realized the extent of the national trouble, and to have felt acutely his inability to retrieve what had been lost. He was also averse to all unnecessary display, and his expenditure on the court and himself was less than that of any of his predecessors or successors. He never wasted the public money on his own person, and that was a great matter. His habits were simple and manly.

Although Taoukwang's reign had been marked by unqualified misfortune, he seems to have derived consolation from the belief that the worst was over, and that as his authority had recovered from such rude shocks it was not likely to experience anything worse. He had managed to extricate himself from a foreign war, which was attended with an actual invasion of a most alarming character, without any diminution of his authority. The symptoms of internal rebellion which had revealed themselves in more than one quarter of the empire had not attained any formidable dimensions, and seemed likely to pass away without endangering the Chinese constitution. Taoukwang may have hoped that while he had suffered much he had saved his family and dynasty from more serious calamities, and that on him alone had fallen the resentment of an offended Heaven. The experience of the next fifteen years was to show how inaccurately he had measured the situation, and how far the troubles of the fifteen years following his death were to exceed those of his reign; for just as he had inherited from his father, Kiaking, a legacy of trouble, so did he pass on to his son an inheritance of misfortune and difficulty, rendered all the more onerous by the pretension of supreme power without the means to support it.

The accession of Prince Yihchoo—who took the name of Hienfung, which means "great abundance," or "complete prosperity"—to the throne threatened for a moment to be disturbed by the ambition of his uncle, Hwuy Wang, who, it will be remembered, had attempted to seize the throne from his brother Taoukwang. This prince had lived in retirement during the last years of his brother's reign, and the circumstances which emboldened him to again put forward his pretensions will not be known until the state history of the Manchu dynasty is published. His attempt signally failed, but Hienfung spared his life, while he punished the ministers, Keying and Muchangah, for their supposed apathy, or secret sympathy with the aspirant to the imperial office, by dismissing them from their posts. When Hienfung became emperor he was less than twenty years of age, and one of his first acts was to confer the title of Prince on his four younger brothers, and to associate them in the administration with himself. This was a new departure in the Manchu policy, as all the previous emperors had systematically kept their brothers in the background. Hienfung's brothers became known in the order of their ages as Princes Kung, Shun, Chun, and Fu, and as Hienfung was the fourth son of Taoukwang, they were also distinguished numerically as the Fifth, Sixth, Seventh, and Eighth princes. Although Hienfung became emperor at a time of great national distress, he was so far fortunate that an abundant harvest, in the year 1850, tended to mitigate it, and by having recourse to the common Chinese practice of ''voluntary contributions,'' a sufficiently large sum was raised to remove the worst features of the prevailing scarcity and suffering. But these temporary and local measures could not improve a situation that was radically bad, or allay a volume of popular discontent that was rapidly developing into unconcealed rebellion.

An imperial proclamation was drawn up by the Hanlin College in which Hienfung took upon himself the whole blame of the national misfortunes, but the crisis had got far beyond a remedy of words. The corruption of the public service had gradually alienated the sympathies of the people. Justice and probity had for a time been banished from the civil service of China. The example of the few men of honor and capacity served but to bring into more prominent relief the faults of the whole class. Justice was nowhere to be found; the verdict was sold to the highest bidder. The guilty, if well provided in worldly goods, escaped scot-free;

the poor suffered for their own frailties as well as the crimes of wealthier offenders.   There was seen the far from uncommon case of individuals sentenced to death obtaining substitutes for the capital punishment.   Offices were sold to men who had never passed an examination, and who were wholly illiterate, and the sole value of office was as the means of extortion.   The nation was heavily taxed, but the taxes to the state were only the smaller part of the sums wrung from the people of the Middle Kingdom.   How was honor, or a sense of duty, to be expected from men who knew that their term of office must be short, and who had to receive their purchase money and the anticipated profit before their post was sold again to some fresh and possibly higher bidder ? The officials waxed rich on ill-gotten wealth, and a few individuals accumulated enormous fortunes, while the government sank lower and lower in the estimation of the people. It lost also in efficiency and striking power.   A corrupt and effeminate body of officers and administrators can serve but as poor defenders for an embarrassed prince and an assailed government against even enemies who are in themselves insignificant and not free from the vices of a corrupt society and a decaying age, and it was only on such that Hienfung had in the first place to lean against his opponents.   Even his own Manchus, the warlike Tartars, who, despite the smallness of their numbers, had conquered the whole of China, had lost their primitive virtue and warlike efficiency in the southern climes which they had made their home.   To them the opulent cities of the Chinese had proved as fatal as Capua to the army of the Carthaginian, and, as the self-immolations of Chapoo and Chinkiangfoo proved to have no successors, they showed themselves unworthy of the empire won by their ancestors.   Eor the first time since the revolt of Wou Sankwei, the Manchus were brought face to face with a danger threatening their right of conquest; yet on the eve of the Taeping Rebellion all Hienfung could think of to oppose his foes with was fine words as to his shortcomings and lavish promises of amendment.

Among the secret societies the Triads were the first to give a political and dynastic significance to their propaganda. The opening sentence of the oath of membership read as follows: "We combine everywhere to recall the Ming and exterminate the barbarians, cut off the Tsing and await the right prince." But as there were none of the Mings left, and as their name had lost whatever hold it may have possessed on the minds of the Chinese people, this proclaimed object tended rather to deter than to invite recruits to the society. Yet if any secret society shared in the origination of the Taeping Rebellion that credit belongs to the Triads, whose anti-Manchu literature enjoyed a wide circulation through Southern China, and they may have had a large share in drafting the programme that the Taeping leader, Tien Wang, attempted to carry out.

The individual on whom that exalted title was subsequently bestowed had a very common origin, and sprang from an inferior race. Hung-tsiuen, such was his own name, was the son of a small farmer near Canton, and he was a *hakka*, a despised race of tramps who bear some resemblance to our gypsies. He was born in the year 1813, and he seems to have passed all his examinations with special credit; but the prejudice on account of his birth prevented his obtaining any employment in the civil service of his country. He was therefore a disappointed aspirant to office, and at such a period it was not surprising that he should have become an enemy of the constituted authorities and the government. As he could not be the servant of the state he set himself the ambitious task of being its master, and with this object in view he resorted to religious practices in order to acquire a popular reputation, and a following among the masses. He took up his residence in a Buddhist monastery; and the ascetic deprivations, the loud prayers and invocations, the supernatural counsels and meetings, were the course of training which every religious devotee adopts as the proper novitiate for those honors based on the superstitious reverence of mankind which are sometimes no

inadequate substitute for temporal power and influence, even
when they fail to pave the way to their attainment.   He left
his place of seclusion to place himself at the head of the largest party of rebels, who had made their headquarters in the
remote province of Kwangsi, and he there proclaimed himself as Tien Wang, which means the Heavenly Prince, and
as an aspirant to the imperial dignity.   Gradually the rebels
acquired possession of the whole of the territory south of the
Canton River, and when they captured the strong and important military station at Nanning the emperor sent three
commissioners, one of them being his principal minister
Saichangah, to bring them to reason, but the result was
not encouraging, and although the Taepings were repulsed
in their attempt on Kweiling, they remained masters of the
open part of the province.   One of the Chinese officers had
the courage to write and tell the emperor that "the outlaws
were neither exterminated nor made prisoners."   Notwithstanding the enormous expenditure on the war and the collection of a large body of troops the imperial forces made no
real progress in crushing the rebels.   Fear or inexperience
prevented them from coming at once to close quarters with
the Taepings, when their superior numbers must have decided the struggle in their favor and nipped a most formidable rebellion in the bud.   That some of Hienfung's officers
realized the position can be gathered from the following letter, written at this period by a Chinese mandarin: "The
whole country swarms with rebels.   Our funds are nearly
at an end, and our troops few; our officers disagree, and the
power is not concentrated.   The commander of the forces
wants to extinguish a burning wagonload of fagots with a
cupful of water.   I fear we shall hereafter have some serious
affair—that the great body will rise against us, and our own
people leave us."   The military operations in Kwangsi lan-
guished during two years, although the tide of war declared
itself, on the whole, against the imperialists; but the rebels
themselves were exposed to this danger—that they were exclusively dependent on the resources of the province, and

that these being exhausted, they were in danger of being compelled to retire into Tonquin. It was at this exceedingly critical moment that Tien Wang showed himself an able leader of men by coming to the momentous decision to march out of Kwangsi, and invade the vast and yet untouched provinces of Central China. If the step was more the pressure of dire need than the inspiration of genius, it none the less forms the real turning-point in the rebellion.

Tien Wang announced his decision by issuing a proclamation, in the course of which he declared that he had received "the Divine commission to exterminate the Manchus, and to possess the empire as its true sovereign"; and, as it was also at this time that his followers became commonly known as Taepings, it may be noted that the origin of this name is somewhat obscure. According to the most plausible explanation it is derived from the small town of that name, situated in the southwest corner of the province of Kwangsi, where the rebel movement seems to have commenced. Another derivation gives it as the style of the dynasty which Tien Wang hoped to found, and its meaning as "Universal peace." Having called in all his outlying detachments and proclaimed his five principal lieutenants by titles which have been rendered as the northern, southern, eastern, western and assistant kings, Tien Wang began his northern march in April, 1852. At the town of Yungan, on the eastern borders of the province of Kwangsi, where he seems to have hesitated between an attack on Canton and the invasion of Hoonan, an event occurred which threatened to break up his force. The Triad chiefs, who had allied themselves with Tien Wang, were superior in knowledge and station to the immediate followers of the Taeping leader, and they took offense at the arrogance of his lieutenants after they had been elevated to the rank of kings. These officers, who possessed no claim to the dignity they had received, assumed the yellow dress and insignia of Chinese royalty, and looked down on all their comrades, especially the Triad organizers, who thought themselves the true originators of the rebellion.

Irritated by this treatment, the Triads took their sudden and secret departure from the Taeping camp, and hastened to make their peace with the imperialists. Of these Triads one chief, named Chang Kwoliang, received an important command, and played a considerable part in the later stages of the struggle.

The defection of the Triads put an end to the idea of attacking Canton, and the Taepings marched to attack Kweiling, where the Imperial Commissioners still remained. Tien Wang's assault was repulsed with some loss, and, afraid of discouraging his troops by any further attempt to seize so strong a place, he marched into Hoonan. Had the imperial commanders, who had shown no inconsiderable capacity in defense, exhibited as much energy in offensive measures, they might then and there have annihilated the power of the Taepings. Had they pursued the Taeping army they might have harassed its rear, delayed its progress, and eventually brought it to a decisive engagement at the most favorable moment. But the Imperial Commissioners did nothing, being apparently well satisfied with having rid themselves of such troublesome neighbors. The advance of the Taepings across the vast province of Hoonan was almost unopposed. The towns were unprepared to resist an assailant, and it was not until Tien Wang reached the provincial capital, Changsha, that he encountered any resistance worthy of the name. Some vigorous preparations had been made here to resist the rebels. Not merely was there a garrison in the place, but it so happened that Tseng Kwofan, a man of considerable ability and of an influential family, was residing near the town. Tseng had held several offices in the public service, and, as a member of the Hanlin, enjoyed a high position and reputation; but he happened to be at his own home in retirement in consequence of the death of a near relation when tidings of the approaching Taepings reached him, and he at once made himself responsible for the defense of Changsha. He threw himself with all the forces his influence or resources enabled him to collect into that town; and at the same time he ordered all the militia of the province to collect and harass the enemy. He called upon all those who had the means to show their duty to the state and sovereign by raising recruits or by promising rewards to those volunteers who would serve in the army against the rebels. Had the example of Tseng Kwofan been generally followed, it is not too much to say that the Taepings would never have got to Nankin. When the rebels reached Changsha, therefore, they found the gates closed, the walls manned, and the town victualed for a siege. They attempted to starve the place into surrender, and to frighten the garrison into yielding by threats of extermination; but when these efforts failed they delivered three separate assaults, all of which were repulsed. After a siege of eighty days, and having suffered very considerable losses, the Taepings abandoned the attack, and on the 1st of December resumed their march northward, which, if information could have been rapidly transmitted, would have soon resulted in their overthrow. On breaking up from before Changsha they succeeded in seizing a sufficient number of junks and boats to cross the great inland lake of Tungting, and on reaching the Yangtsekiang at Yochow they found that the imperial garrison had fled at the mere mention of their approach. The capture of Yochow was important, because the Taepings acquired there an important arsenal of much-needed weapons and a large supply of gunpowder, which was said to have been the property of Wou Sankwei. Thus, well equipped and supplying their other deficiencies by celerity of movement, they attacked the important city of Hankow, which surrendered without a blow. The scarcely less important town of Wouchang, on the southern and opposite bank of the river, was then attacked, and carried after a siege of a fortnight. The third town of Hanyang, which forms, with the others, the most important industrial and commercial hive in Central China, also surrendered without any attempt at resistance, and this striking success at once restored the sinking courage of the Taepings, and made the danger from them to the dynasty again wear an aspect of the most pressing importance.

It would be difficult to exaggerate the effect of this success on the spirits of the Taepings, who had been seriously discouraged before they achieved this gratifying result. The capture of these towns removed all their most serious causes of doubt, and enabled them to repay themselves for the losses and hardships they had undergone, while it also showed that the enterprise they had in hand was not likely to prove unprofitable. After one month's rest at Hankow, and having been joined by many thousands of new followers, the Taepings resolved to pursue their onward course. To tell the truth, they were still apprehensive of pursuit from Tseng Kwofan, who had been joined by the Triad leader, Chang Kwoliang; but there was no ground for the fear, as these officials considered themselves tied to their own province, and unfortunately the report of the success of the imperialists in Hoonan blinded people to the danger in the Yangtse Valley from the Taepings. The Taepings resumed active operations with the capture of Kiukiang and Ganking, and in March, 1853, they sat down before Nankin. The siege continued for a fortnight, but notwithstanding that there was a large Manchu force in the Tartar city, which might easily have been defended against an enemy without artillery, the resistance offered was singularly and unexpectedly faint-hearted. The Taepings succeeded in blowing in one of the gates, the townspeople fraternized with the assailants, and the very Manchus who had defied Sir Hugh Gough in 1842 surrendered their lives and their honor to a force which was nothing more than an armed rabble. The Tartar colony at Nankin, numbering 4,000 families, had evidently lost the courage and discipline which could alone enable them to maintain their position in China. Instead of dying at their posts they threw themselves on the mercy of the Taeping leader, imploring him for pity and for their lives when the gate was blown in by Tien Wang's soldiery. Their cowardice helped them not;

of 20,000 Manchus not one hundred escaped. The tale rests on undoubted evidence. A Taeping who took part in the massacre said, "We killed them all, to the infant in arms; we left not a root to sprout from, and the bodies of the slain we cast into the Yangtse."

The acquisition of Nankin at once made the Taepings a formidable rival to the Manchus, and Tien Wang a contestant with Hienfung for imperial honors. The possession of the second city in the empire gave them the complete control of the navigation of the Yangtsekiang, and thus enabled them to cut off communications between the north and the south of China. To attain this object in a still more perfect manner they occupied Chinkiangfoo at the entrance to the Grand Canal. They also seized Yangchow on the northern bank of the river immediately opposite the place where Sir Hugh Gough had gained his decisive victory in 1842. Such was the terror of the Taepings that the imperial garrisons did not attempt the least resistance, and town after town was evacuated at their approach. Tien Wang, encouraged by his success, transferred his headquarters from Hankow to Nankin, and proclaimed the old Ming city his capital. By rapidity and an extraordinary combination of fortunate circumstances, the Taepings had advanced from the remote province of Kwangsi into the heart of the empire, but it was clear that unless they could follow up their success by some blow to the central government they would lose all they had gained as soon as the Manchus recovered their confidence. At a council of war at Nankin it was decided to send an army against Pekin as soon as Nankin had been placed in a proper state to undergo a protracted siege. Provisions were collected to stand a siege for six or seven years, the walls were repaired and fresh batteries erected. By the end of May, 1853, these preparations were completed, and as the Taeping army had then been raised to a total of 80,000 men, it was decided that a large part of it could be spared for operations north of the Yangtsekiang. That army was increased to a very large total by volunteers who thought an expedition to humble the Manchus at the capital promised much glory and spoil. The progress of this northern army very closely resembled that of the Taepings from Kwangsi to Nankin. They overran the open country, and none of the imperial troops ventured to oppose them, but when any Manchu officer showed valor in defending a walled city they were fain to admit their inadequate engineering skill and military capacity. They attacked Kaifong, the capital of Honan, but were repulsed, and pursuing their former tactics continued their march to Pekin. Having crossed the Hoangho they attacked Hwaiking, where, after being delayed two months, they met with as signal a repulse as at Kaifong. Notwithstanding this further reverse, the Taepings pressed on, and defeating a Manchu force in the Lin Limming Pass, they entered the metropolitan province of Pechihli in September, 1853. The object of their march was plain. Not only did they mystify the emperor's generals, but they passed through an untouched country where supplies were abundant, and they thus succeeded in coming within striking distance of Pekin in almost as fresh a state as when they left Nankin. Such was the effect produced by their capture of the Limming Pass that none of the towns in the southern part of the province attempted any resistance, and they reached Tsing, only twenty miles south of Tientsin, and less than a hundred from Pekin, before the end of October. This place marked the northern limit of Taeping progress, and a reflex wave of Manchu energy bore back the rebels to the Yangtse.

The forcing of the Limming Pass carried confusion and terror into the imperial palace and capital. The fate of the dynasty seemed to tremble in the balance at the hands of a ruthless and determined enemy. There happened to be very few troops in Pekin at the time, and levies had to be hastily summoned from Mongolia. If the Taepings had only shown the same enterprise and rapidity of movement that they had exhibited up to this point, there is no saying that the central government would not have been subverted and the Manchu family extinguished as completely as the Mings. But fortunately for Hienfung, an unusual apathy fell upon the Taepings, who remained halted at Tsing until the Mongol levies had arrived, under their great chief, Sankolinsin. They seem to have been quite exhausted by their efforts, and after one reverse in the open field they retired to their fortified camp at Tsinghai, and sent messengers to Tien Wang for succor. In this camp they were closely beleaguered by Sankolinsin from October, 1853, to March, 1854, when their provisions being exhausted they cut their way out and began their retreat in a southerly direction. They would undoubtedly have been exterminated but for the timely arrival of a relieving army from Nankin. The Taepings then captured Lintsing, which remained their headquarters for some months; but during the remainder of the year 1854 their successes were few and unimportant. They were vigilantly watched by the imperial troops, which had expelled them from the whole of the province of Shantung before March, 1855. Their numbers were thinned by disease as well as loss in battle, and of the two armies sent to capture Pekin only a small fragment ever regained Nankin. While these events were in progress in the region north of Nankin, the Taepings had been carrying their arms up the Yangtse-kiang as far as Ichang, and eastward from Nankin to the sea. These efforts were not always successful, and Tien Wang's arms experienced as many reverses as successes. The important city of Kanchang, the capital of the province of Kiangsi, was besieged by them for four months, and after many attempts to carry it by storm the Taepings were compelled to abandon the task. They were more successful at Hankow, which they recovered after a siege of eighty days. They again evacuated this town, and yet once again, in 1855, wrested it from an imperial garrison.

The establishment of Taeping power at Nankin and the rumor of its rapid extension in every direction had drawn the attention of Europeans to the new situation thus created in China, and had aroused opposite opinions in different sections of the foreign community.   While the missionaries were disposed to regard the Taepings as the regenerators of China, and as the champions of Christianity, the merchants only saw in them the disturbers of peace and the enemies of commerce.   To such an extent did the latter anticipate the ruin of their trade that they petitioned the consuls to suspend, if not withhold, the payment of the stipulated customs to the Chinese authorities.   This proposed breach of treaty was emphatically rejected, and the consuls enjoined the absolute necessity of preserving a strict neutrality between the Taepings and the imperial forces.   But at the same time it became necessary to acquaint the Taeping ruler with the fact that he would be expected to observe the provisions of the Treaty of Nankin as scrupulously as if he were sovereign of China or a Manchu viceroy.   Sir George Bonham, the superintendent of trade and the governor of Hongkong, determined to proceed in person to Nankin, in order to acquaint the Taepings with what would be expected from them, and also to gain necessary information as to their strength and importance by personal observation.   But unfortunately this step of Sir George Bonham tended to help the Taepings by increasing their importance and spreading about the belief that the Europeans recognized in them the future ruling power of China.   It was not intended to be, but it was none the less, an unfriendly act to the Pekin Government, and as it produced absolutely no practical result with the Taepings themselves, it was distinctly a mistaken measure.   Its only excuse was that the imperial authorities were manifesting an increasing inclination to enlist the support of Europeans against the rebels, and it was desirable that accurate information should be obtained beforehand.   The Taotai of Shanghai even presented a request for the loan of the man-of-war at that port, and when he was informed that we intended to remain strictly neutral, the decision was also come to to inform the Taepings of this fact.   Therefore in April, 1853, before the army had left for the northern campaign, Sir George Bonham sailed for Nankin in the "Hermes" man-of-war. On the twenty-seventh of that month the vessel anchored off Nankin, and several interviews were held with the Taeping Wangs, of whom the Northern King was at this time the most influential. The negotiations lasted a week, and they had no result. It was soon made apparent that the Taepings were as exclusive and impracticable as the worst Manchu mandarin, and that they regarded the Europeans as an inferior and subject people. Sir George Bonham failed to establish any direct communication with Tien Wang, who had by this retired into private life, and while it was given out that he was preparing sacred books he was really abandoning himself to the pursuit of profligacy. There is nothing to cause surprise in the fact that the apathy of Tien Wang led to attempts to supersede him in his authority. The Eastern King in particular posed as the delegate of Heaven. He declared that he had interviews with the celestial powers when in a trance, he assumed the title of the Holy Ghost or the Comforter, and he censured Tien Wang for his shortcomings, and even inflicted personal chastisement upon him. If he had had a following he might have become the despot of the Taepings, but as he offended all alike his career was cut short by a conspiracy among the other Wangs, who, notwithstanding his heavenly conferences, murdered him.

At this period one of the most brilliant military exploits of the Taepings was performed, and as it served to introduce the real hero of the whole movement, it may be described in more detail than the other operations, which were conducted in a desultory manner, and which were unredeemed by any exhibition of courage or military capacity. The government had succeeded in placing two considerable armies in the field. One numbering 40,000 men, under the command of Hochun and the ex-Triad Chang Kwoliang, watched Nankin, while the other, commanded by a Manchu general, laid close siege to Chankiang, which seemed on the point of surrender. The Taepings at Nankin determined to effect its relief, and a large force was placed under the orders of an officer named

Li, but whom it will be more convenient to designate by the title subsequently conferred on him of Chung Wang, or the Faithful King. His energy and courage had already attracted favorable notice, and the manner in which he executed the difficult operation intrusted to him fully established his reputation. By a concerted movement with the Taeping commandant of Chankiang, he attacked the imperialist lines at the same time as the garrison made a sortie, and the result was a decisive victory. Sixteen stockades were carried by assault, and the Manchu army was driven away from the town which seemed to lie at its mercy. But this success promised only to be momentary, for the imperialist forces, collecting from all sides, barred the way back to Nankin, while the other Manchu army drew nearer to that city, and its general seemed to meditate attacking Tien Wang in his capital. An imperative summons was sent to Chung Wang to return to Nankin. As the imperialist forces were for the most part on the southern side of the river, Chung Wang crossed to the northern bank and began his march to Nankin. He had not proceeded far when he found that the imperialists had also crossed over to meet him, and that his progress was arrested by their main army under Chang Kwoliang. With characteristic decision and rapidity he then regained the southern bank, and falling on the weakened imperialists gained so considerable a victory that the Manchu commander felt bound to commit suicide. After some further fighting he made good his way back to Nankin. But when he arrived there the tyrant Tung Wang refused to admit him into the city until he had driven away the main imperialist army, which had been placed under the command of Hienfung's generalissimo, Heang Yung, and which had actually seized one of the gates of the city. Although Chung Wang's troops were exhausted they attacked the government troops with great spirit, and drove them back as far as Tanyang, where, however, they succeeded in holding their ground, notwithstanding his repeated efforts to dislodge them. Heang Yung, taking his misfortune too deeply to heart, committed suicide, and thus deprived the emperor of at least a brave officer. But with this success the Taeping tide of victory reached its end, for Chang Kwoliang arriving with the other imperialist army, the whole force fell upon Chung Wang and drove him back into the city with the loss of 700 of his best men, so that the result left of Chung Wang's campaign was the relief of Chankiang and the return to the *status quo* at Nankin. It was immediately after these events that Tung Wang was assassinated, and scenes of blood followed which resulted in the massacre of 20,000 persons and the disappearance of all, except one, of the Wangs whom Tien Wang had created on the eve of his enterprise. Chung Wang seems to have had no part in these intrigues and massacres, and there is little doubt that if the imperialist commanders had taken prompt advantage of them the Taepings might have been crushed at that moment, or ten years earlier than proved to be the case.

While the main Taeping force was thus causing serious danger to the existing government of China, its offshoots or imitators were emulating its example in the principal treaty ports, which brought the rebels into contact with the Europeans. The Chinese officials, without any military power on which they could rely, had endeavored to maintain order among the turbulent classes of the population by declaring that the English were the allies of the emperor, and that they would come to his aid with their formidable engines of war if there were any necessity. Undoubtedly this threat served its turn and kept the turbulent quiet for a certain period; but when it could no longer be concealed that the English were determined to take no part in the struggle, the position of the government was weakened by the oft-repeated declaration that they mainly relied on the support of the foreigners. The first outbreak occurred at Amoy in May, 1853, when some thousand marauders, under an individual named Magay, seized the town and held it until the following November. The imperialists returned in sufficient force in that month and regained possession of the

from taking any further part in it. But the imperialists continued their attack in their own bungling but persistent fashion, and at last the insurgents, having failed to obtain the favorable terms they demanded, made a desperate sortie, when a few made their way to the foreign settlement, where they found safety, but by far the greater number perished by the sword of the imperialists. More than 1,500 insurgents were captured and executed along the highroads, but the two leaders of the movement escaped, one of them to attain great fortune as a merchant in Siam. The imperialists unfortunately sullied their success by grave excesses and by the cruel treatment of the unoffending townspeople, who were made to suffer for the original incapacity and cowardice of the officials themselves. At Canton, which was also visited by the Triads in June, 1854, matters took a different course. The Chinese merchants and shopkeepers combined and raised a force for their own protection, and these well-paid braves effectually kept the insurgents out of Canton. They, however, seized the neighboring town of Fatshan, where the manufacturing element was in strong force, and but for the unexpected energy of the Cantonese they would undoubtedly have seized the larger city too, as the government authorities were not less apathetic here than at Shanghai. The disturbed condition of things continued until February, 1855, when the wholesale executions by which its suppression was marked, and during which a hundred thousand persons are said to have perished, ceased.

The events have now been passed in review which marked the beginning and growth of the Taeping Rebellion, from the time of its being a local rising in the province of Kwangsi to the hour of its leader being installed as a ruling prince in the ancient city of Nankin. But from the growing Taeping Rebellion, which we have now followed down to the year 1856, our attention must be directed to the more serious and important foreign question which had again reached a crisis, and which would not wait on the convenience of the Celestial emperor and his advisers.

CHAPTER XIX

THE SECOND FOREIGN WAR

THE events which caused the second foreign war began to come into evidence immediately after the close of the first; and for the sake of clearness and brevity they have been left for consideration to the same chapter, although they happened while Taoukwang was emperor. After the departure of Sir Henry Pottinger, who was succeeded by Sir John Davis, and the arrival of the representatives of the other European powers, who hastened to claim the same rights and privileges as had been accorded to England, the main task to be accomplished was to practically assert the rights that had been theoretically secured, and to place the relations of the two nations on what may be called a working basis. The consulates were duly appointed, the necessary land for the foreign settlements was acquired, and the war indemnity being honorably discharged, Chusan was restored to the Chinese. With regard to the last matter there was some maneuvering of a not altogether creditable nature, and although the Chinese paid the last-installment punctually to date, Chusan and Kulangsu were not evacuated for some months after the stipulated time. It was said that our hesitation in the former case was largely due to the fear that France would seize it; but this has been permanently removed by the expressed assertion of our prior right to occupy it. A far more gratifying subject is suggested by the harmony of the relations which were established in Chusan between the garrison under Sir Colin Campbell and the islanders, who expressed deep regret at the departure of the English troops. The first members of the consular staff in China were as follows: Mr. G. T. Lay was consul at Canton, Captain George Balfour at Shanghai (where, however, he was soon succeeded by Sir Rutherford Alcock), Mr. Henry Gribble at Amoy, and Mr. Robert Thom at Ningpo. Among the interpreters were the future Sir Thomas Wade and Sir Harry Parkes. Various difficulties presented themselves with regard to the foreign settlements, and the island of Kulangsu at Amoy had to be evacuated because its name was not mentioned in the treaty. At Canton also an attempt was made to extend the boundaries of the foreign settlement by taking advantage of a great conflagration, but in this attempt the Europeans were baffled by the superior quickness of the Chinese, who constructed their new houses in a single night. These incidents showed that the sharpness was not all on one side, and that if the Chinese were backward in conceding what might be legitimately demanded, the Europeans were not averse to snatching an advantage if they saw the chance.

The turbulence of the Canton populace, over whom the officials possessed but a nominal control, was a constant cause of disagreement and trouble. In the spring of 1846 a riot was got up by the mob on the excuse that a vane erected on the top of the flagstaff over the American Consulate interfered with the Fung Shui, or spirits of earth and air; and although it was removed to allay the excitement of the superstitious, the disturbance continued, and several personal encounters took place, in one of which a Chinese was killed. The Chinese mandarins, incited by the mob, demanded the surrender of the man who fired the shot; and that they should have made such a demand, after they had formally accepted and recognized the jurisdiction of consular courts, furnished strong evidence that they had not mastered the lessons of the late war or reconciled themselves to the provisions of the Treaty of Nankin. The fortunate arrival of Keying to "amicably regulate the commerce with foreign countries" smoothed over this difficulty, and the excitement of the Canton mob was allayed without any surrender. It was almost at this precise moment, too, that Taoukwang made the memorable admission that the Christian religion might be tolerated as one inculcating the principles of virtue. But the two pressing and practical difficulties in the foreign question were the opening of the gates of Canton and the right of foreigners to proceed beyond the limits of their factories and compounds. The Chinese wished for many reasons, perhaps even for the safety of the foreigners, to confine them to their settlements, and it might be plausibly argued that the treaty supported this construction. Of course such confinement was intolerable, and English merchants and others would not be prevented from making boating or shooting excursions in the neighborhood of the settlements. The Chinese authorities opposed these excursions, and before long a collision occurred with serious consequences. In March, 1847, a small party of Englishmen proceeded in a boat to Fatshan, a manufacturing town near Canton which has been called the Chinese Birmingham. On reaching the place symptoms of hostility were at once manifested, and the Europeans withdrew for safety to the yamen of the chief magistrate, who happened unfortunately to be away. By this time the populace had got very excited, and the Englishmen were with difficulty escorted in safety to their boat. The Chinese, however, pelted them with stones, notwithstanding the efforts of the chief officer, who had by this time returned and taken the foreigners under his protection. It was due to his great heroism that they escaped with their lives and without any serious injury.

The incident, unpleasant in itself, might have been explained away and closed without untoward consequences if Sir John Davis had not seized, as he thought, a good opportunity of procuring greater liberty and security for Englishmen at Canton. He refused to see in this affair an accident, but denounced it as an outrage, and proclaimed "that he would exact and require from the Chinese Government that British subjects should be as free from molestation and insult in China as they would be in England." This demand was both unreasonable and unjust. It was impossible that the hated foreigner, or "foreign devil," as he was called, could wander about the country in absolute security when the treaty wrung from the emperor as the result of an arduous war confined him to five ports, and limited the emperor's capacity to extend protection to those places. But Sir John Davis determined to take this occasion of forcing events, so that he might compel the Chinese to afford greater liberty to his countrymen, and thus hasten the arrival of the day for the opening of the gates of Canton. On the 1st of April all the available troops at Hongkong were warned for immediate service, and on the following day the two regiments in garrison left in three steamers and escorted by one man-of-war to attack Canton. They landed at the Bogue forts, seized the batteries without opposition and spiked the guns. The Chinese troops, whether surprised or acting under orders from Keying, made no attempt at resistance. Not a shot was fired, not a man was injured among the assailants. The forts near Canton, the very batteries on the island opposite the city, were captured without a blow, and on the 3d of April, 1847, Canton again lay at the mercy of an English force. Sir John Davis then published another notice, stating that "he felt that the moderation and justice of all his former dealings with the government of China lend a perfect sanction to measures which he has been reluctantly compelled to adopt after a long course of misinterpreted forbearance," and made certain demands of the Chinese authorities which may be epitomized as follows: The City of Canton to be opened at two years' date from April 6, 1847; Englishmen to be at liberty to roam for exercise or amusement in the neighborhood of the city on the one condition that they returned the same day; and some minor conditions, to which no exception could be taken. After brief consideration, and notwithstanding the clamor of the Cantonese to be led against the foreigners, Keying agreed to the English demands, although he delivered a side-thrust at the high-handed proceedings of the English officer when he said, "If a mutual tranquillity is to subsist between the Chinese and foreigners, the common feelings of mankind, as well as the just principles of Heaven, must be considered and conformed with."

Keying, by the terms of his convention with Sir John Davis, had agreed that the gates of Canton were to be opened on April 6, 1849, but the nearer that day approached the more doubtful did it appear whether the promise would be complied with, and whether, in the event of refusal, it would be wise to have recourse to compulsion. The officials on both sides were unfeignedly anxious for a pacific solution, but trade was greatly depressed in consequence of the threatening demeanor of the Canton populace. There was scarcely any doubt that the Chinese authorities did not possess the power to compel obedience on the part of the Cantonese to an order to admit Europeans into their city, and on the question being referred to Taoukwang he made an oracular reply which was interpreted as favoring the popular will. "That," he said, "to which the hearts of the people incline is that on which the decree of Heaven rests. Now the people of Kwantung are unanimous and determined that they will not have foreigners enter the city; and how can I post up everywhere my imperial order and force an opposite course on the people?" The English Government was disposed to show great forbearance and refrained from opposing Taoukwang's views. But although the matter was allowed to drop, the right acquired by the convention with Keying was not surrendered; and, as Taoukwang had never formally ratified the promise of that minister, it was considered that there had been no distinct breach of faith on the part of the Chinese Government. The Chinese continued to cling tenaciously to their rights, and to contest inch by inch every concession demanded by the Europeans, and sometimes they were within their written warrant in doing so. Such a case happened at Foochow shortly after the accession of Hienfung, when an attempt was made to prevent foreigners residing in that town, and after a long correspondence it was discovered that the Chinese were so far right, as the treaty specified as the place of foreign residence the *kiangkan* or mart at the mouth of the river, and not the *ching* or town itself. It was at this critical moment that the Chinese were attracted in large numbers by the discovery of gold in California and Australia to emigrate from China, and they showed themselves well capable by their trade organization and close union of obtaining full justice for themselves and an ample recognition of all their rights in foreign countries. The effect of this emigration on Chinese public opinion was much less than might have been expected, and the settlement of the foreign question was in no way simplified or expedited by their influence.

The position of affairs at Canton could not, by the greatest stretch of language, be pronounced satisfactory. The populace was unequivocally hostile; the officials had the greatest difficulty in making their authority respected, and the English Government was divided between the desire to enforce the stipulation as to the opening of the Canton gates, and the fear lest insistence might result in a fresh and serious rupture. Sir George Bonham, who succeeded Sir John Davis, gave counsels of moderation, and when he found that some practical propositions which he made for improved intercourse were rejected he became more convinced that the question must wait for solution for a more convenient and promising occasion.

In 1852 Sir George Bonham returned to England on leave, and his place was taken by Dr. John Bowring, who had officiated for a short period as consul at Canton. His instructions were of a simple and positive character. They were "to avoid all irritating discussions with the authorities of China." He was also directed to avoid pushing arguments on doubtful points in a manner that would fetter the free action of the government; but he was, at the same time, to recollect that it was his duty to carefully watch over and insist upon the performance by the Chinese authorities of their engagements. The proper fulfillment of the latter duty necessarily involved some infringement of the former recommendation; and while the paramount consideration with the Foreign Office was to keep things quiet, it was natural

that the official on the spot should think a great deal, if not
altogether, of how best to obtain compliance to the fullest
extent with the pledges given in the treaty and the subsequent conventions.   Dr. Bowring was not an official to be
deterred from expressing his opinions by fear of headquarters.   He sent home his view of the situation, expressed in
very clear and intelligible language.   "The Pottinger treaties," he said, "inflicted a deep wound upon the pride, but by
no means altered the policy, of the Chinese Government. . . .
Their purpose is now, as it ever was, not to invite, not to
facilitate, but to impede and resist, the access of foreigners.
It must, then, ever be borne in mind, in considering the state
of our relations with these regions, that the two governments
have objects at heart which are diametrically opposed, except
in so far that both earnestly desire to avoid all hostile action,
and to make its own policy, as far as possible, subordinate
to that desire."   At this point a Liberal administration gave
place to a Conservative; but Lord Malmesbury reiterated in
stronger language the instructions of Lord Granville.   "All
irritating discussions with the Chinese should be avoided,
and the existing good understanding must in no way be imperiled."   One of Dr. Bowring's first acts was to write a
letter to the viceroy expressing a desire for an interview,
with the object of suggesting a settlement of pending difficulties; but the viceroy made his excuses.   The meeting did
not take place, and the whole question remained dormant
for two years, by which time not only had Sir John Bowring been knighted and confirmed in the post of governor,
but the viceroy had been superseded by the subsequently
notorious Commissioner Yeh.   Up to this point all Sir John
Bowring's suggestions with regard to the settlement of the
questions pending with the Chinese had been received with
the official reply that he was to abstain from all action, and
that he was not to press himself on the Canton authorities.
But, in the beginning of 1854, his instructions were so far
modified that Lord Clarendon wrote admitting the desira-
bility of "free and unrestricted intercourse with the Chinese

officials," and of "admission into some of the cities of China, especially Canton."

Encouraged by these admissions in favor of the views he had been advancing for some time, Sir John Bowring wrote an official letter to Commissioner Yeh inviting him to an early interview, but stating that the interview must be held within the city of Canton at the viceroy's yamen. It will be noted that what Sir John asked fell short of what Keying had promised. The opening of the gates of Canton was to have been to all Englishmen, but the English Government would at this point have been satisfied if its representative had been granted admission for the purpose of direct negotiation with the Chinese authorities. To the plain question put to him Yeh returned an evasive answer. All his time was taken up with the military affairs of the province, and he absolutely ignored the proposal for holding an interview within the city. The matter had gone too far to be put on one side in this manner, and Sir John Bowring sent his secretary to overcome, if possible, the repugnance of Commissioner Yeh to the interview, and in any case to gain some information as to his objections. As the secretary could only see mandarins of very inferior rank he returned to Hongkong without acquiring any very definite information, but he learned enough to say that Yeh denied that Keying's arrangement possessed any validity. The Chinese case was that it had been allowed to drop on both sides, and the utmost concession Yeh would make was to agree to an interview at the Jinsin Packhouse outside the city walls. This proposition was declared to be inadmissible, when Yeh ironically remarked that he must consequently assume that "Sir John Bowring did not wish for an interview." It was hoped to overcome Chinese finesse with counter finesse, and Sir John Bowring hastened to Shanghai with the object of establishing direct relations with the viceroy of the Two Kiang. After complaining of the want of courtesy evinced by Yeh throughout his correspondence, he expressed the wish to negotiate with any of the other high officials of the empire.

The reply of Eleang, who held this post, and who was believed to be well disposed to Europeans, did not advance matters. He had no authority, he said, in the matter, and could not interfere in what was not his concern. Commissioner Yeh was the official appointed by the emperor to conduct relations with the foreigners, and no other official could assume his functions. Sir John Bowring therefore returned to Hongkong without having effected anything by his visit to Shanghai, but at this moment the advance of the rebels to the neighborhood of Canton seemed likely to effect a diversion that might have important consequences. In a state of apprehension as to the safety of the town, Yeh applied to Sir John Bowring for assistance against the rebels, but this could not be granted, and Sir John Bowring only proceeded to Canton to superintend the preparations made for the defense of the English settlement at that place. All the consuls issued a joint proclamation declaring their intention to remain neutral. The prompt suppression of the rebellion, so far as any danger to Canton went, restored the confidence of the Chinese authorities, and they reverted to their old position on the question of the opening of the gates of Canton.

In June, 1855, Sir John Bowring returned to the subject of official interviews, and made an explicit demand for the reception if not of himself, then at least of the consul at Canton. Yeh took his time before he made any reply, and when he did send one it was to the effect that there was no precedent for an interview with a consul, and that as Sir John had refused to meet him outside the city there was an end of the matter. Mr. Harry Parkes succeeded Mr. Alcock as consul at Canton, and no inconsiderable amount of tact was required to carry on relations with officials who refused to show themselves. But the evil day of open collision could not be averted, and the antagonism caused by clashing views and interests at last broke forth on a point which would have been promptly settled, had there been direct intercourse between the English and Chinese officials.

On October 8, 1856, Mr. Parkes reported to Sir John Bowring at Hongkong the particulars of an affair which had occurred on a British-owned lorcha at Canton. The lorcha "Arrow," employed in the iron trade between Canton and the mouth of the river, commanded by an English captain, and flying the English flag, had been boarded by a party of mandarins and their followers while at anchor near the Dutch Folly. The lorcha—a Portuguese name for a fast sailing boat—had been duly registered in the office at Hongkong, and although not entitled at that precise moment to British protection, through the careless neglect to renew the license, this fact was only discovered subsequently, and was not put forward by the Chinese in justification of their action. The gravity of the affair was increased by the fact that the English flag was conspicuously displayed, and that, notwithstanding the remonstrances of the master, it was ostentatiously hauled down. The crew were carried off prisoners with the exception of two men, left at their own request to take charge of the vessel. Mr. Parkes at once sent a letter to Yeh on the subject of this "very grave insult," requesting that the captured crew of the "Arrow" should be returned to that vessel without delay, and that any charges made against them should be then examined into at the English consulate. In his reply Commissioner Yeh justified and upheld the act of his subordinates. Of the twelve men seized, he returned nine, but with regard to the three whom he detained, he declared one to be a criminal and the others important witnesses. Not merely would he not release them, but he proceeded to justify their apprehension, while he did not condescend to so much as notice the points of the insult to the English flag and of his having violated treaty obligations. Yeh did not attempt to offer any excuse for the proceedings taken in his name. He asserted certain things as facts which, in his opinion, it was sufficient for him to accept that they should pass current. But the evidence on which they were based was not sufficient to obtain credence in the laxest court of justice; but even if it had been conclusive it

would not have justified the removal of the crew from the
"Arrow" when the British flag was flying conspicuously at
her mast. What, in brief, was the Chinese case? It was
that one of the crew had been recognized by a man passing
in a boat as one of a band of pirates who had attacked, ill-
used, and plundered him several weeks before. He had
forthwith gone to the Taotai of Canton, presented a demand
for redress, and that officer had at once given the order for
the arrest of the offender, with the result described. There
is no necessity to impugn the veracity of the Chinaman's
story, but it did not justify the breach of "the ex-territorial
rights of preliminary consular investigation before trial"
granted to all under the protection of the English flag. The
plea of delay did not possess any force either, for the man
could have been arrested just as well by the English consul
as by the mandarins, but it would have involved a damag-
ing admission of European authority in the matter of a
Chinese subject, and the mandarins thought there was no
necessity to curtail their claim to jurisdiction. Commissioner Yeh did not attempt any excuses, and he even declared that "the 'Arrow' is not a foreign lorcha, and, therefore," he said, "there is no use to enter into any discussion
about her."

The question of the nationality of the "Arrow" was
complicated by the fact that its registry had expired ten
days before its seizure. The master explained that this
omission was due to the vessel having been at sea, and
that it was to have been rectified as soon as he returned
to Hongkong. As Lord Clarendon pointed out, this fact
was not merely unknown to the Chinese, but it was also
"a matter of British regulation which would not justify
seizure by the Chinese. No British lorcha would be safe
if her crew were liable to seizure on these grounds." The
history of the lorcha "Arrow" was officially proved to be
as follows: "The 'Arrow' was heretofore employed in trading on the coast, and while so employed was taken by
pirates. By them she was fitted out and employed on the

Canton River during the disturbances between the imperialists and the insurgents. While on this service she was captured by the braves of one of the loyalist associations organized by the mandarins for the support of the government. By this association she was publicly sold, and was purchased by a Chin-chew Hong, a respectable firm at Canton, which also laid out a considerable sum in repairing her and otherwise fitting her out. She arrived at Hongkong about the month of June, 1855, at which time a treaty was on foot (which ended in a bargain) between Fong Aming, Messrs. T. Burd & Co.'s comprador, and Lei-yeong-heen, one of the partners in the Chin-chew Hong, for the purchase of the lorcha by the former. Shortly after the arrival of the vessel at Hongkong she was claimed by one Quantai, of Macao, who asserted that she had been his property before she was seized by the pirates. Of course, the then owner disputed his claim; upon which he commenced a suit in the Vice-Admiralty Court. After a short time, by consent of the parties, the question was referred to arbitration, but the arbitrators could not agree and an umpire was appointed, who awarded that the ownership of the lorcha should continue undisturbed. The ownership of the vessel was then transferred to Fong Aming, and in his name she is registered. These are the simple facts connected with the purchase of the lorcha by a resident of the colony at Hongkong and her registry as a British vessel, and it is from these facts that the Imperial Commissioner Yeh has arrived at an erroneous conclusion as to the ownership of the boat.'' As the first step toward obtaining the necessary reparation, a junk, which was supposed to be an imperial war vessel, was seized as a hostage, and Mr. Parkes addressed another letter to Yeh reminding him that ''the matter which has compelled this menace still remains unsettled.''

Had there been that convenient mode of communication between the governor of Hongkong and the Chinese officials at Canton which was provided for by the Nankin Treaty and the Keying Convention, the ''Arrow'' complication would, in all probability, never have arisen, and it is also scarcely less certain that it would not have produced such serious consequences as it did but for the arrogance of Yeh. He even attempted to deny that the "Arrow" carried the English flag, but this was so clearly proved to be a fact by both English and Chinese witnesses that it ceased to hold a place in the Chinese case. As it was clear that Commissioner Yeh would not give way, and as delay would only encourage him, the admiral on the station, Sir Michael Seymour, received instructions to attack the four forts of the Barrier, and he captured them without loss. Thus, after an interval of fourteen years, was the first blow struck in what may be called the third act of Anglo-Chinese relations, but it would be a mistake to suppose that the "Arrow" case was the sole cause of this appeal to arms. A blue book, bearing the significant title of "Insults to Foreigners," gives a list and narrative of the many outrages and indignities inflicted on Europeans between 1842 and 1856. The evidence contained therein justifies the statement that the position of Europeans in China had again become most unsafe and intolerable. Those who persist in regarding the "Arrow" affair as the only cause of the war may delude themselves into believing that the Chinese were not the most blameworthy parties in the quarrel; but no one who seeks the truth and reads all the evidence will doubt that if there had been no "Arrow" case there would still have been a rupture between the two countries. The Chinese officials, headed by Yeh, had fully persuaded themselves that, as the English had put up with so much, and had acquiesced in the continued closing of the gates of Canton, they were not likely to make the "Arrow" affair a casus belli. Even the capture of the Barrier forts did not bring home to their minds the gravity of the situation.

After dismantling these forts, Sir Michael Seymour proceeded up the river, capturing the fort in Macao Passage, and arriving before Canton on the same day. An ultimatum was at once addressed to Yeh, stating that unless

he at once complied with all the English demands the
admiral would "proceed with the destruction of all the defenses and public buildings of this city and of the government vessels in the river." This threat brought no satisfactory answer, and the Canton forts were seized, their guns
spiked and the men-of-war placed with their broadsides
opposite the city. Then Yeh, far from being cowed, uttered
louder defiance than ever. He incited the population to
make a stubborn resistance; he placed a reward of thirty
dollars on the head of every Englishman slain or captured,
and he publicly proclaimed that there was no alternative but
war. He seems to have been driven to these extremities by
a fear for his own personal safety and official position. He
had no warrant from his imperial master to commit China
to such a dangerous course as another war with the English,
and he knew that the only way to vindicate his proceedings
was to obtain some success gratifying to national vanity.
While Yeh was counting on the support of the people, the
English admiral began the bombardment of the city, directing his fire principally against Yeh's yamen and a part of
the wall, which was breached in two days. After some resistance the breach was carried; a gate was occupied, and
Sir Michael Seymour and Mr. Parkes proceeded to the
yamen of the viceroy, but as it was thought dangerous
to occupy so large a city with so small a force the positions seized were abandoned, although still commanded by
the fire of the fleet. After a few days' rest active operations were resumed against the French Folly fort and a
large fleet of war junks which had collected up the river.
After a warm engagement the vessels were destroyed and
the fort captured. Undaunted by these successive reverses,
Yeh still breathed nothing but defiance, and refused to make
the least concession. There remained no alternative but to
prosecute hostilities with renewed vigor. On the 12th and
13th of November, Sir Michael attacked the Bogue forts on
both sides of the river and captured them with little loss.
These forts mounted 400 guns, but only contained 1,000 men.

Notwithstanding these continuous reverses, the Chinese remained defiant and energetic. As soon as the English admiral left Canton to attack the Bogue forts the Chinese hastened to re-occupy all their positions and to repair the breaches. They succeeded in setting fire to and thus destroying the whole foreign settlement, and they carried off several Europeans, all of whom were put to death and some of them tortured. The heads of these Europeans treacherously seized and barbarously murdered were paraded throughout the villages of Kwangtung, in order to stimulate recruiting and to raise national enthusiasm to a high pitch. Notwithstanding their reverses whenever it became a question of open fighting, the Chinese, by their obstinacy and numbers, at last succeeded in convincing Sir Michael Seymour that his force was too small to achieve any decisive result, and he accordingly withdrew from his positions in front of the city, and sent home a request for a force of 5,000 troops. Meantime the Chinese were much encouraged by the lull in hostilities, and for the time being Yeh himself was not dissatisfied with the result. The Cantonese saw in the destruction of the foreign settlement and the withdrawal of the English fleet some promise of future victory, and at all events sufficient reason for the continued confidence of the patriot Yeh. Curiously enough, there was peace and ostensible goodwill along the coast and at the other treaty ports, while war and national animosity were in the ascendant at Canton. The governor-generals of the Two Kiang and Fuhkien declared over and over again that they wished to abide by the Treaty of Nankin, and they threw upon Yeh the responsibility of his acts. Even Hienfung refrained from showing any unequivocal support of his truculent lieutenant, although there is no doubt that he was impressed by the reports of many victories over the English barbarians with which Yeh supplied him. As long as Yeh was able to keep the quarrel a local one, and to thus shield the central government from any sense of personal danger, he enjoyed the good wishes, if not the active support, of

his sovereign.   But, unfortunately for the success of his
schemes, only the most energetic support of the Pekin Government in money and men could have enabled him to hold
his own; and as he did nothing but report victories in order
to gain a hearing for his policy, he could not grumble when
he was not sent the material aid of which he stood most in
need.   His unreasonable action had done much to unite all
foreign nations against China.   French, American and Spanish subjects, as well as English, had been the victims of Chinese ignorance and cruelty, and they all saw that the success
of Yeh's policy would render their position untenable.

On the receipt of Sir Michael Seymour's request for a
force of 5,000 men, it was at once perceived in London that
the question of our relations with China had again entered
a most important and critical phase.   It was at once decided
to send the force for which the admiral asked; and, while
1,500 men were sent from England and a regiment from the
Mauritius, the remainder was to be drawn from the Madras
army.   At the same time it was considered necessary to send
an embassador of high rank to acquaint the Pekin authorities that, while such acts as those of Yeh would not be tolerated, there was no desire to press too harshly on a country
which was only gradually shaking off its exclusive prejudices.   Lord Elgin was selected for the difficult mission, and
his instructions contained the following five categorical demands, the fourth of which was the most important in its
consequences.

Those instructions were conveyed in two dispatches of
the same date, April 20, 1857.   We quote the following as
the more important passages: ''The demands which you are
instructed to make will be: (1), for reparation of injuries to
British subjects, and, if the French officers should co-operate
with you, for those to French subjects also; (2) for the complete execution at Canton, as well as at the other ports, of
the stipulations of the several treaties; (3) compensation to
British subjects and persons entitled to British protection for
losses incurred in consequence of the late disturbances; (4)

the assent of the Chinese Government to the residence at Pekin, or to the occasional visit to that capital, at the option of the British Government, of a minister duly accredited by the queen to the emperor of China, and the recognition of the right of the British plenipotentiary and chief superintendent of trade to communicate directly in writing with the high officers at the Chinese capital, and to send his communications by messengers of his own selection, such arrangements affording the best means of insuring the due execution of the existing treaties, and of preventing future misunderstandings; (5) a revision of the treaties with China with a view to obtaining increased facilities for commerce, such as access to cities on the great rivers as well as to Chapoo and to other ports on the coast, and also permission for Chinese vessels to resort to Hongkong for purposes of trade from all ports of the Chinese empire without distinction." These were the demands formulated by the English Government for the consent of China, and seven proposals were made as to how they were to be obtained should coercion become necessary. It was also stated that "it is not the intention of her Majesty's Government to undertake any land operations in the interior of the country."

An event of superior, and, indeed, supreme importance occurred to arrest the movement of the expedition to Canton. When Lord Elgin reached Singapore, on June 3, 1857, he found a letter waiting for him from Lord Canning, then Governor-General of India, informing him of the outbreak of the Indian Mutiny, and imploring him to send all his troops to Calcutta in order to avert the overthrow of our authority in the valley of the Ganges, where, "for a length of 750 miles, there were barely 1,000 European soldiers." To such an urgent appeal there could only be one answer, and the men who were to have chastised Commissioner Yeh followed Havelock to Cawnpore and Lucknow. But while Lord Elgin sent his main force to Calcutta, he himself proceeded to Hongkong, where he arrived in the first week of July, and found that hostilities had proceeded to a still more advanced

stage than when Sir Michael Seymour wrote for re-enforcements.   The Chinese had become so confident during the
winter that that officer felt bound to resume offensive measures against them, and having been joined by a few more
men-of-war, and having also armed some merchant ships
of light draught, he attacked a main portion of the Chinese
fleet occupying a very strong position in Escape Creek.   The
attack was intrusted to Commodore Elliott, who, with five
gunboats and the galleys of the larger men-of-war, carried
out with complete success and little loss the orders of his
superior officer.   Twenty-seven armed junks were destroyed,
and the thirteen that escaped were burned the next day.
It was then determined to follow up this success by attacking the headquarters of Yeh's army at Fatshan, the place
already referred to as being some distance from Canton.
By road it is six and by water twelve miles from that city.
The remainder of the Chinese fleet was drawn up in Fatshan
Channel, and the Chinese had made such extensive preparations for its defense, both on land and on the river, that they
were convinced of the impregnability of its position.

The Chinese position was unusually strong, and had been
selected with considerable judgment.   An island named after
the hyacinth lies in midstream two miles from the entrance
to the Fatshan Channel, which joins the main course of the
Sikiang a few miles above the town of that name.   The
island is flat and presents no special advantages for defense,
but it enabled the Chinese to draw up a line of junks across
the two channels of the river, and to place on it a battery of
six guns, thus connecting their two squadrons.   The seventy-
two junks were drawn up with their sterns facing down
stream, and their largest gun bearing on any assailant proceeding up it.   On the left bank of the river an elevated and
precipitous hill had been occupied in force and crowned with
a battery of nineteen guns, and other batteries had been
erected at different points along the river.   There seems no
reason to question the accuracy of the estimate that more
than 300 pieces of artillery and 10,000 men were holding this

position, which had been admirably chosen and carefully
strengthened. The force which Sir Michael Seymour had
available to attack this formidable position slightly exceeded
2,000 men, conveyed to the attack in six gunboats and a
large flotilla of boats. · The English advance was soon known
to the Chinese, who began firing from their junks and batteries as soon as they came within range. Three hundred
marines were landed .to attack the battery on the hill, which
was found not to be so strong as it appeared; for on the
most precipitous side the Chinese, believing it to be unscal-
able, had placed no guns, and those in position could not be
moved to bear on the assailants in that quarter. The marines gained the top with scarcely any loss, and as they
charged over the side the Chinese retired with little loss,
owing to the ill-directed fire of the marines.

Meantime the sailors had attacked the Chinese position
on the river. The tide was at low water, and the Chinese
had barred the channel with a row of sunken junks, leaving
a narrow passage known only to themselves. The leading
English boat struck on the hidden barrier, but the passage
being discovered the other vessels got through. Those boats
which ran aground were gradually floated, one after the
other, by the rising tide, and at last the flotilla, with little
damage, reached the line of stakes which the Chinese had
placed to mark the range of the guns in their junks. At
once the fire from the seventy-two junks and the battery on
Hyacinth Island became so furious and well-directed that
it was a matter of astonishment how the English boats
passed through it. They reached and pierced the line of
junks, of which one after another was given to the flames.
Much of the success of the attack was due to the heroic
example of Commodore Harry Keppel, who led the advance
party of 500 cutlasses, and who gave the Chinese no time to
rest or rally. Having broken the line of junks, he took
up the pursuit in his seven boats, having determined that
the only proof of success could be the capture of Fatshan,
and after four miles' hard rowing he came in sight of the

elaborate defenses drawn up by the Chinese for the security
of that place.   At the short range of a quarter of a mile the
fire of the Chinese guns was tremendous and destructive.
Keppel's own boat was reduced to a sinking state, and had
to be abandoned.   Some of his principal officers were killed,
three of his boats ran aground, and things looked black for
the small English force.   At this critical moment, the Chinese, thinking that they had checked the English attack,
and hearing of the magnitude of their reverse down stream,
thought their best course would be to retire.   Then the few
English boats resumed the attack, and hung on to the
retreating junks like bull-dogs.   Many junks were given
to the flames, and five were carried off under the teeth of
the Fatshan populace; but Keppel's force was too small to
hold that town and put it to the ransom, so the worn-out,
but still enthusiastic force, retired to join the main body
under Sir Michael Seymour, who was satisfied that he had
achieved all that was necessary or prudent with his squadron.   In these encounters thirteen men were killed and
forty wounded, of whom several succumbed to their wounds,
for it was noticed that the Chinese shot inflicted cruel injuries.   The destruction of the Chinese fleet on the Canton
River could not be considered heavily purchased at the cost,
and the extent of the trepidation caused by Commodore
Keppel's intrepidity could not be accurately measured.

Lord Elgin reached Hongkong very soon after this event,
and, although he brought no soldiers with him, he found
English opinion at Hongkong very pronounced in favor of
an attack on Canton with a view of reopening that city
to trade.   But the necessary force was not available, and
Lord Elgin refused to commit himself to this risky course.
Sir Michael Seymour said the attack would require 5,000
troops, and General Ashburnham thought it could be done
with 4,000 men if all were effective, while the whole Hongkong garrison numbered only 1,500, and of these one-sixth
were invalided.   Lord Elgin decided to go to Calcutta, and
ascertain when Lord Canning would be able to spare him

the troops necessary to bring China to reason. He returned to Hongkong on September 20, and he found matters very much as he had left them, and all the English force was capable of was to blockade the river. To supplement the weakness of the garrison a coolie corps of 750 Chinese was organized, and proved very efficient, and toward the end of November troops, chiefly marines, began at last to arrive from England. A fleet of useful gunboats of small draught, under Captain Sherard Osborn, arrived for the purpose of operating against the junks in shallow creeks and rivers. At the same time, too, came the French embassador, Baron Gros, charged with a similar mission to Lord Elgin, and bent on proving once for all that the pretensions of China to superiority over other nations were absurd and untenable.

On December 12, Lord Elgin sent Yeh a note apprising him of his arrival as plenipotentiary from Queen Victoria, and pointing out the repeated insults and injuries inflicted on Englishmen, culminating in the outrage to their flag and the repeated refusal to grant any reparation for their wrongs. But Lord Elgin went on to say that even at this eleventh hour there was time to stay the progress of hostilities by making prompt redress. The terms were plain and simple, and the English demands were confined to two points—the complete execution at Canton of all treaty engagements, including the free admission of British subjects to the city, and compensation to British subjects and persons entitled to British protection for losses incurred in consequence of the late disturbances. To this categorical demand Yeh made a long reply, going over the ground of controversy, reasserting what he wished to believe were the facts, and curtly concluding that the trade might continue on the old conditions, and that each side should pay its own losses. Mr. Wade said that his language might bear the construction that the English consul, Mr. Harry Parkes, should pay all the cost himself. If Commissioner Yeh was a humorist he chose a bad time for indulging his proclivities, and, a sufficient force being available, orders were at once given to attack Canton.   On December 15, Honan was occupied, and ten days were passed in bringing up the troops and the necessary stores, when, all being in readiness, an ultimatum was sent to Yeh that if he would not give way within forty-eight hours the attack would commence.   At the same time every effort was made to warn the unoffending townspeople, so that they might remove to a place of safety.   The attacking force numbered about 5,000 English, 1,000 French, and 750 of the Chinese coolie corps, and it was agreed that the most vulnerable point in the Chinese position was Lin's fort, on the eastern side of the city.   When the attack began, on December 28, this fort was captured in half an hour, and the Chinese retired to the northern hills, which they had made their chief position in 1842.   The destruction of Lin's fort by the accidental explosion of the magazine somewhat neutralized the advantage of its capture.   On the following day the order was given to assault the city by escalade, and three separate parties advanced on the eastern wall.   The Chinese kept up a good fire until the troops were within a short distance, but before the ladders were placed against the wall they abandoned their defenses and fled.   The English troops reformed on the wide rampart of the wall and pursued the Chinese to the north gate, where, being joined by some Manchu troops, the latter turned and charged up to the bayonets of an English regiment.   But they were repulsed and driven out of the city, and simultaneously with this success the fort on Magazine Hill, commanding both the city and the Chinese position on the northern hills, was captured without loss.   In less than two hours the great city of Canton was in the possession of the allies, and the Chinese resistance was far less vigorous and worse directed than on any occasion of equal importance.   Still, the English loss was fourteen killed and eighty-three wounded, while the French casualties numbered thirty-four.   The Chinese had, however, to abandon their positions north of the city, and their elaborate fortifications were blown up.

Although all regular resistance had been overcome, the

greater part of the city remained in possession of the Chinese and of Yeh in person. That official, although in the lowest straits, had lost neither his fortitude nor his ferocity. He made not the least sign of surrender, and his last act of authority was to order the execution of 400 citizens, whom he denounced as traitors to their country. From his yamen in the interior of the city, when he found that the English hesitated to advance beyond the walls, he incited the populace to fresh efforts of hostility, and, in order to check their increasing audacity, it was resolved to send a force into the city to effect the capture of Yeh. On January 5, 1858, three detachments were sent into the native city, and they advanced at once upon the official residences of Yeh and Pihkwei, the governor. The Chinese were quite unprepared for this move, and being taken unawares they offered scarcely any resistance. The yamen was occupied and the treasury captured, while Pihkwei was made prisoner in his own house. The French at the same time attacked and occupied the Tartar city—a vast stone-built suburb which had been long allowed to fall into decay, and which, instead of being occupied, as was believed, by 7,000 Manchu warriors, was the residence of bats and nauseous creatures. But the great object of the attack was unattained, for Yeh still remained at large, and no one seemed to know where he ought to be sought, for all the official buildings had been searched in vain. But Mr. Parkes, by indefatigable inquiry, at last gained a clew from a poor scholar whom he found poring over an ancient classic at the library, undisturbed in the midst of the turmoil. From him he learned that Yeh would probably be found in a yamen situated in the southwest quarter of the city. Mr. Parkes hastened thither with Captain (afterward Admiral) Cooper Key and a party of sailors. They arrived just in time, for all the preparations for flight had been made, and Captain Key caught Yeh with his own hand as he was escaping over the wall. One of his assistants came forward with praiseworthy devotion and declared himself to be Yeh, in the hope of saving his su-

perior; but the deception was at once detected by Mr.
Parkes, who assured Yeh that no harm would be done him.
The capture of Yeh completed the effect of the occupation
of Canton, and the disappearance of the most fanatical opponent of the foreigners insured the tranquillity of the Canton
region, which had been the main seat of disorder, during the
remainder of the war. The government of Canton was then
intrusted to Pihkwei and a commission of one Frenchman
and two Englishmen, and the Chinese admitted it had never
been better governed. Yeh himself was sent to Calcutta,
where he died two years later, and, considering the abundant evidence of his cruel treatment of defenseless prisoners,
he had every reason to consider his punishment lenient.

Having thus settled the difficulty at Canton, it remained
for Lord Elgin to carry out the other part of his task, and
place diplomatic relations between England and China on a
satisfactory basis by obtaining the right of direct communication with Pekin. A letter dated February 11, 1858, was
sent to the senior Secretary of State at Pekin describing
what had occurred in the south, and summarizing what
would be required from the Chinese Government. The
English and French plenipotentiaries also notified that they
would proceed to Shanghai for the purpose of conducting
further negotiations. This letter was duly forwarded to
Pekin by the Governor of Kiangsu, and when Lord Elgin
reached Shanghai on March 30 he found the reply of Yuching, the chief adviser of Hienfung, waiting for him.
Yuching's letter was extremely unsatisfactory. It was
arrogant in its terms and impracticable as to its proposals.
Lord Elgin was told that "no imperial commissioner ever
conducts business at Shanghai," and that it behooved the
English minister to wait at Canton until the arrival of a new
imperial commissioner from Pekin. The only concession the
Chinese made was to dismiss Yeh from his posts, and as he
was a prisoner in the hands of the English this did not mean
much. Lord Elgin's reply to this communication was to
announce his intention of proceeding to the Peiho, and there

negotiating direct with the imperial government. Lord Elgin reached the Gulf of Pechihli about the middle of April, and he again addressed Yuching in the hope of an amicable settlement, and requested that the emperor would appoint some official to act as his plenipotentiary. Three minor officials were appointed, more out of curiosity than from a desire to promote business, but on Lord Elgin discovering that they were of inferior rank and that their powers were inadequate, he declined to see them. But Yuching refused to appoint any others; stating curtly that their powers were ample for the adjustment of affairs, and then Lord Elgin announced that he would proceed up the Peiho to Tientsin. Some delay was caused by the non-arrival of the fleet, which was not assembled in the Gulf of Pechihli, through different causes of delay, until the end of May, or about three weeks after Lord Elgin announced his intention of forcing his way up to Tientsin. There is no doubt that Sir Michael Seymour was in no sense to blame for this delay, but unfortunately it aroused considerable irritation in the mind of Lord Elgin, who sent home a dispatch, without informing his colleague, stating that the delay was "a most grievous disappointment," and attributing it to the supineness of the admiral.

On May 19 the allied fleet proceeded to the mouth of the river, and summoned the commandant to surrender the Taku forts on the following morning. No reply being received, the attack commenced, and after the bombardment had gone on at short range for an hour and a quarter the Chinese gunners were driven from their batteries, and the troops landed, occupying the whole line of forts and intrenched camps. An attempt to injure our fleet by fire-ships miscarried, and considering that the Chinese had some of their best troops present, including a portion of the Imperial Guard, their resistance was not as great as might have been expected. Their general committed suicide, and the Chinese lost the best part of their artillery, which had been removed from Pekin and Tientsin for the defense of the entrance to the Peiho. The fleet proceeded up the river to Tientsin, and Lord Elgin took up his quarters in that city. The Chinese Government was brought to reason by this striking success, and, with his capital menaced, the emperor hastened to delegate full powers to two high commissioners, Kweiliang and Hwashana, both Manchus and dignitaries of the highest birth and rank. Their powers were superior to those granted to Keying at the time of the old war, and they were commanded with affectionate earnestness to show the foreigners that they were competent and willing to grant anything not injurious to China. Nothing could be more satisfactory than the proposals of the new Chinese representatives, and they were anxious to settle everything with the least possible delay. At this point there reappeared upon the scene a man whose previous experience and high position entitled him to some consideration. Less than a week after his first interview with the imperial representatives, Lord Elgin received a letter from Keying, who, it was soon found, had come on a self-appointed mission to induce the English by artifice and plausible representation to withdraw their fleet from the river. His zeal was increased by the knowledge that the penalty of failure would be death, and as his reputation had been very great among Europeans there is no saying but that he might have succeeded had there not been discovered in Yeh's yamen at Canton some of his papers, which showed that he had played a double part throughout, and that at heart he was bitterly anti-foreign. When he found that the English possessed this information he hastened back to Pekin, where he was at once summoned before the Board of Punishment for immediate judgment, and, being found guilty, it was ordered that as he had acted "with stupidity and precipitancy" he should be strangled forthwith. As an act of extreme grace the emperor allowed him to put an end to his existence in consideration of his being a member of the imperial family.

After the departure of Keying, negotiations proceeded very satisfactorily with Kweiliang and Hwashana, and all the points were practically agreed upon, excepting the right to have a resident minister at Pekin. This claim was opposed on several grounds. It was not merely something that had never been heard of, but it would probably be attended with peril to the envoy as well as to the Chinese Government. Then the commissioners wanted to know if he would wear the Chinese dress, if all the powers would have only one minister, and if he would make the kotow? Finding such arguments fail, they asked that the visit of an English embassador to Pekin should be postponed till a more favorable occasion. They made the admission that "there is properly no objection to the permanent residence at Pekin of a plenipotentiary minister of her Britannic Majesty," and they even spoke of sending a return mission to London; but they deprecated the proposal as novel and as specially risky at this moment in consequence of the formidable Taeping Rebellion. These representations did not fail to produce their effect, for it was not to the interest of Europeans generally that the emperor's authority should be subverted on the morrow of his signing a treaty with us. In consequence of these feelings, and with a wish to reciprocate the generally conciliatory attitude of the Chinese officials, Kweiliang and Hwashana were informed that the right would be waived for the present, except that it would be necessary for the English minister to visit Pekin, twelve months later, on the occasion of exchanging the ratifications of the treaty; and so the matter was left pending the arrival of that occasion. While the Treaty of Tientsin provided for the conclusion of a peace that promised to be enduring, and arranged for the future diplomatic relations of the two countries, commissioners were duly appointed to meet at Shanghai and draw up a tariff. But at Tientsin the great crux in the commercial relations between us and the Chinese had been settled by the legalization of opium. It was agreed that opium might be imported into China on payment of thirty tacls, or about fifty dollars, per chest. Experience had shown that leaving the most largely-imported article into China contraband had been both futile and inconvenient, while the Chinese Government was a direct loser by not enjoying a legitimate source of revenue. How general the view had become that the evils of the use of opium were exaggerated, and, even admitting them, that there was no better way of diminishing their effect than by legalizing the import of opium, can be judged by the ready acquiescence of the Chinese commissioners; and here, from many other matured opinions, we may quote the final and deliberate conviction of Sir Henry Pottinger:

"I take this opportunity to advert to one important topic on which I have hitherto considered it right to preserve a rigid silence—I allude to the trade in opium; and I now unhesitatingly declare in this public manner that after the most unbiased and careful observations I have become convinced during my stay in China that the alleged demoralizing and debasing evils of opium have been and are vastly exaggerated. Like all other indulgences, excesses in its use are bad and reprehensible; but I have neither myself seen such vicious consequences as are frequently ascribed to it, nor have I been able to obtain authentic proofs or information of their existence. The great, and perhaps I might say sole, objection to the trade, looking at it morally and abstractedly, that I have discovered, is that it is at present contraband and prohibited by the laws of China, and therefore to be regretted and disavowed; but I have striven—and I hope with some prospect of eventual success—to bring about its legalization; and were that point once effected, I am of opinion that its most objectionable feature would be altogether removed. Even as it now exists it appears to me to be unattended with a hundredth part of the debasement and misery which may be seen in our native country from the lamentable abuse of ardent spirits, and those who so sweepingly condemn the opium trade on that principle need not, I think, leave the shores of England to find a far greater and more besetting evil."

The ink on the Tientsin treaty was scarcely dry before

reasons began to be furnished against the sincerity of the emperor and his desire for peace. Before the fleet left the Peiho workmen were already engaged repairing and re-arming the Taku forts, and the morrow of Lord Elgin's departure from Hongkong witnessed the revival of disturbances round Canton, where the new imperial commissioner Hwang, instead of seeking to restore harmony, had devoted himself to inciting the population to patriotic deeds in emulation of Commissioner Yeh. It was found necessary to take strenuous measures against the turbulent patriots of Kwantung, and to break up their main force in their strong and well-chosen position at Shektsin, which was accomplished by a vigorous attack both on land and water. The suspicion that the Chinese were not absolutely straightforward in their latest dealings with us was confirmed by the discovery at Shektsin of secret imperial edicts, breathing defiance to the foreigners and inciting the people to resistance. These and other facts warned the European authorities on the spot that there was no certainty that the Treaty of Tientsin would be ratified, or that a British envoy would be admitted into the capital for even the temporary business of a diplomatic ceremony. While people in Europe were assuming that the Chinese question might be dismissed for twenty years, the English consuls and commanders in the treaty ports were preparing themselves for a fresh and more vigorous demonstration of Chinese hostility and animosity. The matter that was to prove the sincerity and good faith of the Chinese Government was the reception at Pekin of the English officer intrusted with the duty of exchanging the ratified copies of the treaty. If he were allowed to proceed to Pekin there would be reason for accepting the assurances of the emperor that a permanent arrangement should be effected later on, when it would not injure his dignity or authority.

Mr. Frederick Bruce, who had been secretary to his brother, Lord Elgin, and who had previously served at Hongkong, was appointed her Majesty's representative for the purpose of exchanging the ratifications of the treaty. He was instructed to inform the Chinese officials that, while the British Government would not renounce the right of having a permanent resident minister at Pekin, they were prepared to waive it for a time by allowing diplomatic intercourse to be carried on at Shanghai. But no deviation was to be permitted from the arrangement that the ratifications were to be exchanged at Pekin, and Lord Malmesbury warned the new envoy that "all the arts at which the Chinese are such adepts will be put in practice to dissuade you from repairing to the capital." Mr. Bruce received his instructions on March 1, 1859, and the exchange of ratifications had to be effected before June 26. Mr. Bruce reached Hongkong in April, and he found the air full of unsatisfactory rumors; and when he reached Shanghai the uncertainty was intensified by the presence of Kweiliang and Hwashana, who seemed to think that everything might be settled without a journey to Pekin. They endeavored to get up a discussion on some unsettled details of minor importance, in the hope that the period for the ratification of the treaty might be allowed to expire. Mr. Bruce announced his imminent departure for the Peiho to Kweiliang, and expressed the hope that arrangements would be made for his safe conveyance to and appropriate accommodation at Pekin. Neither Mr. Bruce's instructions nor his own opinion justified any delay in proceeding to the north, and the fleet sent on in advance under the command of Admiral Hope reached the mouth of the Peiho on June 17, three days before Mr. Bruce. The admiral on arrival sent a notification to the Chinese officers in command of the forts that the English envoy was coming. But the reception given to the officers who conveyed this intimation was distinctly unfavorable and even hostile. The two boats sent ashore found that the entrance to the river was effectually barred by a row of iron stakes and by an inner boom, and that a large and excited crowd forbade them to land. A vague promise was given that an opening would be made in the obstructions to admit the passage of the English ships; but on the boats repeating their visit on the succeeding day they found that the small passages had been more effectually secured, and that there could no longer be any doubt that the Chinese did not intend to admit the English envoy. It was therefore determined to make a demonstration with the fleet, and if necessary to resort to force, which it was never doubted would be attended with little risk and crowned with complete success.

On June 25 the attack on the Taku forts began with the removal of the iron stakes forming the outer barrier by the steamer "Opossum," and this part of the operations was performed without a shot being fired. When, however, the eleven ships forming the English fleet reached the inner boom all the Chinese forts and batteries began to fire with an accuracy which showed that the guns had been trained to bear on this precise spot. The result of this unexpectedly vigorous bombardment was soon shown in the damaged condition of our ships. Two gunboats were sunk, all the vessels were more or less damaged, and when, after three hours' cannonade, it was sought to retrieve the doubtful fortune of the day by a land attack, the result only went to accentuate the ill results of the naval engagement. In this disastrous affair more than 800 men were killed and wounded, which, added to the loss of three gunboats, represented a very serious disaster. But the worst of it was that it convinced the emperor and his advisers that they could hold their own against Europeans, and that it placed the extreme party once more in the ascendant at Pekin. Sankolinsin, the Mongol prince who had checked the advance of the Taepings, became master of the situation, and declared that there was nothing to fear from an enemy who had been repulsed by the raw levies of the province while he held the flat country between the Peiho and Pekin with the flower of the Banner army. Mr. Bruce returned to Shanghai, the fleet to Hongkong, and the matter remained suspended until fresh instructions and troops could be received from Europe.

After some hesitation and delay, a plan of joint action was agreed upon in November, 1859, between France and

England, and it was hoped that the whole expeditionary force would have reached its destination by April, 1860. Pending its arrival Mr. Bruce was instructed to present an ultimatum with thirty days' grace demanding an immediate apology, the payment of a large indemnity amounting to $12,000,000 to both England and France, and the ratification of the Treaty of Tientsin. The minister, Pang Wanching, replied, categorically refusing all these requests; and, as neither indemnity nor apology was offered, there remained no alternative but the inevitable and supreme appeal to arms.

The troops which were to form the expedition were mainly drawn from India, and Sir Hope Grant, who had not merely distinguished himself during the Mutiny, but who had served in the first English war with China during the operations round Canton, was appointed to the command of the army; while Admiral Hope, strongly re-enforced in ships, retained the command of the naval forces. A force of five batteries of artillery, six regiments of infantry, two squadrons of cavalry, together with a body of horse and foot from the native army of India, amounting in all to about 10,000 men, was placed at the general's disposal in addition to the troops already in China. The French Government agreed to send another army of about two-thirds this strength to co-operate on the Peiho, and General Montauban was named for the command. The collection of this large expedition brought into prominence the necessity of employing as embassador a diplomatist of higher rank than Mr. Bruce; and accordingly, in February, Lord Elgin and Baron Gros were commissioned to again proceed to China for the purpose of securing the ratification of their own treaty. Sir Hope Grant reached Hongkong in March, 1860, and by his recommendation a stronger native contingent (one Sikh regiment, four Punjab regiments, two Bombay regiments, one Madras regiment of foot, and two irregular regiments of Sikh cavalry, known as Fane's and Probyn's Horse; Sir John Michel and Sir Robert Napier commanding divisions under Sir Hope Grant) was added, raising the English force in the field to more than 13,000 men. A lease was obtained in perpetuity, through the skillful negotiation of Mr. Parkes, of Kowlun and Stonecutter Island, where, from their salubrious position, it was proposed to place the troops on their arrival from India or England. Chusan was occupied the following month without opposition by an English brigade of 2,000 men.

The summer had commenced before the whole of the expedition assembled at Hongkong, whence it was moved northward to Shanghai about a year after the failure of the attack on the forts on the Peiho. A further delay was caused by the tardiness of the French, and July had begun before the expedition reached the Gulf of Pechihli. Then opposite opinions led to different suggestions, and while the English advocated proceeding to attack Pehtang, General Montauban drew up another plan of action. But the exigencies of the alliance compelled the English, who were ready, to wait for the French, who were not, in order that the assault might be made simultaneously. Before that time arrived the French commander had been brought round to the view that the proper plan of campaign was that suggested by the English commander; viz., to attack and capture Pehtang, whence the Taku forts might be taken in the rear. It is somewhat remarkable to observe that no one suggested a second time endeavoring to carry by a front attack these forts, which had in the interval since Admiral Hope's failure been rendered more formidable.

At Pehtang the Chinese had made few preparations for defense, and nothing of the same formidable character as at Taku. The forts on both sides of the river were neither extensive nor well-armed. The garrison consisted largely of Tartar cavalry, more useful for watching the movements of the foreigners than for working artillery when exposed to the fire of the new Armstrong guns of the English. The attacking force landed in boats and by wading, Sir Hope Grant setting his men the example. No engagement took place on the night of disembarkation. When morning broke, a suspicious silence in the enemy's quarters strengthened the belief that Pehtang would not be defended. While the garrison had resolved not to resist an attack, they had contemplated causing their enemy as much loss as if he had been obliged to carry the place by storm by placing shells in the magazine which would be exploded by the moving of some gunlocks put in a spot where they could not fail to be trodden upon. This plot, which was thoroughly in accordance with the practices of Chinese warfare, was fortunately divulged by a native more humane than patriotic, and Pehtang was captured and occupied without the loss of a single man. This success at the commencement enabled the whole of the expedition to land without further delay or difficulty. Three days after the capture of Pehtang, reconnoitering parties were sent out to ascertain what the Chinese were doing, and whether they had made any preparations to oppose an advance toward Taku or Tientsin. Four miles from Pehtang they came in sight of a strongly intrenched camp, where several thousand men opened fire upon the reconnoitering parties with their gingalls, and several men were wounded. The object being only to find out what the Celestial army was doing, and where it was, the Europeans withdrew on discovering the proximity of so strong a force. The great difficulty was to discover a way of getting from Pehtang on to some of the main roads leading to the Peiho; for the whole of the surrounding country had been under water, and was more or less impassable. In fact, the region round Pehtang consisted of nothing but mud, while the one road, an elevated causeway, was blocked by the fortified camp just mentioned as having been discovered by the reconnoitering party. A subsequent reconnaissance, conducted by Colonel (now Lord) Wolseley, revealed the presence of a cart-track which might prove available for the march of troops. This track was turned to advantage for the purpose of taking the Chinese position in flank, and to Sir Robert Napier's division was assigned this, as it proved, difficult operation. When the maneuver of out-flanking had been satisfactorily accomplished, the attack was commenced in front. Here the Chinese stood to their position, but only for a brief time, as the fire from eighteen guns, including some forty-pounders, soon silenced their gingalls, and they precipitately abandoned their intrenchments. While the engagement in front had reached this favorable termination, Sir Robert Napier had been engaged on the right hand with a strong body of Tartar cavalry, which attacked with considerable valor, and with what seemed a possibility of success, until the guns opening upon them and the Sikh cavalry charging them dispelled their momentary dream of victory. The prize of this battle was the village of Sinho with its line of earthworks, one mile north of the Peiho, and about seven miles in the rear of the Taku forts.

The next day was occupied in examining the Chinese position and in discovering, what was more difficult than its capture, how it might be approached. It was found that the village, which formed a fortified square protected by batteries, could be best approached by the river bank, and the only obstacle in this quarter was that represented by the fire of the guns of two junks, supported by a battery on the opposite side of the river. These, however, were soon silenced by the superior fire directed upon them, and the guns were spiked by Captain Willis and a few sailors, who crossed the river for the purpose. The flank of the advance being thus protected, the attack on Tangku itself began with a cannonade from thirty-six pieces of the best artillery of that age. The Chinese fire was soon rendered innocuous, and their walls and forts were battered down. Even then, however, the garrison gave no signs of retreat, and it was not until the Armstrongs had been dragged within a very short distance of the walls, and the foot-soldiers had absolutely effected an entrance, that the garrison thought of their personal safety and turned in flight.

Some days before the battle and capture of Tangku, Lord Elgin received several communications from Hang, the Governor-general of Pechihli, requesting a cessation of hostilities, and announcing the approach of two imperial commissioners appointed for the express purpose of ratifying the Treaty of Tientsin. But Lord Elgin very wisely perceived that it would be impossible to negotiate on fair terms unless the Taku forts were in his possession. The capture of Tangku placed the allied forces in the rear of the northern forts on the Peiho; and those forts once occupied, the others on the southern side would be practically untenable and obliged to surrender at discretion. Several days were passed in preliminary observations and skirmishing. On the one side, the whole of the Tartar cavalry was removed to the southern bank; on the other, a bridge of boats was thrown across the Peiho, and the approach to the northern fort carefully examined up to 600 yards from the wall. At this point the views of the allied generals again clashed. General Montauban wished to attack the southern forts. Sir Hope Grant was determined to begin by carrying the northern. The attack on the chief northern fort commenced on the morning of August 21 with a heavy cannonade; the Chinese, anticipating the plans of the English, were the first to fire. The Chinese fought their guns with extraordinary courage. A shell exploded their principal magazine, which blew up with a terrible report; but as soon as the smoke cleared off they recommenced their fire with fresh ardor. Although even this fort had not been constructed with the same strength in the rear as they all presented in the front, the resistance was most vigorous. A premature attempt to throw a pontoon across the ditch was defeated with the loss of sixteen men. The coolie corps here came to the front, and, rushing into the water, held up the pontoons while the French and some English troops dashed across. But all their efforts to scale the wall were baffled, and it seemed as if they had only gone to self-destruction. While the battle was thus doubtfully contested, Major Anson, who had shown the greatest intrepidity on several occasions, succeeded in cutting the ropes that held up a drawbridge, and an entrance was soon effected within the body of the works. The Chinese still resisted

nobly, and it was computed that out of a garrison of 500
men but 100 escaped. The English loss was 22 killed, and
179, including 21 officers, were wounded. To these figures
must be added the French loss.

There still remained four more forts on the northern side
of the river, and it seemed as if these would offer further
resistance, as the garrisons uttered threats of defiance to a
summons to surrender. But appearances were deceptive,
and for the good reason that all of these forts were only protected in the rear by a slight wall. The French rushed impetuously to the attack, only to find that the garrison had
given up the defense, while a large number had actually
retired. Two thousand prisoners were made, and the fall
of the forts on the northern bank was followed by an immediate summons to those on the southern to surrender; and
as they were commanded by the guns in the former they
yielded with as good a grace as they could muster. The
following day formal occupation was made, and the spoil
included more than 600 cannon of various sizes and degrees
of efficiency. On that day also the fleet, which had during
these operations been riding at anchor off the mouth of the
river, proceeded across the bar, removed the different obstacles that had been intended to hinder its approach, and
Admiral Hope anchored in security off those very forts
which had repulsed him in the previous year, and which
would in all probability have continued to defy any direct
attack from the sea. Let it not be said, therefore, that Sir
Hope Grant's capture of the Taku forts reflected in any way
on the courage or capacity of Admiral Hope for the failure
in 1859.

By this decisive success the road to Tientsin was opened
both by land and by the river. The fleet of gunboats, which
had participated as far as they could without incurring any
undue danger in the attack on the forts, were ordered up the
Peiho; and the English embassador, escorted by a strong
naval and military force, proceeded to Tientsin, where it
would be possible, without any loss of dignity, to resume

negotiations with the Pekin Government. The advanced
gunboats arrived at Tientsin on August 23, and three days
later the greater portion of the expedition had entered that
city. No resistance was attempted, although several batteries and intrenched camps were passed on the way. Precautions were at once taken to make the position of the troops
as secure as possible in the midst of a very large and pre-
sumably hostile population. The people showed, according
to the ideas of Europe, an extraordinary want of patriotic
fervor, and were soon engaged, on the most amicable terms,
in conducting a brisk trade with the invaders of their country; but there was never any doubt that on the first sign of
a reverse they would have turned upon the foreign troops,
and completed by all the means in their power their discomfiture. Several communications passed between the opposite
camps during these days; and when Hang announced the
withdrawal of all Chinese troops from Tientsin he expressed
a wish that the English embassador would not bring many
vessels of war with him. But such requests were made
more with the desire to save appearances than from any
hope that they would be granted. The reality of their fears,
and of their consequent desire to negotiate, was shown by
the appointment of Kweiliang, who had arranged the Treaty
of Tientsin, as high commissioner to provide for the necessary ceremonies in connection with its ratification. Kweiliang
apparently possessed powers of the most extensive character;
and he hastened to inform Lord Elgin, who had taken up
his residence in a beautiful yamen in Tientsin, that he had
received the emperor's authority to discuss and decide everything. In response to this notification the reply was sent
that the three conditions of peace were an apology for the
attack on the English flag at Peiho, the payment of an indemnity, including the costs of the war, and, thirdly, the
ratification and execution of the Treaty of Tientsin, including, of course, the reception at Pekin of the representative
of the Queen of England on honorable terms adequate to
the dignity of that great sovereign. To none of these was

Kweiliang himself disposed to raise any objection. Only in connection with the details of the last-named point was there likely that any difference of opinion would arise; and that difference of opinion speedily revealed itself when it became known that the English insisted on the advance of their army to the town of Tungchow, only twelve miles distant from the walls of Pekin. To the Chinese ministers this simple precaution seemed like exacting the extreme rights of the conqueror, before, too, the act of conquest had been consummated; for already fresh troops were arriving from Mongolia and Manchuria, and the valor of Sankolinsin was beginning to revive. That the Chinese Government had, under the hard taskmaster, necessity, made great progress in its views on foreign matters was not to be denied, but somehow or other its movements always lagged behind the requirements of the hour, and the demands of the English were again ahead of what it was disposed to yield.

If the Chinese Government had promptly accepted the inevitable, and if Kweiliang had negotiated with as much celerity as he pretended to be his desire, peace might have been concluded and the Chinese saved some further ignominy. But it soon became clear that all the Chinese were thinking about was to gain time, and as the months available for active campaigning were rapidly disappearing, it was imperative that not the least delay should be sanctioned. On September 8, Lord Elgin and Sir Hope Grant left Tientsin with an advance force of about 1,500 men; and, marching by the highroad, reached the pretty village of Hosiwu, half-way between that town and the capital. A few days later this force was increased by the remainder of one division, while to Sir Robert Napier was left the task of guarding with the other Tientsin and the communications with the sea. At Hosiwu negotiations were resumed by Tsai, Prince of I, a nephew of the emperor, who declared that he had received authority to conclude all arrangements; but he was curtly informed that no treaty could be concluded save at Tungchow, and the army resumed its advance beyond Hosiwu.

The march was continued without molestation to a point
beyond the village of Matow, but when Sir Hope Grant
approached a place called Chan-chia-wan he found himself
in presence of a large army. This was the first sign of any
resolve to offer military opposition to the invaders since the
capture of the Taku forts, and it came to a great extent in
the manner of a surprise, for by a special agreement with
Mr. Parkes the settlement of the difficulty was to be concluded at Chan-chia-wan in an amicable manner. Instead,
however, of the emperor's delegates, the English commander
found Sankolinsin and the latest troops drawn from Pekin
and beyond the Wall in battle array, and occupying the
very ground which had been assigned for the English encampment.

The day before the English commander perceived that
he was in face of a strong force, Mr. Parkes and some other
officers and civilians had been sent ahead with an escort of
Sikh cavalry to arrange the final preliminaries with the imperial commissioners at Tungchow, both as to where the
camp was to be pitched and also as to the interview between
the respective plenipotentiaries of the opposing powers. This
party proceeded to Tungchow without encountering any opposition or perceiving any exceptional military precautions.
Troops were indeed observed at several points, and officers
in command of pickets demanded the nature of their business
and where they were going, but the reply "To the Commissioners" at once satisfied all inquiries and opened every barrier. The one incident that happened was of happy augury
for a satisfactory issue if the result went to prove the falla-
ciousness of human expectations. A change had in the meanwhile come over the minds of the imperial commissioners,
whether in accordance with the working of a deep and long-
arranged policy, or from the confidence created by the sight
of the numerous warriors drawn from the cradle of the
Manchu race for the defense of the capital and dynasty,
can never be ascertained with any degree of certainty.
Their tone suddenly assumed greater boldness and arro-

gance. To some of the Englishmen it appeared "almost offensive," and it was only after five hours' discussion between Mr. Parkes and the commissioners at Tungchow that some sign was given of a more yielding disposition. The final arrangements were hastily concluded in the evening of September 17 for the arrival of the troops at the proposed camping ground on the morrow, and for the interview that was to follow as soon after as possible. While Mr. Parkes and some of his companions were to ride forward in the morning to apprise Sir Hope Grant of what had been agreed upon, and to point out the site for his camp, the others were to remain in Tungchow with the greater part of the Sikh escort.

On their return toward the advancing English army in the early morning of the following day, Mr. Parkes and his party met with frequent signs of military movement in the country between Tungchow and Chan-chia-wan. Large bodies of infantry and gingall-men were seen marching from all quarters to the town. At Chan-chia-wan itself still more emphatic tokens were visible of a coming battle. Cavalry were drawn up in dense bodies, but under shelter. In a nullah one regiment of a thousand sabers was stationed with the men standing at their horses' heads ready for instant action. At another point a number of men were busily engaged in constructing a battery and in placing twelve guns in position. When the Englishmen gained the plain they found the proposed site of the English camp in the actual possession of a Chinese army, and a strong force of Tartar cavalry, alone reckoned to number six or seven thousand men, scouring the plain. To all inquiries as to what these warlike arrangements betokened no reply was made by the soldiers, and when the whereabout of the responsible general was asked there came the stereotyped answer that "he was many li away." To the most obtuse mind these arrangements could convey but one meaning. They indicated that the Chinese Government had resolved to make another endeavor to avert the concessions demanded from them by the

English and their allies, and to appeal once more to the God
of Battles ere they accepted the inevitable.   When the whole
truth flashed across the mind of Mr. Parkes, the army of Sir
Hope Grant might be, and indeed was, marching into the
trap prepared for it, with such military precautions perhaps
as a wise general never neglected, but still wholly unprepared for the extensive and well-arranged opposition planned
for its reception by a numerous army established in a strong
position of its own choosing.   It became, therefore, of the
greatest importance to communicate the actual state of affairs
to him, and to place at his disposal the invaluable information which the Englishmen returning from Tungchow had
in their possession.   But Mr. Parkes had still more to do.
It was his duty to bring before the Chinese imperial commissioners at the earliest possible moment the knowledge of this
flagrant breach of the convention he had concluded the day
before, to demand its meaning, and to point out the grave
consequences that must ensue from such treacherous hostility; and in that supreme moment, as he had done on the
many other critical occasions of his career in China—at Canton and Taku in particular—the one thought in the mind of
Mr. Parkes was how best to perform his duty.   He did not
forget also that, while he was almost in a place of safety
near the limits of the Chinese pickets, and not far distant
from the advancing columns of Sir Hope Grant, there were
other Englishmen in his rear possibly in imminent peril of
their lives amid the Celestials at Tungchow.

Mr. Parkes rode back, therefore, to that town, and with
him went one English dragoon, named Phipps, and one
Sikh sowar carrying a flag of truce on his spear-point.   We
must leave them for the moment to follow the movements
of the others.   To Mr. Loch was intrusted the task of communicating with Sir Hope Grant; while the remainder of
the party were to remain stationary, in order to show the
Chinese that they did not suspect anything, and that they
were full of confidence.   Mr. Loch, accompanied by two
Sikhs, rode at a hard canter away from the Chinese lines.

He passed through one body of Tartar cavalry without opposition, and reached the advanced guard of the English force in safety. To tell his news was but the work of a minute. It confirmed the suspicions which General Grant had begun to feel at the movements of some bodies of cavalry on the flank of his line of march. Mr. Loch had performed his share of the arrangement. He had warned Sir Hope Grant. But to the chivalrous mind duty is but half-performed if aid is withheld from those engaged in fulfilling theirs. What he had done had proved unexpectedly easy; it remained for him to assist those whose share was more arduous and perilous. So Mr. Loch rode back to the Chinese lines, Captain Brabazon insisting on following him, again accompanied by two Sikhs but not the same who had ridden with him before.

Sir Hope Grant had given him the assurance that unless absolutely forced to engage he would postpone the action for two hours. This small party of four men rode without hesitation, and at a rapid pace, through the skirmishers of the Chinese army. The rapidity of their movements disconcerted the Chinese, who allowed them to pass without opposition and almost without notice. They rode through the streets of Chan-chia-wan without meeting with any molestation, although they were crowded with the mustering men of the imperial army. They gained Tungchow without let or hindrance, after having passed through probably not less than 30,000 men about to do battle with the long hated and now feared foreigners. It may have been, as suggested, that they owed their safety to a belief that they were the bearers of their army's surrender! Arrived at Tungchow, Mr. Loch found the Sikh escort at the temple outside the gates unaware of any danger—all the Englishmen being absent in the town, where they were shopping—and a letter left by Mr. Parkes warning them on return to prepare for instant flight, and saying that he was off in search of Prince Tsai. In that search he was at last successful. He found the high commissioner, he asked the meaning of the change that had taken place, and was told in curt and defiant tones that "there could be no peace, there must be war."

The last chance of averting hostilities was thus shown to be in vain. Prince Tsai indorsed the action of Sankolinsin. Mr. Parkes had only the personal satisfaction of knowing that he had done everything he could to prove that the English did not wish to press their military superiority over an antagonist whose knowledge of war was slight and out of date. He had done this at the greatest personal peril. It only remained to secure his own safety and that of his companions. By this time the whole party of Englishmen had re-assembled in the temple; and Mr. Loch, anxious for Mr. Parkes, had gone into the city and met him galloping away from the yamen of the commissioner. There was no longer reason for delay. Not an Englishman had yet been touched, but between this small band and safety lay the road back through the ranks of Sankolinsin's warriors. From Tung-chow to the advanced post of Sir Hope Grant's army was a ten mile ride; and most of the two hours' grace had already expired. Could it be done? By this time most of the Chinese troops had reached Chan-chia-wan, where they had been drawn up in battle array among the maize-fields and in the nullahs as already described. From Tungchow to that place the country was almost deserted; and the fugitives proceeded unmolested along the road till they reached that town. The streets were crowded partly with armed citizens and peasants, but chiefly with panic-stricken householders; and by this time the horses were blown, and some of them almost exhausted. Through this crowd the seven Englishmen and twenty Sikhs walked their horses, and met not the least opposition. They reached the eastern side without insult or injury, passed through the gates, and descending the declivity found themselves in the rear of the whole Chinese army. The dangers through which they had passed were as nothing compared with those they had now to encounter. A shell burst in the air at this moment, followed by the discharge of the batteries on both sides. The battle had begun. The promised two hours had expired. The fugitives were some ten minutes too late.

The position of this small band in the midst of an Asiatic army actually engaged in mortal combat with their kinsmen may be better imagined than described. They were riding down the road which passed through the center of the Chinese position, and the banks on each side of them were lined with matchlock-men, among whom the shells of the English guns were already bursting. Parties of cavalry were not wanting here, but out in the plain where the Tartar horsemen swarmed in thousands the greatest danger of all awaited them. Their movements were slow, painfully slow, and their progress was delayed by the necessity of waiting for those who were the worst mounted; but they were "all in the same boat, and, like Englishmen, would sink or swim together." In the accumulation of difficulties that stared them in the face not the least seemed to be that they were advancing in the teeth of their own countrymen's fire, which was growing fiercer every minute. In this critical moment men turned to Mr. Parkes, and Captain Brabazon expressed the belief of those present in a cool brave man in arduous extremity when he cried out, "I vote Parkes decides what is to be done." To follow the main road seemed to be certain destruction and death without the power of resisting; for even assuming that some of them could have cut their way through the Tartar cavalry, and escaped from the English shell, they could hardly have avoided being shot down by the long lines of matchlock-men who were ready to fire on them the instant they saw their backs. There was only one possible avenue of escape, and that was to gain the right flank of the army, and endeavor to make their way by a detour round to the English lines. Assuredly this was not a very promising mode of escape, but it seemed to have the greatest chances of success. But when the Chinese, who had up to this regarded their movements without interfering, saw this change in their course, they at once took measures to stop it. A military mandarin said if they persisted in

did so.   A battery was almost in their hands, its officers had
to use their revolvers, when the Sikhs and a few French
dragoons, led by Colonel Foley, the English commissioner
with the French force, gallantly charged them in turn, and
compelled them to withdraw.   Neither side derived much
advantage from this portion of the contest, but the repulse
of the Tartar cavalry enabled the French guns to renew their
fire with great effect on the line of Chinese infantry.   While
the French were thus engaged on the right, the English
troops had begun a vigorous attack on both the center and
the left.   The Chinese appeared in such dense masses, and
maintained so vigorous, but fortunately so ill-directed, a fire,
that the English force made but little progress at either
point.   The action might have been indefinitely prolonged
and left undecided, had not Sir Hope Grant suddenly resolved to re-enforce his left with a portion of his center, and
to assail the enemy's right vigorously.   This latter part of
the battle began with a charge of some squadrons of Probyn's
Horse against the bodies of mounted Tartars moving in the
plain, whom they, with their gallant leader at their head,
routed in the sight of the two armies.   This overthrow of
their chosen fighting-men greatly discouraged the rest of the
Chinese soldiers, and when the infantry advanced with the
Sikhs in front they slowly began to give ground.   But even
then there were none of the usual symptoms of a decisive victory.   The French were so exhausted by their efforts that
they had been compelled to halt, and General Montauban was
obliged to curb his natural impetuosity, and to admit that
he could take no part in the final attack on Chan-chia-wan.
Sir Hope Grant, however, pressed on and occupied the town.
He did not call in his men until they had seized without resistance a large camp about one mile west of the town, where
they captured several guns.   Thus ended the battle of Chan-
chia-wan with the defeat and retreat of the strong army
which Sankolinsin had raised in order to drive the barbarians
into the sea.

  Although the battle was won, Sir Hope Grant, measuring

the resistance with the eye of an experienced soldier, came
to the conclusion that his force was not sufficiently strong
to overawe so obstinate a foe; and accordingly ordered Sir
Robert Napier to join him with as many troops as he could
spare from the Tientsin garrison. Having thus provided for
the arrival of re-enforcements at an early date, he was willing to resume his onward march for Tungchow, where it
was hoped some tidings would be obtained of the missing
officers and men. Two days intervened before any decisive
move was made, but Mr. Wade was sent under a flag of
truce into Tungchow to collect information. But he failed
to learn anything more about Mr. Parkes than that he had
quitted the town in safety after his final interview with
Prince Tsai. Lord Elgin now hastened up from Hosiwu to
join the military headquarters, and on September 21, the
French having been joined by another brigade, offensive
operations were recommenced. The delay had encouraged
the Chinese to make another stand, and they had collected
in considerable force for the defense of the Palikao bridge,
which affords the means of crossing the Peiho west of Tungchow. Here again the battle commenced with a cavalry
charge which, despite an accident that might have had more
serious results, was completely successful. This achievement was followed up by the attack on several fortified positions which were not defended with any great amount of
resolution, and while these matters were in progress on the
side where the English were engaged, the French had carried the bridge with its twenty-five guns in position in very
gallant style. The capture of this bridge and the dispersion
of the troops, including the Imperial Guard, which had been
intrusted with its defense, completed the discomfiture of
the Chinese. Pekin itself lay almost at the mercy of the
invader, and, unless diplomacy could succeed better than
arms, nothing would prevent the hated foreigners violating its privacy not merely with their presence, but in the
most unpalatable guise of armed victors.

The day after the battle at the Palikao bridge came a

letter from Prince Kung, the emperor's next brother, stating
that Prince Tsai and his colleagues had not managed matters
satisfactorily, and that he had been appointed with plenipotentiary powers for the discussion and decision of the peace
question. But the prince went on to request a temporary
suspension of hostilities—a demand with which no general
or embassador could have complied so long as officers were
detained who had been seized in violation of the usages of
war. Lord Elgin replied in the clearest terms that there
could be no negotiations for peace until these prisoners were
restored, and that if they were not sent back in safety the
consequences would be most serious for the Chinese Government. But even at this supreme moment of doubt and danger, the subtlety of Chinese diplomacy would have free play.
Prince Kung was young in years and experience, but his
finesse would have done credit to a gray-haired statesman.
Unfortunately for him, the question had got beyond the
stage for discussion: the English embassador had stated
the one condition on which negotiations would be renewed,
and until that had been complied with there was no need
to give ear to the threats, promises and entreaties even of
Prince Kung. As the prince gave no sign of yielding this
point during the week's delay in bringing up the second
division from Tientsin, Lord Elgin requested Sir Hope
Grant to resume his march on Pekin, from which the advanced guard of the allied forces was distant little more
than ten miles. The cavalry had reconnoitered almost up
to the gates, and had returned with the report that the walls
were strong and in good condition. The danger to a small
army of attempting to occupy a great city of the size and
population of Pekin is almost obvious; and, moreover, the
consistent policy of the English authorities had been to cause
the Chinese people as little injury and suffering as possible.
Should an attack on the city become unavoidable, it was decided that the point attacked should be the Tartar quarter,
including the palace, which occupied the northern half of the
city. By this time it had become known that Parkes and

Loch were living, that they were confined in the Kaou Meaou Temple, near the Tehshun Gate, and that latterly they had been fairly well treated.

In execution of the plan of attack that had been agreed upon, the allied forces marched round Pekin to the northwest corner of the walls, having as their object the Summer Palace of the emperor at Yuen Min Yuen, not quite four miles distant from the city.

On the approach of the foreign army, Hienfung fled in terror from his palace, and sought shelter at Jehol, the hunting residence of the emperors beyond the Wall. His flight was most precipitate; and the treasures of the Summer Palace were left at the mercy of the Western spoilers. The French soldiers had made the most of the start they had obtained, and left comparatively little for their English comrades, who, moreover, were restrained by the bonds of a stricter discipline. But the amount of prize property that remained was still considerable, and, by agreement between the two generals, it was divided in equal shares between the armies. The capture and occupation of the Summer Palace completed the European triumph, and obliged Prince Kung to promptly acquiesce in Lord Elgin's demand for the immediate surrender of the prisoners, if he wished to avoid the far greater calamity of a foreign occupation of the Tartar quarter of Pekin and the appropriation of its vaster collection of treasures.

On October 6, Mr. Parkes wrote from his place of confinement that the French and English detained were to be returned on the 8th of the month, and that the imperial commanders had been ordered at the same time to retire for a considerable distance from Pekin. These promises were carried out. Prince Kung was at last resolved to make all the concessions requisite to insure the speedy conclusion of peace. The restoration of these captives removed what was thought to be the one obstacle to Lord Elgin's discussing the terms on which the invading force would retire and to the respective governments resuming diplomatic relations. It was fortunate for China that the exact fate of the other prisoners was unknown, and that Lord Elgin felt able, in consequence of the more friendly proceedings of Prince Kung, to overlook the earlier treatment of those now returned to him, for the narrative of Mr. Parkes and his fellow prisoners was one that tended to heighten the feeling of indignation at the original breach of faith. To say that they were barbarously ill-used is to employ a phrase conveying a very inadequate idea of the numerous indignities and the cruel personal treatment to which they were subjected. Under these great trials neither of these intrepid Englishmen wavered in their refusal to furnish any information or to make any concession compromising their country. Mr. Loch's part was in one sense the more easy, as his ignorance of the language prevented his replying, but in bodily suffering he had to pay a proportionately greater penalty. The incidents of their imprisonment afford the most creditable testimony to the superiority which the pride of race as well as "the equal mind in arduous circumstance" gives weak humanity over physical suffering. They are never likely to pass out of the public memory; and those who remember the daring and the chivalry which had inspired Mr. Parkes and Mr. Loch on the day when Prince Tsai's treachery and Sankolinsin's mastery were revealed, will not be disposed to consider it exaggerated praise to say that, for an adventure so honorably conceived and so nobly carried out, where the risk was never reckoned and where the penalty was so patiently borne, the pages of history may be searched almost in vain for an event that, in the dramatic elements of courage and suffering, presents such a complete and consistent record of human gallantry and devotion as the capture and subsequent captivity of these English gentlemen and their Sikh companion.

The further conditions as preliminary to the ratification of the Treaty of Tientsin were gradually, if reluctantly, complied with. On October 13 the northeast gate was handed over to the allied troops, but not before Sir Hope

Grant had threatened to open fire on the walls. At the same time Prince Kung returned eight sowars of Fane's Horse and one Frenchman, all the survivors, besides those already surrendered, of the small band which had ridden from Tungchow nearly a month before. The Chinese prince stated in explanation that "a certain number were missing after the fight, or have died of their wounds or of sickness." But the narrative of the Sikhs was decisive as to the fate of the five Englishmen and their own comrades. They had been brutally bound with ropes which, although drawn as tight as human force could draw them, were tightened still more by cold water being poured upon the bands, and they had been maltreated in every form by a cruel enemy, and provided only with food of the most loathsome kind. Some of the prisoners were placed in cages. Lieutenant Anderson, a gallant young officer for whom future renown had been predicted, became delirious and died on the ninth day of his confinement. Mr. De Normann died a week later. What fate befell Captain Barbazon and his French companion, the Abbe de Luc, is uncertain, but the evidence on the subject inclines us to accept as accurate the statement that the Chinese commander in the fight at Palikao, enraged at his defeat, caused them to be executed on the bridge. The soldier Phipps endured for a longer time than Mr. Bowlby the taunts and ill-usage of their jailers, but they at last shared the same fate, dying from the effects of their ill-treatment. The bodies of all the Englishmen, with the exception of Captain Barbazon, were restored, and of most of the Sikhs also. The Chinese officials were more barbarous in their cruelty than even the worst scum among their malefactors; for the prisoners in the jails, far from adding to the tortures of the unfortunate Europeans, did everything in their power to mitigate their sufferings, alleviate their pains, and supply their wants.

The details of these cruel deeds raised a feeling of great horror in men's minds, and, although the desire to arrange the question of peace without delay was uppermost with

Lord Elgin, still it was felt that some grave step was necessary to express the abhorrence with which England regarded this cruel and senseless outrage, and to bring home to the Chinese people and government the fact that Englishmen could not be murdered with impunity. Lord Elgin refused to hold any further intercourse with the Chinese Government until this great crime had been purged by some signal punishment. Sir Hope Grant and he had little difficulty in arriving at the decision that the best mode of expiation was to destroy the Summer Palace. The French commander refused to participate in the act which carried a permanent lesson of political necessity to the heart of the Pekin Government, and which did more than any other incident of the campaign to show Hienfung that the hour had gone by for trifling. On October 18, the threat was carried into execution. The Summer Palace was destroyed by fire, and the sum of $500,000 was demanded and obtained from the Chinese as some compensation for the families of the murdered men. The palace of Yuen Min Yuen had been the scene of some of the worst sufferings of the English prisoners. From its apartments the high mandarins and the immediate courtiers of the emperor had gloated over and enjoyed the spectacle of their foreign prisoners' agony. The whole of Pekin witnessed in return the destruction wrought to the sovereign's abode by the indignant English, and the clouds of smoke hung for days like a vast black pall over the city.

That act of severe but just vengeance consummated, the negotiations for the ratification of the treaty were resumed. The Hall of Ceremonies was selected as the place in which the ratifying act should be performed, while, as some punishment for the hostile part he had played, the palace of Prince Tsai was appropriated as the temporary official residence of Lord Elgin and Baron Gros. The formal act of ratification was performed in this building on October 24. Lord Elgin proceeded in a chair of state, accompanied by his suite, and also by Sir Hope Grant with an escort of 100 officers and 500 troops, through the streets from the Anting Gate to the Hall of Ceremonies. Prince Kung, attended by a large body of civil and military mandarins, was there in readiness to produce the imperial edict authorizing him to attach the emperor's seal to the treaty, and to accept the responsibility for his country of conforming with its terms and carrying out its stipulations. Some further delay was caused by the necessity of waiting until the edict should be received from the emperor at Jehol authorizing the publication of the treaty, not the least important point in connection with its conclusion if the millions of China were to understand and perform what their rulers had promised for them. That closing act was successfully achieved, and more rapidly than had been expected. The Pekinese beheld English troops and officers in residence in their midst for the first time, and when the army was withdrawn and the plenipotentiary, Lord Elgin, transferred to his brother, Mr. Frederick Bruce, the charge of affairs in China as Resident Minister, the ice had been broken in the relations between the officials of the two countries, and the greatest, if not the last, barrier of Chinese exclusiveness had been removed. The last of the allied troops turned their backs upon Pekin on November 9, and the greater portion of the expedition departed for India and Europe just before the cold weather set in. A few days later the rivers were frozen and navigation had become impossible, which showed how narrow was the margin left for the completion of the operations of war.

The object which the more far-seeing of the English residents had from the first hour of difficulty stated to be necessary for satisfactory relations—direct intercourse with the Pekin Government—was thus obtained after a keen and bitter struggle of thirty years. Although vanquished, the Chinese may be said to have come out of this war with an increased military reputation. The war closed with a treaty enforcing all the concessions made by its predecessor. The right to station an embassador in Pekin signified that the greatest barrier of all had been broken down; the old school of politicians were put completely out of court, and a young and intelligent prince, closely connected with the emperor, assumed the personal charge of the foreign relations of the country. As one who had seen with his own eyes the misfortunes of his countrymen, Prince Kung was the more disposed to adhere to what he had promised to perform. Under his direction the ratified Treaty of Tientsin became a bond of union instead of an element of discord between the cabinets of London and Pekin; and a termination was put, by an arrangement carried at the point of the sword, to the constant friction and recrimination which had been the prevailing characteristics of the intercourse for a whole generation. The Chinese had been subjected to a long and bitter lesson. They had at last learned the virtue of submitting to necessity; but although they have profited to some extent both in peace and war by their experience, it requires some assurance to declare that they have even now accepted the inevitable. That remains the problem of the future; but in 1860 Prince Kung came to the sensible conclusion that for that period, and until China had recovered from her internal confusion, there was nothing to be gained and much to be lost by protracted resistance to the peoples of the West. Whatever could be retained by tact and finesse were to form part of the natural rights of China; but the privileges only to be asserted in face of Armstrong guns and rifles were to be abandoned with as good a grace as the injured feeling of a nation can ever display.

CHAPTER XX

THE TAEPING REBELLION

WE left the Taepings supreme at Nankin, but maintaining themselves there with some difficulty against two imperial armies raised by the loyal efforts of the inhabitants of the central provinces. This was at the beginning of 1857; and there is no doubt that if the government had avoided a conflict with the Europeans, and concentrated its efforts and power on the contest with the Taeping rebels, they would have speedily annihilated the tottering fabric of Tien Wang's authority. But the respite of four years secured by the attention of the central government being monopolized by the foreign question enabled the Taepings to consolidate their position, augment their fighting forces, and present a more formidable front to the imperial authorities. When Prince Kung learned from Lord Elgin the full extent of the success of the Taepings on the Yangtse, of which the officials at Pekin seemed to possess a very imperfect and inaccurate knowledge, the Manchu authorities realized that it was a vital question for them to reassert their authority without further delay, but on beginning to put their new resolve into practice they soon experienced that the position of the Taepings in 1861 differed materially from what it was in 1857.

The course of events during that period must be briefly summarized. In 1858 the imperialists under Tseng Kwofan and Chang Kwoliang renewed the siege of Nankin, but as the city was well supplied with provisions, and as the imperialists were well known to have no intention of delivering an assault, the Taepings did not feel any apprehension. After the investment had continued for nearly a year, Chung Wang, who had now risen to the supreme place among the rebels, insisted on quitting the city before it was completely surrounded, with the object of beating up levies and generally relieving the pressure caused by the besiegers. In this endeavor he more than once experienced the unkindness of fortune, for when he had collected 5,000 good troops he was defeated in a vigorous attempt to cut his way through a far larger imperial force. Such, however, was his reputation that the imperial commanders before Nankin sent many of their men to assist the officers operating against him, and Chung Wang, seizing the opportunity, made his way by forced marches back to Nankin, overcoming such resistance

as the enfeebled besiegers were able to offer.   The whole
of the year 1859 was passed in practical inaction, but at its
close the Taepings only retained possession of four towns,
besides Nankin, on the Yangtse.   It again became necessary
for Chung Wang to sally forth and assume the offensive in
the rear and on the line of supplies of the beleaguering imperialists.   His main difficulty was in obtaining the consent
of Tien Wang, who was at this time given over to religious
pursuits or private excesses, and Chung Wang states that
he only consented when he found that he could not stop him.
In January, 1860, Chung Wang began what proved to be a
very remarkable campaign.   He put his men in good humor
by distributing a large sum of money among them, and he
succeeded in eluding the imperial commanders and in mis-
leading them as to his intentions.   While they thought he
had gone off to relieve Ganking, he had really hastened to
attack the important city of Hangchow, where much spoil
and material for carrying on the war might be secured by
the victor.   He captured the city with little or no loss, on
March 19, 1860, but the Tartar city held out until relieved
by Chang Kwoliang, who hastened from Nankin for the
purpose.   Once again the imperial commanders, in their
anxiety to crush Chung Wang, had reduced their force in
front of Nankin to an excessively low condition, and the
Taeping leader, placed in a desperate position, seized the
only chance of safety by hastening from Hangchow to Nankin at full speed, and attacking the imperial lines.   This
battle was fought early in the morning of a cold snowy day
—May 3, 1860—and resulted in the loss of 5,000 imperialists,
and the compulsory raising of the siege.   The Taeping cause
might have been resuscitated by this signal victory if Tien
Wang had only shown himself able to act up to the great
part he assumed, but not merely was he incapable of playing
the part of either a warrior or a statesman, but his petty
jealousy prevented his making use of the undoubted ability
of his lieutenant Chung Wang, who after the greatest of his
successes was forbidden to re-enter Nankin.

The energy and spirit of Chung Wang impelled him to fresh enterprises, and seeing the hopelessness of Tien Wang, he determined to secure a base of operations for himself, which should enable him to hold his own in the warring strife of the realm, and perhaps to achieve the triumph of the cause with which he was associated. It says much for his military energy and skill that he was able to impart new vigor to the Tacping system, and to sustain on a new field his position single-handed against the main forces of the empire. He determined to obtain possession of the important city of Soochow, on the Grand Canal, and not very far distant from Shanghai. On his way to effect this object he gained a great victory over Chang Kwoliang, who was himself killed in the battle. As the ex-Traid chief possessed great energy, his loss was a considerable one for the government, but his troops continued to oppose the advance of the Taepings, and fought and lost three battles before Chung Wang reached Soochow. That place was too large to be successfully defended by a small force, and the imperialists hastily abandoned it. At this critical moment—May, 1860 —Ho Kweitsin, the viceroy of the Two Kiang, implored the aid of the English and French, who were at this moment completing their arrangements for the march on Pekin, against these rebels, and the French were so far favorable to the suggestion that they offered to render the assistance provided the English would combine with them. Mr. Bruce, however, declined the adventure, which is not surprising, considering that we were then engaged in serious hostilities with the Chinese, but the incident remains unique of a country asking another for assistance during the progress of a bitter and doubtful war. The utmost that Mr. Bruce would do was to issue a notification that Shanghai would not be allowed to again fall into the hands of an insurgent force. The viceroy who solicited the aid was at least consistent. He memorialized the Throne, praying that the demands of the Europeans should be promptly granted, and that they should then be employed against the Taepings.

His memorial was ill-timed. He was summoned to Pekin and executed for his very prudent advice. With the possession of Soochow, Chung Wang obtained fresh supplies of money, material, and men, and once more it was impossible to say to what height of success the Taepings might not attain. But Chung Wang was not satisfied with Soochow alone; he wished to gain possession of Shanghai.

Unfortunately for the realization of his project, the Europeans had determined to defend Shanghai at all hazards, but Chung Wang believed either that they would not, or that their army being absent in the north they had not the power to carry out this resolve. The necessity of capturing Shanghai was rendered the greater in the eyes of Chung Wang by its being the base of hostile measures against himself, and by a measure which threatened him with a new peril. The wealthy Chinese merchants of Shanghai had formed a kind of patriotic association, and provided the funds for raising a European contingent. Two Americans, Ward and Burgevine, were taken into their pay, and in July, 1860, they, having raised a force of 100 Europeans and 200 Manila men, began operations with an attack on Sunkiang, a large walled town about twenty miles from Shanghai. This first attack was repulsed with some loss, but Ward, afraid of losing the large reward he was promised for its capture, renewed the attack, and with better success, for he gained possession of a gate, and held it until the whole imperial army had come up and stormed the town. After this success Ward was requested to attack Tsingpu, which was a far stronger place than Sunkiang, and where the Taepings had the benefit of the advice and leading of several Englishmen who had joined them. Ward attacked Tsingpu on August 2, 1860, but he was repulsed with heavy loss. He returned to Shanghai for the purpose of raising another force and two larger guns, and then renewed the attack. It is impossible to say whether the place would have held out or not, but after seven days' bombardment Chung Wang suddenly appeared to the rescue, and, surprising Ward's force, drove it away in utter confusion, and with the loss of all its guns and stores.   Encouraged by this success, Chung Wang then thought the time opportune for attacking Shanghai, and he accordingly marched against it, burning and plundering the villages along the road.   The imperialists had established a camp or stockade outside the western gate, and Chung Wang carried this without any difficulty, but when he reached the walls of the town he found a very different opponent in his path.   The walls were lined with English and French troops, and when the Taepings attempted to enter the city they were received with a warm fire, which quickly sent them to the right-about. Chung Wang renewed the attack at different points during the next four or five days, but he was then obliged to retreat. Before doing so, however, he sent a boasting message that he had come at the invitation of the French, who were traitors, and that he would have taken the city but for the foreigners, as "there was no city which his men could not storm."   At this moment the attention of Chung Wang was called off to Nankin, which the imperialists were investing for a sixth time, under Tseng Kwofan, who had been elevated to the viceroyalty of the Two Kiang.   Tien Wang, in despair, sent off an urgent summons to Chung Wang to come to his assistance, and although he went with reluctance he felt that he had no course but to obey.

Having done what he could to place Nankin in an efficient state of defense, Chung Wang hastened back to Soochow to resume active operations.   It is unnecessary to describe these in detail; but although Chung Wang was twice defeated by a Manchu general named Paochiaou, he succeeded, by rapidity of movement, in holding his own against his more numerous adversaries.   In the meantime an important change had taken place in the situation.   The peace between China and the foreign powers compelled a revision of the position at Shanghai.   Admiral Hope sailed up to Nankin, interviewed the Wangs and exacted from them a pledge that Shanghai should not be attacked for twelve months, and that the Taeping forces should not advance within a radius of thirty miles of that place. In consequence of this arrangement Ward and Burgevine were compelled to desist from recruiting Europeans; but after a brief interval they were taken into the Chinese service for the purpose of drilling Chinese soldiers, a measure from which the most important consequences were to flow, for it proved to be the origin of the Ever-Victorious Army. These preparations were not far advanced when Chung Wang, elated by his capture of Ningpo and Hangchow, resolved to disregard Tien Wang's promise, and make a second attack on Shanghai, the possession of which he saw to be indispensable if his cause was to attain any brilliant triumph. He issued a proclamation that "the hour of the Manchus had come! Shanghai is a little place, and we have nothing to fear from it. We must take Shanghai to complete our dominions." The death of Hienfung seems to have encouraged Chung Wang to take what he hoped would prove a decisive step.

On January 14, 1862, the Taepings reached the immediate vicinity of the town and foreign settlement. The surrounding country was concealed by the smoke of the burning villages, which they had ruthlessly destroyed. The foreign settlement was crowded with thousands of fugitives, imploring the aid of the Europeans to save their houses and property. Their sufferings, which would at the best have been great, were aggravated by the exceptional severity of the winter. The English garrison of two native regiments and some artillery, even when supported by the volunteers, was far too weak to attempt more than the defense of the place; but this it was fortunately able to perform. The rebels, during the first week after their reappearance, plundered and burned in all directions, threatening even to make an attack on Woosung, the port at the mouth of the river, where they were repulsed by the French. Sir John Michel arrived at Shanghai with a small re-enforcement of English troops, and Ward, having succeeded in disciplining two Chinese regiments of about one thousand strong in all, sallied forth

from Sunkiang for the purpose of operating on the rear of
the Taeping forces. Ward's capture of Quanfuling, with
several hundred rebel boats which were frozen up in the
river, should have warned the Taepings that it was nearly
time for them to retire. However, they did not act as prudence would have dictated, and during the whole of February their raids continued round Shanghai. The suburbs
suffered from their attacks, the foreign factories and boats
were not secure, and several outrages on the persons of foreigners remained unatoned for. It was impossible to tolerate
any longer their enormities. The English and French commanders came to the determination to attack the rebels, to
enforce the original agreement with Tien Wang, and to clear
the country round Shanghai of the presence of the Taepings
for the space of thirty miles.

On February 21, therefore, a joint force composed of 336
English sailors and marines, 160 French seamen, and 600
men from Ward's contingent, accompanied by their respective commanders, with Admiral Hope in chief charge, advanced upon the village of Kachiaou, where the Taepings
had strengthened their position and placed guns on the
walls. After a sharp engagement the place was stormed,
Ward's men leading the attack with Burgevine at their
head. The drilled Chinese behaved with great steadiness,
but the Taepings were not to be dismayed by a single defeat.
They even resumed their attacks on the Europeans. On one
occasion Admiral Hope himself was compelled to retire before their superior numbers, and to summon fresh troops to
his assistance. The re-enforcements consisted of 450 Europeans and 700 of Ward's force, besides seven howitzers.
With these it was determined to attack Tseedong, a place of
great strength, surrounded by stone walls and ditches seven
feet deep. The Taepings stood to their guns with great
spirit, receiving the advancing troops with a very heavy fire.
When, however, Ward's contingent, making a detour, appeared in the rear of the place, they hastily evacuated their
positions; but the English sailors had carried the walls, and,

caught between two fires, they offered a stubborn but futile resistance. More than 700 were killed and 300 were taken prisoners. The favorable opinion formed of "the Ever-Victorious Army" by the action at Kachiaou was confirmed by the more serious affair at Tseedong; and Mr. Bruce at Pekin brought it under the favorable notice of Prince Kung and the Chinese Government. Having taken these hostile steps against the rebels, it necessarily followed that no advantage would accrue from any further hesitation with regard to allowing Europeans to enter the imperial service for the purpose of opposing them. Ward was officially recognized, and allowed to purchase weapons and to engage officers. An Englishman contracted to convey 9,000 of the troops who had stormed Ganking from the Yangtse to Shanghai. These men were Honan braves, who had seen considerable service in the interior of China, and it was proposed that they should garrison the towns of Kiangsu accordingly as they were taken from the rebels. The arrival of General Staveley from Tientsin at the end of March, with portions of two English regiments (the 31st and 67th), put a new face on affairs, and showed that the time was at hand when it would be possible to carry out the threat of clearing the country round Shanghai for the space of thirty miles.

The first place to be attacked toward the realization of this plan was the village of Wongkadza, about twelve miles west of Shanghai. Here the Taepings offered only a brief resistance, retiring to some stronger stockades four miles further west. General Staveley, considering that his men had done enough work for that day, halted them, intending to renew the attack the next morning. Unfortunately Ward was carried away by his impetuosity, and attacked this inner position with some 500 of his own men. Admiral Hope accompanied him. The Taepings met them with a tremendous fire, and after several attempts to scale the works they were repulsed with heavy loss. Admiral Hope was wounded in the leg, seven officers were wounded, and seventy men killed and wounded. The attack was repeated in force on the fol-

lowing day, and after some fighting the Taepings evacuated
their stockades. The next place attacked was the village of
Tsipoo; and, notwithstanding their strong earthworks and
three wide ditches, the rebels were driven out in a few hours.
It was then determined to attack Kahding, Tsingpu, Nanjao,
and Cholin, at which places the Taepings were known to
have mustered in considerable strength.

The first place was taken with little resistance, and its
capture was followed by preparations for the attack on
Tsingpu, which were hastened rather than delayed by a
desperate attempt to set fire to Shanghai. The plot was
fortunately discovered in time, and the culprits captured and
summarily executed to the number of two hundred. Early
in May a strong force was assembled at Sunkiang, and proceeded by boat, on account of the difficulties of locomotion,
to Tsingpu. The fire of the guns, in which the expedition
was exceptionally strong, proved most destructive, and two
breaches being pronounced practicable the place was carried
by assault. The rebels fought well and up to the last, when
they found flight impossible. The Chinese troops slew every
man found in the place with arms in his hands. A few days
later Nanjao was captured, but in the attack the French
commander, Admiral Protet, a gallant officer who had been
to the front during the whole of these operations, was shot
dead. The rebels, disheartened by these successive defeats,
rallied at Cholin, where they prepared to make a final stand.
The allied force attacked Cholin on May 20, and an English
detachment carried it almost at the point of the bayonet.
With this achievement the operations of the English troops
came for the moment to an end, for a disaster to the imperial
arms in their rear necessitated their turning their attention
to a different quarter.

The troops summoned from Ganking had at last arrived
to the number of five or six thousand men; and the Futai
Sieh, who was on the point of being superseded to make
room for Li Hung Chang, thought to employ them before
his departure on some enterprise which should redound to his

credit and restore his sinking fortunes. The operation was as hazardous as it was ambitious. The resolution he came to was to attack the city and forts of Taitsan, a place northwest of Shanghai, and not very far distant from Chung Wang's headquarters at Soochow. The imperialist force reached Taitsan on May 12, but less than two days later Chung Wang arrived in person at the head of 10,000 chosen troops to relieve the garrison. A battle ensued on the day following, when, notwithstanding their great superiority in numbers, the Taepings failed to obtain any success. In this extremity Chung Wang resorted to a stratagem. Two thousand of his men shaved their heads and pretended to desert to the imperialists. When the battle was renewed at sunrise on the following morning this band threw aside their assumed character and turned upon the imperialists. A dreadful slaughter ensued. Of the 7,000 Honan braves and the Tartars from Shanghai, 5,000 fell on the field. The consequences of this disaster were to undo most of the good accomplished by General Staveley and his force. The imperialists were for the moment dismayed, and the Taepings correspondingly encouraged. General Staveley's communications were threatened, and he had to abandon his intended plan and retrace his steps to Shanghai.

Chung Wang then laid regular siege to Sunkiang, where Ward was in person, and he very nearly succeeded in carrying the place by escalade. The attempt was fortunately discovered by an English sailor just in time, and repulsed with a loss to the rebels of 100 men. The Taepings continued to show great daring and activity before both Sunkiang and Tsingpu; and although the latter place was bravely defended, it became clear that the wisest course would be to evacuate it. A body of troops was therefore sent from Shanghai to form a junction with Ward at Sunkiang, and to effect the safe retreat of the Tsingpu garrison. The earlier proceedings were satisfactorily arranged, but the last act of all was grossly mismanaged and resulted in a catastrophe. Ward caused the place to be set on fire, when the Taepings, realiz-

ing what was being done, hastened into the town, and assailed the retiring garrison. A scene of great confusion
followed; many lives were lost, and the commandant who
had held it so courageously was taken prisoner. Chung
Wang could therefore appeal to some facts to support his
contention that he had got the better of the Europeans and
the imperialists in the province of Kiangsu.

From the scene of his successes Chung Wang was once
more called away by the timidity or peril of Tien Wang,
who was barely able to maintain his position at Nankin, but
when he hastened off to assist the chief of the Taepings he
found that he was out of favor, and that the jealousy or fear of
his colleagues had brought about his temporary disgrace and
loss of title. Shortly after Chung Wang's departure, Ward
was killed in action and Burgevine succeeded to the command, but it soon became apparent that his relations with
the Chinese authorities would not be smooth. General Ching
was jealous of the Ever-Victorious Army and wished to
have all the credit for himself. Li Hung Chang, who had
been appointed Futai or Governor of Kiangsu, entertained
doubts of the loyalty of this adventurer. Burgevine was a
man of high temper and strong passions, who met the wiles
of the Futai with peremptory demands to recognize the
claims of himself and his band. Nor was this all. Burgevine had designs of his own. Although the project had not
taken definite form in his mind, the inclination was strong
within him to play the part of military dictator with the
Chinese; or failing that, to found an independent authority
on some convenient spot of Celestial territory. The Futai
anticipated, perhaps, more than divined his wishes. In
Burgevine he saw, very shortly after their coming into contact, not merely a man whom he disliked and distrusted, but
one who, if allowed to pursue his plans unchecked, would in
the end form a greater danger to the imperial authority than
even the Taepings. It is not possible to deny Li's shrewd-
ness in reading the character of the man with whom he had
to deal.

The Futai Li, in order to test his obedience, proposed that Burgevine and his men should be sent round by sea to Nankin to take part in the siege of that city. The ships were actually prepared for their conveyance, and the Taotai Wou, who had first fitted out a fleet against the rebels, was in readiness to accompany Burgevine, when Li and his colleague, as suspicious of Burgevine's compliance as they would have been indignant at his refusal, changed their plans and countermanded the expedition. Instead of carrying out this project, therefore, they laid a number of formal complaints before General Staveley as to Burgevine's conduct, and requested the English government to remove him from his command, and to appoint an English officer in his place. The charges against Burgevine did not at this time amount to more than a certain laxness in regard to the expenditure of the force, a disregard for the wishes and prejudices of the Chinese Government, and the want of tact, or of the desire to conciliate, in his personal relations with the Futai. If Burgevine had resigned, all would have been well, but he regarded the position from the standpoint of the adventurer who believes that his own interests form a supreme law and are the highest good. As commander of the Ever-Victorious Army he was a personage to be considered even by foreign governments. He would not voluntarily surrender the position which alone preserved him from obscurity. Having come to this decision, it was clear that even the partial execution of his plans must draw him into many errors of judgment which could not but imbitter the conflict. The reply of the English commander was to the effect that personally he could not interfere, but that he would refer the matter to London as well as to Mr. Bruce at Pekin. In consequence of the delay thus caused the project of removing the force to Nankin was revived, and, the steamers having been chartered, Burgevine was requested to bring down his force from Sunkiang and to embark it at Shanghai. This he expressed his willingness to do on payment of his men, who were two months in arrear, and on the settlement of all outstanding claims. Burgevine was supported by his troops. Whatever his dislike to the proposed move, theirs was immeasurably greater. They refused to move without the payment of all arrears; and on January 2 they even went so far as to openly mutiny. Two days later Burgevine went to Shanghai and had an interview with Takee. The meeting was stormy. Burgevine used personal violence toward the Shanghai merchant, whose attitude was at first overbearing, and he returned to his exasperated troops with the money, which he carried off by force. The Futai Li, on hearing of the assault on Takee, hastened to General Staveley to complain of Burgevine's gross insubordination in striking a mandarin, which by the law of China was punishable with death: Burgevine was dismissed the Chinese service, and the notice of this removal was forwarded by the English general, with a recommendation to him to give up his command without disturbance. This Burgevine did, for the advice of the English general was equivalent to a command, and on January 6, 1863, Burgevine was back at Shanghai. Captain Holland was then placed in temporary command, while the answer of the home government was awaited to General Staveley's proposition to intrust the force to the care of a young captain of engineers, named Charles Gordon. Chung Wang returned at this moment to Soochow, and in Kiangsu the cause of the Taepings again revived through his energy. In February a detachment of Holland's force attacked Fushan, but met with a check, when the news of a serious defeat at Taitsan, where the former Futai Sieh had been defeated, compelled its speedy retreat to Sunkiang. Li had some reason to believe that Taitsan would surrender on the approach of the imperialists, and he accordingly sent a large army, including 2,500 of the contingent, to attack it. The affair was badly managed. The assaulting party was stopped by a wide ditch; neither boats nor ladders arrived. The Taepings fired furiously on the exposed party, several officers were killed, and the men broke into confusion. The heavy guns stuck

who had served with Ward and Burgevine objected to this, and openly refused to obey orders. Fortunately the stores and ammunition were collected, and Major Gordon announced that he would march on the following morning, with or without the mutineers. Those who did not answer to their names at the end of the first half-march would be dismissed, and he spoke with the authority of one in complete accord with the Chinese authorities themselves. The soldiers obeyed him as a Chinese official, because he had been made a tsungping or brigadier-general, and the officers feared to disobey him as they would have liked on account of his commanding the source whence they were paid. The mutineers fell in, and a force of nearly 3,000 men, well-equipped and anxious for the fray, returned to Quinsan, where General Ching had, in the meanwhile, kept the rebels closely watched from a strong position defended by several stockades and supported by the "Hyson" steamer. Immediately after his arrival, Major Gordon moved out his force to attack the stockades which the rebels had constructed on their right wing. These were strongly built; but as soon as the defenders perceived that the assailants had gained their flank they precipitately withdrew into Quinsan itself. General Ching wished the attack to be made on the eastern gate, opposite to which he had raised his own intrenchments, and by which he had announced his intention of forcing his way; but a brief inspection showed Major Gordon that that was the strongest point of the town, and that a direct attack upon it could only succeed, if at all, by a very considerable sacrifice of men. Like a prudent commander Major Gordon determined to reconnoiter; and, after much grumbling on the part of General Ching, he decided that the most hopeful plan was to carry some stockades situated seven miles west of the town, and thence assail Quinsan on the Soochow side, which was weaker than the others. These stockades were at a village called Chumze. On May 30 the force detailed for this work proceeded to carry it out. The "Hyson" and fifty imperial gunboats conveyed the land force, which con-

sisted of one regiment, some guns, and a large body of imperialists. The rebels at Chumze offered hardly the least
resistance; whether it was that they were dismayed at the
sudden appearance of the enemy, or, as was stated at the
time, because they considered themselves ill-treated by their
comrades in Quinsan. The "Hyson" vigorously pursued
those who fled toward Soochow, and completed the effect of
this success by the capture of a very strong and well-built
fort covering a bridge at Ta Edin. An imperialist garrison
was installed there, and the "Hyson" continued the pursuit
to within a mile of Soochow itself.

The defenders of Quinsan itself were terribly alarmed at
the cutting off of their communications. They saw themselves on the point of being surrounded, and they yielded to
the uncontrollable impulse of panic. During the night, after
having suffered severely from the "Hyson" fire, the garrison
evacuated the place, which might easily have held out; and
General Ching had the personal satisfaction, on learning
from some deserters of the flight of the garrison, of leading
his men over the eastern walls which he had wished to assault. The importance of Quinsan was realized on its capture. Major Gordon pronounced it to be the key of Soochow,
and at once resolved to establish his headquarters there,
partly because of its natural advantages, but also and not
less on account of its enabling him to gradually destroy the
evil associations which the men had contracted at Sunkiang.

The change was not acceptable, however, to the force
itself; and the artillery in particular refused to obey orders,
and threatened to shoot their officers. Discipline was, however, promptly reasserted by the energy of the commander,
who ordered the principal ringleader to be shot, and "the
Ever Victorious Army" became gradually reconciled to its
new position at Quinsan. After the capture of Quinsan
there was a cessation of active operations for nearly two
months. It was the height of summer and the new troops
had to be drilled. The difficulty with Ching, who took
all the credit for the capture of Quinsan to himself, was

arranged through the mediation of Dr. Macartney, who had just left the English army to become Li's right-hand man. Two other circumstances occurred to embarrass the young commander. There were rumors of some meditated movement on the part of Burgevine, who had returned from Pekin with letters exculpating him, and who endeavored to recover the command in spite of Li Hung Chang, and there was a further manifestation of insubordination in the force, which, as Gordon said, bore more resemblance to a rabble than the magnificent army it was popularly supposed to be. The artillery had been cowed by Major Gordon's vigor, but its efficiency remained more doubtful than could be satisfactory to the general responsible for its condition, and also relying upon it as the most potent arm of his force. He resolved to remove the old commander, and to appoint an English officer, Major Tapp, in his place. On carrying his determination into effect the officers sent in "a round robin," refusing to accept a new officer. This was on July 25, and the expedition which had been decided upon against Wokong had consequently to set out the following morning without a single artillery officer. In face of the inflexible resolve of the leader, however, the officers repented, and appeared in a body at the camp begging to be taken back, and expressing their willingness to accept "Major Tapp or any one else," as their colonel.

With these troops, part of whom had only just returned to a proper sense of discipline, Gordon proceeded to attack Kahpoo, on the Grand Canal south of Soochow, where the rebels held two strongly-built stone forts. The force had been strengthened by the addition of another steamer, the "Firefly," a sister vessel to the "Hyson." Major Gordon arrived before Kahpoo on July 27; and the garrison, evidently taken by surprise, made scarcely the least resistance. The capture of Kahpoo placed Gordon's force between Soochow and Wokong, the next object of attack. At Wokong the rebels were equally unprepared. The garrison at Kahpoo, thinking only of their own safety, had fled to Soochow,

leaving their comrades at Wokong unwarned and to their
fate. So heedless were the Taepings at this place of all
danger from the north, that they had even neglected to
occupy a strong stone fort situated about 1,000 yards north
of the walls. The Taepings attempted too late to repair their
error, and the loss of this fort caused them that of all their
other stockades. Wokong itself was too weak to offer any
effectual resistance; and the garrison on the eve of the assault ordered for July 29 sent out a request for quarter, which
was granted, and the place surrendered without further
fighting. Meanwhile an event of far greater importance
had happened than even the capture of these towns, although
they formed the necessary preliminary to the investment of
Soochow. Burgevine had come to the decision to join the
Taepings.

Disappointed in his hope of receiving the command,
Burgevine remained on at Shanghai, employing his time
in watching the varying phases of a campaign in which he
longed to take part, and of which he believed that it was
only his due to have the direction, but still hesitating as to
what decision it behooved him to take. His contempt for all
Chinese officials became hatred of the bitterest kind of the
Futai, by whom he had been not merely thwarted but over-
reached, and predisposed him to regard with no unfavorable
eye the idea of joining his fortunes to those of the rebel Taepings. To him in this frame of mind came some of the dismissed officers and men of the Ward force, appealing to his
vanity by declaring that his soldiers remembered him with
affection, and that he had only to hoist his flag for most of
his old followers to rally round him. There was little to
marvel at if he also was not free from some feeling of jealousy at the success and growing fame of Major Gordon, for
whom he simulated a warm friendship. The combination of
motives proved altogether irresistible as soon as he found
that several hundred European adventurers were ready to
accompany him into the ranks of the Taepings, and to endeavor to do for them what they had failed to perform for

the imperialists. On July 15, Dr. Macartney wrote to Major Gordon stating that he had positive information that Burgevine was enlisting men for some enterprise, that he had already collected about 300 Europeans, and that he had even gone so far as to choose a special flag, a white diamond on a red ground, and containing a black star in the center of the diamond. On the 21st of the same month Burgevine wrote to Major Gordon saying that there would be many rumors about him, but that he was not to believe any of them, and that he would come and see him shortly. This letter was written as a blind, and, unfortunately, Major Gordon attached greater value to Burgevine's word than he did to the precise information of Dr. Macartney. He was too much disposed to think that, as the officer who had to a certain extent superseded Burgevine in the command, he was bound to take the most favorable view of all his actions, and to trust implicitly in his good faith. Major Gordon, trusting to his word, made himself personally responsible to the Chinese authorities for his good faith, and thus Burgevine escaped arrest. Burgevine's plans had been deeply laid. He had been long in correspondence with the Taepings, and his terms had been accepted. He proclaimed his hostility to the government by seizing one of their new steamers.

At this very moment Major Gordon came to the decision to resign, and he hastened back to Shanghai in order to place his withdrawal from the force in the hands of the Futai. He arrived there on the very day that Burgevine seized the "Kajow" steamer at Sunkiang, and on hearing the news he at once withdrew his resignation, which had been made partly from irritation at the irregular payment of his men, and also on account of the cruelty of General Ching. Not merely did he withdraw his resignation, but he hastened back to Quinsan, into which he rode on the night of the very same day that had witnessed his departure. The immediate and most pressing danger was from the possible defection of the force to its old leader, when, with the large stores of artillery and ammunition at Quinsan in their possession, not even Shanghai, with its very weak foreign garrison, could be considered safe from attack. As a measure of precaution Major Gordon sent some of his heavy guns and stores back to Taitsan, where the English commander, General Brown, consented to guard them, while he hastened off to Kahpoo, now threatened both by the Soochow force and by the foreign adventurers acting under Burgevine. He arrived at a most critical moment. The garrison was hard pressed. General Ching had gone back to Shanghai, and only the presence of the "Hyson" prevented the rebels, who were well-armed and possessed an efficient artillery, from carrying the fort by a rush. The arrival of Major Gordon with 150 men on board his third steamer, the "Cricket," restored the confidence of the defenders; but there was no doubt that Burgevine had lost a most favorable opportunity, for if he had attacked this place instead of proceeding to Soochow it must have fallen.

General Ching, who was a man of most extraordinary energy and restlessness, resolved to signalize his return to the field by some striking act while Major Gordon was completing his preparations at Quinsan for a fresh effort. His headquarters were at the strong fort of Ta Edin, on the creek leading from Quinsan to Soochow, and having the "Hyson" with him he determined to make a dash to some point nearer the great rebel stronghold. On August 30 he had seized the position of Waiquaidong, where, in three days, he threw up stockades, admirably constructed, and which could not have been carried save by a great effort on the part of the whole of the Soochow garrison. Toward the end of September, Major Gordon, fearing lest the rebels, who had now the supposed advantage of Burgevine's presence and advice, might make some attempt to cut off General Ching's lengthy communications, moved forward to Waiquaidong to support him; but when he arrived he found that the impatient mandarin, encouraged either by the news of his approach or at the inaction of the Taepings in Soochow, had made a still further advance of two miles, so that he was only 1,000 yards distant from the rebel stockades in front of the east gate. Major

Gordon had at this time been re-enforced by the Franco-Chinese corps, which had been well disciplined, under the command of Captain Bonnefoy, while the necessity of leaving any strong garrison at Quinsan had been obviated by the loan of 200 Belooches from General Brown's force. The rebel position having been carefully reconnoitered, both on the east and on the south, Major Gordon determined that the first step necessary for its proper beleaguerment was to seize and fortify the village of Patachiaou, about one mile south of the city wall. The village, although strongly stockaded, was evacuated by the garrison after a feeble resistance, and an attempt to recover it a few hours later by Mow Wang in person resulted in a rude repulse chiefly on account of the effective fire of the "Hyson." Burgevine, instead of fighting the battles of the failing cause he had adopted, was traveling about the country: at one moment in the capital interviewing Tien Wang and his ministers, at another going about in disguise even in the streets of Shanghai. But during the weeks when General Ching might have been taken at a disadvantage, and when it was quite possible to recover some of the places which had been lost, he was absent from the scene of military operations. After the capture of Patachiaou most of the troops and the steamers that had taken it were sent back to Waiquaidong, but Major Gordon remained there with a select body of his men and three howitzers. The rebels had not resigned themselves to the loss of Patachiaou, and on October 1 they made a regular attempt to recover it. They brought the "Kajow" into action, and, as it had found a daring commander in a man named Jones, its assistance proved very considerable. They had also a 32-pounder gun on board a junk, and this enabled them to overcome the fire of Gordon's howitzers and also of the "Hyson," which arrived from Waiquaidong during the engagement. But notwithstanding the superiority of their artillery, the rebels hesitated to come to close quarters, and when Major Gordon and Captain Bonnefoy led a sortie against them at the end of the day they retired precipitately.

At this stage Burgevine wrote to Major Gordon two let-ters—the first exalting the Taepings, and the second written two days later asking for an interview, whereupon he ex-pressed his desire to surrender on the provision of personal safety. He assigned the state of his health as the cause of this change, but there was never the least doubt that the true reason of this altered view was dissatisfaction with his treatment by the Taeping leaders and a conviction of the impossibility of success. Inside Soochow, and at Nankin, it was possible to see with clearer eyes than at Shanghai that the Taeping cause was one that could not be resuscitated. But although Burgevine soon and very clearly saw the hope-lessness of the Taeping movement, he had by no means made up his mind to go over to the imperialists. With a consid-erable number of European followers at his beck and call, and with a profound and ineradicable contempt for the whole Chinese official world, he was loth to lose or surrender the position which gave him a certain importance. He vacil-lated between a number of suggestions, and the last he came to was the most remarkable, at the same time that it revealed more clearly than any other the vain and meretricious char-acter of the man. In his second interview with Major Gor-don he proposed that that officer should join him, and com-bining the whole force of the Europeans and the disciplined Chinese, seize Soochow, and establish an independent au-thority of their own. It was the old filibustering idea, revived under the most unfavorable circumstances, of fight-ing for their own hand, dragging the European name in the dirt, and founding an independent authority of some vague, undefinable and transitory character. Major Gordon list-ened to the unfolding of this scheme of miserable treachery, and only his strong sense of the utter impossibility, and in-deed the ridiculousness of the project, prevented his contempt and indignation finding forcible expression. Burgevine, the traitor to the imperial cause, the man whose health would not allow him to do his duty to his new masters in Soochow, thus revealed his plan for defying all parties, and for deciding the fate of the Dragon Throne. The only reply he received was the cold one that it would be better and wiser to confine his attention to the question of whether he intended to yield or not, instead of discussing idle schemes of "vaulting ambition."

Meantime, Chung Wang had come down from Nankin to superintend the defense of Soochow; and in face of a more capable opponent he still did not despair of success, or at the least of making a good fight of it. He formed the plan of assuming the offensive against Chanzu while General Ching was employed in erecting his stockades step by step nearer to the eastern wall of Soochow. In order to prevent the realization of this project, Major Gordon made several demonstrations on the western side of Soochow, which had the effect of inducing Chung Wang to defer his departure. At this conjuncture serious news arrived from the south. A large rebel force, assembled from Chekiang and the silk districts south of the Taho Lake, had moved up the Grand Canal and held the garrison of Wokong in close leaguer. On October 10 the imperialists stationed there made a sortie, but were driven back with the loss of several hundred men killed and wounded. Their provisions were almost exhausted, and it was evident that unless relieved they could not hold out many days longer. On October 12 Major Gordon therefore hastened to their succor. The rebels held a position south of Wokong, and, as they felt sure of a safe retreat, they fought with great determination. The battle lasted three hours; the guns had to be brought up to within fifty yards of the stockade, and the whole affair is described as one of the hardest fought actions of the war. On the return of the contingent to Patachiaou, about thirty Europeans deserted the rebels, but Burgevine and one or two others were not with them. Chung Wang had seized the opportunity of Gordon's departure for the relief of Wokong to carry out his scheme against Chanzu. Taking the "Kajow" with him, and a considerable number of the foreign adventurers, he reached Monding, where the imperialists were strongly intrenched at the junction of the main creek from Chanzu with the Canal. He attacked them, and a severely contested struggle ensued, in which at first the Taepings carried everything before them. But the fortune of the day soon veered round. The "Kajow" was sunk by a lucky shot, great havoc was wrought by the explosion of a powder-boat, and the imperialists remained masters of a hard-fought field. The defection of the Europeans placed Burgevine in serious peril, and only Major Gordon's urgent representations and acts of courtesy to the Mow Wang saved his life. The Taeping leader, struck by the gallantry and fair dealing of the English officer, set Burgevine free, and the American consul thanked Major Gordon for his great kindness to that misguided officer. Burgevine came out of the whole complication with a reputation in every way tarnished. He had not even the most common courage which would have impelled him to stay in Soochow and take the chances of the party to which he had attached himself. Whatever his natural talents might have been, his vanity and weakness obscured them all. With the inclination to create an infinity of mischief, it must be considered fortunate that his ability was so small, for his opportunities were abundant.

The conclusion of the Burgevine incident removed a weight from Major Gordon's mind. Established on the east and south of Soochow, he determined to secure a similar position on its western side, when he would be able to intercept the communications still held by the garrison across the Taho Lake. In order to attain this object it was necessary, in the first place, to carry the stockades at Wuliungchow, a village two miles west of Patachiaou. The place was captured at the first attack and successfully held, notwithstanding a fierce attempt to recover it under the personal direction of Chung Wang, who returned for the express purpose. This success was followed by others. Another large body of rebels had come up from the south and assailed the garrison of Wokong. On October 26 one of Gordon's lieutenants, Major Kirkham, inflicted a severe defeat upon them, and vigorously pursued them for several miles. The next operation undertaken was the capture of the village of Leeku, three miles north of Soochow, as the preliminary to investing the city on the north. Here Major Gordon resorted to his usual flanking tactics, and with conspicuous success. The rebels fought well; one officer was killed at Gordon's side, and the men in the stockade were cut down with the exception of about forty, who were made prisoners. Soochow was then assailed on the northern as well as on the other sides, but Chung Wang's army still served to keep open communications by means of the Grand Canal. That army had its principal quarters at Wusieh, where it was kept in check by a large imperialist force under Santajin, Li's brother, who had advanced from Kongyin on the Yangtse. Major Gordon's main difficulty now arose from the insufficiency of his force to hold so wide an extent of country; and in order to procure a re-enforcement from Santajin, he agreed to assist that commander against his able opponent Chung Wang. With a view to accomplishing this the Taeping position at Wanti, two miles north of Leeku, was attacked and captured.

At this stage of the campaign there were 13,500 men round Soochow, and of these 8,500 were fully occupied in the defense of the stockades, leaving the very small number of 5,000 men available for active measures in the field. On the other hand, Santajin had not fewer than 20,000, and possibly as many as 30,000 men under his orders. But the Taepings still enjoyed the numerical superiority. They had 40,000 men in Soochow, 20,000 at Wusieh, and Chung Wang occupied a camp, half-way between these places, with 18,000 followers. The presence of Chung Wang was also estimated to be worth a corps of 5,000 soldiers. Had Gordon been free to act, his plan of campaign would have been simple and decisive. He would have effected a junction of his forces with Santajin, he would have overwhelmed Chung Wang's 18,000 with his combined army of double that strength, and he would have appeared at the head of his victorious troops before the bewildered garrison of Wusieh. It would probably have terminated the campaign at a stroke. Even the decisive defeat of Chung Wang alone might have entailed the collapse of the cause now tottering to its fall. But Major Gordon had to consider not merely the military quality of his allies, but also their jealousies and differences. General Ching hated Santajin on private grounds as well as on public. He desired a monopoly of the profit and honor of the campaign. His own reputation would be made by the capture of Soochow. It would be diminished and cast into the shade were another imperial commander to defeat Chung Wang and close the line of the Grand Canal. Were Gordon to detach himself from General Ching he could not feel sure what that jealous and impulsive commander would do. He would certainly not preserve the vigilant defensive before Soochow necessary to insure the safety of the army operating to the north. The commander of the Ever-Victorious Army had consequently to abandon the tempting idea of crushing Chung Wang and to have recourse to slower methods.

On November 19, Major Gordon collected the whole of his available force to attack Fusaiquan, a place on the Grand Canal six miles north of Soochow. Here the rebels had barred the Canal at three different points, while on the banks they occupied eight earthworks, which were fortunately in a very incomplete state. A desperate resistance was expected from the rebels at this advantageous spot, but they preferred their safety to their duty, and retreated to Wusieh with hardly any loss. In consequence of this reverse Chung Wang withdrew his forces from his camp in face of Santajin, and concentrated his men at Monding and Wusieh for the defense of the Grand Canal. The investment of Soochow being now as complete as the number of troops under the imperial standard would allow of, Major Gordon returned to General Ching's stockades in front of that place, with the view of resuming the attack on the eastern gate. General Ching and Captain Bonnefoy had met with a slight repulse there on October 14. The stockade in front of the east gate was known by the name of the Low Mun, and had been strengthened to the best knowledge of the Taeping engineers. Their position was exceedingly formidable, consisting of a line of breastworks defended at intervals with circular stockades. Major Gordon decided upon making a night attack and he arranged his plans from the information provided by the European and other deserters who had been inside. The Taepings were not without their spies and sympathizers also, and the intended attempt was revealed to them. The attack was made at two in the morning of November 27, but the rebels had mustered in force and received Major Gordon's men with tremendous volleys. Even then the disciplined troops would not give way, and encouraged by the example of their leader, who seemed to be at the front and at every point at the same moment, fairly held their own on the edge of the enemy's position. Unfortunately the troops in support behaved badly, and got confused from the heavy fire of the Taepings, which never slackened. Some of them absolutely retired and others were landed at the wrong places. Major Gordon had to hasten to the rear to restore order, and during his absence the advanced guard were expelled from their position by a forward movement led by Mow Wang in person. The attack had failed, and there was nothing to do save to draw off the troops with as little further loss as possible. This was Major Gordon's first defeat, but it was so evidently due to the accidents inseparable from a night attempt, and to the fact that the surprise had been revealed, that it produced a less discouraging effect on officers and men than might have seemed probable. Up to this day Major Gordon had obtained thirteen distinct victories besides the advantage in many minor skirmishes.

Undismayed by this reverse, Major Gordon collected all his troops and artillery from the other stockades, and resolved to attack the Low Mun position with his whole force. He also collected all his heavy guns and mortars and cannonaded the rebel stockade for some time; but on an advance being ordered, the assailants were compelled to retire by the fire which the Taepings brought to bear on them from every available point. Chung Wang had hastened down from Wusieh to take part in the defense of what was rightly regarded as the key of the position at Soochow, and both he and Mow Wang superintended in person the defense of the Low Mun stockade. After a further cannonade the advance was again sounded, but this second attack would also have failed had not the officers and men boldly plunged into the moat or creek and swum across. The whole of the stockades and a stone fort were then carried, and the imperial forces firmly established at a point only 900 yards from the inner wall of Soochow. Six officers and fifty men were killed, and three officers, five Europeans, and 128 men were wounded in this successful attack. The capture of the Low Mun stockades meant practically the fall of Soochow. Chung Wang then left it to its fate, and all the other Wangs except Mow Wang were in favor of coming to terms with the imperialists. Even before this defeat, Lar Wang had entered into communications with General Ching for coming over, and as he had the majority of the troops at Soochow under his orders Mow Wang was practically powerless, although resolute to defend the place to the last. Several interviews took place between the Wangs and General Ching and Li Hung Chang. Major Gordon also saw the former, and had one interview with Lar Wang in person. The English officer proposed as the most feasible plan his surrendering one of the gates. During all this period Major Gordon had impressed on both of his Chinese colleagues the imperative necessity there was, for reasons of both policy and prudence, to deal leniently and honorably by the rebel chiefs. All seemed to be going well. General Ching took an oath of brotherhood with Lar Wang, Li Hung Chang agreed with everything that fell from Gordon's lips. The only one exempted from this tacit understanding was Mow Wang, always in favor of fighting it out and defending the town; and his name was not mentioned for the simple reason that he had nothing to do with the negotiations. For Mow Wang Major Gordon had formed the esteem due to a gallant enemy, and he resolved to spare no effort to save his life. His benevolent intentions were thwarted by the events that had occurred within Soochow. Mow Wang had been murdered by the other Wangs, who feared that he might detect their plans and prevent their being carried out. The death of Mow Wang removed the only leader who was heartily opposed to the surrender of Soochow, and on the day after this chief's murder the imperialists received possession of one of the gates. The inside of the city had been the scene of the most dreadful confusion. Mow Wang's men had sought to avenge their leader's death, and on the other hand the followers of Lar Wang had shaved their heads in token of their adhesion to the imperialist cause. Some of the more prudent of the Wangs, not knowing what turn events might take amid the prevailing discord, secured their safety by a timely flight. Major Gordon kept his force well in hand, and refused to allow any of the men to enter the city, where they would certainly have exercised the privileges of a mercenary force in respect of pillage. Instead of this, Major Gordon endeavored to obtain for them two months' pay from the Futai, which that official stated his inability to procure. Major Gordon thereupon resigned in disgust, and on succeeding in obtaining one month's pay for his men, he sent them back to Quinsan without a disturbance.

The departure of the Ever-Victorious Army for its headquarters was regarded by the Chinese officials with great satisfaction, and for several reasons. In the flush of the success at Soochow both that force and its commander seemed in the way of the Futai, and to diminish the extent of his triumph. Also neither Li nor Ching had the least wish for any of the ex-rebel chiefs, men of ability and accustomed to command, to be taken into the service of the government. Of men of that kind there were already enough. General Ching himself was a sufficiently formidable rival to the Futai, without any assistance and encouragement from Lar

Wang and the others. Li had no wish to save them from the fate of rebels; and although he had promised, and General Ching had sworn to, their personal safety, he was bent on getting rid of them in one way or another. He feared Major Gordon, but he also thought that the time had arrived when he could dispense with him and the foreign-drilled legion in the same way as he had got rid of Sherard Osborn and his fleet. The departure of the Quinsan force left him free to follow his own inclination. The Wangs were invited to an entertainment at the Futai's boat, and Major Gordon saw them both in the city and subsequently when on their way to Li Hung Chang. The exact circumstances of their fate were never known; but nine headless bodies were discovered on the opposite side of the creek, and not far distant from the Futai's quarters. It then became evident that Lar Wang and his fellow Wangs had been brutally murdered. Major Gordon was disposed to take the office of their avenger into his own hands, but the opportunity of doing so fortunately did not present itself. He hastened back to Quinsan, where he refused to act any longer with such false and dishonorable colleagues. The matter was reported to Pekin. Both the mandarins sought to clear themselves by accusing the other; and a special decree came from Pekin conferring on the English officer a very high order and the sum of 10,-000 taels. Major Gordon returned the money, and expressed his regret at being unable to accept any token of honor from the emperor in consequence of the Soochow affair.

A variety of reasons, all equally creditable to Major Gordon's judgment and single-mindedness, induced him after two months' retirement to abandon his inaction and to sink his difference with the Futai. He saw very clearly that the sluggishness of the imperial commanders would result in the prolongation of the struggle with all its attendant evils, whereas, if he took the field, he would be able to bring it to a conclusion within two months. Moreover, the Quinsan force, never very amenable to discipline, shook off all restraint when in quarters and promised to become as dangerous to the government in whose pay it was as to the enemy against whom it was engaged to fight. Major Gordon, in view of these facts, came to the prompt decision that it was his duty, and the course most calculated to do good, for him to retake the field and strive as energetically as possible to expel the rebels from the small part of Kiangsu still remaining in their possession. On February 18, 1864, he accordingly left Quinsan at the head of his men, who showed great satisfaction at the return to active campaigning. Wusieh had been evacuated on the fall of Soochow, and Chung Wang's force retired to Changchow, while that chief himself returned to Nankin. A few weeks later General Ching had seized Pingwang, thus obtaining the command of another entrance into the Taho Lake. Santajin established his force in a camp not far distant from Changchow, and engaged the rebels in almost daily skirmishes. This was the position of affairs when Major Gordon took the field toward the end of February, and he at once resolved to carry the war into a new country by crossing the Taho Lake and attacking the town of Yesing on its western shores. By seizing this and the adjoining towns he hoped to cut the rebellion in two, and to be able to attack Changchow in the rear. The operations at Yesing occupied two days; but at last the rebel stockades were carried with tremendous loss not only to the defenders, but also to a relieving force sent from Liyang. Five thousand prisoners were also taken. Liyang itself was the next place to be attacked; but the intricacy of the country, which was intersected by creeks and canals, added to the fact that the whole region had been desolated by famine, and that the rebels had broken all the bridges, rendered this undertaking one of great difficulty and some risk. However, Major Gordon's fortitude vanquished all obstacles, and when he appeared before Liyang he found that the rebel leaders in possession of the town had come to the decision to surrender. At this place Major Gordon came into communication with the general Paochiaou, who was covering the siege operations against

Nankin, which Tseng Kwofan was pressing with ever-increasing vigor. The surrender of Liyang proved the more important, as the fortifications were found to be admirably constructed, and as it contained a garrison of fifteen thousand men and a plentiful supply of provisions. From Liyang Major Gordon marched on Kintang, a town due north of Liyang, and about half-way between Changchow and Nankin. The capture of Kintang, by placing Gordon's force within striking distance of Changchow and its communications, would have compelled the rebels to suspend these operations and recall their forces. Unfortunately the attack on Kintang revealed unexpected difficulties. The garrison showed extraordinary determination; and although the wall was breached by the heavy fire, two attempts to assault were repulsed with heavy loss, the more serious inasmuch as Major Gordon was himself wounded below the knee, and compelled to retire to his boat. This was the second defeat Gordon had experienced.

In consequence of this reverse, which dashed the cup of success from Gordon's hands when he seemed on the point of bringing the campaign to a close in the most brilliant manner, the force had to retreat to Liyang, whence the commander hastened back with one thousand men to Wusieh. He reached Wusieh on the 25th of March, four days after the repulse at Kintang, and he there learned that Fushan had been taken and that Chanzu was being closely attacked. The imperialists had fared better in the south. General Ching had captured Kashingfoo, a strong place in Chekiang, and on the very same day as the repulse at Kintang, Tso Tsung Tang had recovered Hangchow. Major Gordon, although still incapacitated by his wound from taking his usual foremost place in the battle, directed all operations from his boat. He succeeded, after numerous skirmishes, in compelling the Taepings to quit their position before Chanzu; but they drew up in force at the village of Waisso, where they offered him battle. Most unfortunately, Major Gordon had to intrust the conduct of the attack to his lieu-

tenants, Colonels Howard and Rhodes, while he superintended the advance of the gunboats up the creek. Finding
the banks were too high to admit of these being usefully
employed, and failing to establish communications with the
infantry, he discreetly returned to his camp, where he found
everything in the most dreadful confusion owing to a terrible disaster. The infantry, in fact, had been outmaneuvered and routed with tremendous loss. Seven officers and
265 men had been killed, and one officer and sixty-two men
wounded. Such an overwhelming disaster would have
crushed any ordinary commander, particularly when coming so soon after such a rude defeat as that at Kintang. It
only roused Major Gordon to increased activity. He at once
took energetic measures to retrieve this disaster. He sent
his wounded to Quinsan, collected fresh troops, and, having
allowed his own wound to recover by a week's rest, resumed
in person the attack on Waisso. On April 10 Major Gordon
pitched his camp within a mile of Waisso, and paid his men
as the preliminary to the resumption of the offensive. The
attack commenced on the following morning, and promised
to prove of an arduous nature; but by a skillful flank movement Major Gordon carried two stockades in person, and
rendered the whole place no longer tenable. The rebels
evacuated their position and retreated, closely pursued by
the imperialists. The villagers, who had suffered from
their exactions, rose upon them, and very few rebels
escaped. The pursuit was continued for a week, and the
lately victorious army of Waisso was practically annihilated. The capture of Changchow was to be the next and
crowning success of the campaign. For this enterprise the
whole of the Ever-Victorious Army was concentrated, including the ex-rebel contingent of Liyang. On April 23
Major Gordon carried the stockades near the west gate. In
their capture the Liyang men, although led only by Chinese,
showed conspicuous gallantry, thus justifying Major Gordon's belief that the Chinese would fight as well under their
own countrymen as when led by foreigners. Batteries were

then constructed for the bombardment of the town itself. Before these were completed the imperialists assaulted, but were repulsed with loss. On the following day (April 27) the batteries opened fire, and two pontoon bridges were thrown across, when Major Gordon led his men to the assault. The first attack was repulsed, and a second one, made in conjunction with the imperialists, fared not less badly. The pontoons were lost, and the force suffered a greater loss than at any time during the war, with the exception of Waisso. The Taepings also lost heavily; and their valor could not alter the inevitable result. Changchow had consequently to be approached systematically by trenches, in the construction of which the Chinese showed themselves very skillful. The loss of the pontoons compelled the formation of a cask-bridge; and, during the extensive preparations for renewing the attack, several hundred of the garrison came over, reporting that it was only the Cantonese who wished to fight to the bitter end. On May 11, the fourth anniversary of its capture by Chung Wang, Li requested Major Gordon to act in concert with him for carrying the place by storm. The attack was made in the middle of the day, to the intense surprise of the garrison, who made only a feeble resistance, and the town was at last carried with little loss. The commandant, Hoo Wang, was made prisoner and executed. This proved to be the last action of the Ever-Victorious Army, which then returned to Quinsan, and was quietly disbanded by its commander before June 1.

To sum up the closing incidents of the Taeping war. Tayan was evacuated two days after the fall of Changchow, leaving Nankin alone in their hands. Inside that city there were the greatest misery and suffering. Tien Wang had refused to take any of the steps pressed on him by Chung Wang, and when he heard the people were suffering from want, all he said was, "Let them eat the sweet dew." Tseng Kwofan drew up his lines on all sides of the city, and gradually drove the despairing rebels behind the walls. Chung Wang sent out the old women and children; and let it be recorded to the credit of Tseng Kwotsiuen that he did not drive them back, but charitably provided for their wants, and dispatched them to a place of shelter. In June Major Gordon visited Tseng's camp, and found his works covering twenty-four to thirty miles, and constructed in the most elaborate fashion. The imperialists numbered 80,000 men, but were badly armed. Although their pay was very much in arrear, they were well fed, and had great confidence in their leader, Tseng Kwofan. On June 30, Tien Wang, despairing of success, committed suicide by swallowing golden leaf. Thus died the Hungtsiuen who had erected the standard of revolt in Kwangsi thirteen years before. His son was proclaimed Tien Wang on his death becoming known, but his reign was brief. The last act of all had now arrived. On July 19 the imperialists had run a gallery under the wall of Nankin, and charged it with 40,000 pounds of powder. The explosion destroyed fifty yards of the walls, and the imperialists, attacking on all sides, poured in through the breach. Chung Wang made a desperate resistance in the interior, holding his own and the Tien Wang's palace to the last. He made a further stand with a thousand men at the southern gate, but his band was overwhelmed, and he and the young Tien Wang fled into the surrounding country. In this supreme moment of danger Chung Wang thought more of the safety of his young chief than of himself, and he gave him an exceptionally good pony to escape on, while he himself took a very inferior animal. As the consequence Tien Wang the Second escaped, while Chung Wang was captured in the hills a few days later. Chung Wang, who had certainly been the hero of the Taeping movement, was beheaded on August 7, and the young Tien Wang was eventually captured and executed also, by Shen Paochen. For this decisive victory, which extinguished the Taeping Rebellion, Tseng Kwofan, whom Gordon called "generous, fair, honest and patriotic," was made a Hou, or Marquis, and his brother Tseng Kwotsiuen an Earl.

It is impossible to exaggerate the impression made by

Gordon's disinterestedness on the Chinese people, who elevated him for his courage and military prowess to the pedestal of a national god of war. The cane which he carried when leading his men to the charge became known as "Gordon's wand of victory"; and the troops whom he trained, and converted by success from a rabble into an army, formed the nucleus of China's modern army. The service he rendered his adopted country was, therefore, lasting as well as striking, and the gratitude of the Chinese has, to their credit, proved not less durable. The name of Gordon is still one to conjure with among the Chinese, and if ever China were placed in the same straits, she would be the more willing, from his example, to intrust her cause to an English officer. As to the military achievements of General Gordon in China nothing fresh can be said. They speak indeed for themselves, and they form the most solid portion of the reputation which he gained as a leader of men. In the history of the Manchu dynasty he will be known as "Chinese Gordon"; although for us his earlier sobriquet must needs give place, from his heroic and ever-regrettable death, to that of "Gordon of Khartoum."

CHAPTER XXI

THE REGENCY

WHILE the suppression of the Taeping Rebellion was in progress, events of great interest and importance happened at Pekin. It will be recollected that when the allied forces approached that city in 1860, the Emperor Hienfung fled to Jehol, and kept himself aloof from all the peace negotiations which were conducted to a successful conclusion by his brother, Prince Kung. After the signature of the convention in Pekin, ratifying the Treaty of Tientsin, he refused to return to his capital; and he even seems to have hoped that he might, by asserting his imperial prerogative, transfer the capital from Pekin to Jehol, and thus evade one of the principal concessions to the foreigners. But if this was impossible, he was quite determined, for himself, to have nothing to do with them, and during the short remainder of his life he kept his court at Jehol. While his brother was engaged in meeting the difficulties of diplomacy, and in arranging the conditions of a novel situation, Hienfung, by collecting round his person the most bigoted men of his family, showed that he preferred those counselors who had learned nothing from recent events, and who would support him in his claims to undiminished superiority and inaccessibility. Prominent among the men in his confidence was Prince Tsai, who had taken so discreditable a part in the arrest of Parkes and his companions at Tungchow, and among his other advisers were several inexperienced and impetuous members of the Manchu family. They were all agreed in the policy of recovering, at the earliest possible moment, what they considered to be the natural and prescriptive right of the occupant of the Dragon Throne to treat all other potentates as in no degree equal to himself. No respect for treaties would have deterred them from reasserting what had solemnly been signed away, and the permanent success of the faction at Jehol would have entailed, within a comparatively short period, the outbreak of another foreign war. But the continued residence of the emperor at Jehol was not popular with either his own family or the inhabitants of Pekin. The members of the Manchu clan, who received a regular allowance during the emperor's residence at Pekin, were reduced to the greatest straits, and even to the verge of starvation, while the Chinese naturally resented the attempt to remove the capital to any other place. This abnegation of authority by Hienfung, for his absence meant nothing short of that, could not have been prolonged indefinitely, for a Chinese emperor has many religious and secular duties to perform which no one else can discharge, and which, if not discharged, would reduce the office of emperor to a nonentity. Prince Tsai and his associates had no difficulty in working upon the fears of this prince, who held the most exalted idea of his own majesty, at the same time that he had not the power or knowledge to vindicate it.

While such were the views prevailing in the imperial circle at Jehol, arrangements were in progress for the taking up of his residence at Pekin of the British minister. After Lord Elgin's departure, his brother, Sir Frederick Bruce, who was knighted for his share in the negotiations, was appointed first occupant of the post of minister in the Chinese capital, and on March 22, 1861, he left Tientsin for Pekin. Mr. Wade accompanied Sir Frederick as principal secretary, and the staff included six student interpreters, whose ranks, constantly recruited, have given many able men to the public service. Before Sir Frederick reached the capital, the Chinese minister had taken a step to facilitate the transaction of business with the foreign representatives. Prince Kung —and the credit of the measure belongs exclusively to him— will always be gratefully remembered by any foreign writer on modern China as the founder of the department known as the Tsungli Yamen, which he instituted in January, 1861. This department, since its institution, has very fully answered all the expectations formed of it; and, although it is erroneous to represent it as in any sense identical with the Chinese government, or as the originating source of Chinese policy, it has proved a convenient and well-managed vehicle for the dispatch of international business. Prince Kung became its first president, and acted in that capacity until his fall from power in 1884.

Before long, reports began to be spread of the serious illness of the emperor. In August, Prince Kung hastened to Jehol, the object of his journey being kept secret. The members of the Tsungli Yamen were observed by the foreign officials to be pre-occupied, and even the genial Wansiang could not conceal that they were passing through a crisis. Not merely was Hienfung dying, but it had become known to Prince Kung and his friends that he had left the governing authority during the minority of his son, a child of less than six years of age, to a board of regency composed of eight of the least intelligent and most arrogant and self-seeking members of the imperial family, with Prince Tsai at their head. The emperor died on August 22. A few hours later the imperial decree notifying the last wishes of the ruler as to the mode of government was promulgated. The board of regency assumed the nominal control of affairs, and Hienfung's son was proclaimed emperor under the style of Chiseang. In all of these arrangements neither Prince Kung nor his brothers, nor the responsible ministers at the capital, had had the smallest part. It was an intrigue among certain members of the imperial clan to possess themselves of the ruling power, and for a time it seemed as if their intrigue would be only too successful. Nothing happened during the months of September and October to disturb their confidence, for they remained at Jehol, and at Pekin the routine of government continued to be performed by Prince Kung. That statesman and his colleagues employed the interval in arranging their own plan of action, and in making sure of the fidelity of a certain number of troops. Throughout these preparations Prince Kung was ably and energetically supported by his brother, Prince Chun, by his colleague, Wansiang, and by his aged father-in-law, the minister Kweiliang. But the conspirators could not keep the young emperor at Jehol indefinitely, and when, at the end of October, it became known that he was on the point of returning to Pekin, it was clear that the hour of conflict had arrived. At Jehol the Board of Regency could do little harm; but once its pretensions and legality were admitted at the capital, all the ministers would have to take their orders from it, and to resign the functions which they had retained. The main issue was whether Prince Kung or Prince Tsai was to be supreme. On November 1 the young emperor entered his capital in state. A large number of soldiers, still dressed in their white mourning, accompanied their sovereign from Jehol; but Shengpao's garrison was infinitely more numerous, and thoroughly loyal to the cause of Prince Kung. The majority of the regents had arrived with the reigning prince; those who had not yet come were on the road, escorting the dead body of Hienfung toward its resting-place. If a blow was to be struck at all now was the time to strike it. The regents had not merely placed themselves in the power of their opponent, but they had actually brought with them the young emperor, without whose person Prince Kung could have accomplished little. Prince Kung had spared no effort to secure, and had fortunately succeeded in obtaining, the assistance and co-operation of the Empress Dowager, Hienfung's principal widow, named Tsi An. Her assent had been obtained to the proposed plot before the arrival in Pekin, and it now only remained to carry it out. On the day following the entry into the capital, Prince Kung hastened to the palace, and, producing before the astonished regents an Imperial Edict ordering their dismissal, he asked them whether they obeyed the decree of their sovereign, or whether he must call in his soldiers to compel them. Prince Tsai and his companions had no choice save to signify their acquiescence in what they could not prevent; but, on leaving the chamber in which this scene took place, they hastened toward the emperor's apartment in order to remonstrate against their dismissal, or to obtain from him some counter-edict reinstating them in their positions. They were prevented from carrying out their purpose, but this proof of contumacy sealed their fate. They were promptly arrested, and a second decree was issued ordering their degradation from their official and hereditary rank. To Prince Kung and his allies was intrusted the charge of trying and punishing the offenders.

The next step was the proclamation of a new regency, composed of the two empresses, Tsi An, principal widow of Hienfung, and Tsi Thsi, mother of the young emperor. Two precedents for the administration being intrusted to an empress were easily found by the Hanlin doctors during the Ming dynasty, when the Emperors Chitsong and Wanleh were minors. Special edicts were issued and arrangements made for the transaction of business during the continuance of the regency, and as neither of the empresses knew Manchu, it was specially provided that papers and documents, which were always presented in that language, should be translated into Chinese. Concurrently with these measures for the settlement of the regency happened the closing scenes in the drama of conspiracy which began so successfully at Jehol and ended so dramatically at Pekin. For complete success and security it was necessary that all the ringleaders should be captured, and some of them were still free.

The bravest, if not the ablest, of the late Board of Regency, Sushuen, remained at large. He had been charged with the high and honorable duty of escorting the remains of Hienfung to the capital. It was most important that he should be seized before he became aware of the fate that had befallen his colleagues. Prince Chun volunteered to capture the last, and in a sense the most formidable, of the intriguers himself, and on the very day that the events described happened at Pekin he rode out of the capital at the head of a body of Tartar cavalry. On the following night Prince Chun reached the spot where he was encamped, and, breaking into the house, arrested him while in bed. Sushuen did not restrain his indignation, and betrayed the ulterior plans entertained by himself and his associates by declaring that Prince Chun had been only just in time to prevent a similar fate befalling himself. He was at once placed on his trial with the other prisoners, and on November 10 the order was given in the emperor's name for their execution. Sushuen was executed on the public ground set apart for that purpose; but to the others, as a special favor from their connection with the imperial family, was sent the silken cord, with which they were permitted to put an end to their existence. In the fate of Prince Tsai may be seen a well merited retribution for his treachery and cruelty to Sir Harry Parkes and his companions.

Another important step which had to be taken was the alteration of the style given to the young emperor's reign. It was felt to be impolitic that the deposed ministers should retain any connection whatever in history with the young ruler. Were Hienfung's son to be handed down to posterity as Chiseang there would be no possibility of excluding their names and their brief and feverish ambition from the national annals. After due deliberation, therefore, the name of Tungche was substituted for that of Chiseang, and meaning, as it does, "the union of law and order," it will be allowed that the name was selected with some proper regard for the circumstances of the occasion. Prince Kung was rewarded with many high offices and sounding titles in addition to the post of chief minister under the two empresses. He was made president of the Imperial Clan Court in the room of Prince Tsai, and the title of Iching Wang, or Prince Minister, was conferred upon him. His stanch friends and supporters, Wansiang, Paukwen, and Kweiliang, were appointed to the Supreme Council. Prince Chun, to whose skill and bravery in arresting Sushuen Prince Kung felt very much indebted, was also rewarded. With these incidents closed what might have proved a grave and perilous complication for the Chinese Government. Had Prince Kung prematurely revealed his plans there is every reason to suppose that he would have alarmed and forewarned his rivals, and that they, with the person of the emperor in their possession, would have obtained the advantage. His patience during the two months of doubt and anxiety while the emperor remained at Jehol was matched by the vigor and promptitude that he displayed on the eventful 2d of November. That his success was beneficial to his country will not be disputed by any one, and Prince Kung's name must be permanently remembered both for having commenced, and for having insured the continuance of diplomatic relations with England and the other foreign powers.

The increased intercourse with Europeans not merely led to greater diplomatic confidence and to the extension of trade, but it also induced many foreigners to offer their services and assistance to the Pekin government during the embarrassment arising from internal dissension. At first these persons were, as has been seen, encouraged and employed more in consequence of local opinion in the treaty-ports than as a matter of State policy. But already the suggestion had been brought forward in more than one form for the employment of foreigners, with the view of increasing the resources of the government by calling in the assistance of the very agency which had reduced them. A precedent had been established for this at an earlier period—before, in fact, the commencement of hostilities—by the appointment of Mr. Horatio N. Lay to direct and assist the local authorities in the collection of customs in the Shanghai district. Mr. Lay's experience had proved most useful in drawing up the tariff of the Treaty of Tientsin, and his assistance had been suitably acknowledged. In 1862, when the advantages to be derived from the military experience of foreigners had been practically recognized by the appointment of Europeans to command a portion of the army of China, and in pursuance of a suggestion made by the present Sir Robert Hart in the previous year, it was thought desirable for many reasons that something should also be done to increase the naval resources of the empire, and Mr. Lay was intrusted with a commission for purchasing and collecting in Europe a fleet of gunboats of small draught, which could be usefully employed for all the purposes of the Pekin Government on the rivers and shallow estuaries of the country. Mr. Lay, who undertook the commission, said: "This force was intended for the protection of the treaty-ports, for the suppression of piracy then rife, and for the relief of this country from the burden of 'policing' the Chinese waters"; but its first use in the eyes of Prince Kung was to be employed against the rebels and their European supporters, of whom Burgevine was the most prominent. Captain Sherard Osborn, a distinguished English naval officer, was associated with Mr. Lay in the undertaking. An Order of Council was issued on August 30, 1862, empowering both of these officers to act in the matter as delegates of the Chinese. Captain Osborn and Mr. Lay came to England to collect the vessels of this fleet, and the former afterward returned with them to China in the capacity of their commodore. The transaction was not well managed from the very commencement. Mr. Lay wrote in August, 1862, to say that he had chosen as the national ensign of the Chinese navy "a green flag, bearing a yellow diagonal cross," and he wrote again to request that an official notification should appear in the "Gazette." Had his request been complied with, there would have been very strong reason for assuming that the English Government was prepared to support and facilitate every scheme for forcing the Chinese to accept and submit to the exact method of progress approved of and desired by the European servants of their government, without their taking any part in the transaction save to ratify terms that might be harsh and exorbitant. Fortunately, the instinctive caution of our Foreign Office was not laid aside on this occasion. Mr. Lay was informed that no notice could appear in the "London Gazette" except after the approval of the Pekin authorities had been expressed; and Prince Kung wrote, on October 22, to say that the Chinese ensign would be of "yellow ground, and on it will be designed a dragon with his head toward the upper part of the flag." Mr. Lay preceded the vessels—seven gunboats and one store-ship—and arrived at Pekin in May, 1863.

Prince Kung had been most anxious for the speedy arrival of the flotilla; and the doubtful fortune of the campaign in Kiangsu, where the gunboats would have been invaluable, rendered him extremely desirous that they should commence active operations immediately on arrival. But he found, in the first place, that Mr. Lay was not prepared to accept the appointment of a Chinese official as joint commander, and in the second place, that he would not receive orders from any of the provincial authorities. Such a decision was manifestly attended with the greatest inconvenience to China; for only the provincial authorities knew what the interests of the State demanded, and where the fleet might co-operate with advantage in the attacks on the Taepings. Unless Captain

Osborn were to act on the orders of Tsen Kwofan, and particularly of Li Hung Chang, it was difficult to see of what possible use he or his flotilla could be to China. The founders of the new Chinese navy claimed practically all the privileges of an ally, and declined the duties devolving on them as directing a department of the Chinese administration. Of course, it was more convenient and more dignified for the foreign officers to draw their instructions and their salaries direct from the fountain-head; but if the flotilla was not to be of any practical use to China it might just as well never have been created. The fleet arrived in safety, but remained inactive. The whole summer and autumn of 1863, with its critical state of affairs round Soochow, passed away without anything being done to show what a powerful auxiliary Mr. Lay's ships might be. The ultimate success of those operations without the smallest co-operation on the part of Captain Osborn or his flotilla virtually sealed its fate. In October, Wansiang, in the name of the Foreign Office, declared that the Chinese could not recognize or ratify the private arrangement between Mr. Lay and his naval officer, and that it was essential for Captain Osborn to submit to receive his instructions from the provincial authorities. In the following month Mr. Lay was summarily dismissed from the Chinese service, and it was determined, after some delay and various counter suggestions, to send back the ships to Europe, there to be disposed of. The radical fault in the whole arrangement had been Mr. Lay's wanting to take upon himself the responsibility not merely of Inspector-General of Customs, but also of supreme adviser on all matters connected with foreign questions. The Chinese themselves were to take quite a subordinate part in their realization, and were to be treated, in short, as if they did know how to manage their own affairs. Mr. Lay's dreams were suddenly dispelled, and his philanthropic schemes fell to the ground. Neither Prince Kung nor his colleagues had any intention to pave the way for their own effacement.

After Mr. Lay's departure, the Maritime Customs were

placed under the control of Mr. Robert Hart, who had acted during Mr. Lay's absence in Europe. This appointment was accompanied by the transfer of the official residence from Pekin to Shanghai, which was attended with much practical advantage. Already the customs revenue had risen to three millions, and trade was steadily expanding as the rebels were gradually driven back, and as the Yangtsekiang and the coasts became safer for navigation. Numerous schemes were suggested for the opening up of China by railways and the telegraph; but they all very soon ended in nothing, for the simple reason that the Chinese did not want them. They were more sincere and energetic in their adoption of military improvements.

The anxieties of Prince Kung on the subject of the dynasty, and with regard to the undue pretensions and expectations of the foreign officials who looked on the Chinese merely as the instruments of their self-aggrandizement, were further increased during this period by the depredations of the Nienfei rebels in the province of Shantung. During these operations Sankolinsin died, leaving Tseng Kwofan in undisputed possession of the first place among Chinese officials. Sankolinsin, when retreating after a reverse, was treacherously murdered by some villagers whose hospitality he had claimed.

The events of this introductory period may be appropriately concluded with the strange stroke of misfortune that befell Prince Kung in the spring of 1865, and which seemed to show that he had indulged some views of personal ambition. The affair had probably a secret history, but if so the truth is hardly likely to be ever known. The known facts were as follows: On April 2, 1865, there appeared an edict degrading the prince in the name of the two regent-empresses. The charge made against him was of having grown arrogant and assumed privileges to which he had no right. He was at first "diligent and circumspect," but he has now become disposed "to overrate his own importance." In consequence, he was deprived of all his appointments and dismissed from the scene of public affairs. Five weeks after his fall, however, Prince Kung was reinstated, on May 8, in all his offices, with the exception of that of President of the Council. This episode, which might have produced grave complications, closed with a return to almost the precise state of things previously existing. There was one important difference. The two empresses had asserted their predominance. Prince Kung had hoped to be supreme, and to rule uncontrolled. From this time forth he was content to be their minister and adviser, on terms similar to those that would have applied to any other official.

The year 1865, which witnessed this very interesting event in the history of the Chinese Government, beheld before its close the departure of Sir Frederick Bruce from Pekin, and the appointment of Sir Rutherford Alcock, who had been the first British minister to Japan during the critical period of the introduction of foreign intercourse with that country, to fill the post of Resident Minister at Pekin. Sir Rutherford Alcock then found the opportunity to put in practice some of the honorable sentiments to which he had given expression twenty years before at Shanghai. When Sir Rutherford left Yeddo for Pekin, the post of Minister in Japan was conferred on Sir Harry Parkes, who had been acting as consul at Shanghai since the conclusion of the war. The relations between the countries were gradually settling down on a satisfactory basis, and the appointment of a Supreme Court for China and Japan at Shanghai, with Sir Edmund Hornby as Chief Judge, promised to enforce obedience to the law among even the unsettled adventurers of different nationalities left by the conclusion of the Taeping Rebellion and the cessation of piracy without a profitable pursuit.

While the events which have been set forth were happening in the heart of China, other misfortunes had befallen the executive in the more remote quarters of the realm, but resulting none the less in the loss and ruin of provinces, and in the subversion of the emperor's authority. Two great uprisings of the people occurred in opposite directions, both commencing while the Taeping Rebellion was in full force, and continuing to disturb the country for many years after its suppression. The one had for its scene the great south-western province of Yunnan; the other the two provinces of the northwest, Shensi and Kansuh, and extending thence westward to the Pamir. They resembled each other in one point, and that was that they were instigated and sustained by the Mohammedan population alone. The Panthays and the Tungani were either indigenous tribes or foreign immigrants who had adopted or imported the tenets of Islam. Their sympathies with the Pekin Government were probably never very great, but they were impelled in both cases to revolt more by local tyranny than by any distinct desire to cast off the authority of the Chinese; but, of course, the obvious embarrassment of the central executive encouraged by simplifying the task of rebellion. The Panthay rising calls for description in the first place, because it began at an earlier period than the other, and also because the details have been preserved with greater fidelity. Mohammedanism is believed to have been introduced into Yunnan in or about the year 1275, and it made most progress among the so-called aboriginal tribes, the Lolos and the Mantzu. The officials were mostly Chinese or Tartars, and, left practically free from control, they more often abused their power than sought to employ it for the benefit of the people they governed. In the very first year of Hienfung's reign (1851) a petition reached the capital from a Mohammedan land proprietor in Yunnan named Ma Wenchu, accusing the emperor's officials of the gravest crimes, and praying that "a just and honest man" might be sent to redress the wrongs of an injured and long-suffering people. The petition was carefully read and favorably considered at the capital; but beyond a gracious answer the emperor was at the time powerless to apply a remedy to the evil. Four years passed away without any open manifestation of the deep discontent smoldering below the surface. But in 1855 the Chinese and

the Mohammedan laborers quarreled in one of the principal
mines of the province, which is covered with mines of gold,
iron, and copper.   It seems that the greater success of the
Mohammedans in the uncertain pursuit of mining had roused
the displeasure of the Chinese.   Disputes ensued, in which
the Mussulmans added success in combat to success in mining; and the official appointed to superintend the mines, instead of remaining with a view to the restoration of order,
sought his personal safety by precipitate flight to the town
of Yunnan.   During his absence, the Chinese population
raised a levy *en masse*, attacked the Mohammedans who
had gained a momentary triumph, and compelled them by
sheer weight of numbers to beat a hasty retreat to their own
homes in a different part of the province.   This success was
the signal for a general outcry against the Mohammedans,
who had long been the object of the secret ill-will of the
other inhabitants.   Massacres took place in several parts of
Yunnan, and the followers of the Prophet had to flee for
their lives.

Among those who were slain during these popular disorders was a young chief named Ma Sucheng; and when the
news of his murder reached his native village, his younger
brother, Ma Sien, who had just received a small military
command, declared his intention to avenge him, and fled to
join the Mohammedan fugitives in the mountains.   In this
secure retreat they rallied their forces, and, driven to desperation by the promptings of want, they left their fastnesses
with the view of regaining what they had lost.   In this they
succeeded better than they could have hoped for.   The Chinese population experienced in their turn the bitterness of
defeat; and the mandarins had the less difficulty in concluding a temporary understanding between the exhausted
combatants.   Tranquillity was restored, and the miners resumed their occupations.   But the peace was deceptive, and
in a little time the struggle was renewed with increased fury.
In this emergency the idea occurred to some of the officials
that an easy and efficacious remedy of the difficulty in which

they found themselves would be provided by the massacre
of the whole Mussulman population. In this plot the foremost part was taken by Hwang Chung, an official who bitterly hated the Mohammedans. He succeeded in obtaining
the acquiescence of all his colleagues with the exception of
the viceroy of the province, who exposed the iniquity of the
design, but who, destitute of all support, was powerless to
prevent its execution. At the least he resolved to save his
honor and reputation by committing suicide, and he and his
wife were found one morning hanging up in the hall of the
yamen. His death simplified the execution of the project
which his refusal might possibly have prevented. May 19,
1856, was the date fixed for the celebration of this Chinese
St. Bartholomew. But the secret had not been well kept.
The Mohammedans, whether warned or suspicious, distrusted the authorities and their neighbors, and stood vigilantly on their guard. At this time they looked chiefly to a
high priest named Ma Tesing for guidance and instruction.
But although on the alert, they were, after all, taken to some
extent by surprise, and many of them were massacred after
a more or less unavailing resistance. But if many of the
Mussulmans were slain, the survivors were inspired with a
desperation which the mandarins had never contemplated.
From one end of Yunnan to the other the Mohammedans,
in face of great personal peril, rose by a common and spon-
taneous impulse, and the Chinese population was compelled
to take a hasty refuge in the towns. At Talifoo, where the
Mohammedans formed a considerable portion of the population, the most desperate fighting occurred, and after three
days' carnage the Mussulmans, under Tu Wensiu, were left
in possession of the city. The rebels did not remain without
leaders, whom they willingly recognized and obeyed; for the
kwanshihs, or chiefs, who had accepted titles of authority
from the Chinese, cast off their allegiance and placed themselves at the head of the popular movement. The priest Ma
Tesing was raised to the highest post of all as Dictator, but
Tu Wensiu admitted no higher authority than his own

within the walls of Talifoo. Ma Tesing had performed the pilgrimage to Mecca, he had resided at Constantinople for two years, and his reputation for knowledge and saintliness stood highest among his co-religionists.

While Ma Tesing exercised the supremacy due to his age and attainments, the young chief Ma Sien led the rebels in the field. His energy was most conspicuous, and in the year 1858 he thought he was sufficiently strong to make an attack upon the city of Yunnan itself. His attack was baffled by the resolute defense of an officer named Lin Tzuchin, who had shown great courage as a partisan leader against the insurgents before he was intrusted with the defense of the provincial capital. Ma Sien was compelled to beat a retreat, and to devote himself to the organization of the many thousand Ijen or Lolos recruits who signified their attachment to his cause. For the successful defense of Yunnan, Lin was made a Titu, and gradually collected into his own hands such authority as still remained to the emperor's lieutenants. On both sides preparations were made for the renewal of the struggle, but before the year 1858 ended Ma Sien met with a second repulse at the town of Linan. The year 1859 was not marked by any event of signal importance, although the balance of success inclined on the whole to the Mussulmans. But in the following year the Mohammedans drew up a large force, computed to exceed 50,000 men, round Yunnanfoo, to which they laid vigorous siege. The imperialists were taken at a disadvantage, and the large number of people who had fled for shelter into the town rendered the small store of provisions less sufficient for a protracted defense. Yunnanfoo was on the point of surrender when an event occurred which not merely relieved it from its predicament, but altered the whole complexion of the struggle. The garrison had made up its mind to yield. Even the brave Lin had accepted the inevitable, and begun to negotiate with the two rebel leaders, Ma Sien and the priest Ma Tesing. Those chiefs, with victory in their gossip, manifested an unexpected and surprising moderation. Instead of demanding from Lin a complete and unconditional surrender, they began to discuss with him what terms could be agreed upon for the cessation of the war and the restoration of tranquillity to the province. At first it was thought that these propositions concealed some intended treachery, but their sincerity was placed beyond dispute by the suicide of the mandarin Hwang Chung, who had first instigated the people to massacre their Mohammedan brethren. The terms of peace were promptly arranged, and a request was forwarded to Pekin for the ratification of a convention concluded under the pressure of necessity with some of the rebel leaders. The better to conceal the fact that this arrangement had been made with the principal leader of the disaffected, Ma Sien changed his name to Ma Julung, and received the rank of general in the Chinese service; while the high priest accepted as his share the not inconsiderable pension of two hundred taels a month. It is impossible to divine the true reasons which actuated these instigators of rebellion in their decision to go over to the side of the government. They probably thought that they had done sufficient to secure all practical advantages, and that any persistence in hostilities would only result in the increased misery and impoverishment of the province. Powerful as they were, there were other Mohammedan leaders seeking to acquire the supreme position among their co-religionists; and foremost among these was Tu Wensiu, who had reduced the whole of Western Yunnan to his sway, and reigned at Talifoo. The Mohammedan cause, important as it was, did not afford scope for the ambitions of two such men as Ma Julung and Tu Wensiu. The former availed himself of the favorable opportunity to settle this difficulty in a practical and, as he shrewdly anticipated, the most profitable manner for himself personally, by giving in his adhesion to the government.

This important defection did not bring in its train any certainty of tranquillity. Incited by the example of their leaders, every petty officer and chief thought himself deserving of the highest honors, and resolved to fight for his own hand. Ma Julung left Yunnanfoo for the purpose of seizing a neighboring town which had revolted, and during his absence one of his lieutenants seized the capital, murdered the viceroy, and threatened to plunder the inhabitants. Ma Julung was summoned to return in hot haste, and as a temporary expedient the priest Ma Tesing was elected viceroy. When Ma Julung returned with his army he had to lay siege to Yunnanfoo, and although he promptly effected an entrance into the city, it took five days' hard fighting in the streets before the force in occupation was expelled. The insurgent officer was captured, exposed to the public gaze for one month in an iron cage, and then executed in a cruel manner. Ma Tesing was deposed from the elevated position which he had held for so short a time, and a new Chinese viceroy arrived from Kweichow. The year 1863 opened with the first active operations against Tu Wensiu, who, during these years of disorder in Central Yunnan, had been governing the western districts with some prudence. It would have been better if they had not been undertaken, for they only resulted in the defeat of the detachments sent by Ma Julung to engage the despot of Talifoo. Force having failed, they had recourse to diplomacy, and Ma Tesing was sent to sound Tu Wensiu as to whether he would not imitate their example and make his peace with the authorities. These overtures were rejected with disdain, and Tu Wensiu proclaimed his intention of holding out to the last, and refused to recognize the wisdom or the necessity of coming to terms with the government. The embarrassment of Ma Julung and the Yunnan officials, already sufficiently acute, was at this conjuncture further aggravated by an outbreak in their rear among the Miaotze and some other mountain tribes in the province of Kweichow. To the difficulty of coping with a strongly placed enemy in front was thus added that of maintaining communications through a hostile and difficult region. A third independent party had also come into existence in Yunnan, where an ex-Chinese official named Liang

Shihmei had set up his own authority at Linan, mainly, it was said, through jealousy of the Mohammedans taken into the service of the government. The greatest difficulty of all was to reconcile the pretensions of the different commanders, for the Chinese officials, and the Futai Tsen Yuying in particular, regarded Ma Julung with no friendly eye. With the year 1867, both sides having collected their strength, more active operations were commenced, and Ma Julung proceeded in person, at the head of the best troops he could collect, to engage Tu Wensiu. It was at this time that the imperialists adopted the red flag as their standard in contradistinction to the white flag of the insurgents. A desultory campaign ensued, but although Ma Julung evinced both courage and capacity, the result was on the whole unfavorable to him; and he had to retreat to the capital, where events of some importance had occurred during his absence in the field. The viceroy, who had been stanchly attached to Ma Julung, died suddenly and under such circumstances as to suggest a suspicion of foul play; and Tsen Yuying had by virtue of his rank of Futai assumed the temporary discharge of his duties. The retreat of Ma Julung left the insurgents free to follow up their successes; and, in the course of 1868, the authority of the emperor had disappeared from every part of the province except the prefectural city of Yunnanfoo. This bad fortune led the Mussulmans who had followed the advice and fortunes of Ma Julung to consider whether it would not be wise to rejoin their co-religionists, and to at once finish the contest by the destruction of the government. Had Ma Julung wavered in his fidelity for a moment they would have all joined the standard of Tu Wensiu, and the rule of the Sultan of Talifoo would have been established from one end of Yunnan to the other; but he stood firm and arrested the movement in a summary manner.

Tu Wensiu, having established the security of his communications with Burma, whence he obtained supplies of arms and munitions of war, devoted his efforts to the capture of Yunnanfoo, which he completely invested. The garrison was reduced to the lowest straits before Tsen Yuying resolved to come to the aid of his distressed colleague. The loss of the prefectural town would not merely entail serious consequences to the imperialist cause, but he felt it would personally compromise him as the Futai at Pekin. In the early part of 1869, therefore, he threw himself into the town with three thousand men, and the forces of Tu Wensiu found themselves obliged to withdraw from the eastern side of the city. A long period of inaction followed, but during this time the most important events happened with regard to the ultimate result. Ma Julung employed all his artifice and arguments to show the rebel chiefs the utter hopelessness of their succeeding against the whole power of the Chinese empire, which, from the suppression of the Taeping Rebellion, would soon be able to be employed against them. They felt the force of his representations, and they were also oppressed by a sense of the slow progress they had made toward the capture of Yunnanfoo. Some months after Tsen Yuying's arrival, those of the rebels who were encamped to the north of the city hoisted the red flag and gave in their adhesion to the government. Then Ma Julung resumed active operations against the other rebels, and obtained several small successes. A wound received during one of the skirmishes put an end to his activity, and the campaign resumed its desultory character. But Ma Julung's illness had other unfortunate consequences; for during it Tsen Yuying broke faith with those of the rebel leaders who had come over, and put them all to a cruel death. The natural consequence of this foolish and ferocious act was that the Mohammedans again reverted to their desperate resolve to stand firmly by the side of Tu Wensiu. The war again passed into a more active phase. Ma Julung had recovered from his wounds. A new viceroy, and a man of some energy, was sent from Pekin. Lin Yuchow had attracted the notice of Tseng Kwofan among those of his native province who had responded to his appeal to defend Hoonan against the Tae-

pings sixteen years before; and shortly before the death of
the last viceroy of Yunnan, he had been made Governor
of Kweicho. To the same patron at Pekin he now owed
his elevation to the viceroyalty. It is said that he had lost
the energy which once characterized him; but he brought
with him several thousand Hoonan braves, whose courage
and military experience made them invaluable auxiliaries
to the embarrassed authorities in Yunnan. In the course
of the year 1870 most of the towns in the south and the
north of Yunnan were recovered, and communications were
reopened with Szchuen. As soon as the inhabitants perceived that the government had recovered its strength, they
hastened to express their joy at the change by repudiating
the white flag which Tu Wensiu had compelled them to
adopt. The imperialists even to the last increased the difficulty of their work of pacification by exhibiting a relentless
cruelty; and while the inhabitants thought to secure their
safety by a speedy surrender, the Mussulmans were rendered more desperate in their resolve to resist. The chances
of a Mohammedan success were steadily diminishing when
Yang Yuko, a mandarin of some military capacity, who had
begun his career in the most approved manner as a rebel,
succeeded in capturing the whole of the salt-producing district which had been the main source of their strength. In
the year 1872 all the preliminary arrangements were made
for attacking Talifoo itself. A supply of rifles had been received from Canton or Shanghai, and a few pieces of artillery had also arrived. With these improved weapons the
troops of Ma Julung and Tsen Yuying enjoyed a distinct
advantage over the rebels of Talifoo. The horrors of war
were at this point increased by those of pestilence, for the
plague broke out at Puerh on the southern frontier, and,
before it disappeared, devastated the whole of the province,
completing the effect of the civil war, and ruining the few
districts which had escaped from its ravages. The direct
command of the siege operations at Talifoo was intrusted to
Yang Yuko, a hunchback general, who had obtained a repu-

tation for invincibility; and when Tsen Yuying had completed his own operations he also proceeded to the camp before the Mohammedan capital for the purpose of taking part in the crowning operation of the war.

Tu Wensiu and the garrison of Talifoo, although driven to desperation, could not discover any issue from their difficulties. They were reduced to the last stage of destitution, and starvation stared them in the face. In this extremity Tu Wensiu, although there was every reason to believe that the imperialists would not fulfill their pledges, and that surrender simply meant yielding to a cruel death, resolved to open negotiations with Yang Yuko for giving up the town. The emperor's generals signified their desire for the speedy termination of the siege, at the same time expressing acquiescence in the general proposition of the garrison being admitted to terms. Although the Futai and Yang Yuko had promptly come to the mutual understanding to celebrate the fall of Talifoo by a wholesale massacre, they expressed their intention to spare the other rebels on the surrender of Tu Wensiu for execution and on the payment of an indemnity. The terms were accepted, although the more experienced of the rebels warned their comrades that they would not be complied with. On January 15, 1873, Tu Wensiu, the original of the mythical Sultan Suliman, the fame of whose power reached England, and who had been an object of the solicitude of the Indian government, accepted the decision of his craven followers as expressing the will of Heaven, and gave himself up for execution. He attired himself in his best and choicest garments, and seated himself in the yellow palanquin which he had adopted as one of the few marks of royal state that his opportunities allowed him to secure. Accompanied by the men who had negotiated the surrender, he drove through the streets, receiving for the last time the homage of his people, and out beyond the gates to Yang Yuko's camp. Those who saw the cortege marveled at the calm indifference of the fallen despot. He seemed to have as little fear of his fate as consciousness of his surroundings. The truth soon became evident. He had baffled his enemies by taking slow poison. Before he reached the presence of the Futai, who had wished to gloat over the possession of his prisoner, the opium had done its work, and Tu Wensiu was no more. It seemed but an inadequate triumph to sever the head from the dead body, and to send it preserved in honey as the proof of victory to Pekin. Four days after Tu Wensiu's death, the imperialists were in complete possession of the town, and a week later they had taken all their measures for the execution of the fell plan upon which they had decided. A great feast was given for the celebration of the convention, and the most important of the Mohammedan commanders, including those who had negotiated the truce, were present. At a given signal they were attacked and murdered by soldiers concealed in the gallery for the purpose, while six cannon shots announced to the soldiery that the hour had arrived for them to break loose on the defenseless townspeople. The scenes that followed are stated to have surpassed description. It was computed that 30,000 men alone perished after the fall of the old Panthay capital, and the Futai sent to Yunnanfoo twenty-four large baskets full of human ears, as well as the heads of the seventeen chiefs.

With the capture of Talifoo the great Mohammedan rebellion in the southwest, to which the Burmese gave the name of Panthay, closed, after a desultory struggle of nearly eighteen years. The war was conducted with exceptional ferocity on both sides, and witnessed more than the usual amount of falseness and breach of faith common to Oriental struggles. Nobody benefited by the contest, and the prosperity of Yunnan, which at one time had been far from inconsiderable, sank to the lowest possible point. A new class of officials came to the front during this period of disorder, and fidelity was a sufficient passport to a certain rank. Ma Julung, the Marshal Ma of European travelers, gained a still higher station; and notwithstanding the jealousy of his colleagues, acquired practical supremacy in the province.

The high priest, Ma Tesing, who may be considered as the prime instigator of the movement, was executed or poisoned in 1874 at the instigation of some of the Chinese officials. Yang Yuko, the most successful of all the generals, only enjoyed a brief tenure of power. It was said that he was dissatisfied with his position as commander-in-chief, and aspired to a higher rank. He also was summoned to Pekin, but never got further than Shanghai, where he died, or was removed. But although quiet gradually descended upon this part of China, it was long before prosperity followed in its train.

About six years after the first mutterings of discontent among the Mohammedans in the southwest, disturbances occurred in the northwest provinces of Shensi and Kansuh, where there had been many thousand followers of Islam since an early period of Chinese history. They were generally obedient subjects and sedulous cultivators of the soil; but they were always liable to sudden ebullitions of fanaticism or of turbulence, and it was said that during the later years of his reign Keen Lung had meditated a wholesale execution of the male population above the age of fifteen. The threat, if ever made, was never carried out, but the report suffices to show the extent to which danger was apprehended from the Tungan population. The true origin of the great outbreak in 1862 in Shensi seems to have been a quarrel between the Chinese and the Mohammedan militia as to their share of the spoil derived from the defeat and overthrow of a brigand leader. After some bloodshed, two imperial commissioners were sent from Pekin to restore order. The principal Mohammedan leader formed a plot to murder the commissioners, and on their arrival he rushed into their presence and slew one of them with his own hand. His coreligionists deplored the rash act, and voluntarily seized and surrendered him for the purpose of undergoing a cruel death. But although he was torn to pieces, that fact did not satisfy the outraged dignity of the emperor. A command was issued in Tungche's name to the effect that all those who persisted in following the creed of Islam should perish by the sword. From Shensi the outbreak spread into the adjoining province of Kansuh; and the local garrisons were vanquished in a pitched battle at Tara Ussu, beyond the regular frontier. The insurgents did not succeed, however, in taking any of the larger towns of Shensi, and after threatening with capture the once famous city of Singan, they were gradually expelled from that province. The Mohammedan rebellion within the limits of China proper would not, therefore, have possessed more than local importance but for the fact that it encouraged a similar outreak in the country further west, and that it resulted in the severance of the Central Asian provinces from China for a period of many years.

The uprising of the Mohammedans in the frontier provinces appealed to the secret fears as well as to the longings of the Tungan settlers and soldiers in all the towns and military stations between Souchow and Kashgar. The sense of a common peril, more perhaps than the desire to attain the same object, led to revolts at Hami, Barkul, Urumtsi, and Turfan, towns which formed a group of industrious communities half-way between the prosperous districts of Kansuh on the one side and Kashgar on the other. The Tungani at these towns revolted under the leading of their priests, and imitated the example of their co-religionists within the settled borders of China by murdering all who did not accept their creed. After a brief interval, which we may attribute to the greatness of the distance, to the vigilance of the Chinese garrison, or to the apathy of the population, the movement spread to the three towns immediately west of Turfan, Karashar, Kucha, and Aksu, where it came into contact with, and was stopped by, another insurrectionary movement under Mohammedan, but totally distinct, auspices. West of Aksu the Tungan rebellion never extended south of the Tian Shan range. The defection of the Tungani, who had formed a large proportion, if not the majority, of the Chinese garrisons, paralyzed the strength of the Celestials in Central Asia. Both in the districts dependent on Ili, and in those ruled from Kashgar and Yarkand, the Chinese were beset by many great and permanent difficulties. They were with united strength a minority, and now that they were divided among themselves almost a hopeless minority. The peoples they governed were fanatical, false, and fickle. The ruler of Khokand and the refugees living on his bounty were always on the alert to take the most advantage of the least slip or act of weakness on the part of the governing classes. Their machinations had been hitherto baffled, but never before had so favorable an opportunity presented itself for attaining their wishes as when it became known that the whole Mohammedan population was up in arms against the emperor, and that communications were severed between Kashgar and Pekin. The attempts made at earlier periods on the part of the members of the old ruling family in Kashgar to regain their own by expelling the Chinese have been described. In 1857 Wali Khan, one of the sons of Jehangir, had succeeded in gaining temporary possession of the city of Kashgar, and seemed for a moment to be likely to capture Yarkand also. He fell by his vices. The people soon detested the presence of the man to whom they had accorded a too hasty welcome. After a rule of four months he fled the country, vanquished in the field by the Chinese garrison, and followed by the execrations of the population he had come to deliver. The invasion of Wali Khan further imbittered the relations between the Chinese and their subjects; and a succession of governors bore heavily on the Mohammedans. Popular dissatisfaction and the apprehension in the minds of the governing officials that their lives might be forfeited at any moment to a popular outbreak added to the dangers of the situation in Kashgar itself, when the news arrived of the Tungan revolt, and of the many other complications which hampered the action of the Pekin ruler. We cannot narrate here the details of the rebellion in Kashgar. Its influence on the history of China would not sanction such close exactitude. But in the year 1863 the Chinese officials had become so alarmed at their isolated position that they resolved to adopt the desperate expedient of massacring all the Mohammedans or Tungani in their own garrisons. The amban and his officers were divided in council and dilatory in execution. The Tungani heard of the plot while the governor was summoning the nerve to carry it out. They resolved to anticipate him. The Mohammedans at Yarkand, the largest and most important garrison in the country, rose in August, 1863, and massacred all the Buddhist Chinese. Seven thousand men are computed to have fallen. A small band fled to the citadel, which they held for a short time; but at length, overwhelmed by numbers, they preferred death to dishonor, and destroyed themselves by exploding the fort with the magazine. The defection of the Tungani thus lost Kashgaria for the Chinese, as the other garrisons and towns promptly followed the example of Yarkand; but they could not keep it for themselves. The spectacle of this internal dissension proved irresistible for the adventurers of Khokand, and Buzurg, the last surviving son of Jehangir, resolved to make another bid for power and for the recovery of the position for which his father and kinsmen had striven in vain. The wish might possibly have been no more attained than theirs, had he not secured the support of the most capable soldier in Khokand, Mahomed Yakoob, the defender of Ak Musjid against the Russians. It was not until the early part of the year 1865 that this Khoja pretender, with his small body of Khokandian officers and a considerable number of Kirghiz allies, appeared upon the scene. Then, however, their success was rapid. The Tungan revolt in Altyshahr resolved itself into a movement for the restoration of the Khoja dynasty. In a short time Buzurg was established as ruler, while his energetic lieutenant was employed in the task of crushing the few remaining Chinese garrisons, and also in cowing his Tungan allies, who already regarded their new ruler with a doubtful eye. By the month of September in the same year that witnessed the passage of the invading force through the Terek defile, the triumph of

the Khoja's arms was assured. A few weeks later Mahomed Yakoob deposed his master, and caused himself to be
proclaimed ruler in his stead. The voice of the people ratified the success of the man; and in 1866 Mahomed Yakoob,
or Yakoob Beg, received at the hands of the Ameer of
Bokhara the proud title of Athalik Ghazi, by which he was
long known. The Mohammedan rising spread still further
within the limits of Chinese authority in Central Asia.

While the events which have been briefly sketched were
happening in the region south of the great Tian Shan range,
others of not less importance had taken place in Ili or Kuldja,
which, under Chinese rule, had enjoyed uninterrupted peace
for a century. It was this fact which marked the essential
difference between the Tungan rebellion and all the disturbances that had preceded it. The revolution in the metropolitan province was complicated by the presence of different
races, just as it had been in Kashgaria by the pretensions of
the Khoja family. A large portion of the population consisted of those Tarantchis who were the descendants of the
Kashgarians deported on more than one occasion by the
Chinese from their own homes to the banks of the Ili; and
they had inherited a legacy of ill-will against their rulers
which only required the opportunity to display itself. The
Tungan—or Dungan, as the Russians spell it—element was
also very strong, and colonies of the Sobo and Solon tribes,
who had been emancipated from their subjection to the
Mongols by the Emperor Kanghi for their bravery, further
added to the variety of the nationalities dwelling in this
province. It had been said with some truth that the Chinese
ruled in this quarter of their dominions on the old principle
of commanding by the division of the subjected; and it had
been predicted that they would fall whenever any two of the
dependent populations combined against them. There is
little difficulty in showing that the misfortunes of the Chinese were due to their own faults. They neglected the
plainest military precautions, and the mandarins thought
only of enriching themselves. But the principal cause of the

destruction of their power was the cessation of the supplies which they used to receive from Pekin. The government of these dependencies was only possible by an annual gift from the imperial treasury. When the funds placed at the disposal of the Ili authorities were diverted to other uses, it was no longer possible to maintain the old efficiency of the service. Discontent was provided with a stronger argument at the same time that the executive found itself embarrassed in grappling with it.

The news of the Mohammedan outbreak in China warned the Tungani in Ili that their opportunity had come. But although there were disturbances as early as January, 1863, these were suppressed, and the vigilance of the authorities sufficed to keep things quiet for another year. Their subsequent incapacity, or hesitation to strike a prompt blow, enabled the Mohammedans to husband their resources and to complete their plans. A temporary alliance was concluded between the Tungani and the Tarantchis, and they hastened to attack the Chinese troops and officials. The year 1865 was marked by the progress of a sanguinary struggle, during which the Chinese lost their principal towns, and some of their garrisons were ruthlessly slaughtered after surrender. The usual scenes of civil war followed. When the Chinese were completely vanquished and their garrisons exterminated, the victors quarreled among themselves. The Tungani and the Tarantchis met in mortal encounter, and the former were vanquished and their chief slain. When they renewed the contest, some months later, they were, after another sanguinary struggle, again overthrown. The Tarantchis then ruled the state by themselves, but the example they set of native rule was, to say the least, not encouraging. One chief after another was deposed and murdered. The same year witnessed no fewer than five leaders in the supreme place of power; and when Abul Oghlan assumed the title of Sultan the cup of their iniquities was already full. In the year 1871 an end was at last put to these enormities by the occupation of the province by a

Russian force, and the installation of a Russian governor. Although it is probable that they were only induced to take this step by the fear that if they did not do so Yakoob Beg would, the fact remains that the Russian Government did a good thing in the cause of order by interfering for the restoration of tranquillity in the valley of the Ili.

The Mohammedan outbreaks in southwestern and northwestern China resulted, therefore, in the gradual suppression of the Panthay rebellion, which was completed in the twelfth year of Tungche's reign, while the Tungan rising, so far as the Central Asian territories were concerned, remained unquelled for a longer period. The latter led to the establishment of an independent Tungan confederacy beyond Kansuh, and also of the kingdom of Kashgaria ruled by Yakoob Beg. The revolt in Ili, after several alternations of fortune, resulted in the brief independence of the Tarantchis, who were in turn displaced by the Russians under a pledge of restoring the province to the Chinese whenever they should return. Judged by the extent of territory involved, the Mohammedan rebellion might be said to be not less important than the Taeping; but the comparison on that ground alone would be really delusive, as the numerical inferiority of the Mohammedans rendered it always a question only of time for the central power to be restored.

The young Emperor Tungche, therefore, grew up amid continual difficulties, although the successes of his principal lieutenants afforded good reason to believe that, so far as they arose from rebels, it was only a question of time before they would be finally removed. The foreign intercourse still gave cause for much anxiety, although there was no apprehension of war. It would have been unreasonable to suppose that the relations between the foreign merchants and residents and the Chinese could become, after the suspicion and dangers of generations, absolutely cordial. The commercial and missionary bodies, into which the foreign community was naturally divided, had objects of trade or religion to advance, which rendered them apt to take an unfavorable view of the progress made by the Chinese Government in the paths of civilization, and to be ever skeptical even of its good faith. The main object with the foreign diplomatic representatives became not more to obtain justice for their countrymen than to restrain their eagerness, and to confine their pretensions to the rights conceded by the treaties. A clear distinction had to be drawn between undue coercion of the Chinese Government on the one hand, and the effectual compulsion of the people to evince respect toward foreigners and to comply with the obligations of the treaty on the other. Instances repeatedly occurred in reference to the latter matter, when it would have been foolish to have shown weakness, especially as there was not the least room to suppose that the government possessed at that time the power and the capacity to secure reparation for, or to prevent the repetition of, attacks on foreigners. Under this category came the riot at Yangchow in the year 1868, when some missionaries had their houses burned down, and were otherwise maltreated. A similar outrage was perpetrated in Formosa; but the fullest redress was always tendered as soon as the executive realized that the European representatives attached importance to the occurrence. The recurrence of these local dangers and disputes served to bring more clearly than ever before the minds of the Chinese ministers the advisability of taking some step on their own part toward an understanding with European governments and peoples. The proposal to depute a Chinese embassador to the West could hardly be said to be new, seeing that it had been projected after the Treaty of Nankin, and that the minister Keying had manifested some desire to be the first mandarin to serve in that novel capacity. But when the Tsungli Yamen took up the question it was decided that in this as in other matters it would be expedient to avail themselves in the first place of foreign mediation. The favorable opportunity of doing so presented itself when Mr. Burlinghame retired from his post as minister of the United States at Pekin. In the winter of 1867–68 Mr. Burlinghame accepted an appointment

CHINA—20

as accredited representative of the Chinese Government to eleven of the principal countries of the world, and two Chinese mandarins and a certain number of Chinese students were appointed to accompany him on his tour. The Chinese themselves did not attach as much importance as they might have done to his efforts, and Mr. Burlinghame's mission will be remembered more as an educational process for foreigners than as signifying any decided change in Chinese policy. His death at St. Petersburg, in March, 1870, put a sudden and unexpected close to his tour, but it cannot be said that he could have done more toward the elucidation of Chinese questions than he had already accomplished, while his bold and optimistic statements, after awakening public attention, had already begun to produce the inevitable reaction.

In 1869 Sir Rutherford Alcock retired, and was succeeded in the difficult post of English representative in China by Mr. Thomas Wade, whose services have been more than once referred to. In the very first year of his holding the post an event occurred which cast all the minor aggressive acts that had preceded it into the shade. It may perhaps be surmised that this was the Tientsin massacre—an event which threatened to re-open the whole of the China question, and which brought France and China to the verge of war. It was in June, 1870, on the eve of the outbreak of the Franco-Prussian War, that the foreign settlements were startled by the report of a great popular outbreak against foreigners in the important town of Tientsin. At that city there was a large and energetic colony of Roman Catholic priests, and their success in the task of conversion, small as it might be held, was still sufficient to excite the ire and fears of the literary and official classes. The origin of mob violence is ever difficult to discover, for a trifle suffices to set it in motion. But at Tientsin specific charges of the most horrible and, it need not be said, the most baseless character were spread about as to the cruelties and evil practices of those devoted to the service of religion. These rumors were diligently circulated, and it need not cause wonder if, when the mere cry of "Fan-

quai"—Foreign Devil—sufficed to raise a disturbance, these
allegations resulted in a vigorous agitation against the missionaries, who were already the mark of popular execration.
It was well known beforehand that an attack on the missionaries would take place unless the authorities adopted very
efficient measures of protection. The foreign residents and
the consulates were warned of the coming outburst, and a
very heavy responsibility will always rest on those who
might, by the display of greater vigor, have prevented the
unfortunate occurrences that ensued. At the same time,
allowing for the prejudices of the Chinese, it must be allowed
that not only must the efforts of all foreign missionaries be
attended with the gravest peril, but that the acts of the
French priests and nuns at Tientsin were, if not indiscreet, at
least peculiarly calculated to arouse the anger and offend the
superstitious predilections of the Chinese. That the wrong
was not altogether on the side of the Chinese may be gathered from an official dispatch of the United States Minister,
describing the originating causes of the outrage: "At many
of the principal places in China open to foreign residence, the
Sisters of Charity have established institutions, each of which
appears to combine in itself a foundling hospital and orphan
asylum. Finding that the Chinese were averse to placing
children in their charge, the managers of these institutions
offered a certain sum per head for all the children placed
under their control, to be given to them; it being understood
that a child once in their asylum no parent, relative, or
guardian could claim or exercise any control over it. It has
for some time been asserted by the Chinese, and believed by
most of the non-Catholic foreigners residing here, that the
system of paying bounties induced the kidnaping of children
for these institutions for the sake of the reward. It is also
asserted that the priests or sisters, or both, have been in the
habit of holding out inducements to have children brought
to them in the last stages of illness for the purpose of being
baptized *in articulo mortis*. In this way many children
have been taken to these establishments in the last stages

of disease, baptized there, and soon after taken away dead. All these acts, together with the secrecy and seclusion which appear to be a part and parcel of the regulations which govern institutions of this character everywhere, have created suspicions in the minds of the Chinese, and these suspicions have engendered an intense hatred against the sisters."

At that time Chung How, the superintendent of trade for the three northern ports, was the principal official in Tientsin; but although some representations, not as forcible however as the occasion demanded, were made to him by M. Fontanier, the French Consul, on June 18, three days before the massacre, no reply was given and no precautions were taken. On the 21st a large crowd assembled outside the mission house. They very soon assumed an attitude of hostility, and it was clear that at any moment the attack might begin. M. Fontanier hastened off in person to Chung How, but his threats seem to have been as unavailing as his arguments. On his return he found the attack on the point of commencing. He made use of menaces, and he fired a shot from his revolver, whether in self-defense or in the heat of indignation at some official treachery will never be known. The mob turned upon him, and he was murdered. The Chinese then hastened to complete the work they had begun. Chung How, like Surajah Dowlah, was not to be disturbed, and the attack on the mission house and consulate proceeded, while the officials responsible for order remained inactive. Twenty-one foreigners in all were brutally murdered under circumstances of the greatest barbarity, while the number of native converts who fell at the same time can never be ascertained.

The Tientsin massacre was followed by a wave of anti-foreign feeling over the whole country; but although an official brought out a work—entitled "Death-blow to Corrupt Doctrine"—which obtained more than a passing notoriety, and notwithstanding that some members of the imperial family, and notably, as it was stated, Prince Chun, regarded the movement with favor, the arguments of Prince Kung and the more moderate ministers carried the day, and it was resolved to make every concession in the power of the government for the pacific settlement of the dispute that had arisen with France. The outbreak of the war between France and Germany, while it contributed to a peaceful settlement of the question, rendered the process of diplomacy slow and dubious. The Tsungli Yamen, as soon as it realized that nothing short of the dispatch of a mission of apology to Europe would salve the injured honor of France, determined that none other than Chung How himself should go to Paris to assure the French that the government deplored the popular ebullition and had taken no part in it. The untoward result of the great war for France embarrassed her action in China. Chung How's assurances were accepted, the proffered compensation was received; but the Chinese were informed that in recognition of France's moderation, and in return for the reception of their envoy by M. Thiers, the right of audience should be conceded to the French minister resident at Pekin. The Audience Question naturally aroused the greatest interest at Pekin, where it agitated the official mind not merely because it signified another concession to force, but also because it promised to produce a disturbing effect on the mind of the people. The young emperor was growing up, and might be expected to take a direct share in the administration at an early date. It was not an idle apprehension that filled the minds of his ministers lest he might lay the blame on them for having cast upon him the obligation of receiving ministers of foreign States in a manner such as they had never before been allowed to appear in the presence of the occupant of the Dragon Throne. The youth of the sovereign served to postpone the question for a short space of time, but it was no longer doubtful that the assumption of personal authority by the young Emperor Tungche would be accompanied by the reintroduction, and probably by the settlement, of the Audience Question. It was typical of the progress Chinese statesmen were making that none of them seemed to consider the possibility of distinctly refusing this privilege. Its concession was only post-poned until after the celebration of the young emperor's marriage.

It had been known for some time that the young ruler had fixed his affections on Ahluta, a Manchu lady of good family, daughter of Duke Chung, and that the empresses had decided that she was worthy of the high rank to which she was to be raised. The marriage-ceremony was deferred on more than one plea until after the emperor had reached his sixteenth birthday, but in October, 1872, there was thought to be no longer any excuse for postponement, and it was celebrated with great splendor on the 16th of that month. The arrangements were made in strict accordance with the precedent of the Emperor Kanghi's marriage in 1674, that ruler having also married when in occupation of the throne, and before he had attained his majority. It was stated that the ceremonial was imposing, that the incidental expenses were enormous, and that the people were very favorably impressed by the demeanor of their young sovereign. Four months after the celebration of his marriage the formal act of conferring upon Tungche the personal control of his dominions was performed. In a special decree issued from the Board of Rites the emperor said that he had received "the commands of their majesties the two empresses to as-sume the superintendence of business." This edict was directed to the Foreign ministers, who in return presented a collective request to be received in audience. Prince Kung was requested "to take his Imperial Majesty's orders with reference to their reception." The question being thus brought to a crucial point, it was not unnatural that the Chinese ministers should make the most vigorous resistance they could to those details which seemed to and did encroach upon the prerogative of the emperor as he had been accus-tomed to exercise it. For, in the first place, they were no longer free agents, and Tungche had himself to be consid-ered in any arrangement for the reception of foreign envoys. The discussion of the question assumed a controversial character, in which stress was laid on the one side upon the necessity of the kotow even in a modified form, while on the other it was pointed out that the least concession was as objectionable as the greatest, and that China would benefit by the complete settlement of the question. It says a great deal for the fairness and moderation of Prince Kung and the ministers with him that, although they knew that the foreign governments were not prepared to make the Audience Question one of war, or even of the suspension of diplomatic relations, they determined to settle the matter in the way most distasteful to themselves and most agreeable to foreigners. On June 29, 1873, Tungche received in audience the ministers of the principal powers at Pekin, and thus gave completeness to the many rights and concessions obtained from his father and grandfather by the treaties of Tientsin and Nankin. The privilege thus secured caused lively gratification in the minds of all foreign residents, to whom it signified the great surrender of the inherent right to superiority claimed by the Chinese emperors, and we have recently seen that it has been accepted as a precedent.

The sudden death of Tseng Kwofan in the summer of 1872 removed unquestionably the foremost public man in China. After the fall of Nankin he had occupied the highest posts in the empire, both at that city and in the metropolis. He was not merely powerful from his own position, but from his having placed his friends and dependents in many of the principal offices throughout the empire. At first prejudiced against foreigners, he had gradually brought himself to recognize that some advantage might be derived from their knowledge. But the change came at too late a period to admit of his conferring any distinct benefit on his country from the more liberal policy he felt disposed to pursue with regard to the training of Chinese youths in the science and learning of the West. It was said that had he been personally ambitious he might have succeeded in displacing the Tartar regime. But such a thought never assumed any practical shape in his mind, and to the end of his days Tseng Kwofan was satisfied to remain the steadfast supporter and adherent of the Manchus. In this respect he has been closely imitated by his most distinguished lieutenant, Li Hung Chang, who succeeded to some of his dignities and much of his power.

Another of Tseng's proteges, Tso Tsung Tang, had been raised from the viceroyalty of Chekiang and Fuhkien to that of Shensi and Kansuh. The promotion was of the more doubtful value, seeing that both those provinces were in the actual possession of the rebels; but Tso threw himself into the task of reconquering them with remarkable energy, and within two years of his arrival he was able to report that he had cleared the province of Shensi of all insurgents. He then devoted his attention to the pacification of Kansuh; and after many desultory engagements proceeded to lay siege to the town of Souchow, where the Mohammedans had massed their strength. At the end of the year 1872 the imperial army was drawn up in front of this place, but Tso does not seem to have considered himself strong enough to deliver an attack, and confined his operations to preventing the introduction of supplies and fresh troops into the town. Even in this he was only partially successful, as a considerable body of men made their way in, in January, 1873. In the following month he succeeded in capturing, by a night attack, a temple outside the walls, upon which the Mohammedans placed considerable value. The siege continued during the whole of the summer, and it was not until the month of October that the garrison was reduced to such extremities as to surrender. The chiefs were hacked to pieces, and about four thousand men perished by the sword. The women, children, and old men were spared, and the spoil of the place was handed over to the soldiery. It was Tso's distinctive merit that, far from being carried away by these successes, he neglected no military precaution, and devoted his main efforts to the reorganization of the province. In that operation he may be left employed for the brief remainder of Tungche's reign; but it may be said that in

1874 the campaign against Kashgaria had been fully decided upon. A thousand Manchu cavalry were sent to Souchow. Sheepskins, horses, and ammunition in large quantities were also dispatched to the far west, and General Kinshun, the Manchu general, was intrusted with the command of the army in the field.

The year 1874 witnessed an event that claims notice. There never has been much good will between China and her neighbors in Japan. The latter are too independent in their bearing to please the advocates of Chinese predominance, at the same time that their insular position has left them safe from the attack of the Pekin Government. The attempt made by the Mongol, Kublai Khan, to subdue these islanders had been too disastrous to invite repetition. In Corea the pretensions of the ruler of Yeddo had been repelled, if not crushed; but wherever the sea intervened the advantage rested more or less decisively with him. The island of Formosa is dependent upon China, and the western districts are governed by officials duly appointed by the Viceroy of Fuhkien. But the eastern half of the island, separated from the cultivated districts by a range of mountains covered with dense if not impenetrable forests, is held by tribes who own no one's authority, and who act as they deem fit. In the year 1868 or 1869 a junk from Loochoo was wrecked on this coast, and the crew were murdered by the islanders. The civil war in Japan prevented any prompt claim for reparation, but in 1873 the affair was revived, and a demand made at Pekin for compensation. The demand was refused, whereupon the Japanese, taking the law into their own hands, sent an expedition to Formosa. China replied with a counter demonstration, and war seemed inevitable. In this crisis Mr. Wade offered his good services in the interests of peace, and after considerable controversy he succeeded in bringing the two governments to reason. The Chinese paid an indemnity of half a million taels, and the Japanese evacuated the island.

In all countries governed by an absolute sovereign it is

as interesting as it is difficult to obtain some accurate knowledge of the character of the autocrat. A most important
change had been effected in the government of China, yet
it is impossible to discover what its precise significance was,
or to say how far it influenced the fortunes of the country.
The empresses had retired into private life, and for a time
their regency came to an end. Prince Kung was only the
minister of a young prince who had it in his power to guide
affairs exactly as he might feel personally disposed. Prince
Kung might be either the real governor of the state or only
the courtier of his nephew. It depended solely on that
prince's character. There were not wanting signs that
Tungche had the consciousness, if not the capacity, of supreme power, and that he wished his will to be paramount.
Such evidence as was obtainable agreed in stating that he
was impatient of restraint, and that the prudent reflections
of his uncle were not overmuch to his fancy. On September 10 the young ruler took the world into his confidence
by announcing in a Vermilion Edict that he had degraded
Prince Kung and his son in their hereditary rank as princes
of the empire, for using "language in very many respects
unbecoming." Whether Tungche took this very decided
step in a moment of pique or because he perceived that
there was a plan among his chief relatives to keep him in
leading-strings, must remain a matter of opinion. At the
least he must have refused to personally retract what he
had done, for on the very following day (September 11) a
decree appeared from the two empresses reinstating Prince
Kung and his son in their hereditary rank and dignity,
and thus reasserting the power of the ex-regents.

Not long after this disturbance in the interior of the palace, of which only the ripple reached the surface of publicity, there were rumors that the emperor's health was in a
precarious state, and in the month of December it became
known that Tungche was seriously ill with an attack of
smallpox. The disease seemed to be making satisfactory
progress, for the doctors were rewarded; but on December

18 an edict appeared ordering or requesting the empresses dowager to assume the personal charge of the administration. Six days later another edict appeared which strengthened the impression that the emperor was making good progress toward recovery. But appearances were deceptive, for, after several weeks' uncertainty, it became known that the emperor's death was inevitable. On January 12, 1875, Tungche "ascended upon the Dragon, to be a guest on high," without leaving any offspring to succeed him. There were rumors that his illness was only a plausible excuse, and that he was really the victim of foul play; but it is not likely that the truth on that point will ever be revealed. Whether he was the victim of an intrigue similar to that which had marked his accession to power, or whether he only died from the neglect or incompetence of his medical attendants, the consequences were equally favorable to the personal views of the two empresses and Prince Kung. They resumed the exercise of that supreme authority which they had resigned little more than twelve months. The most suspicious circumstance in connection with this event was the treatment of the young Empress Ahluta, who, it was well known, was pregnant at the time of her husband's death. Instead of waiting to decide as to the succession until it was known whether Tungche's posthumous child would prove to be a son or a daughter, the empresses dowager hastened to make another selection and to place the young widow of the deceased sovereign in a state of honorable confinement. Their motive was plain. Had Ahluta's child happened to be a son, he would have been the legal emperor, as well as the heir by direct descent, and she herself could not have been excluded from a prominent share in the government. To the empresses dowager one child on the throne mattered no more than another; but it was a question of the first importance that Ahluta should be set on one side. In such an atmosphere there is often grievous peril to the lives of inconvenient personages. Ahluta sickened and died. Her child was never born. The chari-

table gave her credit for having refused food through grief for her husband, Tungche. The skeptical listened to the details of her illness with scorn for the vain efforts to obscure the dark deeds of ambition. In their extreme anxiety to realize their own designs, and at the same time not to injure the constitution, the two empresses had been obliged to resort to a plan that could only have been suggested by desperation. For the first time since the Manchu dynasty occupied the throne it was necessary to depart from the due line of succession, and to make the election of the sovereign a matter of individual fancy or favor instead of one of inheritance. The range of choice was limited; for the son of Prince Kung himself, who seemed to enjoy the prior right to the throne, was a young man of sufficient age to govern for himself; and moreover his promotion would mean the compulsory retirement from public life of Prince Kung, for it was not possible in China for a father to serve under his son, until Prince Chun, the father of the present reigning emperor, established quite recently a precedent to the contrary. The name of Prince Kung's son, if mentioned at all, was only mentioned to be dismissed. The choice of the empresses fell upon Tsai Tien, the son of Prince Chun or the Seventh Prince, who on January 13 was proclaimed emperor. As he was of too tender an age to rule for himself, his nomination served the purposes of the two empresses and their ally, Prince Kung, who thus entered upon a second lease of undisputed power.

CHAPTER XXII

THE REIGN OF KWANGSU

THUS after a very brief interval the governing power again passed into the hands of the regents who had ruled the state so well for the twelve years following the death of Hienfung. The nominal emperor was a child of little more than three years of age, to whom was given the style of "Kwangsu," or "illustrious succession," and the empresses could look forward to many years of authority in the name of so young a sovereign. The only opposition to their return to power seems to have come from the palace eunuchs, who had asserted themselves during the brief reign of Tungche and hoped to gain predominance in the imperial councils. But they found a determined mistress in the person of Tsi An, the Eastern Empress, as she was also called, who took vigorous action against them, punishing their leaders with death and effectually nipping in the bud all their projects for making themselves supreme.

The return of the empresses to power was followed by a great catastrophe in the relations between England and China. For the moment it threw every other matter into the shade, and seemed to render the outbreak of war between the two countries almost inevitable. In the year 1874 the government of India, repenting of its brief infatuation for the Panthay cause, yet still reluctant to lose the advantages it had promised itself from the opening of Yunnan to trade, resolved upon sending a formal mission of explory under Colonel Horace Browne, an officer of distinction, through Burma to that province. The difficulties in the way of the undertaking seemed comparatively few, as the King of Burma was friendly and appeared disposed at that time to accept his natural position as the dependent of Calcutta. The Pekin authorities also were outwardly not opposed to the journey; and the only opposition to be apprehended was from the Yunnan officials and people.

It was thought desirable, with the view of preparing the way for the appearance of this foreign mission, that a representative of the English embassy at Pekin, having a knowledge of the language and of the ceremonial etiquette of the country, should be deputed to proceed across China and meet Colonel Browne on the Burmese frontier. The officer selected for this delicate and difficult mission was Mr. Raymond Augustus Margary, who to the singular aptitude he had displayed in the study of Chinese added a buoyant spirit and a vigorous frame that peculiarly fitted him for the long and lonely journey he had undertaken across China. His reception throughout was encouraging. The orders of the Tsungli Yamen, specially drawn up by the Grand Secretary Wansiang, were explicit, and not to be lightly ignored. Mr. Margary performed his journey in safety; and, on January 26, 1875, only one fortnight after Kwangsu's accession, he joined Colonel Browne at Bhamo. A delay of more than three weeks ensued at Bhamo, which was certainly unfortunate. Time was given for the circulation of rumors as to the approach of a foreign invader along a disturbed frontier held by tribes almost independent, and whose predatory instincts were excited by the prospect of rich plunder, at the same time that their leaders urged them to oppose a change which threatened to destroy their hold on the caravan route between Bhamo and Talifoo. When, on February 17, Colonel Browne and his companions approached the limits of Burmese territory, they found themselves in face of a totally different state of affairs from what had existed when Mr. Margary passed safely through three weeks before. The preparations for opposing the English had been made under the direct encouragement, and probably the personal direction, of Lisitai, a man who had been a brigand and then a rebel, but who at this time held a military command on the frontier.

As Colonel Browne advanced he was met with rumors of the opposition that awaited him. At first these were discredited, but on the renewed statements that a large Chinese force had been collected to bar his way, Mr. Margary rode forward to ascertain what truth there was in these rumors. The first town on this route within the Chinese border is Momein, which, under the name of Tengyue, was once a military station of importance, and some distance east of it again is another town, called Manwein. Mr. Margary set out on February 19, and it was arranged that only in the event of his finding everything satisfactory at Momein was he to proceed to Manwein.

Mr. Margary reached Momein in safety, and reported in a letter to Colonel Browne that all was quiet at that place, and that there were no signs of any resistance. That letter was the last news ever received from Mr. Margary. On February 19 he started from Momein, and the information subsequently obtained left no doubt that he was treacherously murdered on that or the following day at Manwein. An ominous silence followed, and Colonel Browne's party delayed its advance until some definite news should arrive as to what had occurred in front, although the silence was sufficient to justify the worst apprehensions. Three days later the rumor spread that Mr. Margary and his attendants had been murdered. It was also stated that an army was advancing to attack the English expedition; and on February 22 a large Chinese force did make its appearance on the neighboring heights. There was no longer any room to doubt that the worst had happened, and it only remained to secure the safety of the expedition. The Chinese numbered several thousand men under Lisitai in person, while to oppose them there were only four Europeans and fifteen Sikhs. Yet superior weapons and steadfastness carried the day against greater numbers. The Sikhs fought as they retired, and the Chinese, unable to make any impression on them, abandoned an attack which was both perilous and useless.

The news of this outrage did not reach Pekin until a month later, when Mr. Wade at once took the most energetic measures to obtain the amplest reparation in the power of the Pekin Government to concede. The first and most necessary point in order to insure not merely the punishment of the guilty, but also that the people of China should not have cause to suppose that their rulers secretly sympathized with the authors of the attack, was that no punitive measures should be undertaken, or, if undertaken, recognized, until a special Commission of Inquiry had been appointed to investigate the circumstances on the spot. Mr. Margary was an officer of the English Government traveling under

efforts on its capture. He moved forward his army to Guchen, 200 miles west of Barkul, where he established a fortified camp and a powder factory, and took steps to ascertain the strength and intentions of the enemy. Toward the end of July the Chinese army resumed its march. The difficulties of the country were so great that the advance guards of the opposing armies did not come into contact until August 10. The Chinese general seems to have attempted on that date a night surprise; but although he gained some success in the encounter which ensued, the result must have been doubtful, seeing that he felt obliged to call off his men from the attack. It was only, however, to collect his forces for the delivery of a decisive blow. On August 13 a second battle was fought with a result favorable to the Chinese. Two days later the enemy, who held a fortified camp at Gumti, were bombarded out of it by the heavy artillery brought from the coasts of China for the purposes of the war, and after twenty-four hours' firing three breaches were declared to be practicable. The place was carried by storm at the close of four hours' fighting and slaughter, during which 6,000 men were stated to have been killed. Kinshun followed up his victory by a rapid march on Urumtsi. That town surrendered without a blow, and many hundred fugitives were cut down by the unsparing Manchu cavalry, which pursued them along the road to Manas, their last place of shelter. As soon as the necessary measures had been taken for the military protection of Urumtsi, the Chinese army proceeded against Manas. Their activity, which was facilitated by the favorable season of the year, was also increased by the rumored approach of Yakoob Beg with a large army to the assistance of the Tungani. At Manas the survivors of the Tungan movement proper had collected for final resistance, and all that desperation could suggest for holding the place had been done. Kinshun appeared before Manas on September 2. On the 7th his batteries were completed, and he began a heavy fire upon the northeast angle of the wall. A breach of fourteen feet having been made, the order to assault was given, but the stormers were repulsed with the loss of 100 killed. The operations of the siege were renewed with great spirit on both sides. Several assaults were subsequently delivered; but although the Chinese always gained some advantage at the beginning they never succeeded in retaining it. In one of these later attacks they admitted a loss of 200 killed alone. The imperial army enjoyed the undisputed superiority in artillery, and the gaps in its ranks were more than filled by the constant flow of re-enforcements from the rear. The siege gradually assumed a less active character. The Chinese dug trenches and erected earthworks. They approached the walls by means of galleries in readiness to deliver the attack on any symptom of discouragement among the besieged. On October 16 a mine was sprung under the wall, making a wide breach; but although the best portion of the Chinese army made two assaults on separate occasions, they were both repulsed with loss. Twelve days later another mine was sprung, destroying a large portion of the wall; but when the Chinese stormers endeavored to carry the remaining works, they were again driven back with heavy loss, including two generals killed in the breach. Although thus far repulsed, the imperialists had inflicted very heavy losses on the besieged, who, seeing that the end of their resources was at hand, that there was no hope of succor, and that the besiegers were as energetic as ever, at last arrived at the conclusion that they had no choice left save to surrender on the best terms they could obtain. On November 4, after a two months' siege, Haiyen, as the Chinese named the Mohammedan leader, came out and offered to yield the town. His offer seems to have been partly accepted, and on the 6th of the month the survivors of the brave garrison, to the number of between two and three thousand men, sallied forth from the west gate. It was noticed as a ground of suspicion that all the men carried their weapons, and that they had placed their old men, women and children in the center of their phalanx as if they contemplated rather a sortie than a tame and unresisting surrender. The Chinese commanders were not indisposed to deal with the least suspicious circumstances as if they meant certain treachery. The imperialists gradually gathered around the garrison. The Mohammedans made one bold effort to cut their way through. They failed in the attempt, and were practically annihilated on the ground. Those men who were taken by the cavalry were at once beheaded, whether in the city or among those who had gone forth, but the aged, the women and the children were spared by Kinshun's express orders. All the leaders taken were tortured before execution as rebels, and even the bodies of the dead chiefs were exhumed in order that they might be subjected to indignity. The siege of Manas was interesting both for the stubbornness of the attack and defense, and also as marking the successful termination of the Chinese campaign against the Tungani. With its capture, those Mohammedans who might be said to be Chinese in ways and appearance ceased to possess any political importance. It would not be going much too far to say that they no longer existed. The movement of rebellion which began at Hochow in 1862 was thus repressed in 1876, after having involved during those fourteen years the northwestern provinces of China, and much of the interior of Asia, in a struggle which, for its bitter and sanguinary character, has rarely been surpassed.

The successes of the Chinese gave their generals and army the confidence and prestige of victory, and the overthrow of the Tungani left them disengaged to deal with a more formidable antagonist. The siege of Manas had been vigorously prosecuted in order that the town might be taken before the army of Yakoob Beg should arrive. The Athalik Ghazi may have believed that Manas could hold out during the winter, for his movements in 1876 were leisurely, and betrayed a confidence that no decisive fighting would take place until the following spring. His hopes were shown to be delusive, but too late for practical remedy. Manas had fallen before he could move to its support. The Chinese had crushed the Tungani, and were in possession of the mountain passes. They were gathering their whole strength to fall upon him, and to drive him out of the state in which he had managed to set up a brief authority. While the events recorded had been in progress, Yakoob Beg had been ruling the state of Kashgaria with sufficient vigor and wisdom to attract the observation of his great neighbors, the governments of England and Russia. He had shown rare skill in adapting circumstances to suit his own ends. The people passively accepted the authority which he was prepared to assert with his Khokandian soldiery, and the independent state of Kashgaria might have continued to exist for a longer period had the Chinese not returned. But in 1875 the arrival of Kinshun at Barkul showed Yakoob Beg that he would have to defend his possessions against their lawful owners, while the overthrow of the Tungani and the capture of their strongholds, in 1876, carried with them a melancholy foreboding of his own fate. The Athalik Ghazi made his preparations to take the field, but there was no certainty in his mind as to where he should make his stand. He moved his army eastward, establishing his camp first at Korla and then moving it on to Turfan, 900 miles distant from Kashgar. The greatest efforts of this ruler only availed to place 15,000 men at the front, and the barrenness of the region compelled him to distribute them. The Ameer was at Turfan with 8,500 men and twenty guns. His second son was at Toksoun, some miles in the rear, at the head of 6,000 more and five guns. There were several smaller detachments between Korla and the front. Opposed to these was the main Chinese army under Kinshun at Urumtsi, while another force had been placed in the field at Hami by the energy of Tso, and intrusted to the direction of a general named Chang Yao. No fighting took place until the month of March, 1877, and then the campaign began with a rapid advance by Chang Yao from Hami to Turfan. The Kashgarians were driven out of Pidjam, and compelled, after a battle, to evacuate Turfan.

The Chinese records do not help us to unravel the events of the month of April. The campaign contained no more striking or important episodes, and yet the reports of the generals have been mislaid or consigned to oblivion. The Athalik Ghazi fought a second battle at Toksoun, where he rejoined his son's army, but with no better fortune. He was obliged to flee back to his former camp at Korla. After the capture of Turfan the Chinese armies came to a halt. It was necessary to reorganize the vast territory which they had already recovered, and to do something to replenish their arsenals. During five months the Celestials stayed their further advance, while the cities were being re-peopled and the roads rendered once more secure. Tso Tsung Tang would leave nothing to chance. He had accomplished two of the three parts into which his commission might be naturally divided. He had pacified the northwest and overthrown the Tungani, and he would make sure of his ground before attempting the third and the most difficult of all. And while the Chinese viceroy had, for his own reasons, come to the very sensible conclusion to refresh his army after its arduous labors in the limited productive region situated between two deserts, the stars in their courses fought on his side.

Yakoob Beg had withdrawn only to Korla. He still cherished the futile scheme of defending the eastern limits of his dominion, but with his overthrow on the field of battle the magic power which he had exercised over his subjects vanished. His camp became the scene of factious rivalry and of plots to advance some individual pretension at the cost of the better interests and even the security of the State. The exact details of the conspiracy will never be known, partly from the remoteness of the scene, but also on account of the mention of persons of whom nothing was, or is ever likely to be, known. The single fact remains clear that Yakoob Beg died at Korla on May 1, 1877, of fever according to one account, of poison administered by Hakim Khan Torah according to another. Still the Chinese did not even then advance, and Yakoob's sons were left to contest with Hakim Khan Torah over the dismembered fragments of their father's realm. A bitter and protracted civil war followed close upon the disappearance of the Athalik Ghazi. On the removal of his dead body for sepulture to Kashgar his eldest son, Kuli Beg, murdered his younger brother over their father's bier. It was then that Hakim Khan came prominently forward as a rival to Kuli Beg, and that the Mohammedans, weak and numerically few as they were, divided themselves into two hostile parties. While the Chinese were recruiting their troops and repairing their losses, the enemy were exhausting themselves in vain and useless struggles. In June, 1877, Hakim Khan was signally defeated and compelled to flee into Russian territory, whence on a later occasion he returned for a short time in a vain attempt to disturb the tranquillity of Chinese rule. When, therefore, the Chinese resumed their advance much of their work had been done for them. They had only to complete the overthrow of an enemy whom they had already vanquished, and who was now exhausted by his own disunion. The Chinese army made no forward movement from Toksoun until the end of August, 1877. Liu Kintang, to whom the command of the advance had been given, did not leave until one month later; and when he arrayed his forces he found them to number about 15,000 men. It had been decided that the first advance should not be made in greater force, as the chief difficulty was to feed the army, not to defeat the enemy.

The resistance encountered was very slight, and the country was found to be almost uninhabited. Both Karashar and Korla were occupied by a Chinese garrison, and the district around them was intrusted to the administration of a local chief. Information that the rebel force was stationed at the next town, Kucha, which is as far beyond Korla as that place is from Toksoun, induced Liu Kintang to renew his march and to continue it still more rapidly. A battle was fought outside Kucha in which the Chinese were victorious, but not until they had overcome stubborn resistance. However, the Chinese success was complete, and with Kucha in their power they had simplified the process of attacking Kashgar itself. A further halt was made at this town to enable the men to recover from their fatigue, to allow fresh troops to come up, and measures to be taken for insuring the security of communications with the places in the rear. At Kucha also the work of civil administration was intrusted to some of the local notables. The deliberation of the Chinese movements, far from weakening their effect, invested their proceedings with the aspect of being irresistible. The advance was shortly resumed. Aksu, a once flourishing city within the limits of the old kingdom of Kashgar, surrendered at the end of October. Ush Turfan yielded a few days later. The Chinese had now got within striking distance of the capital of the state. They had only to provide the means of making the blow as fatal and decisive as possible. In December they seized Maralbashi, an important position on the Kashgar Darya, commanding the principal roads to both Yarkand and Kashgar. Yarkand was the chief object of attack. It surrendered without a blow on December 21. A second Chinese army had been sent from Maralbashi to Kashgar, which was defended by a force of several thousand men. It had been besieged nine days, when Liu Kintang arrived with his troops from Yarkand. A battle ensued, in which the Mohammedans were vanquished, and the city with the citadel outside captured. Several rebel leaders and some eleven hundred men were said to have been executed; but Kuli Beg escaped into Russian territory. The city of Kashgar was taken on December 26, and one week later the town of Khoten, famous from a remote period for its jade ornaments, passed into the hands of the race who best appreciated their beauty and value. The Chinese thus brought to a triumphant conclusion the campaigns undertaken for the reassertion of their authority over the Mohammedan populations which had revolted. They had conquered in this war by the superiority of their weapons and their organization, and not by an over-

KANG, THE REFORMER

China

whelming display of numbers. Although large bodies of troops were stationed at many places, it does not seem that the army which seized the cities of Yarkand and Kashgar numbered more than twenty thousand men. Having vanquished their enemy in the field, the Celestials devoted all their attention to the reorganization of what was called the New Dominion, the capital of which after much deliberation was fixed at Urumtsi. Their rule has been described by a Mussulman as being both very fair and very just.

Having conquered Eastern Turkestan, the Chinese next took steps for the recovery of Ili. Without the metropolitan province the undertaking of Tso Tsung Tang would lack completeness, while indeed many political and military dangers would attend the situation in Central Asia. But this was evidently a matter to be effected in the first place by negotiation, and not by violence and force of arms. Russia had always been a friendly and indeed a sympathetic neighbor. In this very matter of Ili she had originally acted with the most considerate attention for China's rights, when it seemed that they had permanently lost all definite meaning, for she had declared that she would surrender it on China sending a sufficient force to take possession, and now this had been done. It was, therefore, by diplomatic representations on the part of the Tsungli Yamen to the Russian Minister at Pekin that the recovery of Ili was expected in the first place to be achieved. At about the same time the Russian authorities at Tashkent came to the conclusion that the matter must rest with the Czar, and the Chinese official world perceived that they would have to depute a Minister Plenipotentiary to St. Petersburg.

The official selected for the difficult and, as it proved, dangerous task of negotiating at St. Petersburg, was that same Chung How who had been sent to Paris after the Tientsin massacre. He arrived at Pekin in August, 1878, and was received in several audiences by the empresses while waiting for his full instructions from the Tsungli Yamen. He did not leave until October, about a month after the

Marquis Tseng, Tseng Kwofan's eldest son, set out from Pekin to take the place of Kwo Sungtao as Minister in London and Paris. Chung How reached St. Petersburg in the early part of the following year, and the discussion of the various points in question, protracted by the removal of the court to Livadia, occupied the whole of the summer months. At last it was announced that a treaty had been signed at Livadia, by which Russia surrendered the Kuldja valley, but retained that of the Tekes, which left in her hands the command of the passes through the Tian Shan range into Kashgar. Chung How knew nothing about frontiers or military precautions, but he thought a great deal about money. He fought the question of an indemnity with ability, and got it fixed at five million roubles, or little more than half that at which it was placed by the later treaty. There was never any reason to suppose that the Chinese Government would accept the partial territorial concession obtained by Chung How. The first greeting that met Chung How on his return revealed the fate of his treaty. He had committed the indiscretion of returning without waiting for the Edict authorizing his return, and as the consequence he had to accept suspension from all his offices, while his treaty was submitted to the tender mercies of the grand secretaries, the six presidents of boards, the nine chief ministers of state, and the members of the Hanlin. Three weeks later, Prince Chun was specially ordered to join the Committee of Deliberation. On January 27, Chung How was formally cashiered and arrested, and handed over to the Board of Punishment for correction. The fate of the treaty itself was decided a fortnight later. Chung How was then declared to have "disobeyed his instructions and exceeded his powers." On March 3 an edict appeared, sentencing the unhappy envoy to "decapitation after incarceration." This sentence was not carried out, and the reprieve of the unlucky envoy was due to Queen Victoria's expression of a hope that the Chinese Government would spare his life.

At the same time that the Chinese refused their ratification to Chung How's treaty, they expressed their desire for another pacific settlement, which would give them more complete satisfaction. The Marquis Tseng was accordingly instructed to take up the thread of negotiation, and to proceed to the Russian capital as Embassador and Minister Plenipotentiary. Some delay ensued, as it was held to be doubtful whether Russia would consent to the reopening of the question. But owing to the cautious and well-timed approaches of the Marquis Tseng, the St. Petersburg Foreign Office acquiesced in the recommencement of negotiations, and, after six months' discussion, accepted the principle of the almost unqualified territorial concession for which the Chinese had stood firm. On February 12, 1881, these views were embodied in a treaty, signed at St. Petersburg, and the ratification within six months showed how differently its provisions were regarded from those of its predecessor. With the Marquis Tseng's act of successful diplomacy the final result of the long war in Central Asia was achieved. The Chinese added Ili to Kashgar and the rest of the New Dominion, which at the end of 1880 was made into a High Commissionership and placed under the care of the dashing General Liu Kintang.

The close of the great work successfully accomplished during the two periods of the Regency was followed within a few weeks by the disappearance of the most important of the personages who had carried on the government throughout these twenty years of constant war and diplomatic excitement. Before the Pekin world knew of her illness, it heard of the death of the Empress Dowager Tsi An, who as Hienfung's principal widow had enjoyed the premier place in the government, although she had never possessed a son to occupy the throne in person. In a proclamation issued in her name and possibly at her request, Tsi An described the course of her malady, the solicitude of the emperor, and urged upon him the duty of his high place to put restraint upon his grief. Her death occurred on April 18, from heart disease, when she was only forty-five, and her funeral obsequies were as splendid as her services demanded. For herself she had always been a woman of frugal habits, and the successful course of recent Chinese history was largely due to her firmness and resolution. Her associate in the Regency, Tsi Thsi, who has always been more or less of an invalid, still survives.

The difficulty with Russia had not long been composed, when, on two opposite sides of her extensive dominion, China was called upon to face a serious condition of affairs. In Corea, "the forbidden land" of the Far East, events were forced by the eagerness and competition of European states to conclude treaties of commerce with that primitive kingdom, and perhaps, also, by their fear that if they delayed Russia would appropriate some port on the Corean coast. To all who had official knowledge of Russia's desire and plan for seizing Port Lazareff, this apprehension was far from chimerical, and there was reason to believe that Russia's encroachment might compel other countries to make annexations in or round Corea by way of precaution. Practical evidence of this was furnished by the English occupation of Port Hamilton, and by its subsequent evacuation when the necessity passed away; but should the occasion again arise the key of the situation will probably be found in the possession not of Port Hamilton or Quelpart, but of the Island of Tsiusima. Recourse was had to diplomacy to avert what threatened to be a grave international danger; and although the result was long doubtful, and the situation sometimes full of peril, a gratifying success was achieved in the end. In 1881 a draft commercial treaty was drawn up, approved by the Chinese authorities and the representatives of the principal powers at Pekin, and carried to the court of Seoul for acceptance and signature by the American naval officer, Commodore Schufeldt. The Corean king made no objection to the arrangement, and it was signed with the express stipulation that the ratifications of the treaty were to be exchanged in the following year. Thus was it harmoniously arranged at Pekin that Corea was to issue from her hermit's cell, and open her ports to trading countries under the guidance and encouragement ·of China. There can be no doubt that if this arrangement had been carried out, the influence and the position of China in Corea would have been very greatly increased and strengthened. But, unfortunately, the policy of Li Hung Chang—for if he did not originate, he took the most important part in directing it—aroused the jealousy of Japan, which has long asserted the right to have an equal voice with China in the control of Corean affairs; and the government of Tokio, on hearing of the Schufeldt treaty, at once took steps not merely to obtain all the rights to be conferred by that document, to which no one would have objected, but also to assert its claim to control equally with China the policy of the Corean court. With that object, a Japanese fleet and army were sent to the Seoul River, and when the diplomatists returned for the ratification of the treaty, they found the Japanese in a strong position close to the Corean capital. The Chinese were not to be set on one side in so open a manner, and a powerful fleet of gunboats, with 5,000 troops, were sent to the Seoul River to uphold their rights. Under other circumstances, more especially as the Chinese expedition was believed to be the superior, a hostile collision must have ensued, and the war which has so often seemed near between the Chinese and Japanese would have become an accomplished fact; but fortunately the presence of the foreign diplomatists moderated the ardor of both sides, and a rupture was averted. By a stroke of judgment, the Chinese seized Tai Wang Kun, the father of the young king, and the leader of the anti-foreign party, and carried him off to Pekin, where he was kept in imprisonment for some time, until matters had settled down in his own country. The opening of Corea to the Treaty Powers did not put an end to the old rivalry of China and Japan in that country, of which history contains so many examples; and, before the Corean question was definitely settled, it again became obtrusive. Such evidence as is obtainable points to the conclusion that Chinese influence was gradually getting the better of Japanese in the country, and the attack on the Japanese legation in 1884 was a striking revelation of popular antipathy or of an elaborate anti-Japanese plot headed by the released Chinese prisoner, Tai Wang Kun.

At the opposite point of the frontier China was brought face to face with a danger which threatened to develop into a peril of the first magnitude, and in meeting which she was undoubtedly hampered by her treaties with the general body of foreign powers and her own peculiar place in the family of nations. It is the special misfortune of China that she cannot engage in any, even a defensive, war with a maritime power without incurring the grave risk, or indeed the practical certainty, that if such a war be continued for any length of time she must find herself involved with every other foreign country through the impossibility of confining the hostility of her own subjects to one race of foreigners in particular. In considering the last war with a European country in which China was engaged, due allowance must be made for these facts, and also for the anomalous character of that contest, when active hostilities were carried on without any formal declaration of war—a state of things which gave the French many advantages. Toward the end of the year 1882, the French Government came to the decision to establish a "definite protectorate" over Tonquin. Events had for some time been shaping themselves in this direction, and the colonial ambition of France had long fixed on Indo-China as a field in which it might aggrandize itself with comparatively little risk and a wide margin of advantage. The weakness of the kingdom of Annam was a strong enough temptation in itself to assert the protectorate over it which France had, more or less, claimed for forty years; but when the reports of several French explorers came to promote the conviction that France might acquire the control of a convenient and perhaps the best route into some of the richest provinces of interior China without much difficulty, the temptation became irresistible. French activity in Indo-China was heightened by the declaration of Garnier, Rocher, and others, that the Songcoi, or Red River, furnished the best means of communicating with Yunnan, and tapping the wealth of the richest mineral province in China. The apathy of England in her relations with Burma, which presented, under its arrogant and obstructive rulers, what may have seemed an insuperable obstacle to trade intercourse between India and China, afforded additional inducement to the French to act quickly; and, as they felt confident of their ability and power to coerce the court of Hue, the initial difficulties of their undertaking did not seem very formidable. That undertaking was, in the first place, defined to be a protectorate of Annam, and, as the first step in the enterprise, the town of Hanoi, in the delta of the Red River, and the nominal capital of Tonquin, was captured before the end of the year 1882.

Tonquin stood in very much the same relationship to China as Corea; and, although the enforcement of the suzerain tie was lax, there was no doubt that at Pekin the opinion was held very strongly that the action of France was an encroachment on the rights of China. But if such was the secret opinion of the Chinese authorities, they took no immediate steps to arrest the development of French policy in Tonquin by proclaiming it a Chinese dependency, and also their intention to defend it. It is by no means certain that the prompt and vigorous assertion of their rights would have induced the French to withdraw from their enterprise, for its difficulties were not revealed at first; but if China is to make good her hold over such dependencies, she must be prepared to show that she thinks them worth fighting for. While Li Hung Chang and the other members of the Chinese Government were deliberating as to the course they should pursue, the French were acting with great vigor in Tonquin, and committing their military reputation to a task from which they could not in honor draw back. During the whole of the year 1883 they were engaged in military operations with the Black Flag irregulars, a force half piratical and half patriotic, who represented the national army of the country. It was believed at the time, but quite erroneously, that the Black Flags were paid and incited by the Chinese. Subsequent evidence showed that the Chinese authorities did not take even an indirect part in the contest until a much later period. After the capture of Hanoi, the French were constantly engaged with the Black Flags, from whom they captured the important town of Sontay, which was reported to be held by imperial Chinese troops, but on its capture this statement was found to be untrue. The French were in the full belief that the conquest of Tonquin would be easily effected, when a serious reverse obliged them to realize the gravity of their task. A considerable detachment, under the command of Captain Henri Riviere, who was one of the pioneers of French enterprise on the Songcoi, was surprised and defeated near Hanoi. Riviere was killed, and it became necessary to make a great effort to recover the ground that had been lost. Fresh troops were sent from Europe, but before they arrived the French received another check at Phukai, which the Black Flags claimed as a victory because the French were obliged to retreat.

Before this happened, the French had taken extreme measures against the King of Annam, of which state Tonquin is the northern province. The king of that country, by name Tuduc, who had become submissive to the French, died in July, 1883, and after his death the Annamese, perhaps encouraged by the difficulties of the French in Tonquin, became so hostile that it was determined to read them a severe lesson. Hue was attacked and occupied a month after the death of Tuduc, and a treaty was extracted from the new king which made him the dependent of France. When the cold season began in Tonquin, the French forces, largely increased, and commanded by Admiral Courbet, renewed operations, and on December 11 attacked the main body of the Black Flags at Sontay, which they had reoccupied and strengthened. They offered a desperate and well-sustained resistance, and it was only with heavy loss that the French succeeded in carrying the town. The victors were somewhat recompensed for their hardships and loss by the magnitude of the spoil, which included a large sum of money. Desultory fighting continued without intermission; Admiral Courbet was superseded by General Millot, who determined to signalize his assumption of the command by attacking Bacninh, which the Black Flags made their head-quarters after the loss of Sontay. On March 8, he attacked this place at the head of 12,000 men, but so formidable were its defenses that he would not risk an attack in front, and by a circuitous march of four days he gained the flank of the position, and thus taken at a disadvantage the Black Flags abandoned their formidable lines, and retreated without much loss, leaving their artillery, including some Krupp guns, in the hands of the victors. At this stage of the question diplomacy intervened, and on May 11 a treaty of peace was signed by Commander Fournier, during the ministry of M. Jules Ferry, with the Chinese Government. One of the principal stipulations of this treaty was that the French should be allowed to occupy Langson and other places in Tonquin. When the French commander sent a force under Colonel Dugenne to occupy Langson it was opposed in the Bacle defile and repulsed with some loss. The Chinese exonerated themselves from all responsibility by declaring that the French advance was premature, because no date was fixed by the Fournier Convention, and because there had not been time to transmit the necessary orders. On the other hand, M. Fournier declared on his honor that the dates in his draft were named in the original convention. The French Government at once demanded an apology, and an indemnity fixed by M. Jules Ferry, in a moment of mental excitement, at the ridiculous figure of $50,000,000. An apology was offered, but such an indemnity was refused, and eventually France obtained one of only $800,000.

After the Bacle affair hostilities were at once resumed, and for the first time the French carried them on not only against the Black Flags, but against the Chinese. M. Jules

Ferry did not, however, make any formal declaration of war against China, and he thus gained an advantage of position for his attack on the Chinese which it was not creditable to French chivalry to have asserted. The most striking instance of this occurred at Foochow, where the French fleet, as representing a friendly power, was at anchor above the formidable defenses of the Min River. In accordance with instructions telegraphed to him, the French admiral attacked those places in reverse and destroyed the forts on the Min without much difficulty or loss, thanks exclusively to his having been allowed past them as a friend. The French also endeavored to derive all possible advantage from there being no formal declaration of war, and to make use of Hongkong as a base for their fleet against China. But this unfairness could not be tolerated, and the British minister at Pekin, where Sir Harry Parkes had in the autumn of 1883 succeeded Sir Thomas Wade, issued a proclamation that the hostilities between France and China were tantamount to a state of war, and that the laws of neutrality must be strictly observed. The French resented this step, and showed some inclination to retaliate by instituting a right to search for rice, but fortunately this pretension was not pushed to extremities and the war was closed before it could produce any serious consequences. The French devoted much of their attention to an attack on the Chinese possessions in Formosa and the occupation of Kelung; a fort in the northern part of that island was captured, but the subsequent success of the French was small. The Chinese displayed great energy and resource in forming defenses against any advance inland from Kelung or Tamsui, and the French Government was brought to face the fact that there was nothing to be gained by carrying on these desultory operations, and that unless they were prepared to send a large expedition, it was computed of not less than 50,000 men, to attack Pekin, there was no alternative to coming to terms with China. How strong this conviction had become may be gathered from the fact that the compulsory retreat, in March, 1885, of the

French from before Langson, where some of the Chinese regular troops were drawn up with a large force of Black and Yellow Flags—the latter of whom were in Chinese pay —did not imperil the negotiations which were then far advanced toward completion. On June 9 of the same year a treaty of peace was signed by M. Patenotre and Li Hung Chang which gave France nothing more than the Fournier Convention.

The military lessons of this war must be pronounced inconclusive, for the new forces which China had organized since the Pekin campaign were never fully engaged, and the struggle ended before the regular regiments sent to Langson had any opportunity of showing their quality. But the impression conveyed by the fighting in Formosa and the northern districts of Tonquin was that China had made considerable progress in the military art, and that she possessed the nucleus of an army that might become formidable. But while the soldiers had made no inconsiderable improvement, as much could not be said of the officers, and among the commanders there seemed no grasp of the situation, and a complete inability to conduct a campaign. Probably these deficiencies will long remain the really weak spot in the Chinese war organization, and although they have men who will fight well, the only capacity their commanders showed in Tonquin and Formosa was in selecting strong positions and in fortifying them with consummate art. But as the strongest position can be turned and avoided, and as the Chinese, like all Asiatics, become demoralized when their rear is threatened, it cannot be denied that, considerable progress as the Chinese have made in the military art, they have not yet mastered some of its rudiments. All that can be said is that the war between France and China was calculated to teach the advisability of caution in fixing a quarrel upon China. Under some special difficulties from the character of the war and with divided counsels at Pekin, the Chinese still gave a very good account of themselves against one of the greatest powers of Europe.

During the progress of this struggle a *coup d'état* was effected at Pekin of which at the time it was impossible to measure the whole significance. In July, 1884, the Chinese world was startled by the sudden fall and disgrace of Prince Kung, who had been the most powerful man in China since the Treaty of Pekin. A decree of the empress-regent appeared dismissing him from all his posts and consigning him to an obscurity from which after nine years he has not yet succeeded in emerging. The causes of his fall are not clear, but they were probably of several distinct kinds. While he was the leader of the peace party and the advocate of a prompt arrangement with France, he was also an opponent of Prince Chun's desire to have a share in the practical administration of the state, or, at least, an obstacle in the way of its realization. Prince Chun, who was a man of an imperious will, and who, on the death of the Eastern Empress, became the most important personage in the palace and supreme council of the empire, was undoubtedly the leader of the attack on Prince Kung, and the immediate cause of his downfall. Prince Kung, who was an amiable and well intentioned man rather than an able statesman, yielded without resistance, and indeed he had no alternative, for he had no following at Pekin, and his influence was very slight except among Europeans. Prince Chun then came to the front, taking an active and prominent part in the government, making himself president of a new board of national defense and taking up the command of the Pekin Field Force, a specially trained body of troops for the defense of the capital. He retained possession of these posts after his son assumed the government in person, notwithstanding the law forbidding a father serving under his son, which has already been cited, and he remained the real controller of Chinese policy until his sudden and unexpected death in the first days of 1891. Some months earlier, in April, 1890, China had suffered a great loss in the Marquis Tseng, whose diplomatic experience and knowledge of Europe might have rendered his country infinite service in the future. He was the chosen colleague of Prince Chun, and he is said to have gained the ear of his young sovereign. While willing to admit the superiority of European inventions, he was also an implicit believer in China's destiny and in her firmly holding her place among the greatest powers of the world. In December, 1890, also died Tseng Kwo Tsiuen, uncle of the marquis, and a man who had taken a prominent and honorable part in the suppression of the Taeping Rebellion.

In 1885 an important and delicate negotiation between England and China was brought to a successful issue by the joint efforts of Lord Salisbury and the Marquis Tseng. The levy of the lekin or barrier tax on opium had led to many exactions in the interior which were injurious to the foreign trade and also to the Chinese Government, which obtained only the customs duty raised in the port. After the subject had been thoroughly discussed in all its bearings a convention was signed in London, on July 19, 1885, by which the lekin was fixed at eighty taels a chest, in addition to the customs due of thirty taels, and also that the whole of this sum should be paid in the treaty port before the opium was taken out of bond. This arrangement was greatly to the advantage of the Chinese Government, which came into possession of a large revenue that had previously been frittered away in the provinces, and much of which had gone into the pockets of the mandarins. This subject affords the most appropriate place for calling attention to the conspicuous services rendered, as Director-General of Chinese Customs during more than thirty years, by Sir Robert Hart, who, on the premature death of Sir Harry Parkes, was appointed British Minister at Pekin, which post, for weighty reasons, he almost immediately resigned. It is impossible to measure the consequences and important effect of his conduct and personal influence upon the policy and opinion of China, while his work in the interests of that country has been both striking and palpable. To his efforts the central government mainly owes its large and increasing cash revenue, and when some candid Chinese historian sums up the work done for his country by foreigners, he will admit that, what Gordon did in war and Macartney in diplomacy, Hart accomplished in those revenue departments which are an essential element of strength, and we must hope that this truthful chronicler will also not forget to record that all these loyal servants were English, members of a race which, after fighting China fairly, frankly held out the hand of friendship and alliance. In connection with this subject it may be noted that the emperor issued an edict in 1890 formally legalizing the cultivation of opium, which, although practically carried on, was nominally illegal. An immediate consequence of this step was a great increase in the area under cultivation, particularly in Manchuria, and so great is the production of native opium now becoming that that of India may yet be driven from the field as a practical revenge for the loss inflicted on China by the competition of Indian tea. But at all events these measures debar China from ever again posing as an injured party in the matter of the opium traffic. She has very rightly determined to make the best of the situation and to derive all the profit she can by taxing an article in such very general use and consumption; but there is an end to all representations like those made by prominent officials from Commissioner Lin to Prince Kung and Li Hung Chang, that the opium traffic was iniquitous, and constituted the sole cause of disagreement between China and England.

During these years the young Emperor Kwangsu was growing up. In February, 1887, in which month falls the Chinese New Year, it was announced that his marriage was postponed in consequence of his delicate health, and it was not until the new year of 1889, when Kwangsu was well advanced in his eighteenth year, that he was married to Yeh-ho-na-la, daughter of a Manchu general named Knei Hsiang, who had been specially selected for this great honor out of many hundred candidates. The marriage was celebrated with the usual state, and more than $5,000,000 is said to have been expended on the attendant ceremonies. At the same time the empress-regent issued her farewell edict and passed into retirement, but there is reason to believe that she continued to exercise no inconsiderable influence over the young emperor.

The marriage and assumption of governing power by the Emperor Kwangsu brought to the front the very important question of the right of audience by the foreign ministers resident at Pekin. This privilege had been conceded by China at the time of the Tientsin massacre, and it had been put into force on one occasion during the brief reign of Tungche. The time had again arrived for giving it effect, and, after long discussions as to the place of audience and the forms to be observed, Kwangsu issued, in December, 1890, an edict appointing a day soon after the commencement of the Chinese New Year for the audience, and also arranging that it should be repeated annually on the same date. In March, 1891, Kwangsu gave his first reception to the foreign ministers, but after it was over some criticism and dissatisfaction were aroused by the fact that the ceremony had been held in the Tse Kung Ko, or Hall of Tributary Nations. As this was the first occasion on which Europeans saw the young emperor, the fact that he made a favorable impression on them is not without interest, and the following personal description of the master of so many millions may well be quoted. "Whatever the impression 'the Barbarians' made on him the idea which they carried away of the Emperor Kwangsu was pleasing and almost pathetic. His air is one of exceeding intelligence and gentleness, somewhat frightened and melancholy looking. His face is pale, and though it is distinguished by refinement and quiet dignity it has none of the force of his martial ancestors, nothing commanding or imperial, but is altogether mild, delicate, sad and kind. He is essentially Manchu in features, his skin is strangely pallid in hue, which is, no doubt, accounted for by the confinement of his life inside these forbidding walls and the absence of the ordinary pleasures and pursuits of youth, with the constant discharge of onerous, complicated and difficult duties of state which, it must be remembered, are, according to imperial Chinese etiquette, mostly transacted between the hours of two and six in the morning. His face is oval shaped with a very long narrow chin and a sensitive mouth with thin, nervous lips; his nose is well shaped and straight, his eyebrows regular and very arched, while the eyes are unusually large and sorrowful in expression. The forehead is well shaped and broad, and the head is large beyond the average."

Owing to the dissatisfaction felt at the place of audience, which seemed to put the Treaty Powers on the same footing as tributary states, the foreign ministers have endeavored to force from the Tsungli Yamen the formal admission that a more appropriate part of the imperial city should be assigned for the ceremony; but as the Powers themselves were not disposed to lay too much stress on this point, no definite concession has yet been made, and the Chinese ministers have held out against the pressure of some of the foreign representatives. But, although no precise alteration has been made in the place of audience, the question has been practically settled by a courteous concession to the new English minister, Mr. O'Conor, who succeeded Sir John Walsham in 1892, and it is gratifying to feel that this advantage was gained more by tact than by coercion. When Mr. O'Conor wished to present his credentials to the emperor, it was arranged that the emperor should receive him in the Cheng Kuan Tien Palace, which is part of the imperial residence of Peace and Plenty within the Forbidden City. The British representative, accompanied by his secretaries and suite in accordance with arrangement, proceeded to this palace on December 13, 1892, and was received in a specially honorable way at the principal or imperial entrance by the officials of the court. Such a mark of distinction was considered quite unique in the annals of foreign diplomacy in China, and has since been a standing grievance with the other ministers at Pekin. It was noticed by those present that the emperor took a much greater interest in the ceremony than on previous occasions, and that he showed special attention as Prince Ching, the President of the Yamen, translated the letter from Queen Victoria. This audience, which lasted a considerable time, was certainly the most satisfactory and encouraging yet held with the Emperor Kwangsu by any foreign envoy, and it also afforded opportunity of confirming the favorable impression which the intelligence and dignified demeanor of the Emperor Kwangsu have made on all who have had the honor of coming into his presence. One incident in the progress of the audience question deserves notice, and that was the emperor's refusal, in 1891, to receive Mr. Blair, the United States Minister, in consequence of the hostile legislation of that country against China. The anti-foreign outbreak along the Yangtsekiang, in the summer of 1891, was an unpleasant incident, from which at one time it looked as if serious consequences might follow; but the ebullition fortunately passed away without an international crisis, and it may be hoped that the improved means of exercising diplomatic pressure at Pekin will render these attacks less frequent, and their settlement and redress more rapid.

During the last ten years events in Central Asia and Burma have drawn England and China much more closely together, and have laid the basis of what it must be hoped will prove a firm and durable alliance. If suspicion were laid aside and candid relations established on the frontier, it should not be difficult to maintain an excellent understanding with China, and at the present moment every difficulty has been smoothed over with the exception of that on the Burmese frontier. It is to be hoped that not less success will be obtained in this quarter than in Sikhim and Hunza, and Mr. O'Conor's convention of Pekin in July, 1886, recognizing China's right to receive a tribute mission from Burma once in ten years went far to prove the extent of concession England would make to China. It is divulging what cannot long be kept secret, to explain the circumstances under which Mr. O'Conor's convention was signed, and the unusual concession made by a British Government of admitting its liability to send a tribute mission. The Chefoo Convention, closing the Yunnan incident, contained a promise from the Chinese Government to allow an English mission to pass through Tibet. Years passed without any attempt to give effect to this stipulation, but at last, in 1884, Mr. Colman Macaulay, a member of the Indian Civil Service, obtained the assent of his government to requesting the permission of the Chinese Government to visit Lhasa. He went to Pekin and he came to London, and he obtained the necessary permission and the formal passport of the Tsungli Yamen; and there is no doubt that if he had set off for Tibet with a small party, he would have been honorably received and passed safely through Tibet to India. On the other hand there is no doubt that such a visit would have presented no feature of special or striking importance. It would have been an interesting individual experience, but scarcely an international landmark. This modest character for his long-cherished project did not suit Mr. Macaulay, and unmindful of the adage that there may be a slip betwixt the cup and the lip, he not merely delayed the execution of his visit, but he made ostentatious preparations for an elaborate mission, and he engaged many persons with scientific qualifications to accompany him, with the view of examining the mineral resources of Tibet. The Chinese themselves did not like, and had never contemplated, such a mission, but their dissatisfaction was slight in comparison with the storm it raised in Tibet; and the Chinese Government was thus brought face to face with a position in which it must either employ its military power to coerce the Tibetans, who made preparations to oppose the Macaulay mission by force of arms, or acquiesce in the Tibetans ignoring its official passports, and thus provoke a serious complication with this country. Such was the position of the Tibetan question when Burma was annexed in January, 1886, and negotiations followed with China for the adjustment of her claims in the country. Negotiations were carried on, in the first place by Lord Salisbury, and in the second by Lord Rosebery, with the Chinese minister in London, and the draft of more than one convention was prepared. Among such contemplated arrangements were the dispatch of a mission from Burma to China, and of a return one from China; the appointment of the Head Priest of Mandalay as the person to send the mission, thus making it a purely native matter, outside the participation of the British Government; and the concession of material advantages on the Irrawaddy and in the Shan country, as the equivalent for the surrender of the tribute. It is probable that one of these three arrangements would have been carried out, but that, on certain points being referred to Pekin, the knowledge came to the ears of the British Government that if the Tibetan mission were withdrawn, the Chinese would be content with the formal admission of their claim to receive the tribute mission from Burma in accordance with established usage. As both governments wanted a speedy settlement of the question, the Chinese, with the view of allaying the rising agitation in Tibet and getting rid of a troublesome question, and the English not less anxious to have the claims of China in Burma defined in diplomatic language, the convention which bears Mr. O'Conor's name was drawn up and signed with quite remarkable dispatch. For the abandonment of the Macaulay mission, and the recognition of their right to receive the tribute mission from Burma, the authorities at Pekin were quite, at the moment, willing to forego material claims such as a port on the Irrawaddy. Diplomacy has not yet said the last word on this matter, and the exact frontier between Burma and China has still to be delimited, but the fixing of a definite date for the dispatch of the first mission from Mandalay to Pekin, which is timed to set out in January, 1894, is in itself of hopeful augury for the settlement of all difficulties. When this matter is composed there will be no cloud in the sky of Anglo-Chinese relations, and that such an auspicious result will be obtained is not open to serious doubt. The most gratifying fact in the history of China during the last ten years is the increasing sympathy and tacit understanding between the two great empires of England and China in Asia, which must in time constitute an effective alliance against any common danger in that continent, and the aggressive policy of Russia.

THE WAR WITH JAPAN AND SUBSEQUENT EVENTS

WE have seen that, up to 1892, it had been customary to receive the representatives of foreign powers in the Tse Kung Ko, or Hall of Tributary Nations. Naturally, much dissatisfaction was provoked by the selection of a place of audience which seemed to put the Treaty Powers on the same footing as tributary states, and, accordingly, the foreign ministers undertook to exact from the Tsungli Yamen, or Board for Foreign Affairs, the designation of a more suitable locality in the imperial city for the annual ceremony. The proposed innovation was resisted for some time; but when Sir Nicolas O'Conor was appointed British Minister at Pekin, an exception was made in his favor, and a place of superior importance to the Hall of Tributary Nations was chosen for the presentation of his credentials. The Emperor Kwangsu agreed to receive him in the Cheng Kuan Tien Palace, or pavilion which forms part of the imperial residence of Peace and Plenty within the Forbidden City. In pursuance of this arrangement, the British representative, attended by his suite, proceeded to this pavilion on December 13, 1892, and was received at the principal entrance by the high court officials. It was also noted that the emperor took a greater interest in the ceremony than on preceding occasions, and followed with attention the reading of Queen Victoria's letter, by Prince Ching, then president of the Tsungli Yamen. Thenceforth, there was observed with every year a decided improvement in the mode of receiving foreign diplomatists, and, eventually, the imperial audience was supplemented with an annual dinner given by the Board for Foreign Affairs. Through the personal reception accorded by the Emperor of China to Prince Henry of Prussia on May 15, 1898, the audience question was finally settled in favor of the right of foreign potentates to rank on an equality with the so-called Son of Heaven.

We come now to the most memorable event in the modern history of China since the Taeping Rebellion; to wit, the war with Japan. In order to comprehend, however, the causes of this contest between the two chief races of the Far East, it is necessary to review the development of the Corean question which gave rise to it. There seems to be no doubt that Japan derived its first civilizing settlers, and most of its arts and industries, from the Corean peninsula. It is certain that, for centuries, the intercourse between the two countries was very close, and that more than one attempt was made by Japanese rulers to subjugate Corea. The latest and most strenuous endeavor to that end was made near the end of the sixteenth century, and, although it resulted in a temporary occupation of the peninsula, the Japanese troops were eventually withdrawn, and Corea resumed its former status of a kingdom tributary to the Celestial Empire. Thenceforth, for almost three centuries, Corea and Tonquin bore, in theory, precisely the same relation to the Middle Kingdom. In each instance, the practical question was whether China was strong enough to make good her nominal rights. The outcome of her resistance to French aggression in Tonquin had shown that there, at least, she had no such power. But, in the subsequent ten years, efforts had been made to organize an efficient army and navy, and the belief was entertained at Pekin that China was at all events strong enough to uphold her claims in Corea, which was, geographically and strategically, of far more importance to the Middle Kingdom than was Tonquin. Yet, while it was evident that Corea would not be renounced without a struggle, the Pekin authorities, for some years, met the Japanese encroachments with a weak and vacillating policy. As early as 1876, the Mikado's advisers entered

on a course which obviously aimed at the attainment of commercial, if not, also, political, ascendency in the Hermit
Kingdom. An outrage having been committed upon some
of her sailors, Japan obtained, by way of reparation from
the court of Seoul, the opening of the port of Fushan to her
trade. Four years later, Chemulpo, the port of Seoul, was
also opened. These forward steps on the part of the Japanese aroused the Chinese to activity, and, in 1881, a draft
commercial treaty was prepared by the Chinese authorities
in council with the representatives of the principal powers
at Pekin, and sent to Seoul, where it was accepted. The
Japanese alleged, however, that they possessed a historical
right to an equal voice with China in the Corean peninsula,
and that, consequently, the treaty to which we have just
referred required their ratification. To sustain this claim,
the Japanese allied themselves with the Progressive party
in Corea, a move which compelled the Chinese to lean upon
the Reactionists, who were opposed to the concessions lately
made to foreigners, and who, as events were to show, were
preponderant in the Hermit Kingdom. In June, 1882, the
Corean Reactionists attacked the Japanese Legation at Seoul,
murdered some members of it, and compelled the survivors
to flee to the sea-coast. Thereupon, the Mikado sent some
troops to exact reparation, and the Chinese, on their part,
dispatched a force to restore order. A compromise was
brought about, and, for two years, Japanese and Chinese
soldiers remained encamped beside one another under the
walls of the Corean capital. In December, 1884, however,
a second collision occurred between the Japanese and the
Coreans, the latter being, this time, assisted by the Chinese. The Mikado's subjects were again compelled to take
to flight. The Tokio Government now resolved upon firm
measures, and, while it exacted compensation from the Coreans, it sent Count Ito Hirobumi to China to bring about
an accommodation with the Pekin Government. At that
conjuncture, there is no doubt that China possessed advantages in the Corean peninsula that were lacking to the Japa-

nese. Not only was she popular with the majority of the people, but the Treaty Powers were more disposed to act through her than through Japan in order to secure the general extension of trade with the Hermit Kingdom. Those advantages, nevertheless, were thrown away by an agreement which the shortsighted advisers of the Chinese emperor were persuaded to accept. Li Hung Chang was appointed the Chinese Plenipotentiary to negotiate with Count Ito, and, after a short conference, a convention was signed at Tientsin on April 18, 1885. The provisions of the convention were: first, that both countries should withdraw their troops from Corea; secondly, that no more officers should be sent by either country to drill the Corean army; and, thirdly, that if, at any future time, either of the two countries should send troops to Corea, it must inform the other. It is manifest that, by this agreement, China, practically, acquiesced in Japan's assertion of an equal right to control the Hermit Kingdom. Thenceforth, it was impossible to speak of Corea as being a vassal state of the Celestial Empire.

For some nine years, nevertheless, after the conclusion of the Tientsin agreement, there were no dangerous disturbances in the Peninsular Kingdom. In the early part of 1894, however, Kim-Ok-Kiun, a reformer, and the leader of the Corean uprising in 1884, was assassinated at Shanghai, and it subsequently transpired that the murder had been committed by the order of the Corean authorities. It is certain that honors and rewards were bestowed upon the assassin on his return to the Hermit Kingdom, while the body of his victim was drawn and quartered as that of a traitor. Just at this juncture, the Tonghaks, a body of religious reformers, having failed to obtain certain concessions, revolted, and, by the end of May, achieved so much success over the Corean forces that the Seoul Government became alarmed, and sent to China for assistance. In response to the request, some two thousand Chinese troops were disembarked on June 10 at Asan, a seaport some distance south of the Corean capital, and a few Chinese men-of-war were dispatched to the coast of the peninsula. Formal notice of these proceedings was given to Japan under the terms of the Tientsin Convention. Thereupon, the Mikado's Government decided to undertake a like interposition, and acted with so much energy that, within forty-eight hours after the arrival of the Chinese at Asan, they had placed at Seoul a much superior force. They were thus able to dominate the court, although it was in entire sympathy with China. The Pekin Government now made the mistake of reviving its pretensions to regard the Hermit Kingdom as a vassal state. These pretensions Japan refused to tolerate, on the ground, first, that she had never admitted them, and, secondly, that the Tientsin Convention recognized an equality of rights in the two states. The Japanese also called attention to the misrule that prevailed in Corea, and proposed that the Chinese should join them in carrying out needful reforms. To this proposal China could not accede, being hampered by her alliance with the reactionary party at Seoul; consequently, Japan undertook the execution of the task alone. As a first step in that direction, the Japanese got possession of the person of the Corean ruler, and compelled him to act as the instrument of his captors. The initial document which he was constrained to sign was an order that the Chinese troops, who had come at his invitation, should leave the country. The seizure of the king's person, which occurred on July 23, 1894, was followed by two successful acts of aggression. On the 25th, the Japanese squadron attacked the Chinese transport "Kowshing," conveying fresh soldiers to Asan, and its escort of warships. In the engagement one Chinese man-of-war was sunk, one was disabled, and 1,200 soldiers were destroyed on the "Kowshing," which was torpedoed. On July 29, the Japanese general Oshima, at the head of a small force, made a night attack upon the Chinese fortified camp at Song Hwang, and carried the place with a loss to their opponents of 500 killed and wounded. These preliminary encounters were followed by a declaration of war on

August 1, 1894. During the ensuing six weeks, Japan poured her troops into the peninsula, while the Chinese fleet, instead of harassing the enemy, remained in the harbors of Port Arthur and Wei-hai-Wei. On September 15, the Japanese army in Corea was strong enough to detach a corps of 14,000 men to attack the Chinese position at Pingyang, a town on the northern banks of the Paidong River. The passage of the river was difficult, and the Chinese might have overwhelmed the Japanese when crossing it, but they took no measures to this end, and the battle began at sunrise on the day just named. There were five forts to be captured, and some of them were vigorously defended, nor was it until night set in that the garrison finally determined upon evacuating the place. In the battle itself and the retreat, over 2,000 Chinese were killed, to say nothing of the wounded and the prisoners. The Japanese themselves lost 162 killed, 438 wounded and 33 missing, and there seems to be no reason to doubt that, had all the Chinese officers been capable of the valor displayed by the general Tso-pao-kuei, the Japanese would have been repulsed. As it was, the battle proved decisive, for not a Chinaman paused until he had reached the other side of the Yalu River, which forms the northwest boundary of Corea.

On the very day of the fight at Pingyang, a number of Chinese war vessels, under the command of Admiral Ting, were transporting troops to the mouth of the Yalu, where the Chinese were assembling a second army. On its return from this task, it was encountered, September 17, off the island of Haiyang, by a Japanese squadron under Admiral Ito. Ostensibly, the two fleets were evenly matched. They each numbered ten fighting vessels, and, if two of the Chinese ships possessed a more powerful armament, the Japanese were superior in steam power. It was to quickness in maneuvering that the Japanese admiral trusted for victory, and his first attack consisted mainly in circling around the Chinese squadron. He was careful, also, to reserve his fire until only two miles separated him from his adversaries.

After a duel with the Japanese "Matsushima," the Chinese flagship "Tingyuen" was severely damaged, and only saved from sinking by the intervention of her sister ship, the "Chenyuen." These two ironclads, together with the torpedo boats, succeeded in making their escape, but five of the Chinese vessels were sunk or destroyed. In men, the Chinese lost 700 killed or drowned and 300 wounded, while the Japanese lost 115 killed and 150 wounded. The result of this victory was that the Chinese never afterward attempted to dispute the control of the sea, and their water communication with the Yalu was effectually cut off.

After the battle of Pingyang, the Japanese army halted, and it was not until after they received re-enforcements under Marshal Yamagata that they resumed their forward movement. On October 10 their advance guard reached the Yalu, a river broad and difficult of passage, behind which was stationed a considerable Chinese army, which, however, after a nominal resistance, soon retreated. In the abandoned positions on the northern bank of the Yalu, the Japanese captured a vast quantity of material of war, including 74 cannons, over 4,000 rifles, and more than 4,000,000 rounds of ammunition. It was supposed that the retreating Chinese force would make a stand at Feng Hwang, but, on reaching that town, October 30, the Japanese found it evacuated, and were informed that the Chinese soldiers had dispersed.

While Marshal Yamagata was beginning the invasion of China from the direction of Corea, another Japanese army, under Marshal Oyama, had landed on the Liau-Tung, or Regent's Sword Peninsula, with the aim of capturing the Chinese naval station of Port Arthur. Even in Chinese hands, this was a redoubtable stronghold. It had 300 guns in position, and the garrison numbered some 10,000 men, while the attacking force did not exceed 13,000, although we should bear in mind that it was aided by the Japanese fleet. After landing at the mouth of the Huhua-Yuan River, about 100 miles north of Port Arthur, the Japanese advanced south, and took the fortified city of Chinchow, without incurring any loss. The next day they reached Talienwan, where the Chinese had five heavily armed batteries, and a considerable garrison, which, however, on the approach of the enemy, abandoned the post without firing a shot. In the forts at this point were found over 120 cannons, two and a half million rounds of ammunition for the artillery and nearly 34,000,000 rifle cartridges. On November 20, 1894, the Japanese army was drawn up in front of Port Arthur, and the fleet prepared to co-operate in the action. The attack began in the morning of November 22, and, although, in one quarter, the Chinese offered sturdy resistance, yet, by the end of the day, with the loss of no more than 18 men killed and 250 wounded, the Japanese were in possession of the strongest position in China, a naval fortress and arsenal on which $30,000,000 had been spent.

Throughout December the force under Marshal Yamagata pushed forward into Manchuria, but met there with more vigorous opposition than it had hitherto encountered. In the fight at Kangwasai, the Japanese lost 400, and, in the capture of the town of Kaiting, 300 killed and wounded. About the middle of January, 1895, the Japanese began operations against Wei-hai-Wei, the naval stronghold on the northern coast of Shantung, in which the remnant of China's fleet had taken refuge. Although not so strong as Port Arthur, this harbor is considered one of the keys to the Gulf of Pechihli. On January 20, the Japanese troops began to land at Yungchang, a little west of the point to be attacked, and, on the 26th, they appeared at the gates of Wei-hai-Wei. About half of the beleaguered garrison consisted of 4,000 sailors from the fleet, under Admiral Ting, who was to show himself a leader of courage and energy. The assault on the land side of Wei-hai-Wei began on January 29, and continued throughout that and the following day. At certain points, where Admiral Ting's squadron was able to act with effect, the Japanese were repulsed, but, eventually, the whole of the land garrison fled panic-stricken to Chefoo. Even then Ting's squadron and the island force continued to resist, and it was not until February 9, when almost all the vessels had been taken or sunk, that he consented to capitulate, after receiving a telegram from Li Hung Chang to the effect that no help could be given him. No sooner were the terms of capitulation agreed upon than Admiral Ting retired to his cabin and took a fatal dose of opium. He had held out for three weeks, whereas Port Arthur had been lost in a day. The war continued for a few weeks longer, the Japanese pursuing their advance in Manchuria, and capturing the two places which are collectively called Newchwang, thus threatening Pekin. They now possessed an army of 100,000 men ready to advance upon the Chinese capital. As there was no reason to suppose that Pekin could be successfully defended, the necessity of concluding peace as promptly as possible was recognized. To that end it was needful to appoint a plenipotentiary whose name would convince the Japanese Government that the Chinese were in earnest in their overtures. The only two men who possessed the requisite qualifications were Prince Kung and Li Hung Chang. The former, however, being a prince of the imperial family, and the uncle of the reigning emperor, Kwangsu, could not be induced to submit to the humiliation of proceeding to Japan and suing for peace. The only possible selection, therefore, was Li Hung Chang, who was, accordingly, appointed plenipotentiary. He reached Shimonoseki on March 20, 1895, and, four days after his arrival, the success of his mission was greatly promoted by the attempt of a fanatic to assassinate him during his conference with Count Ito, the Japanese representative. The wound was not very serious, but the outrage caused a unanimous expression of sympathy and regret on the part of the Japanese people, and the Mikado sent his own physician to attend the wounded minister. To attest their sorrow for this incident, the Japanese at once granted an armistice, and the terms of peace which they at first proposed were materially mitigated. On April 17, the

Treaty of Shimonoseki was signed, and, on May 8, the ratifications were exchanged at Chefoo. The terms of the original treaty were these: First, China was to surrender Formosa and the Pescadores Islands and the southern part of the Shingking province, including the Liau-Tung, or Regent's Sword Peninsula, and of course, also, the naval fortress of Port Arthur. China was likewise to pay in eight installments a money indemnity of 200,000,000 Kuping taels, or, say, $160,000,000. She was also to grant certain commercial concessions, including the admission of ships under the Japanese flag to the Chinese lakes and rivers, and the appointment of consuls. In view of the completeness of Japan's triumph, these conditions could not be considered onerous, but they, undoubtedly, disturbed the balance of power in the Far East, and, had they been permitted to stand, would have effectually thwarted Russia's plan of advancing southward, and of obtaining an ice-free port. The Czar's Government, accordingly, determined to interpose, and, having secured the co-operation of its French ally, and also of Germany, it presented to the Mikado, in the name of the three powers, a request that he should waive that part of the Shimonoseki Treaty which provided for the surrender of the Liau-Tung Peninsula. It was proposed that, in return for the renunciation of this territory on the Chinese mainland, the pecuniary indemnity should be increased by $30,000,000, and that Wei-hai-Wei should be retained until the whole sum should have been paid. The demand was, obviously, one that could not be rejected without war against the three interposing powers, and the odds were too great for Japan to face without the assistance of Great Britain, which Lord Rosebery, then prime minister, did not see fit to offer. The Mikado, accordingly, submitted to the loss of the best part of the fruits of victory, retaining only Formosa and the Pescadores, the value of which is, as yet, undetermined; with the money indemnity, however, Japan has been enabled so greatly to strengthen her fleet that, when all the vessels building for her are completed, she will take rank as a naval power of the first class in the Pacific.

For some time after the revision of the Shimonoseki Treaty, the Chinese seem to have imagined that the Czar had intervened from disinterested motives, but Count Cassini, the Russian minister at Pekin, eventually made it clear that the interposition would not be gratuitous. In what form the payment for Russia's services should be made was, for some time, the subject of debate, but, before Li Hung Chang left China in the spring of 1896, as a special embassador to attend the coronation of Nicholas II. at Moscow, the heads of a convention had been drawn up, and, on Li's arrival in Russia, he signed an agreement which embodied the concessions to be made to the Czar in return for his services. This secret treaty gave Russia the control of the Liau-Tung Peninsula, which she had ostensibly saved, at the cost to China of $30,000,000, and the St. Petersburg Government was also to be allowed to build a branch of the Trans-Siberian Railway through Manchuria to Talienwan and Port Arthur. A period of eighteen months elapsed before the details of this momentous agreement became known. On the return of Li Hung Chang to Pekin, he not only failed to recover the viceroyship of Chihli, but he found his relations with the Emperor Kwangsu quite as unsatisfactory as they had been after his return from Shimonoseki. He was restored, indeed, to a seat on the Tsungli Yamen, or Board of Foreign Affairs, but, for twelve months, it seemed as if, despite the support of the Empress-Dowager Tsi An, his influence would never revive.

The two years that followed the Shimonoseki Treaty gave a breathing spell to China, and should have been devoted to energetic reforms in the military and naval administration. As a matter of fact, nothing had been accomplished, when, in 1897, a blow fell which brought the Middle Kingdom face to face with the prospect of immediate partition. In November of that year, without any preliminary notice or warning to the Pekin Government, two German men-of-war entered the harbor of Kiao Chou, and ordered the commandant to give up the place in reparation for the murder of two German missionaries in the province of Shantung. Germany refused to evacuate Kiao Chou unless due reparation should be made for the outrage on the missionaries, and unless, further, China would cede to her the exclusive right to construct railways and work mines throughout the extensive and populous province of Shantung. This, of course, was equivalent to the demarcation of a sphere of influence. For a time, the Pekin Government showed itself recalcitrant, but, in January, 1898, it consented to lease Kiao Chou to Germany for ninety-nine years, and to make the required additional concession of exclusive rights in Shantung. Russia, on her part, did not wait long after the German seizure of Kiao Cho , to put forward her claim for compensation on account of the services rendered in the matter of the revision of the Shimonoseki Treaty. The terms of the Cassini agreement were now gradually revealed. In December, 1897, the St. Petersburg Government announced that the Chinese had given permission to the Russian fleet to winter at Port Arthur; in February, 1898, Russia added Talienwan to Port Arthur, but essayed to disarm criticism by declaring that the first-named port would be opened to the ships of all the great powers like other ports on the Chinese mainland. This promise was subsequently qualified, and on March 27 a convention was signed at Pekin giving the Russians the "usufruct" of Port Arthur and Talienwan, which, practically, meant that Russia had obtained those harbors unconditionally, and for an indefinite period. France, on her part, obtained possession of the port of Kwangchowfoo, which is the best outlet to the sea for the trade of the southern province of Kwangsi; she also secured a promise that the island of Hainan should not be ceded to any other power; and, finally, she gained a recognition of her claim, first advanced in 1895, to a prior right to control the commercial development of the province of Yunnan. This claim is as reasonable as that put forward by Germany with reference to the province of Shantung, but it is incompatible with the northeastward development of British Burma. While these acts, which, virtually, amounted to mutilations of the Middle Kingdom, were being committed by Germany, Russia and France, England undertook to assert the principle of the "open door," the principle, namely, that, whatever territorial concessions might be made by the Pekin Government, no nation could be deprived of its treaty rights in the ports ceded. That is to say, American citizens, British subjects, or the subjects of any other power which has a treaty with China containing "the most favored nation" clause, must be allowed to enjoy precisely the same rights in Talienwan, Kiao Chou and Kwangchowfoo as they would have enjoyed had not those places been surrendered to Russia, Germany and France respectively. This principle could only have been enforced by war, in which England would have needed the assistance of Japan; but Japan was not yet ready to engage in a contest, for the reason that she still had to receive $60,000,000 of the war indemnity due from China, and because the war vessels which she had ordered to be constructed in foreign shipyards were not yet sufficiently near completion. Being thus constrained to abandon the hope of maintaining its treaty rights in the ceded parts of China, the British Foreign Office changed its ground and fell back on the policy of exacting an equivalent for the advantages gained by Russia, Germany and France. In the pursuance of this policy it obtained Wei-hai-Wei, which, as we have said, is one of the two keys to the Gulf of Pechihli. It is, however, very inferior to Port Arthur; only by the expenditure of a large sum of money could it be made a naval fortress of high rank, and, even then, it would require a large garrison for its protection. This was not all that England gained, however; she secured a promise from the Pekin Government that the valley of the Yangtsekiang should never be alienated to any foreign power except Great Britain. The limits of the valley, nevertheless, were not defined, and the Pekin authorities have acted on the hypothesis that the covenant against alienation did not debar them from giving commercial and industrial privileges within the basin to the subjects of European powers other than England. The right to build, for instance, a railway from Pekin to Hangchow has been conferred upon a syndicate nominally Belgian, in which, however, it is understood that Russia is deeply interested. On the other hand, in spite of protests from St. Petersburg, the privilege of extending to Newchwang in Manchuria the railway which already extends some distance in a northeasterly direction from Tientsin, has been secured by a British corporation.

In September, 1898, a palace revolution occurred at Pekin. For some time, the Emperor Kwangsu had been known to be under the influence of a highly intelligent and progressive Cantonese named Kang Yu Wei. At the latter's suggestion, edicts were put forth decreeing important administrative reforms which would have deprived the mandarins of their opportunities of embezzlement, and also indicating an intention to reorganize the educational system of China upon European models. The necessity of such changes is obvious enough if China is to follow Japan in the path of progress, but it is equally plain that the advocacy of them would render the Emperor obnoxious to the whole body of mandarins and of the literati. The unpopularity caused by his proposed innovations proved fatal to Kwangsu; for the party at court, headed by the Empress-Dowager Tsi An, took advantage of it to arrest and imprison him. Kang Yu Wei, having received warning of the conspiracy, had fled, and succeeded in gaining an asylum under the British flag, but many of the Emperor's personal followers were put to death. On September 22, appeared an edict ostensibly signed by Kwangsu announcing that he had requested the Empress-Dowager to resume authority over the affairs of State. The immediate effect of the *coup d'état* was to place all power at Pekin in the hands of Manchus least friendly to the adoption of European ideas, and more willing to lean upon Russia than upon any other foreign power. The early restoration to high office of Li Hung Chang, who had, for some time, been a useful tool of the St. Petersburg Government, and who is a favorite of the Empress-Dowager, was a foregone conclusion.

Soon after, the rumor flashed around the world that the young Emperor, at the instigation of the Empress-Dowager and her advisers, had swallowed a fatal dose of opium. Such credence did this report gain in the capitals of Christendom that a dozen other silly tales followed, culminating in the ludicrous story that Li Hung Chang and the Empress-Dowager had eloped. But the young Emperor was afterward seen alive, though he was in more frail health than ever. It was not to the interest of that shrewd old woman whom Bismarck once dubbed "the only man in China" to have the putative occupant of the throne killed. He was necessary as the figure-head whose name must be signed to her most odious decrees, and he was too completely in her power to be able to thwart her plans. From 1898 to 1900 the palace at Pekin was the scene of countless political intrigues. Every important foreign government was plotting to secure special consideration. The Empress-Dowager and her advisers were playing off one power against another, while all Europe, outside of Russia, had an uneasy conviction that the Czar's Government was secretly and exultantly gathering all the diplomatic plums. The only decisive victory gained between the powers was the achievement of Secretary of State Hay in obtaining the pledge of the nations that, no matter what spheres of influence were created in China, the "open door" policy should be applied to them all.

Early in 1900, whispers of the impending Boxer troubles began to reach the outer world. Little attention was paid to them. They were regarded only as the symptoms of another of those more or less important internal disorders that have ever harassed the Celestial Government. The Empress-Dowager gave the most engaging assurances of the continued safety of all alien sojourners in the realm. Her policy toward the powers was one of extreme conciliation. Yet as the weeks went on the Boxers grew in strength, prestige and power. They proselyted vigorously in many provinces, though their greatest strength was in the province of Shantung, where they originated many generations ago. They came into existence first as a kind of Masonic order, and many of their rites are said to bear a grotesque resemblance to those of the Freemasons, thus suggesting the possibility of great antiquity and foreign origin. Their belief is a curious blending of Oriental religions, child-like superstitions, politics and fanatical hatred of foreigners. They practice many mysteries, the parent of which is hypnotism—a thing in itself wholly inexplicable to the mind of the Chinese peasant or coolie. Susceptible persons are made the subjects of these Boxer hypnotists. To the accompaniment of weird rites and much hocus-pocus a subject is thrown into a trance by a Boxer hypnotist in the presence of a multitude of possible converts. While in this trance the subject is made to proclaim supposed communications from the gods. The Boxer literature of 1900 abounded in the most marvelous messages from on high that were so obtained. Other subjects were made to endure thrusts from knives and cuts from swords, and their invulnerability to pain while in the hypnotic condition was used to persuade the credulous masses that Boxers were proof against death by assassination or in battle. It was especially promised that at the propitious moment 8,000,000 spirit soldiers would descend from heaven to aid in sweeping the last barbarian from the soil of China. Secret orders had gone out from the Regent to prepare everywhere to resist foreign invasion. This speedily leaked out, both to the officials and to the masses, and its effect in inflaming the popular mind can be readily understood. All the while the Celestial Government made outward show of suppressing the "rebels." Officials who openly consorted with the Boxers were degraded, summoned to Pekin, cautioned to be outwardly more circumspect and sent elsewhere to higher posts. Leading Boxers were secretly brought to Pekin, where they gave exhibitions of their mysteries before the Empress-Dowager and Prince Tuan, the father of Pu Chun, a lad of fourteen, who had been named as successor to the throne. Both of these keen and aged intriguers saw in the Boxers tools that could be used to further their own ends—or else they dreaded a tidal wave that could not be resisted. General Nieh, who commanded the military at the capital, took his orders for the suppression of the Boxers so seriously that in an encounter he killed several of them. For this carelessness he was promptly reprimanded from the palace. After that he was careful to provide his troops with blank cartridges.

The propaganda swept over Shantung and the other infected provinces with the rapidity of a prairie fire. Not men alone were enrolled; the young women were persuaded to join. As the men and youths were known as the "Brothers of the Long Sword," so were the women called by the name of the "Sisters of the Red Lantern." Thus the organization took its root at the very hearth-side. Yu Hien, a Manchu governor who had supplied some of the Boxers with long swords, in order that they might butcher the builders of the German railway, was called to Pekin and decorated with a breastplate. Immediately afterward he was assigned to the governorship of the Shansi province, where he soon afterward distinguished himself by causing or permitting the slaughter of more than half a hundred missionaries and native converts to a number that cannot be accurately estimated. In Shantung and other provinces white men and women, as well as native converts, fell under the long swords as the Boxers continued to roll on to Pekin. Recruits to the new "patriotic" movement poured in by thousands. Yellow boatmen who found themselves out of work because the hated foreigners had introduced steam navigation on the Peiho River, joined the new standard in the desperation of starvation. Drivers of native carts and coolies who had formerly existed by carrying prodigious burdens great distances on their backs had found themselves thrown out of employment by the operation of the railway between Tong-ku and Pekin; they, too, and their women, allied themselves with the movement that was to forever drive out the barbarian who wanted to build railroads.

At last even the foreigners in sacred Pekin took alarm. The heads of the different Legations petitioned the Tsungli Yamen for permission to have marine guards sent to Pekin from the fleets of the world already assembled off the Taku forts at the mouth of the Peiho, the river waterway from the sea to the capital. With characteristic Oriental diplo- macy the Yamen half consented, yet parleyed, and so the negotiations went on for weeks. The crash came on May 27, when Boxers tore up the railway to Paoting Fu, burned the station houses, killed some of the Belgian employés and barely failed to bag the entire lot. Now the foreign Minis- ters and naval commanders acted with tardy decision. Small Legation guards of marines, aggregating not more than 450 officers and men, were rushed to Pekin by special train. Hardly had the train passed when the tracks were torn up —behind it—by infuriated Boxers. Communication between the Legations and the outside world was cut off. The siege had begun. China stood arrayed against the entire civilized world, the vicious, implacable aggressor in the most exten- sive and horrible transgression of the inviolability of em- bassy known to history. It is a curious fact that during the first few days of the siege the Boxers and their friends, the rabble, were the assailants. The unorganized rabble vanished first from the scene. After them the Boxers faded gradually from view. Then the government's Imperial sol- diery took stations just beyond the defenses of the besieged foreigners in Pekin, and for two months maintained an un- ceasing effort to crush out the few hundred indomitable ones whom they had thought at their mercy. On June 9, all the buildings belonging to foreigners in the southern or Chinese part of the city, were burned, the owners being compelled to flee to the Legations. Missionaries came flocking in. A naval force from all the fleets, numbering some two thou- sand men, set out from Tientsin by rail, in the expectation

fully all that they could for the common defense. In espe-
cial they sewed bags of silk, cotton and other fabrics, and
filled them with earth. These bags were used in constructing the walls of the defenses. Commanding points on the
Legation walls were occupied at great hazard by the marines.
Frequent sorties were made for the purpose of capturing cannon from the enemy, or for driving back over-bold Chinese.
Superintended by an American marine, some of the defenders constructed a cannon out of an old brass pump. As the
weeks wore on food became scarcer. Horses and mules to
the number of eighty were killed and sparingly eaten. At
the last there were but three or four of the animals left.
The barrels of meal with which the besiegers had stocked
themselves were used to the very bottoms when relief came.
Despite the excellence of the defenses many of the officers
and men were killed and wounded, and the civilians were
hardly more fortunate. By day there was unending sharp-
shooting by concealed Chinese without, and by night the
greatest horror of all; for then the besiegers made their
most desperate assaults, generally with a prelude of artillery fire fiendishly well served. It seemed to those despairing ones within the Legation walls as though each rush of
the enemy must be the final act of the tragedy. Making the
night awful with their yells, countless thousands of Chinese
would swarm forward. Only their compact masses made
continued defense possible. The marines would fire as
fast as they could load, while the incessant play of the defenders' machine guns carried wholesale death to the assailants. Yet such courage did the Chinese display that it
seemed impossible to much longer keep them at a distance.

In the meantime the world was chafing over the slow approach of formidable relief to Pekin. From the Philippines
a few thousand American troops were sent, and General
Adna R. Chaffee was hastened across the Pacific to command them. The other seven powers that had taken part
in the defense of the foreigners at Pekin sent various con-
tingents. All the way to Tientsin these troops were vigor-

ously opposed by the Chinese. The foreigners at this city were in as much danger as those at the capital. Gordon Hall, the largest building in the foreign settlement, was made the headquarters of the menaced aliens. It was not until the 23d of June that the Russians made their welcome appearance at Tientsin in considerable force. After them came the troops of other nationalities. But the Chinese still held the formidable citadel. It was three weeks later that this great fortress fell into the hands of the allies, and then only on the second day of the most ferocious fighting. The American forces engaged were the Ninth United States Infantry and a picked body of American marines. They were brigaded with British troops under General Dorward. French and Japanese troops fought close to our men and had practical illustration of the superb work of the American regular infantry. On the morning of the second day of the attack upon the citadel the Japanese charged one of the gates and blew it in with high explosives after the second attempt. The citadel fell and was occupied by the allies.

Within a few days an army numbering some fifteen thousands troops was organized, equipped and started on the eighty-mile march to the capital. For purposes of transportation the river route was followed. The ground between Tientsin and Pekin became the theater of operations in a campaign in which the battles steadily decreased in severity. The whipping at Tientsin had had its effect. The Chinese lost confidence in themselves with every succeeding engagement. At length, on the 13th of August, the allied armies, marching from Tung Chow, reached the positions assigned to them outside the Chinese capital. Knowing the proximity of the hostile force, the Chinese made the fiercest assault of all on the Legations that night. The noise of attack and defense was plainly audible in the foreign camps. Though it had been agreed to defer the attack upon Pekin until the next day, the Russian troops moved forward without delay. It was fortunate that they did so, for the reminder of the allies joined in the assault. At midnight the watchers at the British Legation heard the din of opening battle, during a lull in the attack upon themselves, and shouted across the compound the glorious news that relief was almost within rifle range. Discouraged by repeated thrashings from inferior numbers, the Chinese did not long hold out. By morning the allies were fighting their way through the outer streets of Pekin. At ten o'clock in the morning, amid the most deafening cheers from the lately besieged, the gates of the British Legation were thrown open to admit a company of mounted Sikhs who came as the advance guard of safety. Later in the day our Minister, Mr. E. H. Conger, and his secretary, Mr. Squiers, had the delight of welcoming General Chaffee and the American troops. While attacking the Imperial Palace, Captain Reilly, of the United States Artillery, was killed. His death was the most notable that befell our forces, with the single exception of the splendid Liscum, colonel of the Ninth, who fell in the attack on the Tientsin citadel.

Soon after the rescue of the Legation a strong force went to the aid of the French Cathedral, which had held out all these weeks. Another body of troops was sent to the Methodist compound, where many white and native Christians had held out for the same length of time. While the Methodists were well equipped for defense, they had singularly escaped any severity of attack.

Of course the Empress-Dowager, the Emperor and all the court suite were gone by the time that the allies found themselves in possession of this Babylon of the East. They had escaped to Singan-fu, an ancient imperial city which had on former occasions sheltered the royal family from threatening storm. An important strategic point in itself, the route thither could be guarded by a comparative handful of determined soldiers, for the way lay through tortuous mountain passes. Here China's court awaited the turn of events, ready to parley over its own merited punishment. As soon as the foreign military commanders had pause for breath they divided the city into zones for government, each nation represented taking the responsibility for order in its own zone. The time had now come for soldiers to show what they knew of civil administration. In the American, British and Japanese zones life, property and justice were notably secure. Courts were instituted, and all lawlessness, whether of whites or natives, was rigorously suppressed. The allies entered Pekin to find it almost a deserted city. In a few weeks it was again a metropolis. There was one blot, however, upon the fair name of Christendom. Certain sections of the city were sacked by soldier looters, a work in which they were most cheerfully assisted by many of the civilian foreigners. In justification it has been urged that the outrageous conduct of the Chinese in attacking the Legations and the outlying missions called for a punishment so severe that it would not be forgotten in generations. There were the murders of scores of foreign missionaries and laymen and thousands of native Christians to avenge. There was the destruction of much property belonging to Europeans and Americans to be punished. Undoubtedly, General Chaffee did more than any other commander among the allies to stop looting. In the end his edicts became so potent that most American soldiers were compelled to buy their trophies from the looting troops of other nationalities.

There were many punitive expeditions sent out to points within a few days' march of Pekin, the most notable being that to Paoting-fu. A spectacle arranged with great solemnity was the memorable march of troops representing the eight allies through the Forbidden City. This is the innermost part of Pekin, the Chinese Holy of Holies, wherein no man but the Emperor is supposed to set his foot. A reverent Chinaman would expect to be struck dead by heaven for the sacrilege of entering the Forbidden City. It was therefore important that the allies should complete the humiliation of the Chinese by marching hostile troops through the sacred precincts.

Immediately after the occupation of Pekin the question

of the partition of China came up among the powers. The United States were foremost in their contention that there must be no division, but that a stable Chinese Government must be established and supported. To this proposition Great Britain gave ready assent. Japan, too, objected to division. The other powers, influenced, doubtless by a dread that partition would only bring about additional perplexities— even disasters—followed the programme initiated by the United States. The Empress-Dowager, finding herself powerless for further mischief, prevailed upon her chief advisers to allow her to appoint plenipotentiaries to negotiate terms of peace. Upon Li Hung Chang, China's greatest statesman, and the aged Prince Ching, who in the most trying times had shown himself desirous of conciliating the civilized nations, fell the task of wringing from the powers such concessions—or rather, such mild terms of punishment —as were possible. At first these negotiations were carried on with the military commanders; afterward the diplomatic representatives took up the tangled skein. China's representatives fought with all the skill of Oriental diplomacy. Couriers were ever in motion between the court and China's negotiators. Every pretext for delay was seized. The first victory gained by the powers was the admission of China's liability for damages, actual and punitive. After that numerous conferences were held to determine the sums to be paid each of the powers, and the method of guaranteeing payment. Another demand made, and lately admitted, was that China abandon the antiquated system of "likin" charges and follow the tariff system of the civilized world. All of the powers are to be admitted on the same footing as to customs charges and all internal taxes on foreign merchandise are to be abolished. China has further consented to take her place among the civilized nations of the earth, observing all the obligations that are binding upon the fraternity of nations. In other words, her peace commissioners have virtually agreed that this great empire was in the wrong, and that henceforth unrestricted trade and all other features of modern civilization shall be as fully recognized in China as elsewhere. Railways are to be built wherever there appears to be a good opportunity for them; telegraph lines are to span the empire; religious toleration is to be established in thorough earnest; modern science is to be encouraged, and reform such as Japan eagerly seized at is to be permitted, and even encouraged, in China. How much sincerity there was in these promises only the future can show. The experience of the past has proved that the Chinese are ready guarantors in times of adversity. They have always been equally ready to forget as soon as the cloud of danger passed over.

Early in 1901 it was deemed advisable by the powers to remove the greater part of the allied army that had poured into China. There were two reasons for this decision: In the first place, the danger was over, or was believed to be, and the Chinese were considered to be sufficiently cowed; in the second place the imperial court refused to return to Pekin while a foreign army of occupation held the city. As the powers had decided that it was of prime importance to retain Kwangsu upon the throne, it was necessary to make any concession that would bring the court back to Pekin. The embarkation of troops was therefore begun, each power leaving only enough soldiers to constitute a guard for its Legation. It is a noteworthy fact, however, that this was the first time in the records of the world when nations found it necessary to combine for the defense of their Legations. China, the oldest nation in the world, had to learn the amenities of international life from nations which, excepting Japan, had existed but a few centuries apiece.

So well had the American district of Pekin been governed by General Chaffee and his subordinates that, just before the departure of the American troops, a delegation of Pekin merchants waited upon the American commander. They presented him with a petition bearing five thousand signatures praying that the American troops remain to govern Pekin. The request, of course, could not be granted.

THE FUTURE OF CHINA

IT is obvious that arterial communication is the first organic need of all civilized States, and pre-eminently of a country so vast and various in its terrestrial conditions as is China. This need has been recognized by the ablest of its rulers, who, from time to time, have made serious efforts to connect the most distant parts of the empire by both land and water routes. The Grand Canal, or Yunho ("River of Transports"), is pronounced as memorable a monument of human industry in its way as is the Great Wall. It is not, however, a canal in the Western sense of the word, but merely, as Richthofen has explained, "a series of abandoned river beds, lakes and marshes, connected one with another by cuttings of no importance, fed by the Wanho in Shantung, which divides into two currents at its summit, and by other streams and rivers along its course. A part of the water of the Wanho descends toward the Hoangho and Gulf of Pe- chihli; the larger part runs south in the direction of the Yangtse." The Grand Canal links Hangchow, a port on the East China Sea, south of the Yangtse, with Tientsin in Chihli, where it unites with the Peiho, and thus may be said to extend to Tungchow in the neighborhood of Pekin. When the canal was in order, before the inflow of the Yel- low River failed, there was uninterrupted water communica- tion from Pekin to Canton, and to the many cities and towns met with on the way. For many years past, however, and especially since the carriage of tribute-rice by steamers along the coast began, repairs of the Grand Canal have been prac- tically abandoned. The roads in China, confined generally to the northern and western sections of the country, are described as the very worst in the world. The paving, according to Baber, "is of the usual Chinese pattern, rough bowlders and blocks of stone being laid somewhat loosely together on the surface of the ground; 'good for ten years and bad for ten thousand,' as the Chinese proverb admits. On the level plains of China, where the population is sufficiently affluent to subscribe for occasional repairs, the system has much practical value. But, in the Yunnan mountains, the roads are never repaired; so far from it, the indigent natives extract the most convenient blocks to stop the holes in their hovel walls, or to build a fence on the windward side of their poppy patches. The rains soon undermine the pavement, especially where it is laid on a steep incline; sections of it topple down the slope, leaving chasms a yard or more in depth." Where traveling by water is impossible, sedan chairs are used to carry passengers, and coolies with poles and slings transport the luggage and goods. The distances covered by the sedan chair porters are remarkable, being sometimes as much as thirty-five miles a day, even on a journey extending over a month. The transport animals—ponies, mules, oxen and donkeys—are strong and hardy, and manage to drag carts along the execrable roads. The ponies are said to be admirable, and the mules unequaled in any other country. The distances which these animals will cover on the very poorest of forage are surprising.

The rapid adoption of steamers along the coast and on the Yangtse has paved the way for railways. Shallow steamers have yet to traverse the Poyang and the Tungting Lakes, which lie near the Yangtse, and Peiho and Canton Rivers, as well as many minor streams. It is the railway, however, that is the supreme necessity. Mr. Colquhoun has pointed out that, except along the Yangtse for the thousand-odd miles now covered by steamers, there is not a single trade route of importance in China where a railway would not pay. Especially would a line from Pekin carried through the heart of China to the extreme south, along the existing trade routes, be advantageous and remunerative. The enormous traffic carried on throughout the Celestial Empire in the face of appalling difficulties, on men's backs, or by caravans of mules or ponies, or by the rudest of carts and wheelbarrows, must be, some day, undertaken by railways. In the judgment of careful observers, too much stress should not be laid on the introduction of the locomotive for strategic purposes. The capital aim of railway construction should be, they think, the development of the interprovincial trade of China, the interchange of the varied products of a country which boasts so many climates and soils. This would bring prosperity to the people, render administrative reforms possible, and open China for the Chinese quite as much as for the European merchant or manufacturer. From the viewpoint of Chinese interests, the most useful lines would be two that should connect Pekin, Tientsin and all the northern part of the country with central and southern China. Trunk lines could be constructed for this purpose without any difficulty. They would pass along the old trade tracks, and would encounter populous cities the whole way. Through eastern Shansi and Honan, for example, to Hangchow on the Yangtse; thence to the Si Kiang and Canton; such lines would be shafts driven through the heart of the Middle Kingdom, connecting the North and the South. For the entire distance, some 1,300 or 1,400 miles, the extent, fertility and variety of the soil are described as remarkable. From the North, abounding in cotton and varieties of grain and pulse, to the South, where many vegetable products of the Orient are met, the redundancy of the population is a striking feature. A constant succession of villages, towns and cities would be transformed into a picture of bustle and business.

The internal economical conditions of China to-day are very much the same as were those of India when railways were introduced. The only difference is that the Chinese people are better off per man, and that the Chinese and Indo-Chinese, unlike the natives of India, are born travelers and traders. Yet, even in India, contrary to expectation, the passenger traffic on the railways has, from the first, exceeded the goods traffic. In 1857, the number of passengers carried by railway in India was 2,000,000; in 1896, it had risen to 160,000,000. In the first named year, the quantity of goods transported was 253,000 tons; in 1896, it was 32,500,000 tons. There has been witnessed in India during those forty years an expansion of commerce which, at the outset of the period, would have been deemed incredible. The imports and exports rose in that time from 400,000,000 to 2,000,000,000 rupees. Forty years ago, India was merely a dealer in drugs, dyes and luxuries; now she is one of the largest purveyors of food grains, fibers, and many other staples. Few persons are aware how favorably the earnings of Indian railways compare with those of other countries. The average earnings of railways in the United States are 3 per cent; in Great Britain, 3.60 per cent; in India, 5.46 per cent. This in spite of the fact that, in India, a man can travel 400 miles within twenty-four hours for the sum of $2.08. The policy of low charges has answered well, the people, on its adoption, at once having begun to travel and to send their produce by rail. In China, also, low rates will be a necessity. Another fact of importance to China is that, out of the 260,000 people employed on Indian railways, 95.66 per cent are natives. Only the higher posts are held by Europeans. In China, the proportions would probably be even more in favor of the native element.

Mr. Colquhoun, who is a high authority, has no doubt that, as Richthofen anticipated years ago, China will eventually be directly connected with Europe via Hami, Lanchow and Sian. "No direct connection of this kind," says Richthofen, "is possible south of the Wei basin, and any road to the north of it would have to keep entirely north of the Yellow River and run altogether through desert countries." The same reason which confined the commerce of China with the West during thousands of years to the natural route via Hami will be decisive as regards railway communication also. In respect of natural facilities, and because of the

and steam navigation. So far as railways are concerned,
Burma should be connected with Tali and Yunnanfoo,
Yunnanfoo with Nanning, Canton with Kaulun. This
would thoroughly open the whole of Southern China lying
between Burma and the British colony of Hongkong.
Yunnanfoo should also be connected to the northeast with
Suifoo on the upper Yangtse, the navigation limit of that
waterway. Steam navigation should at once be extended to
Nanning and to Suifoo, and also, wherever it may be practicable, throughout all inland waters. Next in importance
to the creation of proper communication is the question of
taxation. All travelers, in Southern China especially, dwell
on the obstacles to trade resulting from the collection of so
many various imposts. The British Government should insist on its treaty rights, especially the enforcement, successfully accomplished by the French Government, of the transit-
pass system. It is, finally, the conviction of all competent
students of the subject that it is from Burma, on the one
hand, and from Shanghai and Hongkong on the other, that
England must, by the aid of steam applied overland and by
water, practically occupy the upper Yangtse region, which
will be found to be the key to a dominant position in China.

In some comments on China's prospective commercial
development, Mr. Colquhoun, the latest first-hand observer,
sets forth some statistics which are of interest not only to
Englishmen but to Americans. He shows that in 1896 the
total net value of imports and of exports was £55,768,500,
and the total gross value £57,274,000, of which the British
dominions contributed £39,271,000, leaving for all other
nations £18,003,000. Of this aggregate Russia contributed
£2,856,000, the rest of Europe £4,585,000, Japan £4,705,000,
and other countries, including the United States, £5,767,000.
The percentage of the carrying trade of the Middle Kingdom
under foreign flags was: British, 82.04; German, 7.49;
French, 2.00; Japanese, 1.34; Russian, 0.59; other countries, 5.54. The percentage of dues and duties paid under
foreign flags was as follows: British, 76.04; German, 10.12;

French, 2.95; Japanese, 2.28; Russian, 1.90; all other nations, 6.71. It appears, then, that Great Britain not only carries eighty-two per cent of the total foreign trade with China, but pays seventy-two per cent of the revenue resulting from that trade. Until recently, British subjects were at liberty to carry on business at but eighteen ports in China. They were Newchwang, Tientsin, Chifui, on the northern coast; Chungking, Ichang, Hankow, Kiukiang, Wehu, Chinkiang and Shanghai, on the Yangtse River; Ningpo, Wenchow, Foochow, Amoy, Swatow, Canton, Hoihow (Kiungchow) and Pakhoi, on the coast south of the Yangtse. To these must be now added Shansi on the Yangtse, between Ichang and Hankow; Hangchow and Soochow, two inland cities near Shanghai; Woochow and Sanshui on the West River, and Ssumao and Lungchow in the south. It is also reported that three other ports have been very recently opened; viz., Yochow, on the Tungting Lake; Chungwang, on the Gulf of Pechihli, and Funing in Fuhkien.

Let us now proceed to demonstrate how deeply the United States are concerned in the China question from the industrial point of view. Inasmuch as, owing to the fact that Americans now manufacture more than they consume, they are compelled to embark on a foreign policy and to look increasingly to foreign markets, they cannot but feel that the future of the Middle Kingdom is a matter of vital importance to themselves. It is manifest that the Pacific slope, though at present playing but a small part, is destined to be more profoundly affected by the development of China than is any other section of the American republic. Our Pacific States are possessed of enormous natural resources; their manufactures have quadrupled in twenty years, and will, in the course of time, find a most advantageous market in the Far East. When the Nicaragua Canal shall have been dug, the Atlantic States will also be brought into close connection with China and with the rest of Eastern Asia. The volume of the United States traffic with China already represented a considerable part of the foreign trade of the empire in 1896.

While the imports from China received by the United States have increased but slowly, the exports from the last-named country to the Middle Kingdom have increased 126 per cent in ten years, and are more than fifty per cent greater than the exports of Germany to the same market. The export of American cotton cloths to China amounted to $7,485,000 in 1897, or nearly one-half the entire value of cotton cloths sent abroad by the United States. The export of kerosene oil from the States to China now ranks second in importance to that of cotton goods, and is likely to increase at a rapid rate. The Chinese demand for the illuminating fluid is quickly growing, and the delivery of it from the United States to China has more than trebled in value during the past ten years. That is to say, it has risen from $1,466,000 in 1888 to $4,498,000 in 1897. The Russian oil has hitherto been the only serious foreign competitor of the American product, but the Langkat oil is coming to some extent into use. The exports of American wheat flour to China reached a value in 1897 of $3,390,000, and those of chemicals, dyes, etc., $1,000,000. At present, the export trade of the United States to China is confined mainly to cottons and mineral oils; that is to say, it is largely restricted to commodities which would be hard to sell in any Chinese port where the conditions of equal trade did not prevail. It would probably prove impossible to sell them in any Asiatic port controlled by Russia or by France. It follows that, although England has most to lose by the partition of China, even though she should receive a large share of territory, the United States are also deeply interested in the question, for their trade is already considerable, and is likely, under favorable circumstances, to undergo great expansion.

Let us, finally, examine the Chinese question from a political point of view. We concur with Mr. Colquhoun in believing that Englishmen are now at the parting of the ways, and that their failure to take the right course in the Far East will mean the loss of England's commercial supremacy, and, eventually, the disintegration of the British

Empire. He maintains that, since November 16, 1896, when the German government was compelled by Bismarck's revelations to disclose the drift of its future policy, it has been apparent that there is an increasing tendency toward co-operation in the Near East and the Far East between Germany and Russia, and therefore, also, between those powers and France, which is Russia's ally. The understanding is based upon mutual interest, territorial in the case of Russia, commercial in that of Germany, and political in the case of France. The cornerstone of the combination is Russia, whose goodwill is sought for at all costs by France, in a lesser degree by Germany, and, latterly, even by Austria-Hungary. The chief aim of the combination is the reduction of England to a secondary position, politically and commercially. In China, the outcome of the coalition has been to isolate England completely. For some years past, her efforts to secure concessions at Pekin have been frustrated by Russia and France. Meanwhile, these two countries, and, more lately, Germany as well, have secured for themselves solid advantages. Japan, on her part, since she was compelled to submit to a revision of the Shimonoseki treaty, has been watching silently and preparing anxiously for eventualities. England's official optimists talked in 1895, however, as they still talk, of the successes gained, the "rectification" of the Burmo-Chinese frontier and the incomplete "opening" of the West River. As a matter of fact, the British Government has done little or nothing to establish overland railway communication from Burma to China, or to reach China "from behind," as Lord Salisbury called it; and the Upper Yangtse, the main artery of China, has remained practically unopened. Such, indeed, is the situation at this writing.

To understand the present situation, which is the natural sequel of 1895, it is needful, first of all, to recognize the fact that Russia is, at this moment, the protector of China against all comers, and that France supports her firmly, while Germany, having once taken the decisive step of placing herself alongside Russia, is likely to follow the czar's lead for two sufficient reasons; namely, for fear of displeasing the Russian ally of France, and because concessions are not likely to be obtained at Pekin by Germany, if the latter country places itself in direct and open opposition to the St. Petersburg government. Russian influence has, for some time past, been omnipotent at Pekin, mainly through the kindly assistance rendered to China in 1895, followed up by what has been practically an offensive and defensive league. The nature of the understanding between Russia and the Middle Kingdom has, indeed, for some time been patent to all the world except Englishmen, the chief features of it being: First, an offensive and defensive alliance; secondly, branch railways through Manchuria; thirdly, the refortification of Port Arthur and Talienwan, both to be paid for by China, and either or both of these harbors to be placed at Russia's disposal whenever they may be required. It is true that China has denied the existence of any agreement except that concerning the northern Manchurian Railway, but Russia has never denied anything except the accuracy of the version of the so-called "Cassini" Convention, published by a Shanghai paper. Apart from the existence of any written contract, the facts speak for themselves. Russia, having had a prior lien on Kiao Chou, it is obvious that Germany could not have seized that harbor in opposition to Russia. Again, what is to prevent Germany from discovering some day that Kiao Chou does not "meet her requirements," in which event what is there to hinder Russia from taking over Kiao Chou and giving Germany another port? Provision has, in truth, been made to enable Germany to treat Kiao Chou as a negotiable bill of exchange.

There is really nothing unforeseen in the recent evolution of affairs in the Far East. On the contrary, it has been clearly indicated by various writers in the past fifty years. As far back as 1850, Meadows wrote: "China will not be conquered by any Western power until she becomes the Persia of some future Alexander the Great of Russia, which is the Macedon of Europe. England, America and France will, if they are wise, wage, severally or collectively, a war of exhaustion with Russia rather than allow her to conquer China, for, when she has done that, she will be mistress of the world." In reply to those who ridicule the policy of "guarding against imaginary Russian dangers in China," he said: "Many may suppose the danger to be too remote to be a practical subject for the present generation. The subject is most practical at the present hour, for, as the English, Americans and French now deal with China, and with her relations to Russia, so the event will be. For those to whom 'it will last our time' is a word of practical wisdom, this volume is not written." Again, a few years later, Meadows wrote: "The greatest, though not nearest, danger of a weak China lies precisely in those territorial aggressions of Russia which she began two centuries ago, and which, if allowed to go on, will speedily give her a large and populous territory, faced with Sveaborgs and Sebastopols on the seaboard of Eastern Asia. Let England, America and France beware how they create a sick giant in the Far East. China is a world-necessity." Foreshadowing the gradual extension of Russia into China, and the time when the former country would become dominant at Pekin, and when, with all Manchuria organized behind her, she would occupy the whole of the Yellow River basin, Meadows expressed the belief that, should that occasion occur, no combination of powers would then be able to thwart Russia's purpose. "With 120,000,000 Chinese to work or fight for her, nothing would stand between Russia and the conquest of the rest of the Celestial Empire; not China alone, but Europe itself would then be dominated, and it would cost the Russian Emperor of China but little trouble to overwhelm the Pacific States of the New World." Such was the forecast of a writer whose name is to-day forgotten.

What are the advantages which Russia possesses over England in dealing with China? There is, in the first place, the advantage of proximity. The Chinese people in the northern provinces, and especially at the capital, which is not far from the Great Wall, undoubtedly discriminate between Russians and other foreigners. Like other Orientals, they only believe what they see; and Russia is seen and realized on the northern frontier. Besides the effect of contact, the Russians possess a gift in dealing with the Chinese. The affinities and analogies which the Russians and Chinese exhibit have been depicted by Michie in his book on the "Siberian Overland Route." "Analogies in the manners, customs and modes of thought of the two races are constantly turning up, and their resemblance to the Chinese has become a proverb among the Russians themselves. The Russians and the Chinese are peculiarly suited to each other in the commercial as well as in the diplomatic departments. They have an equal disregard for truth, for the Russian, in spite of his fair complexion, is, at the bottom, more than half Asiatic. There is nothing original about this observation, but it serves to explain how it is that the Russians have won their way into China by quiet and peaceable means, while we have always been running our heads against a stone wall, and never could get over it without breaking it down. The Russians meet the Chinese as Greek meets Greek; craft is encountered with craft, politeness with politeness, and patience with patience. They understand each other's character thoroughly, because they are so closely alike." Michie went on to say that "when either a Russian or a Chinese meets a European, say an Englishman, he instinctively recoils from the blunt, straightforward, up-and-down manner of coming to business at once, and the Asiatic either declines a contest which he cannot fight with his own weapons, or, seizing the weak point of his antagonist, he angles for him until he wearies him into acquiescence. As a rule, the Asiatic has the advantage. His patient equanimity and heedlessness of the waste of time are too much for the impetuous haste of the European. This characteristic of the Russian trading classes has enabled them to insinuate themselves into the confidence of the Chinese; to fraternize and identify themselves with them, and, as it were, to make common cause with them in their daily life; while the Western European holds himself aloof, and only comes in contact with the Chinese when business requires it; for, in all the rest, a great gulf separates them in thoughts, ideas and the aims of life.''

Of interest, also, as showing how history repeats itself, are the observations made nearly forty years ago by Lockhart, a missionary, after a long residence in China. Lockhart wrote: ''The Russian Government anticipated us, not in the knowledge of the advantages of close commercial and political relations with an empire so enormous in its resources, but in the employment of those arguments that alone could render a vain and effeminate State sensible of their value. . . The map of all the Russias, published at St. Petersburg, now includes that vast portion of Central Asia heretofore constituting the outlying provinces of the Chinese empire beyond the Great Wall. Having placed a mission in the Chinese capital and organized an overwhelming army in Chinese Tartary, with magazines of warlike resources, Russia easily secured a permanent footing in region after region, till she had dominated over, and then obtained the cession of, all the intervening space, leaving the conquest of the entire Chinese empire to the time when it should please the reigning Czar to order his Cossacks to take possession. It is impossible to state with any precision the amount of moral or material support which the Chinese emperor received from his imperial brother and formidable neighbor, and which encouraged him to the obstinate resistance that he offered to the demands of England and France [in 1860]; but a slight acquaintance with Russian policy must satisfy any one that, having established itself as a favored nation, Russia could not regard with complacency any attempt made by another nation to share such advantages.'' Comprehending, therefore, the Chinese character, perceiving clearly that the present Manchu dynasty is unable to perform the elementary functions of an organized society, that Pekin is another Teheran or Constantinople, that, while the people are sound, the courts and the officials are corrupt, Russia has studied and gained over certain influential persons and applied skillfully the maxim, *divide et impera*. What China is taught night and day is that Russia is a land power, and, therefore, alone can protect China; that she keeps her promises and threats; that, with England, on the other hand, it is always a case of *vox et præterea nihil*. In short, Russia protects China in a peculiar sense, that is to say, for a price, to be paid to Russia or even to her friends. The dominating idea instilled into the Chinese court and bureaucracy, which, in the absence of a strong policy on England's part, are in a hypnotized condition, is to be saved from Japan. The great object of Russian policy is to utilize China for territorial and political expansion.

What would China be worth to Russia? This question is answered by Mr. Colquhoun at considerable length. What the utilization of China would mean can be realized, he says, only by a full appreciation of the extraordinary resources of that country, judged from various points of view. The Celestial Empire has the men with which to create armies and navies; the materials, especially iron and coal, requisite for the purposes of railway and steam navigation; all the elements, in fact, out of which to evolve a great living force. One thing alone is wanting, namely, the will, the directing power, which, absent from within, is now being applied from without. That supplied, there are to be found in abundance within China itself the capacity to carry out, the brains to plan, the hands to work. When, moreover, it is understood that not merely is the soil fertile, but that the mineral resources, the greatest, perhaps, in the whole world, are, as yet, practically untouched, the merest surface being scratched; when we further consider the volume of China's population, the ability and enterprise, and, above all, the intense vitality of the people, as strong as ever after four millenniums; when we reflect on the general characteristics of the race; it seems indisputable that the Chinese, under wise direction, are destined to dominate the whole of Eastern Asia, and, may be, to play a leading part in the affairs of the world. Even although the Celestial Empire appears to be now breaking up, it is capable, under tutelage, of becoming reconsolidated. Often before now, when conquered, has China either thrown off the yoke or absorbed its conquerors. But never before has the conqueror come, as does the Czar to-day, in the guise of a great organizing force. To much the same effect wrote Michie, whose opinion is of weight, and from whom we have already quoted: "The theory that China's decadence is due to the fact that she has long since reached maturity and has outlived the natural term of a nation's existence does not hold good. The mass of the people have not degenerated; they are as fresh and vigorous as ever they were; it is the government only that has become old and feeble; a change of dynasty may yet restore to China the luster which belongs legitimately to so great a nation. The indestructible vitality of Chinese institutions has preserved the country unchanged throughout many revolutions. The high civilization of the people and their earnestness in the pursuit of peaceful industry have enabled them to preserve their national existence through more dynastic changes than perhaps any other country or nation has experienced." Mr. Colquhoun, for his own part, testifies that, in peaceful pursuits, in agriculture, in the arts and manufactures, no limit can be placed to the capabilities of China. Even in the paths of war, he deems it difficult to foretell what, under skillful direction, may not be accomplished. It is true that, touching this point, there is a wide difference of opinion. Prjevalski said, apropos of the Tonquin campaign: "She [China] lacks the proper material; she lacks the life-giving spirit. Let Europeans supply the Chinese with any number of arms that they please: let them exert themselves ever so energetically to train Chinese soldiers: let them even supply leaders: the Chinese Army will, nevertheless, even under the most favorable conditions, never be more than an artificially created, mechanically united, unstable organism. Subject it but once to the serious test of war, speedy dissolution will overtake such an army, which could never hope for victory over a foe animated with any real spirit." On the other hand, high testimony has been borne by other travelers and military critics to the excellent quality of China's raw material for military purposes. Wingrove Cooke, the "Times" correspondent with the allied forces in 1857–58, who is generally accounted one of the best critics of Chinese men and affairs; Count d'Escayrac de Lauture, one of the Pekin prisoners in 1859–60; Chinese Gordon and Lord Wolseley, have all spoken highly of the courage and endurance of the Chinese soldier. The following summary of his capabilities was given by one who had had experience with Gordon's "Ever-Victorious Army": "The old notion is pretty well got rid of that they are at all a cowardly people, when properly paid and efficiently led; while the regularity and order of their habits, which dispose them to peace in ordinary times, give place to a daring bordering on recklessness in times of war. Their intelligence and capacity for remembering facts render them well fitted for use in modern warfare, as do also the coolness and the calmness of their disposition. Physically, they are, on the average, not so strong as Europeans, but considerably more so than most of the other races of the East; and, on a cheap diet of rice, vegetables, salt fish and pork, they can go through a vast amount of fatigue whether in a temperate climate or a tropical one, where Europeans are ill fitted for exertion. Their wants are few; they have no caste prejudices and hardly any appetite for intoxicating liquors."

It is Mr. Colquhoun's opinion, based upon prolonged observation, that, if China were conquered by Russia, organized, disciplined and led by Russian officers and Russian administrators, an industrial and military organization would be developed which India could not face, and which would shake to its foundations the entire fabric of the British Empire. If, he says, the Chinese failed to profit by their numerical superiority and their power of movement in Tonquin, it must be remembered that they were as ill-equipped and supplied and nearly as unorganized and unofficered as they were in the Chino-Japanese war. Transport, commissariat, tents, medical service, all the paraphernalia employed in organized army work, were then, as in the late campaign, absolutely unknown. Notwithstanding the unfavorable judgment of Prjevalski that the Chinese are animated by neither military nor patriotic spirit, the conviction of many observers is that, however undisciplined they proved themselves in the Chino-Japanese war; however badly the undrilled, unfed, unled Chinamen in uniform compared with the highly organized troops of Japan, their capabilities, as the components of a fighting machine, should be rated exceedingly high. The apparent inconsistencies of the Chinese can, in all likelihood, be reconciled. That they offer excellent military material when shaped and guided by foreigners may be pronounced certain. If they come from the Manchurian provinces or from Shantung, they are found to be steady, willing to be taught and amenable to discipline, of splendid physique and able to bear hardships and cold without a murmur. If from Honan, they exhibit many of the best characteristics of highland races—courage and loyalty to their own leader—but they are more difficult to manage, and they are not steady in any sense of the word. The southern Chinese seem to be held generally in low esteem, but one should not forget that the best fighters of the Taeping army were the men from the Canton province, and that, as seamen, the coast populations of Southern China are unequaled. The western highlanders, whether Mohammedans or not, are men of good physique, and would make good fighting material. The Mongolians are horsemen from their early years, and are suitable for light cavalry of the Cossack type.

Like the Central Asian peoples, the Chinese possess in a high degree the virtue of passive bravery. At first the Russians, in their contests in Central Asia, expended much time and wasted many lives in besieging towns. They acted with caution, throwing up approaches and opening trenches. This method, however, was presently abandoned for that of open escalade, as, for instance, at Tashkend, Khojand and Uratapa. Finally, the plan was adopted of storming breaches, to permit of which breaching batteries would be thrown up at very close quarters, after which, a favorable time being chosen, the place would be carried by storm. From every point of view, this proved to be the most effective method. The Chinaman, as has been proved repeatedly, is like other Central Asiatics in this respect, that, under cover, he sustains the heaviest fire with indifference; he never surrenders except under bold assaults, which he cannot withstand.

What is the conclusion to which the observations of all first-hand students of China have conducted them? Their conclusion is that it is a question of vital importance, a matter of commercial life and death, for England to maintain and consolidate herself in the Yangtse basin, which cannot possibly be done except by an effective occupation of the upper Yangtse, and by developing in every possible way her communications along that watercourse, and by the West River from Hongkong, also by railway connection with Upper Burma and through that province with India. Mr. Colquhoun, for his part, also believes it to be high time that countries like the United States, Australasia and Germany should set themselves to watch with attention, not to say anxiety, the situation in the Far East. He advises them to reflect upon the history of the ancient empire formed by Genghis Khan and his successors, for that history is repeating itself to-day. Russia is conquering by modern methods the kingdoms of Genghis and Kublai Khan, and the Russian Czar, once emperor of China, will take the place of the Tartar conquerors who carried fire and sword beyond the Carpathians and the Vistula and throughout eastern, western and southern Asia.

THE END